# FAIR PLAY

## A Daniel Dorling reader
## on social justice

First published in Great Britain in 2012 by

The Policy Press
University of Bristol
Fourth Floor
Beacon House
Queen's Road
Bristol BS8 1QU
UK

t: +44 (0)117 331 4054
f: +44 (0)117 331 4093
tpp-info@bristol.ac.uk
www.policypress.co.uk

North America office:
The Policy Press
c/o The University of Chicago Press
1427 East 60th Street
Chicago, IL 60637, USA
t: +1 773 702 7700
f: +1 773-702-9756
e:sales@press.uchicago.edu
www.press.uchicago.edu

British Library Cataloguing in Publication Data
A catalogue record for this book is available from the British Library.

Library of Congress Cataloging-in-Publication Data
A catalog record for this book has been requested.

ISBN 978 1 84742 879 0 paperback
ISBN 978 1 84742 880 6 hardcover

Cover design by The Policy Press
Front cover: image kindly supplied by www.alamy.com
Printed and bound in Great Britain by Hobbs, Southampton
The Policy Press uses environmentally responsible print partners

To my brothers,
Anthony and Tristan Dorling

# Contents

# Sources of extracts

The following research centres, journals, publishers, newspapers, trade unions, trusts and websites all generously gave permission for previously published work to be included here. Many thanks to all.

## Section I: Inequality and poverty

1   Prime suspect: murder in Britain
    From: *Criminal obsessions: why harm matters more than crime* (second edition), (2008) pp 24–40, Centre for Crime and Justice Studies.

2   The dream that turned pear-shaped
    From: 'Inequalities in Britain 1997–2006' (2006) *Local Economy*, vol 21 no 4, pp 353–61, Sage.

3   The soul searching within New Labour
    From: 'The soul searching within New Labour', (2007) *Local Economy*, vol 22, no 4, pp 317–24, Sage.

4   Unequal Britain
    From: 'Unequal Britain' (2007) *Socialist Worker*, Issue 2061, 28th July 2007.

5   Axing the child poverty measure is wrong
    From: 'Axing the child poverty measure is wrong', (2010) *The Guardian/Observer*.

## Section II: Injustice and ideology

6   Brutal budget to entrench inequality
    From: 'Brutal budget to entrench inequality', (2010) *Socialist Review*, 349, July/August, p 5.

7   New Labour and inequality: Thatcherism continued?
    From: 'New Labour and inequality: Thatcherism continued? (2010) *Local Economy*, vol 25, nos 5/6, pp 397–413. Sage.

8   All in the mind? Why social inequalities persist
    From: 'All in the mind? Why social inequalities persist', (2010) *Public Policy Research*, vol 16, no 4, pp 226-231, Wiley.

9   Glass conflict: David Cameron's claim to understand poverty
    From: 'Glass conflict: David Cameron's claim to understand poverty and his wish to 'eradicate dependency' seem wide of the mark', (2010) *Roof Magazine*, vol 35, no 1, p 10, Shelter.

10  Clearing the poor away
    From: 'Clearing the poor away', (2010) *Socialist Review*, November.

## Section III: Race and identity

11  Ghettos in the sky
    From: 'Why Trevor is wrong about race ghettos', (2005) *The Guardian/Observer*.

# Foreword

When I agreed to write the foreword to this book it seemed obvious how I should go about it. I would approach it with rigorous journalistic detachment, as if what it has to say has no direct impact on me or on my life. After thinking about it, though, I reached the conclusion that this would be dishonest. There is no way for me to read this book – or any others by the author for that matter – without it resonating on a personal level.

You see, I was born into that stratum of society many of the more privileged among us would refer to – without a hint of irony - as the "underclass". Therefore, the lack of a level playing field that this book deconstructs is much more than an abstraction to me.

In the early 1980s, during the brutal years of Thatcherism, my father became unemployed. He would never work again. On many occasions my siblings and I were painfully aware of what it felt like to have no money for basic provisions. We were aware too of the fact that receiving free school meals placed us in a particular category of people somewhere towards the bottom of an already deprived community. And we were also conscious of the humiliation of borrowing money from the "tick man" who visited weekly to collect what he'd lent us at extortionate rates of interest. All so we would have some presents at Christmas.

We had no washing machine. We were often envious of our friends whose fathers had jobs and we were certainly envious of the middle class people we never got to meet because they lived in "better" areas and didn't send their kids to the same schools as us.

There is more to being "poor" or "disadvantaged" than statistics alone can ever tell us. That is why *Fair play*, with its emphasis on marrying abstract ideas about social exclusion to the experience of it, and on laying bare the cultural manifestations of elitism that underpin contemporary Britain, matters.

Can't you see that the poorest people in society only think they are poor? Compare them with the genuinely impoverished of decades past and really, they are pretty well off. So the argument of some people goes. Those who propagate this kind of reasoning tend to bolster their contentions with facts such as the number of so-called poor people who own mobile phones, or a television or any other kind of electronic luxury you might care to mention like – say – a washing machine. Within this perspective resides the attitude that the modern poor and marginalised should stop their whingeing, get off their pizza-gorging backsides and accrue multiple low-paying jobs, and grin and bear their fates in the face of abject exploitation. So the argument goes.

There are better people than I capable of demolishing this kind of logic and one of them is Danny Dorling. In book after book he manages to obliterate the specious arguments and entrenched prejudices that sustain elitism - and its apologists. Yet again, here is a book from Dorling that consummately dismantles what we think we know about poverty, social exclusion, mobility (or the lack of it) education and hierarchy, wellbeing, wealth inequalities and all their myriad corollaries.

Across a series of discrete chapters – mainly carefully edited extracts from previously published work in magazines, newspapers and elsewhere – you the reader are treated to the unravelling of the ideologies that sustain a society where the gap between rich and poor widens under the so-called "progressive" government that was New Labour. You are also guided through the (indisputably important) whys, hows and consequences of unrelenting momentous social changes and political hubris that have seen a country that, for all its problems in 1978, was more equal then than it is now.

Our politicians may talk the talk on social equality and "poverty of opportunity" as some like to refer to it, but they merely tinker. Under New Labour there were some encouraging developments of which the minimum wage, a calculable focus on child poverty, improved maternity rights, and progressive projects such as Sure Start are just a few. But to their great shame, their "*progressive*" era also shepherded in the conditions that cultivated a jump in wealth inequalities between the very top and very bottom of our society. If you were born poor under the New Labour government you can bet you are probably staying poor. In a decade's time, who knows what your prospects will be thanks to the coalition government in power when this book is published.

*Fair play* is about chronicling what Dorling terms "the tenacity of unfairness". It is about confronting that most stubborn of social norms: the idea that the poor are the architects of their own misfortune. For those of you reading this book that have known what it is like to live in poverty in modern Britain (despite its status as an extraordinarily wealthy country in global terms) the charts and numbers and analysis on offer will be much more than analytical aids or abstract rationale. The analysis will be a valuable and comprehensible framework within which you can place your own experience.

It is no coincidence that often the most vigorous defenders of the view that the poor should (as Norman Tebbit once put it so acidly) "get on their bikes" hail from low-income backgrounds. These are often the people who have clambered their way out of the social cesspit they were born into and who can't for a moment contemplate why, for every one of them, there are thousands left behind: excluded, hopeless, shunned and ignored. I did it so why not the rest?

There are multiple studies – many of them referenced in this book – that document the social attitudes, structures and political forces, that have brought Britain to a place where it ranks high among wealthy nations on income and health inequalities and where there is scant evidence to suggest that this will change any time soon. As Dorling says, "The prejudice that preserves poverty remains stronger in Britain than in most of the rest of the rich world. [...] Labour introduced and continued to extol a populist and punitive approach [to poverty], labelling benefit claimants as potentially feckless. [...] Permitting rising inequality and stoking prejudices against the poor sets a precedent for the next government which heavily outweighs the many gains made."

It takes sound reasoning and robust evidence to shed light on the reality of inequality, social injustice and any notions of 'fairness' we might have as a society. However, it also takes a singular ability to unpick and demystify the complex social forces and contradictory messages that swirl about us each and every day. This is exactly what *Fair play* does.

As America's second president, John Adams so eloquently put it, "Facts are stubborn things; and whatever may be our wishes, our inclinations, or the dictates of our passion, they cannot alter the state of facts and evidence."

*Mary O'Hara*
*Journalist and Alistair Cooke Fulbright Scholar*

# Acknowledgements

Thanks to Alison Shaw at The Policy Press for persevering with the idea of an edited collection and helping to ensure it was not too large a collection. Laura Vickers at Policy put in hours way beyond what was agreed in chasing up copyright clearances for reprinting all these papers and especially to help secure permission to include the images used throughout the book including many not used in the original publications. Jo Morton and Laura Greaves edited the text and ensured that the work from so many sources was tidied up, allowing it to be reproduced throughout this whole book to a similar quality. Dave Worth typeset all the text and illustrations. The images shown here are from the collections of iStockphoto and Super-Stock images.

Vassiliki (Vicky) Yiagopoulou, was very kind in searching out the images used at the start of each section and chapter. Paul Coles redrew all the graphs, tables and maps shown here without ever asking when the apparently limitless stream of requests would end (although he did raise an eyebrow at times!). Bronwen Dorling read an early draft and convinced me not to be as mean to the world's elite economists in print as I was in that first draft (what you are just about to read is me being kind to them). David Dorling did the same and suggested which parts of my previously published papers were so boring that you should be spared reading them and thus helped in the extracting of sections. Finally, although they are not always reproduced below to save on space and your time, many of the papers reprinted here had their own acknowledgment sections to anonymous referees, journal editors, to colleagues who had helped me earlier with work and so on and on. It is quite shocking to step back and list everyone you owe favours to. I am very grateful for all the help.

For any human creation – from a humble book to a complicated television, to generating fair play in a school playground – many of us might think we know how it works, but a single person could hardly ever put a good book together from beginning to end, let alone make a television on their own, or bring up and organise many schools classes of children so they play well in the open air. Books, like machines, like playgrounds, like villages, towns, cities, countries and international organisations reveal what it is that human beings are really good at – working together. We are just very bad at acknowledging that. Especially in our more selfish and individualistic of cultures. To say "when I wrote my book" is to help prolong the myths that we can do much at all on our own. We are almost all of us guilty at various times of suggesting that we contribute a great deal more than our fair share, and guilty of complaining about the apparent deficiencies of others. Almost everyone who does contribute more than their fair share will never get to read a book like this. So, we need to start learning better how to play fair.

# Introduction

## What the book is about

This book is a collection of several previously published academic papers, a book review, a lecture, many newspaper and magazine articles, a few previously unpublished pieces and some material that until now had only appeared online in web publications. What is included here errs towards material published in more recent times, concerning very recent events and, in a few cases, a short extract from a longer piece is included to ensure that the whole book is easier to read because all the parts are easily digestible. In some cases I have included some additional material not previously published alongside the original piece. Usually this has been done to provide more sources than the original publication format allowed. Newspapers tend not to allow footnotes. The whole text has also been lightly edited to bring it all to a similar style, and to standardize formatting and referencing. There is a foreword on page xi, very kindly written by Mary O'Hara, someone a little more detached than I am from this work.

The book is arranged in nine sections into which the fifty-two chapters have been ordered. The sections range from writing on social mobility and educational immobility, to ideas over injustices in general, and the ideologies which prolong them. There is a common theme of the tenacity of unfairness in most of the material and also of how it matters where you live and move to in terms of what happens to you and yours. The title of the book comes from playing around with various ideas about fairness. The sections divide the material roughly by subject, telling a story that begins with talking about the circumstances in which we find ourselves, and ending with what we can do about it. None of these articles was originally written to be placed with the others, but they have been ordered to try to tell a series of stories, and each section, each set of stories, is introduced with a very short story explaining the thinking across each particular set of papers.

The chapter titles are taken from the original titles of each paper or a shorter subsection of those original titles. Many of the chapters were jointly authored and some have been reprinted before, so a footnote is usually given at the start of each chapter detailing who was involved in the writing and where else it might have appeared. Editorial notes have also been inserted to update information to include details from 2011 in various places.

## Who the book is for

The idea of this book is that it should be something you can easily hold in your hand, something you might want to read from start to end, which is why it is 120,000 words in length, with an index for looking up issues of interest and to allow cross-referencing. It is arranged as a book for people who want a book to read, not a reference work, so each chapter has been included because it is short and hopefully readable. As a consequence most papers I have published in medical journals are excluded, as are longer and sometimes stodgy pieces in more worthy journals and almost all book chapters I have written in recent years (they are too long). I have also left out a great many papers on mapping world distributions which are very similar to each other (each looking at a different topic by using maps of the same style from the website www.worldmapper.org that my colleagues and I have been working on during most of the last decade). Another mechanism used to cut down the selection is to ensure that most of the articles here are quite recent, and to be included they have had to have been on a topic that could be grouped in sections worth reading together.

The book is for students in the social sciences, both undergraduate and postgraduate, who are interested in how arguments can be made that range across a wide variety of fields, across a variety of print media and of subjects. *Fair play*[1] is also targeted at that small group of the general public interested in topics like this and so aims, in title and choice of subjects, to be popular and accessible. The book had been put together with journalists and political commentators in mind as well. This is partly why the vast majority of the material here comes from work published mostly in the last five years, if not in the last two years. It is also collated here to save other academics time. If you want to know what I *think* I think – read this collection.

Most academics in elite universities and many university students do have access to most of the material reprinted here through their online library subscriptions to journals, but by including only a small section of papers here (and by taking extracts from a few more) I am, in effect, saying "if you

---

[1] The book was originally to be titled *Playing fair*. "Fair play" sounds a little more posh, but it means the same thing. If the book were aimed at younger adults, or a less select group of adults, it would be titled differently.

were going to read anything of what I've done, if I were you I would read this.". Finally it is far cheaper and easier for someone to buy and read this book than it is for them to print out even a section of this work from the web; it is far more enjoyable to read it on paper than on a computer screen (or even on a hand-held Kindle although you might dispute that depending on how you are reading this right now!). Put in book form here, you can remember where it is you read it, and can use the index to find something you only half remember. The book ends with a half page bibliography showing what is included and excluded and where there is access on the web for those who wish to read the full versions of any truncated articles, or for those who wish to grab graphics from anything shown here, put their own copy in Endnote, some other library software, or do whatever they may wish with it. The book also has an accompanying website where many of the figures are made freely available including the data from which they were derived. At www.shef.ac.uk/sasi a link can be found to that website.

## Why was the book put together?

*Fair play* concerns contesting the need to live in an increasingly unfair world, and beginning that contestation locally by illustrating just how unfair life in Britain is. Britain is a place where many people like to pride themselves on 'sticking to the rules', but where we recently discovered that large numbers of our representatives in parliament often broke their own rules on expense claims. Our MPs felt themselves to be above the rest of us. In Britain our governing parties often appear not to have the majority of the population's interests at heart, despite needing that majority to place them in power.

*Fair play*, as the titles of the sections of the book reveals, is about issues of inequality and poverty; about injustice and ideology; race and identity; education and hierarchy; elitism and geneticism; mobility and employment; bricks and mortar; wellbeing and misery; advocacy and action. However, in the remainder of this introduction this book begins not with Britain, but with a story of Nobel Laureates sitting around a lunch bench on a college campus in the United States of America. This story is required to explain why we need to be so vigilant to ensure that others really do have our best interests at heart, to ensure that they do not look down on us.

The key question underlying *Fair play* is the question of equality. Just how inherently equal are people? If people are created, conceived, even born, pretty much equal, then they do not deserve to be treated as differently as they are. The outcomes described in this book would, in this case, be grossly unjust. However, if there are great differences in different people's capabilities to learn, to understand, to create and to command, then much of the outcomes of the ways in which we organise society can be justified, and we are 'playing fair'. It would be fine then to look down on some people and up to others.

Ideologically our world is currently dominated by men who believe that they are particularly smart and that, although they might care for others, others can never quite be like them. Until very recently all women were part of that excluded group. Most people on the planet remain similarly excluded, the majority of them still women, but now excluded more through their poverty than their gender. The argument that we are all quite equal, all just as capable of being stupid as we are capable of being smart, begins with a story of five men – Joe, Karl, Ken, Paul and Larry – and a discussion two of them had over smartness.

## Is he smart like us?

Academia, understandably, is full of people who think that they are very clever. From the most downtrodden of lecturers in the most obscure institutions tucked away in the back of beyond, to those at the very peaks of recognition, almost all of them men, sitting in great seats of learning in the most eminent of learned institutions, there tends to be a common arrogance and conceit. This is hardly surprising to find in places where the stock-in-trade is the setting and passing of examinations. Places where collegiality is professed but comparison and constant competition is practised. The result has been termed 'smartism' and smartism can lead to a failure to play fair. Smartism makes us all more stupid.

In economics, until Elinor Ostrom was awarded a prize "for her analysis of economic governance, especially the commons" along with Oliver E. Williamson "for his analysis of economic governance, especially the boundaries of the firm", not a single woman had been awarded the Sveriges Riksbank Prize in Economic Sciences (in Memory of Alfred Nobel) despite a prize having been awarded to one or more people every year since 1969.[2] The way debate in universities still tends to play out is a very masculine way, even in the social sciences where far more women work than in science or even the more human of humanities.

Before 2009 the most radical the Nobel Committee could be was to award a prize to someone like Joe Stiglitz. Joe is described as one of the few non-neoliberals to have been awarded the prize, and as being almost on "the side of the angels",[3] so he is picked here for showing how widespread

---

[2] Dorling, D. (2010) 'Putting men on a pedestal: Nobel prizes as superhuman myths?', *Significance*, vol 7, no 3, pp 142–4.

[3] George, S. (2008) *Hijacking America: How the religious and secular right changed what Americans think*, Cambridge: Polity Press (page 20, footnote for details on Joe and the prize, the angels comment coming from page 37 and being a little unspecific as to who is on-side or off-side with great precision when it comes to the angel team).

'smartism' is. It is necessary to name all these luminaries here as, if they were not named and the sources to these statements not referenced, then you may not believe that such conversations take place amongst the male intelligentsia (and no doubt amongst some women too). "But is he smart like us?" is a comment attributed to Nobel Laureate Joe, overheard as he was talking to Carl Shapiro.[4] It was revealed by Ken Rogoff later when he was having an argument with Joe.[5] The comment was said to have been made over a meal at Princeton University, one of the most eminent of learned institutions in the world.

## How to identify smartness

Joe was asking Carl, at lunch in Princeton, whether a man called Paul Volcker was 'smart'. Paul Volcker has been described as the cigar-stomping chair of the Federal Reserve who raised interest rates in America in 1979, to reduce what he saw as the great evil of inflation. Incidentally, that inflation began, if you are looking for the immediate cause, with oil price rises as Iranian workers went on strike. For the causes behind the cause you need to know why they went on strike and why oil prices had been so low before they did. In response, in the United States, Paul apparently raised interest rates in the "full knowledge that a deepened recession would result."[6] But is was not that which concerned Joe or Carl over lunch. What they wanted to know was whether Paul was 'one of them', one of the 'smart ones'.

To answer Joe's question in the round, we now know that whether you think someone else is 'smart like you' depends on the extent to which you like them. In experiments of the assessment of a fictional Intelligence Quotient (IQ) score, it was found by psychologists that for someone to ascribe a high score to someone else "required much more evidence when the person was an unbearable pain in the ass than when the person was funny, kind and friendly."[7] Carl's reply is not recorded, but the 'clever' reply would be, 'if you like him, then he's smart like us'.

If you do a little detective work you will find that the man Carl and Joe were discussing, Paul Volker, despite the stomping, is often described as one of the more likeable of well known economists. Whether that is damning him with faint praise, or whether that gave him an advantage that day when his ears should have been burning, I leave to your imagination. Often economists appear not to want to be liked. Paul is blamed for bringing the

---

[4] Rogoff, K. (2002) 'An open letter to Joseph Stiglitz', 2007, from www.imf.org/external/np/vc/2002/070202.htm
[5] Kay, J. (2004) (2nd edn) *The truth about markets: Why some nations are rich but most remain poor*, London: Penguin, p 381.
[6] Smith, N. (2005) *The endgame of globalization*, Abingdon: Routledge, p 132.
[7] Gilbert, D. (2006) *Stumbling on happiness*, London: Harper Collins, p 170.

United States economy to a halt to squeeze inflation, and consequently being responsible for raising unemployment greatly. This was when he was running the Central Bank of the United States.[8] I don't want to add to the casting of aspersions here, what I want to do is to highlight what kind of discussions occur at the very apex of power in the social sciences and amongst policy-makers. These are just those discussions for which there is documentation.

I don't know whether Paul ever got the job or prize that Joe wondered if he was smart enough for. There is no record of why they were discussing his smartness. But whether he did or *not* will have probably depended as much on whether those judging him *really* thought him smart, not on any great actual differentiation by smartness but, as new research is beginning to teach us, on whether they found him likeable.[9] These men were playing a game no more or less sophisticated than that played by millions of children in school yards worldwide. They were deciding whether to include Paul in their gang or not. Their gang happened to be a very exclusive gang, but it was a gang nevertheless. The question was, were they playing fair?

## From the politics of the playground to world stage politics

Maybe because of, maybe regardless of, what Joe and Carl thought of Paul, by November 24th 2009 Paul was heading Barak Obama's Economic Recovery Advisory Board along with another fourteen men (and one woman: Laura D'Andrea Tyson). When heading the board Paul clashed with a man called Larry Summers, who was then director of the White House National Economic Council and another character in this short story. It was because of Larry that we now know all about that conversation over lunch in Princeton, but it is a tangled story. Playground politics can be as complex as the real thing because often the real thing is as much about the playground in which the elite have fun and get hurt, as it is about some mythical place high on a hill where our betters organise our futures for the common good.

Joe's comment was made public by a third man at that lunch table, Ken Rogoff,[10] reportedly in retaliation for Joe's lack of respect for Ken's mate Larry (Joe had 'dissed' Larry). Larry, then also known as United States Deputy

---

[8] Irvin, G. (2008) *Super rich: The rise of inequality in Britain and the United States*, Cambridge: Polity Press, p 75.

[9] For some strange reason whether he is apparently likeable or not alternates on different days as opposing forces on the internet edit his biography. His Wikipedia entry by 8 May 2008 no longer described him as 'a lovely man', but this former chairman of the Federal Reserve was awarded that title on the same web page a day earlier.

[10] Later (and now former) chief economist at the International Monetary Fund (*Guardian* newspaper, 20 August 2008, page 22, described as 'the nutty professor' himself on page 23).

Secretary, Lawrence Summers, was a man who had described building free capital markets into the basic architecture of the world economy as "…our [the USA's] most crucial international priority".[11] Larry advocated being able to buy, sell, run and ruin the services which other nations were reliant on through building those free capital markets into the global economic architecture. Joe had had the audacity to describe actions such as Larry's as "…a curious blend of ideology and bad economics, dogma that sometimes seemed to be thinly veiling special interests".[12]

Joe was roundly lauded by those more aligned towards the political left as being correct to be suspicious of Larry's ideas and other propositions more commonly associated with the right. It remains the case, though, that just as Joe appears to believe that only a few people are as smart as he is, so too he imagines that economic theory provides a good lens through which to view the human world, but particularly his kind of economics. Moreover, since Joe's criticism of the World Bank, "…the Bank has become increasingly insistent, even strident, although it has made serious attempts to moderate its language, soften its image and mollify its critics".[13] And so Joe's intervention helped the World bank repackage its image.

While these man argue with one another they are also engaged in what can be seen as a common task: justifying various inequalities while arguing against others. Some want a more equal world, others think greater inequalities are inevitable, almost all believe they are much smarter than most of us.

Between his posts as Deputy Secretary and then Whitehouse Economic Council director, Larry Summers went on to become president of Harvard University, and was sacked for saying "…that innate differences between men and women might be one reason fewer women succeed in science and math careers".[14] Shortly after that Larry became a key advisor to President Obama, he is best remembered for having fallen asleep as the president was talking.[15] By 2011 he had been replaced and *The Economist* magazine was running stories entitled "Did Larry Summers ruin everything?".[16] These were stories concerning the advice he gave Barack Obama. If we put people on pedestals which none of us are (so able as to be) able to balance atop

---

[11] Ball, S.J. (2008) *The education debate*, Bristol: The Policy Press, p 33, quoting Lawrence Summers' words of 2001.

[12] Ibid, p 33, quoting Joe Stiglitz from 2002.

[13] Ibid, p 33, quoting Philip Jones writing in 2007.

[14] Bombardieri, M. (2005) 'Summers' remarks on women draw fire', *Boston Globe*, 17 January, www.boston.com/news/local/articles/2005/01/17/summers_remarks_on_women_draw_fire/

[15] Ward, J. (2009) 'Larry Summers falls asleep while Obama talks', *The Washington Times*, 23 April, www.washingtontimes.com/weblogs/potus-notes/2009/apr/23/larry-summers-falls-asleep-while-obama-talks/

[16] *The Economist* (2010) 'Did Larry Summers ruin everything?', blog, 20 January, www.economist.com/blogs/freeexchange/2011/01/economic_policy

we should not be surprised to see the great and the good so often fall off. Just two years before his fall from grace, the *New York Times* had quoted one 'top economist' saying of another: "Larry Summers is one of the world's most brilliant economists."[17]

## The antidote to playground politics

We need an antidote to talk of people being the "most brilliant" in one breath and then being labelled as idiotic in another. We need a way of not becoming obsessed with whether others are "smart like us" or much "smarter than us" or "not as smart as us". We need ways of thinking which help others not suggest so often that just a few are at the forefront of humanity. What the examples above illustrate is that we need "…a change in social ethos, a change in the attitudes people sustain towards each other in the thick of daily life, [this] is necessary for producing equality…".[18]

Elitism is everywhere, clearly a core tenant of belief among the right-wing, but widespread even among supposedly progressive economists in the United States, and also readily found across almost the whole gamut of British politics. In Britain elitism is part of "… the Fabian tradition, [which] to some extent reproduces the mandarin fantasy of a public domain administered by a benign, disinterested, patrician elite".[19] The left-wing mandarin fantasy, with its nuances of (and pretence towards) elite Chinese meritocracy, is that a few should be specially selected by examination to rule over the multitudes.

I do not believe that only some of you are "smart like us". I do not believe that we, those who get to write books, are that smart – any of us. I do not believe that what we produce is the product of much more than the teaching we have received, our collaboration with others, hard work, the hard work of all those whose work we read, what we hear on radio and in lectures, what we see on TV, careful editing (by others), careful further checking (usually by others), all of which ends up having just a few people's names within any book being acknowledged, and even fewer in collections such as this.

Literally hundreds of different people have edited the texts printed below; family, friends, colleagues, editors, sub-editors, copy-editors and many

---

[17] Calmes, J. (2009) 'Obama's economic circle keeps tensions high', *New York Times*, 7 June, www.nytimes.com/2009/06/08/us/politics/08team.html?_r=1, full quote: 'Larry Summers is one of the world's most brilliant economists', said Mr. Orszag, who along with Mr. Geithner, successfully resisted Mr. Summers's attempts early on to control their access to Mr. Obama. 'He enriches any discussion he participates in, which is particularly valuable given the complexity and importance of the challenges currently facing us'.

[18] Cohen, G. A. (2002) *If you're an egalitarian how come you're so rich*, Cambridge, MA: Harvard University Press, p 3.

[19] Gilbert, J. (2007) 'Social democracy and anti-capitalist theory', *Renewal: A Journal of Social Democracy*, vol 15, no 4, 38-45. (page 42).

professional proof-readers. Dozens and dozens of people have been involved in deciding what is included and what is not: referees, commissioning editors, publishers of all kinds. I rarely disagree with them, after all, who am I to disagree? But if they are lucky they get inadequate acknowledgements, usually anonymous. We are not very good at fair play. That is why we invent rules to structure the games we play, to try to increase fairness, to try to make us behave better than we otherwise might. It is when we see other people not playing by the rules of humanity that we need to work harder to ensure fair play.

# SECTION I
# Inequality and poverty

The first chapter in this book concerns murder. Murder fascinates. Could we be murdered? Could we murder? Murder is the most individualised of crimes. Few people see murder as largely a product of inequality and poverty despite murder rates being so much higher in more unequal countries and despite the poor being so much more likely to be the victims of murder than those living on modest, average, generous or high incomes. The murder rate in Britain doubled in the first three decades of my life, from 1968 to 1998. With many colleagues I have studied the statistics on murder and I lay a large part of the blame for that rise in murder in Britain on the harm that was inflicted on poorer men born after 1965, those men who came of age in the years 1984 and beyond. Chapter 1 explains why I came to this particular view, and then points the finger at the government policies of 1979–97 that coincided with the greatest rise in inequality, poverty and murder.

What matters most where inequality and poverty are concerned is what we do. Two papers from the journal *Local Economy* are reprinted next in this section both concerning how the New Labour government, when in power, failed to turn around the growth in inequality and injustice that was reflected in so many poor outcomes, not least the huge increase in direct and indirect violence – of which the doubling of murder rates was just the most visible tip of the iceberg of harm. Next comes an article reprinted from the *Socialist Worker* newspaper giving a summary of the results of growing inequalities as revealed by comparing poverty surveys from 1968–69, 1983, 1990, and 1999 with more recent statistics. This is followed by an article first published in the *Guardian* newspaper concerned with how the new Coalition government's immediate response to tackling poverty and injustice was to appoint Frank Field, a Labour MP, to cast doubt on how poverty is measured and whether the poor really lack money.

Writing in 2011, it feels as if we have turned the clock back again to 1980, the year after Mrs Thatcher came to power and the year in which Ronald Reagan entered the White House. Some things are worse. Now the Conservatives are being aided by the Liberal Democrats in a way David Steel's Liberal Party would never have acted in the early 1980s. Now we are behaving with callousness despite knowing the likely outcomes of cutting most from the poor. In 1980 mass unemployment and widespread poverty were faded memories from 50 years in the past. Today we have fewer excuses to be stupid. But the prejudice that preserves poverty remains stronger in Britain than in most of the rest of the world.

# 1

# Prime suspect: murder in Britain[1]

*Prison Service Journal*, (2006) no 166, pp 3-10

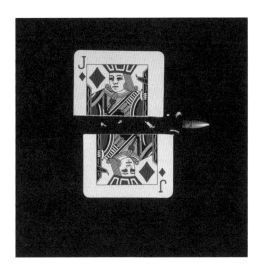

## Introduction

Murder is part of our everyday lives. Depending on the television schedules, we are exposed to far more fictional murders per day in Britain than actually occur across the whole country in a week, a month or even a year. The few actual murders that take place (between one and two a day on average) are brought vividly to our attention through newspapers, radio and television news. Murder sells the media. It buys votes through fear. Its presence almost certainly leads to many of us curtailing our daily activities, treating strangers in strange ways, avoiding travelling through parts of towns and cities, worrying who our children will meet. Our daily exposure to the fact and fiction of murder seeps into our subconscious and alters our attitudes and

---

[1] Note – Murder and manslaughter are not distinguished in the statistics used here, which strictly speaking concern homicide, although that term is more well known in the United States. This article was last reproduced in the *Prison Service Journal* from a book chapter in, Hillyard, P., Pantazis, C., Tombs, S., Gordon, D. and Dorling, D. (eds) (2005) *Criminal Obsessions: Why Harm Matters More Than Crime*, London: Centre for Crime and Justice Studies, which was itself derived from an earlier academic paper: Shaw, M., Tunstall, H. and Dorling, D. (2005) *Increasing inequalities in risk of murder in Britain: Trends in the demographic and spatial distribution of murder, 1981-2000. Health and Place*, 11, 45-54. A couple of the more technical paragraphs have been turned into footnotes in this version to make the paper more readable as a first chapter.

behaviour. The majority of people in Britain have traditionally favoured a return of the death sentence for the perpetrators of this rarest of crimes. They would sanction this murder, because they see murder as the isolated acts of individuals and so they think that if you kill the killer the killing goes away. What, though, really lies behind murder?

A classic, and ever more popular, way in which murder is portrayed is through the eyes of its victims. The pathologist has taken a lead role in the story of murder that they tell through the bodies and reconstructed lives of their silent witnesses, second only to the murder detective. What would we see if we were to take that approach, but not with one murder, a dozen, or even a hundred or so, but with the thousands of murders that have taken place across the whole country over many years? Such an approach has the disadvantage of reducing each event to just a short series of facts, and turning detailed individual stories into numbers and rates. However, it has the advantage of preventing extrapolation from just a few events to produce unjustified generalisations and encourages us to look deeper for the root causes of murder. It also makes us treat each murdered victim as equal, rather than concentrating on the most complex, unusual or topical of murders, and it can be turned back into individual stories of particular people in places and times. This chapter attempts to illustrate the advantages of such an approach to the study of murder. To follow this story you need to follow the twists and turns of homicide statistics, social indices, and population estimates, rather than modus operandi, suspects, bodies and weapons; but this is just as much a murder story as the conventional one. Here, however, is a factual story of 13,000 murders rather than one, and of a search for underlying rather than superficial causes.

This chapter is structured through asking five simple questions:

- who was murdered?
- when were they murdered?
- where were they murdered?
- with what were they murdered? and, finally,
- why were they murdered?

The killer, as is traditional, is not revealed until the end and, as is tradition, there is a twist to the plot. But, although this story is told in a dispassionate way, it is a story of real people and actual events. The story behind the thousands of murder stories is more a testament to our shared inhumanity than a thriller. Murder, behind the headlines, is the story of the connected consequences to our collective actions. Murder, despite being the rarest of crimes, tells us in the round a great deal about millions of us who will never be even remotely connected to such a death directly.

## *Who was murdered?*

Between January 1981 and December 2000, approximately 13,140 people were murdered in Britain, on average 1.8 per day. The number is approximate because about 13 per cent of deaths which were initially recorded as murder are later determined not to have been murders and thus the numbers are revised periodically (these deaths have been excluded here). Similarly, deaths not thought to have been murders can subsequently be reclassified as murder. Figure 1 shows the rates of murder in Britain by single year of age and sex.[2]

Figure 1 tells us many things. The overall 20 year average British murder rate that can be calculated from it of 12.6 murders per year per million people is of little meaning for anything other than international comparisons (British rates are low), for reassuring the population (99.88 per cent of people are not murdered), or for scaring them (you are 176 times more likely to be murdered than win the lottery with one ticket). More usefully, the rate for men, at 17 per million per year is roughly twice that for women (at nine per million per year). The single age group with the highest murder rate are boys under the age of one (40 per million per year) and then men aged 21 (38 per million per year). A quarter of all murders are of men aged between 17 and 32. A man's chance of being murdered doubles between the age of 10 and 14, doubles again between 14 and 15, 15 and 16, 16 and 19 and then does not halve until age 46 and again by age 71 to be roughly the same then as it stood at age 15. Rates rise slightly at some very old ages for both men and women although at these ages the numbers of deaths attributed to murder are very small (as the population falls).

We often tend to concentrate far more upon the characteristics of the direct perpetrators and the immediate circumstances leading up to murder than on the characteristics of the victims or the longer-term context in which murder occurs. For instance, 50 per cent of female homicide victims killed by men are killed by their current or former male partner; it is almost always parents but occasionally other family or acquaintances who kill

---

[2] Figure 1 was constructed through examining all the records of deaths in England, Wales and Scotland and identifying those where the cause of death was either recorded as homicide (according to the *International Classification of Diseases [ICD] ninth revision*, E960-E969) or death due to injury by other and unspecified means (E988.8) which mainly turn out later to be homicides (Noble and Charlton, 1994). Each of these deaths was then given a probability of being a murder according to the year in which death occurred such that the total number of deaths classified here as murder sums exactly in England and Wales to the number of offences currently recorded as homicides per year (Flood-Page and Taylor, 2003, Table 1.01; see also Home Office, 2001). It was assumed that the annual probabilities that a death initially recorded as homicide remains being viewed as homicide would be applicable also to deaths in Scotland, although the system of initially coding cause of death differs in that country. The population denominators used to calculate the rates shown in Figure 1 are derived from mid-year estimates of the population and the data have been smoothed for death occurring over age two.

infants; and alcohol is a factor in just over half of murders by men of men (Brookman and Maguire, 2003). However, researchers commissioned to consider the short-term causes of homicide also know that:

> … there is evidence of a strong correlation between homicide rates and levels of poverty and social inequality, and it may be that, in the long-run, significant and lasting reductions in homicide can best be achieved by strategies which take this fully into account. (Brookman and Maguire, 2003, p 2)

**Figure 1:** Rate of murder per million per year, in Britain, 1981-2000, by sex and age

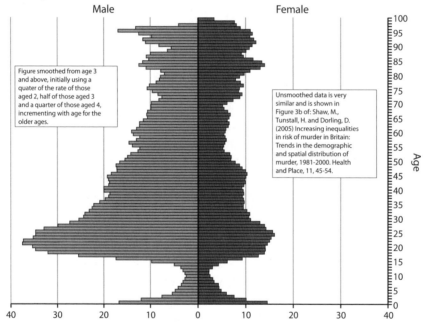

Figure 1 suffers from only telling us what the chances of an average person of particular age and sex are of being murdered in Britain in a year. For any particular person those rates will vary dramatically according to knowing more about exactly who they are, where they live and so on. Before turning to those facts the next step is to determine the importance of when they were murdered.

*When were they murdered?*

Both the number of murders and the rate of murder have doubled in England and Wales in the 35 years since the official series began. Figure 2 shows this series (Flood-Page and Taylor, 2003, Table 1.01). It is very likely that the numbers for the last two years will be reduced as some of these offences come to be no longer regarded as homicide in the future, but it is unlikely that they will be reduced by much. Thus, until recent years the increase in the murder rate was slowly falling. In the first half of the 1970s the smoothed murder rate rose by 22 per cent in five years, it rose by 13 per cent in the subsequent five years, by four per cent in the first half of the 1980s, three per cent in the latter half of the 1980s, eight per cent in the first half of the 1990s and 14 per cent in the latter half of that decade. In answer to the question of when, victims are more likely to have been murdered more recently.

**Figure 2:** Offences currently recorded as homicide, England and Wales, 1967-2001

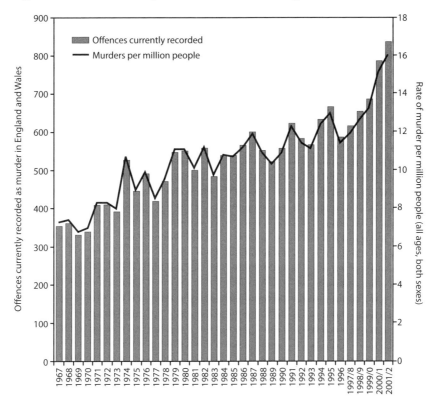

*Note:* The bars are number of murders now thought to have been committed in that year taking into account later reclassifications and acquittals (scale on left hand axis), the line is the rate of murder per million people (for which the scale is provided on the right hand axis).

At first glance, Figure 2 appears to imply that murder rates have risen. However, for the majority of the population this turns out, on closer inspection, not to be the case. From here on, data for deaths occurring in the years 2001 or 2002 will not be used as we cannot yet be sure of their reliability.[3] Instead the four five-year time periods from 1981 to 2000 will be compared (see Rooney and Devis, 1999 for more details of time trends). It is important to remember that in calculating a murder rate it is not only the number of people who are murdered that changes over time, but also the number of people living who could be murdered.

Figure 3 shows the percentage changes in the murder rates that taken together all contribute to the overall change shown in Figure 2. Most strikingly, for all ages of women, other than infant girls, the murder rate has either fallen or hardly changed; for women aged 65 to 69 it fell to less than half its early 1980s levels. Murder rates have also fallen for men aged 60 and above and boys under five. For a majority of the population, given their ages and sexes, their chances of being murdered have fallen over time, in some cases considerably. How then has the overall rate increased? For all males aged between five and 59, murder rates have increased significantly.

**Figure 3:** Change in the murder rate, Britain, 1981–1985 to 1996–2000 by age group and sex

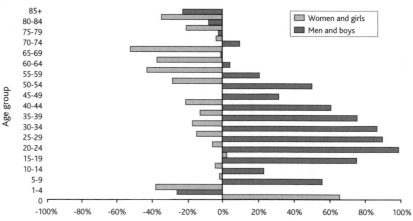

Change in the murder rate in Britain, 1981-1985 to 1996-2000

---

[3] Editorial note: When this article was first written it was too early to tell if there really was a "murder spike" at the start of the twenty-first century. However, the murders attributed to Dr Harold Shipman, the deaths of cockle pickers in Morecambe bay declared to be homicide, those of some fifty people hidden in a lorry trying to evade immigration control, the "7/7" murders in London, and several lone gun-man killing sprees, all made analysis of murder trends in recent years practically impossible when considering the use of murder as a marker of wider social trends, other than the trends of our increased inhumanity made even more evident when doctors treat patients as sub-human, officials make immigration illegal, and fanatical young men kill themselves while trying to kill as many others as possible.

At the extreme they have doubled for men aged 20 to 24 over the course of these two decades. The increase in the murder rate of men, and particularly young men is enough to more than outweigh the decreases that most groups have experienced over time. Of course, this is not true of all people, and so we next turn to where these changes have occurred.

### Where were they murdered?

Having considered who is most likely to be murdered given their age and sex and how these rates are changing over time, the next step in the process is to consider where these murders take place. As already touched on, it is obvious to the public at large, and to criminologists who consider murder in detail, that place matters. Living in the United States is more dangerous no matter whatever age you are, compared with Britain. But then there are many places within the US with lower murder rates than places in Britain. Places are far harder to categorise than people's ages or sex, or time. However, we know that the key component to what makes one place more dangerous to live in than another is poverty. The poorer the place you live in, the more likely you are to be murdered. But just how much more likely and how is that changing?

In Britain the most sensible measure of poverty is the Breadline Britain index, which can be used to calculate, for each ward in the country, the proportion of households living in poverty (Gordon, 1995)[4]. The results of applying this methodology are simple to interpret and also remarkable. They are shown in Table 1. The first line of this table indicates that in the least poor areas of Britain, we find that for every 100 people we would expect to be murdered given how many people live there, only 54 were murdered at the start of the 1980s and only 50 by the end, a fall of four per 100 expected (or four per cent).

---

[4] Fortunately for this study the index was calculated at the mid-point of the period we are interested in using, among other information, the results of the 1991 Census for over 10,000 local wards in Britain. For each ward we know the proportion of households living in poverty at that time. This tends to change very slowly over time and thus we can divide the country up into 10 groups of wards ranging from those within which people suffer the highest rates of poverty to those in which poverty is most rare. Next, for each of the four time periods we are concerned with, we make use of the changing number of people by their age and sex living in each of these 10 groups of areas. Given that information, and applying the murder rates that people experienced in the first period throughout, we can calculate how many people we would expect to be murdered in each decile area taking into account the changing composition of the populations of those areas. Finally, if we divide the number of people actually murdered in those areas at those times by the number we would expect if place played no part, we derive a standardised mortality ratio (SMR) for each area at each time.

**Table 1:** Standardised mortality ratios (SMRs) for murder in Britain, by ward poverty, 1981–2000

| Area | 1981–85 | 1986–90 | 1991–95 | 1996–00 | Change (%) |
|---|---|---|---|---|---|
| Least poor (10) | 54 | 59 | 55 | 50 | −4 |
| Decile 9 | 67 | 65 | 67 | 60 | −7 |
| Decile 8 | 62 | 69 | 68 | 66 | 4 |
| Decile 7 | 74 | 85 | 72 | 81 | 7 |
| Decile 6 | 79 | 77 | 83 | 88 | 9 |
| Decile 5 | 95 | 95 | 95 | 103 | 8 |
| Decile 4 | 112 | 122 | 125 | 130 | 18 |
| Decile 3 | 119 | 130 | 148 | 147 | 28 |
| Decile 2 | 151 | 166 | 191 | 185 | 34 |
| Most poor (1) | 243 | 261 | 271 | 282 | 39 |
| Ratio | 4.50 | 4.42 | 4.89 | 5.68 | |

*Note*: Expected values are based on 1981–85 national rates (100 is the national average)

In the five years 1981-85, people living in the poorest ten per cent of wards in Britain were four and a half times more likely to be murdered than those living in the least poor 10 per cent. Furthermore, the SMR for murder rises monotonically (always in the same direction) with poverty: for every increase in poverty there is a rise in the murder rate, such that people living in the poorest tenth of Britain were 143 per cent more likely than average to be murdered. This rose in the successive five year periods to 161 per cent, 171 per cent and then 182 per cent above the average SMR of 100. Most surprisingly, despite the overall national doubling of the murder rate over this time, people living in the least poor 20 per cent of Britain saw their already very low rates of murder fall further. The increase in murder was concentrated almost exclusively in the poorer parts of Britain and most strongly in its poorest tenth of wards. By the 1990s the excess deaths due to murder in the poorest half of Britain amounted to around 200 per year, that is murders that would not occur if these places experienced average rates. Just over half of that number related to excess murders amongst the poorest tenth of the population. The rise in murder in Britain has been concentrated almost exclusively in men of working age living in the poorest parts of the country.

### With what were they murdered?

What is causing these murders? How are they being committed? Is it a rise in the use of guns? These are superficial questions. It is what lies behind the murder rate that matters. A rise in drug use? Again superficial, it's what might lie behind that. Nevertheless, it is worth looking at how people by place are killed if only to help dispel some myths. The cause of death by method is specified on the death certificates of a proportion of those who are murdered. In many cases the exact cause is unspecified. If we take those cases for which a cause is specified then five main causes account for almost all murders: a fight (ICD E960), poison (ICD E962), strangling (ICD E963), use of firearms (ICD E965) or cutting (ICD E966). Figure 4 shows the proportion of murders attributed to these methods and all other causes for all murders in each ward of Britain grouped by poverty rate between 1981 and 2000.

**Figure 4:** Methods of murder by ward poverty, Britain, 1981–2000

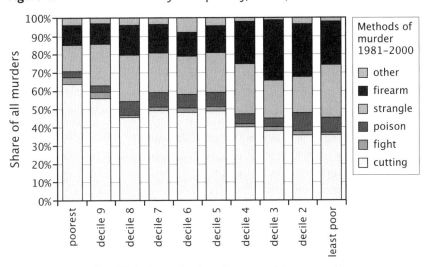

Wards of Britain ranked and grouped into equal
population sized groups by poverty rates

The most important myth to dispel is that of gun crimes being a key factor behind the high murder rates in poor areas. Firearms account for only 11 per cent of murders in the poorest wards of Britain compared to 29 per cent of murders in the least poor areas. The more affluent an area, the more likely it is that guns will be used when murders are committed. The simple reason for this is that there are more guns in more affluent areas. There might be more legal shotguns rather than illegal handguns over the 20 years, but mortality is raised by roughly an additional five murders a year (roughly one extra murder per million people living there). There has been no change in the proportion of murders committed with firearms in richer areas, despite the introduction of legislation designed to limit their use.

The most common way in which people are murdered in the poorest fifth of areas in Britain is through being cut with a knife or broken glass/bottle or (in only four per cent of cases, but still the largest proportion of any decile area) in a fight – usually through kicking. A higher proportion of people are poisoned or strangled in more affluent areas. In fact the use of poison in murder has increased its share by 15 per cent in the least poor areas over the 20 years. Perhaps those murders still occurring in more affluent areas are becoming a little more premeditated there? In almost all areas the proportion of murders attributable to strangling is falling. This may well reflect the fall in the murder rate of women by men. This brief summary has concentrated on what is changing. In the round, however, much the same methods of murder are used now as were used 20 years ago, just more often in poorer areas and less often in the less poor parts of Britain.

### Why are they murdered?

Our final, fifth, question is 'why?' Why are some people much more likely to be murdered than others and why are the rates of murder in Britain changing as they are? These are the most difficult of all the questions to address, but clearly the most important. In a way, the answer to the second part of the question – why are the rates changing as they are? – can help answer the first – why are some people much more likely to be murdered? Table 2, is complicated but attempts to show how the changes can be examined in much more detail to try to uncover the reasons behind the rising overall murder rate.

Table 2 shows the murder rate of all men in Britain by age from 11 to 50. The table begins in 1993 because this was the first year in which deaths were recorded by year of occurrence rather than registration (year-on-year variations are unreliable before then). The rates have been smoothed slightly to make them more reliable, which has the effect of reducing the highest rates slightly. The first line of the table shows that the murder rate of 11-year-old boys has fluctuated between one and three per million over these eight years while the murder rate of the group now most at risk of murder, 21 year old men, has risen from 31 per million in 1993 to 51 per million by 2000. The figures in the table are shaded to allow for easier reading and it is the pattern to the shading that provides our clue as to why murder rates are rising. The shading forms a triangle and, on these kinds of figures a triangle indicates what is known as a cohort effect. A cohort effect is something which affects people born in a particular year or group of years.

Take a man born in 1960. At age 33, in 1993, his cohort suffered a murder rate of 24 per million; this went up and down slightly as he aged but was still 24 per million by the time he was 40 in 2000. The murder rates that these, now older, men experience in Britain are not falling as they age, and, in general, each successive cohort is starting out with a higher murder rate at around age 20 to 21 and carrying that forward. However, for one particular group of men their murder rate is actually generally increasing as they age – men aged 35 or below in 2000, men born in 1965 and after. Why should they be different to men born in 1964 or before? Most men born in 1965 left school at the age of 16 in the summer of 1981 (some may have left at 15 slightly earlier, only a small minority carried on to take

**Table 2:** Murder rates per million in Britain, by age/cohort, 1993–2000

| Age | 1993 | 1994 | 1995 | 1996 | 1997 | 1998 | 1999 | 2000 |
|-----|------|------|------|------|------|------|------|------|
| 11 | 1 | 1 | 3 | 3 | 2 | 1 | 1 | 3 |
| 12 | 1 | 2 | 4 | 5 | 3 | 2 | 3 | 5 |
| 13 | 2 | 3 | 6 | 6 | 4 | 3 | 4 | 6 |
| 14 | 5 | 5 | 6 | 7 | 6 | 4 | 5 | 7 |
| 15 | 7 | 8 | 11 | 12 | 10 | 9 | 11 | 11 |
| 16 | 13 | 13 | 17 | 19 | 17 | 17 | 19 | 17 |
| 17 | 21 | 21 | 23 | 24 | 25 | 26 | 27 | 26 |
| 18 | 24 | 24 | 27 | 28 | 28 | 31 | 35 | 35 |
| 19 | 24 | 25 | 30 | 31 | 28 | 30 | 37 | 42 |
| 20 | 26 | 29 | 32 | 33 | 30 | 32 | 41 | 49 |
| 21 | 31 | 33 | 34 | 34 | 35 | 36 | 42 | 51 |
| 22 | 32 | 34 | 34 | 32 | 33 | 32 | 34 | 42 |
| 23 | 29 | 31 | 33 | 31 | 27 | 27 | 30 | 34 |
| 24 | 26 | 29 | 33 | 33 | 29 | 27 | 30 | 33 |
| 25 | 28 | 30 | 33 | 34 | 31 | 27 | 27 | 30 |
| 26 | 27 | 29 | 31 | 30 | 28 | 26 | 29 | 31 |
| 27 | 21 | 23 | 27 | 27 | 24 | 25 | 33 | 36 |
| 28 | 20 | 21 | 26 | 24 | 21 | 26 | 35 | 38 |
| 29 | 23 | 23 | 23 | 20 | 23 | 30 | 36 | 37 |
| 30 | 24 | 25 | 24 | 24 | 26 | 30 | 30 | 31 |
| 31 | 23 | 24 | 26 | 27 | 27 | 26 | 27 | 30 |
| 32 | 24 | 25 | 25 | 24 | 25 | 27 | 29 | 31 |
| 33 | 24 | 28 | 25 | 21 | 23 | 27 | 30 | 32 |
| 34 | 22 | 27 | 26 | 22 | 21 | 24 | 31 | 39 |
| 35 | 19 | 25 | 27 | 21 | 17 | 22 | 30 | 36 |
| 36 | 20 | 27 | 29 | 22 | 18 | 21 | 25 | 26 |
| 37 | 21 | 26 | 28 | 23 | 20 | 19 | 21 | 24 |
| 38 | 20 | 23 | 26 | 25 | 21 | 18 | 21 | 25 |
| 39 | 20 | 23 | 26 | 26 | 23 | 22 | 24 | 25 |
| 40 | 22 | 23 | 24 | 25 | 25 | 25 | 25 | 24 |
| 41 | 24 | 22 | 22 | 23 | 26 | 25 | 23 | 24 |
| 42 | 22 | 22 | 21 | 21 | 24 | 23 | 22 | 27 |
| 43 | 17 | 20 | 19 | 17 | 19 | 22 | 23 | 25 |
| 44 | 15 | 18 | 19 | 16 | 18 | 23 | 22 | 18 |
| 45 | 15 | 19 | 20 | 19 | 19 | 21 | 18 | 13 |
| 46 | 16 | 18 | 19 | 19 | 18 | 17 | 15 | 15 |
| 47 | 15 | 17 | 17 | 16 | 15 | 16 | 18 | 18 |
| 48 | 13 | 15 | 16 | 14 | 16 | 20 | 21 | 19 |
| 49 | 14 | 16 | 15 | 14 | 17 | 21 | 22 | 20 |
| 50 | 17 | 18 | 15 | 14 | 16 | 17 | 17 | 18 |

*Notes*: The statistics in this table are the murder rates per million per year of all men in Britain by single year of age and by the year in which they were murdered (due to small number problems the statistics have been smoothed by two passes of a simple two dimensional binomial filter). To aid reading, the table cells are shaded by value. A bold line demarcates the cohort of 1965 who were aged 28 in 1993 and 35 in 2000.

A Levels. The summer of 1981 was the first summer for over 40 years that a young man living in a poor area would find work or training very scarce, and it got worse in the years that followed. When the recession of the early 1980s hit, mass unemployment was concentrated on the young, they were simply not recruited. Over time the harm caused in the summer of 1981 was spread a little more evenly; life became more difficult for slightly older men, while most of the younger men were, eventually, employed. However, the seeds that were sown then; that date at which something changed to lead to the rise in murders in the rest of the 1980s and 1990s, can still be seen through the pattern of murder by age and year shown in the figure. Above the cohort of the 1965 line, shown in bold in Table 2, murder rates for men tend to rise as they age.

Table 2 concerns all men, there are too few murders and we know with too little accuracy the numbers of men by single year of age living in each ward in the country in each year to be able to produce the same exhibit for men living in poor areas. Nevertheless, we can be almost certain that this rise is concentrated in the poorest parts of Britain and is far greater there. Most worryingly, in the most recent years the rates for the youngest men have reached unprecedented levels. If these men carry these rates with them as they age, or worse, if their rates rise as have those before them, overall murder rates in Britain will continue to rise despite still falling for the majority of the population in most places.

There is no natural level of murder. Very low rates of murder can fall yet lower as we have seen for older women and in the more affluent parts of the country. For murder rates to rise in particular places, and for a particular group of people living there, life in general has to be made more difficult to live, people have to be made to feel more worthless. Then there are more fights, more brawls, more scuffles, more bottles and more knives and more young men die. These are the same groups of young men for whom suicide rates are rising, the same groups of which almost a million left the country in the 1990s unknown to the authorities, presumably to find somewhere better to live. These are the same young men who saw many of their counterparts, brought up in better circumstances and in different parts of Britain gain good work, or university education, or both, and become richer than any similarly sized cohort of such young ages in British history. The lives of men born since 1964 have polarised, and the polarisation, inequality, curtailed opportunities and hopelessness have bred fear, violence and murder.

Why is the pattern so different for women? One explanation could be that the rise in opportunities (amongst them work, education and financial independence) for women outweighed the effects of growing inequalities. Extreme 'domestic' violence leading to murder, almost always of women, has fallen dramatically over this time period. Women's rates of suicide are also falling for all age groups of women and there has been no exodus of young women from Britain as the 2001 census revealed had occurred for men. Women working in the sex industry still suffer very high rates of murder, but to attempt to identify these deaths through the postcodes of the victims would be taking ecological analysis a step too far. There were also several hundred people, mostly elderly women, murdered by Harold Shipman and these deaths are not included in any of the figures here (he wrote the death certificates and only a few cases were formally investigated at his trial – and thus officially reclassified as murders). But even taking these into account, the fall in extreme violence suffered by women in Britain implies that when a group gains more self-worth, power, work, education and opportunity, murder falls.

## Conclusion

Murder is a social marker. The murder rate tells us far more about society and how it is changing than each individual murder tells us about the individuals involved. The vast majority of the 13,000 murders that have been considered here were not carefully planned and executed crimes; they were acts of sudden violence, premeditated only for a few minutes or seconds, probably without the intent to actually kill in many cases (often those involved were drunk). There will have been hundreds of thousands of similar incidents over this time period that could just as easily have led to murder, but did not. There will have been millions of serious fights, and assaults beyond this and beyond that tens of millions, even hundreds of millions of minor acts of violence and intimidation. Murders are placed at the tip of this pyramid of social harm and their changing numbers and distributions provide one of the key clues as to where harm is most and least distributed. Behind the man with the knife is the man who sold him the knife, the man who did not give him a job, the man who decided that his school did not need funding, the man who closed down the branch plant where he could have worked, the man who decided to reduce benefit levels so that a black economy grew, all the way back to the woman who only noticed 'those inner cities' some six years after the summer of 1981, and the people who voted to keep her in office. The harm done to one generation has repercussions long after that harm is first acted out. Those who perpetrated the social violence that was done to the lives of young men starting some 20 years ago are the prime suspects for most of the murders in Britain.

### Endnote

This paper was originally published as a chapter in the booklet *Criminal Obsessions: Why Harm Matters More Than Crime* published by the Crime and Society Foundation in 2005. The day after the booklet was published *The Times* newspaper ran a story on the research. Referring to the last sentence of that story I sent a letter to *The Times* that day but they did not have space to print it. Below is what it said. The patterns to the trends in murder suggest that threats of violence are not what deters violence. Similarly, record rises in the incarceration rates of young men have been accompanied by the rise in violence reported above. The rise in incarceration is not due to the rise in the murder rate of young men. Only a tiny minority of men who are in prison are convicted of murder or attempted murder. Neither killing nor locking up the killer makes the killing go away. Instead, when a group gains more respect they become more powerful and are less likely to become victims. Take away respect and you increase vulnerability.

Dear Sir

Your report on my Crime and Society Foundation study (Alcohol fuels murder rate for young men, *The Times*, 17 October) ended with the statement that it "found that the number and rate of murder had doubled since 1967 – just after hanging was abolished." The study made no link between the abolition of hanging and the rise in the national murder rate. The only mention of hanging in the report was that it is false to think that "if you kill the killer the killing goes away." National murder rates rose not only after 1967, but after 1969, 1970, 1973, 1975, 1977, 1978, 1979, 1981 and so on. The date of 1967 was included in the report because that was when the Home Office data series began. The view that abolishing hanging increased the overall murder rate does not explain why murder rates reduced for almost all groups of women, children and pensioners over this period. Indeed the United States, where the death penalty is still in use in many states, reports much higher rates of murder than does the UK.

Yours sincerely,

Danny Dorling

## References

Barclay, G. and Travers, C. (2002) *International comparisons of criminal justice statistics 2000*, Issue 05/02, 12 July 2000, Home Office (Report was originally hosted at www.homeoffice.gov.uk/rds/pdfs2/ hosb502.pdf).

Baumer, E., Lauritsen, R., Rosenfield, R. and Wright, R. (1998) 'The influence of crack cocaine on robbery, burglary, and homicide rates: a cross-city longitudinal analysis', *Journal of Research in Crime and Delinquency*, 35, pp 316–40.

Bleetman, A., Perry, C.H., Crawford, R. and Swann, I.J. (1997) 'Effect of Strathclyde police initiative "Operation Blade" on accident and emergency attendances due to assault', *Journal of Accident and Emergency Medicine*, vol 14, no 3, pp 153–6.

Blumstein, A., Rivara, F.P. and Rosenfeld, R. (2000) 'The rise and decline of homicide – and why', *Annual Review of Public Health*, 21, p 505.

Bowling, B. (1999) 'The rise and fall of New York murder: zero tolerance or crack's decline?', *British Journal of Criminology*, vol 39, no 4, pp 531–54.

Brookman, F. and Maguire, M. (2003) *Reducing homicide: Summary of a review of the possibilities*, Home Office Research Development and Statistics Directorate Occasional Paper No. 84 (www.homeoffice.gov.uk/rds/ pdfs2/ occ84homicide.pdf) (Now moved to national web archives).

Chervyakov, V.V., Shkolnikov, V.M., Pridemore, W.A. and McKee, M. (2002) 'The changing nature of murder in Russia', *Social Science and Medicine*, vol 55, no 10, pp 1713–24.

Cubbin, C., LeClere, F.B. and Smith, G.S. (2000) 'Socioeconomic status and injury mortality: individual and neighbourhood determinants', *Journal of Epidemiology and Community Health*, no 54, pp 517–24.

Duncan, C., Jones, K. and Moon, G. (1998) 'Context, composition and heterogeneity: using multilevel models in health research', *Social Science and Medicine*, no 42, pp 817–30.

Durkheim, E. (1999) *Suicide: A study in sociology*, London: Routledge [First published 1897].

Felson, R.B. and Messner, S.F. (1996) 'To kill or not to kill? Lethal outcomes in injurious attacks', *Criminology*, vol 34, no 4, pp 519–45.

Flood-Page, F. and Taylor, J. (eds) (2003) *Crime in England and Wales 2001/2002: Supplementary volume*, London: Home Office Research Development and Statistics Directorate.

Gordon, D. (1995) 'Census based deprivation indices: their weighting and validation', *Journal of Epidemiology and Community Health*, no 49 (Supplement 2), pp 39–44.

Griffiths, C. (2003) 'The impact of Harold Shipman's unlawful killings on mortality statistics by cause in England and Wales', *Health Statistics Quarterly*, no 19, pp 5–9.

Gunnell, D., Wehner, H. and Frankel, S. (1999) 'Sex differences in suicide trends in England and Wales', *Lancet*, no 353, pp 556–7.

Harris, A.R., Thomas, S.H., Fisher, G.A., and Hirsch, D.J. (2002) 'Murder and medicine: the lethality of criminal assault 1960–1999', *Homicide Studies*, vol 6, no 2, pp 128–66.

Helmuth, L. (2000) 'Has America's tide of violence receded for good?', *Science*, no 5479 (28 July 2000) pp 582–5.

Karmen, A. (1996) *Research into the reasons why the murder rate has dropped so dramatically in New York City 1994–5*, Second Progress Report, New York: John Jay College of Criminal Justice.

Lattimore, P., Trudeau, J., Riley, J., Leiter, J. and Edwards, S. (1997a) *A study of homicide in eight US cities*, NIJ Intramural Research Project, Washington, DC: National Institute of Justice.

Lattimore, P., Trudeau, J., Riley, J., Leiter, J. and Edwards, S. (1997b). *Homicide in eight US cities: Trends, context, and policy implications*, Washington, DC: National Institute of Justice.

Lester, D. (2002) 'Murder rates in the regions of Germany', *Psychological Reports*, vol 90, no 2, pp 446–446.

Macdonald, G. (2002) 'Violence and health: the ultimate public health challenge', *Health Promotion International*, vol 17, no 4, pp 293–95.

Mackenbach, J.P. (2002) 'Income inequality and population health', *British Medical Journal*, 324, pp 1–2.

Noble, B. and Charlton, J. (1994) 'Homicides in England and Wales', *Population Trends*, no 75, pp 26–29.

O'Kane, M. (2002) 'Mean streets', *The Guardian*, 16 September, pp 1–4.

Pickett, K.E. and Pearl, M. (2001) 'Multilevel analysis of neighbourhood socioeconomic context and health outcomes: a critical review', *Journal of Epidemiology and Community Health*, no 55, pp 111–22.

Pridemore, W.A. (2003) 'Demographic, temporal, and spatial patterns of homicide rates in Russia', *European Sociological Review*, vol 19, no 1, pp 41–49.

Richards, P. (1999) *Homicide statistics*, House of Commons Research Paper 99/56.

Rooney, C. and Devis, T. (1999) 'Recent trends in deaths from homicide in England and Wales', *Health Statistics Quarterly*, no 3, pp 5–13.

Saunderson, T., Haynes, R. and Langford, I. (1998) 'Urban rural variations in suicides and undetermined deaths in England and Wales', *Journal of Public Health Medicine*, no 20, 261–7.

Shaw, M., Dorling, D., Gordon, D. and Davey Smith, G. (1999) *The widening gap: Health inequalities and policy in Britain*, Bristol: The Policy Press.

Shaw, M., Gordon, D., Dorling, D., Mitchell, R. and Davey Smith, G. (2000) 'Increasing mortality differentials by residential area level of poverty: Britain 1981–1997', *Social Science and Medicine*, vol 51, no 1, pp 151–3.

Shepherd, J. (1994) 'Preventing injuries from bar glasses', *British Medical Journal*, no 308, pp 932–3.

Wagstaff, A. and van Doorslaer, E. (2000) 'Income inequality and health: what does the literature tell us?', *Annual Review of Public Health*, no 21, pp 543–67.

Wallace, D. and Wallace, R. (1998) 'Scales of geography, time and population: the study of violence as a public health problem', *American Journal of Public Health*, vol 88, no 12, pp 1853–8.

Warburton, A.L. and Shepherd, J.P. (2000) 'Effectiveness of toughened glassware in terms of reducing injury in bars: a randomised controlled trial', *Injury Prevention*, no 6, pp 36–40.

Ward, H., Day, S. and Weber, J. (1999) 'Risky business: health and safety in the sex industry over a 9 year period', *Sexually Transmitted Infection*, vol 75, no 5, pp 340–3.

Whitley, E., Gunnell, D., Dorling, D. and Davey Smith, G. (1999) 'Ecological study of social fragmentation, poverty and suicide', *British Medical Journal*, no 319, pp 1034–7.

WHO (World Health Organization)(2002) *World report on violence and health.* Geneva: WHO.

Wilkinson, R. (1992) 'Income distribution and life expectancy', *British Medical Journal*, no 304, pp 165–8.

Wilkinson, R. (1996) *Unhealthy societies: The afflictions of inequality*, London: Routledge.

Wilson Huang, W.S. (1995) 'A cross-national analysis on the effect of moral individualism on murder rates', *International Journal of Offender Therapy and Comparative Criminology*, vol 39, no 1, pp 63–75.

# 2

# The dream that turned pear-shaped[1]

*Local Economy* (2006) vol 21, no 4, pp 353–61

For international readers I'm afraid (as the English tend to say) that this is a very British tale beginning with a very British piece of slang, so I had better define at least one of my terms:

"Pear-shaped (noun) ...

The third meaning is mostly limited to the United Kingdom. It is used to describe a situation that went awry, perhaps horribly wrong. A failed bank robbery, for example, could be said to have 'gone pear-shaped'.

The phrase seems to visualise the original plan as a perfect circle, but for some reason, this became distorted in the execution. Hence the outcome was more pear-shaped.

The origin for this use of the term is in dispute...."

[source: www.answers.com/topic/pear-shaped]

---

[1] Original title began: *Inequalities in Britain 1997–2006.*

The dream, the perfect-policy-circle that was going to deliver so much was fully recognised to be pear-shaped only in the tenth year of its dreaming. The dream was that inequalities would be reduced by a government committed to social justice. This included all kinds of inequalities, but it made sense in the journal this chapter was first published in to begin with those concerning economic geography:

On the 20th of March 2006 *The Financial Times* published the results of its investigation which…

> "…uncovered a startling picture of underperformance in the very regions of the country the government came to office vowing to revitalise. The stark message of the statistics is that regional and local economies under Mr Blair's government have become divergent more quickly than under Margaret Thatcher, generally seen as the premier whose policies did most to entrench the north-south divide." (Giles, 2006)

The growing divide they found was not just between regions of the country but "at the level of parts of UK cities and small rural areas … the richest areas benefited from faster growth since 1997 than poorer areas" (*ibid*). The newspaper quoted Professor Andrew Henley of Swansea University as saying that it was "shocking, really" and that "we have had more dispersion between 1995 and 2001 than between 1977 and 1995", and that developments since 1997 are pointing towards the growth of "extremely productive breakaway regions including London, the South-East and a few cities elsewhere, a few intermediate areas – and a big rump of poor performance". In short, a pear-shaped picture of economic development was emerging in Britain, where the bulk of the population was destined to live in underperforming regions from which the 'productive' winners are moving further and further away. Where, though, are these winner and loser places and peoples? Which are the 'few cities elsewhere' and what do they have that the rest lack to beat the bulge?

In work towards helping to produce the statistics for the then Office of the Deputy Prime Minister's *State of the English cities* report (Parkinson et al. 2006), with colleagues in the Social and Spatial Inequalities Group (SASI, 2006) at Sheffield University we produced a very simple league table (Table 1). A version of the table is reproduced here sorted by which cities have risen fastest to slowest in the league since around the year 1997. The average score for a city is simply the normalised average of five measures of well-being: life expectancy, education (% with university degrees), low worklessness (reflected in low Job Seeker's Allowance/Income Support claim rates), low poverty (using the Poverty and Social Exclusion measure) and average housing prices. The score is expressed in units akin to life expectancy and is now highest for Cambridge at 82.3 and lowest for Liverpool at 64.7. The cities we compare are the largest as defined by their built up area in England. Note Scotland, Wales and Northern Ireland are not included here. Despite this omission, it is evident from Table 1 (and by just looking within England) that those cities where chances have improved the most have been mainly in the south. To aid interpretation the table is shaded by whether each city is in the north or the south of this country. The north is dark.

**Table 1:** Key state of the city indicators, sorted by change and an overall score given

| City | Life Exp. 2001–2003 | 2001 % of adults with a degree | %working age claiming JSA/IS 2003 | poverty by PSE 1999–2001 % | Average housing price 2003 £s | Average score 2003 | Change in score over time |
|---|---|---|---|---|---|---|---|
| Brighton | 78.4 | 29 | 9.3 | 27 | 212,361 | 77.6 | 6.8 |
| Oxford | 79.2 | 37 | 6.1 | 30 | 255,181 | 80.9 | 6.7 |
| London | 78.6 | 30 | 10.3 | 33 | 283,387 | 77.5 | 6.7 |
| Cambridge | 79.5 | 41 | 5.1 | 29 | 244,862 | 82.3 | 5.6 |
| York | 79.4 | 23 | 5.4 | 25 | 147,513 | 78.2 | 5.4 |
| Reading | 79.6 | 26 | 4.7 | 20 | 211,794 | 81.5 | 5.3 |
| Bournemouth | 79.7 | 17 | 7.1 | 21 | 214,296 | 79.1 | 5.0 |
| Southampton | 78.8 | 19 | 6.9 | 25 | 172,585 | 76.9 | 4.9 |
| Crawley | 79.6 | 19 | 4.8 | 22 | 205,506 | 79.8 | 4.7 |
| Aldershot | 79.0 | 22 | 3.7 | 17 | 238,991 | 81.9 | 4.6 |
| Bristol | 78.9 | 23 | 7.7 | 25 | 160,708 | 77.1 | 4.6 |
| Warrington | 77.9 | 17 | 6.8 | 23 | 119,668 | 75.1 | 4.6 |
| Southend | 79.0 | 13 | 7.5 | 19 | 186481 | 77.6 | 4.2 |
| Milton Keynes | 78.2 | 18 | 6.6 | 25 | 161,625 | 76.0 | 4.2 |
| Derby | 78.1 | 18 | 10.5 | 27 | 114,280 | 73.1 | 4.2 |
| Worthing | 78.8 | 16 | 6.4 | 20 | 186,992 | 78.0 | 4.1 |
| Swindon | 78.2 | 15 | 6.6 | 22 | 150,689 | 76.0 | 4.1 |
| Northampton | 78.2 | 17 | 7.8 | 24 | 135,871 | 75.1 | 4.1 |
| Newcastle | 77.1 | 16 | 12.8 | 34 | 111,220 | 69.2 | 4.1 |
| Portsmouth | 78.8 | 16 | 6.6 | 25 | 157,145 | 76.2 | 4.0 |
| Norwich | 79.8 | 18 | 7.5 | 27 | 138,187 | 76.3 | 3.9 |
| Coventry* | 77.8 | 16 | 10.9 | 28 | 111,165 | 72.0 | 3.8 |
| Hastings | 77.4 | 15 | 13.4 | 25 | 163,128 | 72.3 | 3.7 |
| Preston | 77.7 | 17 | 7.2 | 26 | 97,038 | 73.6 | 3.6 |
| Manchester | 76.7 | 19 | 11.6 | 30 | 119,569 | 70.9 | 3.6 |
| Sheffield | 77.9 | 16 | 10.4 | 33 | 96,328 | 70.8 | 3.6 |
| Ipswich | 79.0 | 16 | 10.1 | 25 | 134,514 | 74.7 | 3.5 |
| Plymouth | 78.1 | 13 | 9.8 | 28 | 118,978 | 72.4 | 3.5 |
| Wakefield | 77.5 | 14 | 9 | 28 | 110,407 | 72.1 | 3.5 |
| Gloucester | 78.4 | 16 | 8.5 | 22 | 141,690 | 75.5 | 3.4 |

* Yes, Coventry is in the north of England (just).

| City | Life Exp. 2001–2003 | 2001 % of adults with a degree | %working age claiming JSA/IS 2003 | poverty by PSE 1999–2001 % | Average housing price 2003 £s | Average score 2003 | Change in score over time |
|------|------|------|------|------|------|------|------|
| Nottingham | 77.5 | 18 | 9.8 | 28 | 123,663 | 72.7 | 3.4 |
| Birkenhead | 77.9 | 13 | 12.2 | 29 | 95,632 | 70.6 | 3.3 |
| Sunderland | 76.6 | 12 | 12.4 | 34 | 91,322 | 67.8 | 3.2 |
| Leeds | 78.2 | 19 | 8.9 | 32 | 119,262 | 72.8 | 3.1 |
| Middlesbrough | 77.1 | 12 | 13.1 | 32 | 81,760 | 68.4 | 3.1 |
| Doncaster | 77.3 | 11 | 10.6 | 30 | 82,267 | 69.8 | 3.0 |
| Barnsley | 77.2 | 10 | 10.8 | 32 | 79,492 | 68.9 | 3.0 |
| Telford | 77.9 | 13 | 9 | 27 | 115,722 | 72.6 | 2.9 |
| Chatham | 77.7 | 12 | 7.7 | 23 | 142,374 | 74.2 | 2.8 |
| Liverpool | 75.7 | 14 | 18 | 36 | 87,607 | 64.7 | 2.8 |
| Wigan | 76.5 | 12 | 8.6 | 27 | 88,946 | 70.7 | 2.6 |
| Grimsby | 77.6 | 10 | 11.5 | 28 | 77,898 | 70.0 | 2.6 |
| Rochdale | 76.4 | 14 | 12.2 | 31 | 92,523 | 68.8 | 2.5 |
| Leicester | 78.0 | 17 | 11 | 28 | 124,812 | 72.6 | 2.3 |
| Bolton | 76.8 | 15 | 10.4 | 29 | 89,281 | 70.4 | 2.3 |
| Blackpool | 77.2 | 13 | 8.9 | 24 | 103,656 | 72.5 | 2.2 |
| Birmingham | 77.4 | 14 | 12.8 | 33 | 122,794 | 69.7 | 2.2 |
| Peterborough | 77.5 | 14 | 9.5 | 28 | 123,089 | 72.1 | 2.1 |
| Luton | 77.2 | 14 | 9.7 | 28 | 143,698 | 72.2 | 2.0 |
| Mansfield | 77.1 | 9 | 9.4 | 28 | 94,749 | 70.4 | 2.0 |
| Blackburn | 75.8 | 14 | 12.7 | 30 | 70,969 | 67.8 | 1.9 |
| Huddersfield | 77.2 | 15 | 8.7 | 29 | 97,815 | 71.6 | 1.8 |
| Stoke | 76.9 | 11 | 10.3 | 29 | 78,834 | 69.7 | 1.7 |
| Burnley | 76.8 | 12 | 10.7 | 31 | 55,879 | 68.7 | 1.5 |
| Bradford | 76.9 | 13 | 11.5 | 33 | 75919 | 68.6 | 1.4 |
| Hull | 76.6 | 12 | 17.1 | 33 | 72374 | 66.0 | 1.4 |

In describing the playing field that was formed as a result of long-term social trends that have, in the main, been exacerbated since 1997, we suggested that English cities can appear in a series of leagues when the data in Table 1 is sorted by the 2003 score and considered in the round. A "premier league" of four cities with high average scores from 80.9 to 82.3 is clear (including Oxford and Cambridge), followed by 18 "first division cities" with scores from 74.2 to 79.8 (from Crawley to Chatham, including London and Bristol). There is a gap and then a "second division" of 14 cities scoring between 71.6 and 73.6 (from Preston to Huddersfield, including Leeds and Nottingham), followed by a "third division" from 70.9 to 70.4 (headed by Manchester and down to Bolton), and a "fourth division" from Grimsby to Middlesbrough, including Birmingham, and Newcastle); with Blackburn, Sunderland; and then Hull; and then Liverpool following below division four. Almost all southern cities are in the premier league or first division of Table 1. Less than a half dozen are found in the second division and none below that.

Division two downwards is dominated by cities in the North of England. All that changes since 1997 have achieved is to exacerbate these inequalities in the variations in life chances between these cities. This is seen before we even consider that in general the life chances gains have also been greater outside of the built up areas of these cities – in their commuting hinterlands (especially the hinterlands of the more southern cities).

Brighton, Oxford and Cambridge are the star performers matching the growth of London. In the north only York stands out as comparable. York is in a way becoming a southern enclave in the north of England – again. A millennia ago when William the Conqueror marched north he was handed the keys to the city of York on his arrival, built two castles, and made the city his base for conquering the rest of the north of England. There are very long historical roots as to why some places find themselves a little higher or lower on the league than they might otherwise be placed. After York, growth in the round has been fastest in Reading, Bournemouth, Southampton, Crawley, Aldershot and Bristol; all cities with relatively quick connections to London (which is also part of York's advantage being on the East Coast Mainline). There is really only one star economic performing city in Britain – London. It just happens to have people commuting to it, or dependent on it, from a range of nearby towns and cities and so those areas often rank high too. The map below is thus possibly as good a guide as anything to future economic prospects in the short term in Britain. Note that in the south, towns like Hastings do a little bit worse than might be expected, other

**Figure 1:** Travel time by fastest morning train to the capital, 2005 (England only, from the largest cities, conventional and population mapped)

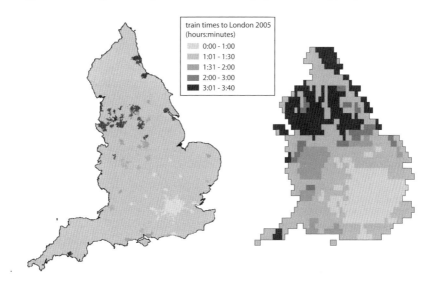

than for their slightly slower commuting times, and perhaps if we stretch the possible importance of their history of poor geographical connections.

Government,[2] at least that large part that does not believe its own spin (Dorling et al, 2002), knows this is happening. The party of government know it even better, being based and strongest in those very areas where people are losing out the most relative to others. Most cabinet ministers know that their constituents are losing out compared to the norm (let alone as compared with the best-off). So how does government cope with this reality, especially in the run-up to the tenth anniversary of the 1997 landslide? One way is to convince themselves that the present would have been far more unequal, had the landslide and the policies that could be implemented as a result of it not occurred. That is very possible, but that becomes a weaker defence to use as more time passes. Saying that at least nowhere appears to have fared absolutely worse (on balance if not in every instance) under your watch is no great claim to achievement – even if under other circumstances immiseration might have been more absolute than relative. Another way that government can cope with their failure is to blame someone else – and when you run out of other politicians to blame – you can turn to the victims of your policy failure.

Suppose we take the five areas used to construct the league table above. The first is life expectancy where the statistics show we are moving away from, rather than approaching or meeting, the two main government targets to reduce health inequalities. Firstly, inequalities in infant mortality by class have increased. Thankfully no-one has yet blamed working class babies for not trying hard enough to live through their first year of life as compared to the efforts of middle class newborns. Secondly, inequalities in life expectancy between areas have been rising steadily under New Labour (and they pledged to reduce those inequalities too). Here some parts of government believe folk can be blamed for this trend. Taking a day-off from supporting United States foreign policy on Wednesday July 26th, 2006, the Prime Minister travelled to Nottingham to tell the population that "we can't slim for you". There is a very long history to the disingenuous turn on public health policy that took Labour from its position in 1997, when Tessa Jowell, the then Minister for Public Health, criticised the health strategy of the previous administration for "its excessive emphasis on lifestyle issues" which "cast the responsibility back on to the individual" (Jowell, 1997). It took just under ten years to turn around the promise not to blame the victim.

Take (next) adults with a degree and you find that the greatest absolute increases in access to university education have been amongst those children

---

[2] Editorial note: This chapter was originally published in 2006 so it is the then Labour government which is being referred to here. It is worth noting that after that government lost power in 2010, the poorest areas of Britain were allowed to become even poorer by the new administration.

already most likely to go; and this despite initiatives to widen access. It may well have been worse without those initiatives. The gap in access to universities, let alone the gap in access to particular groups of universities, could have grown far wider had there not been a change in government – but that gap widened after 1997 and we have yet to see it narrow (Dorling, 2006). And who is blamed? The universities say it is the secondary schools. The secondary schools blame primary schools, and they in turn the home environment. 'Sure Start' is then supposed to cure all ills there. Meanwhile the quota on how many children can get to university is set rigidly by the centre.

Were all the children of Britain to excel above our wildest expectations the numbers of university places are fixed, any mechanism to ensure a fairer distribution of what is available is not working. Attendance of private school has risen year on year since 1997, mainly to ensure that those whose parents are richer can continue to take most places while the rest are told they have failed – sorry, blamed – for not being clever enough. Quite what is clever about having parents who can pay for your pieces of paper by proxy is never fully explained – but there are so many more victims yet to blame, so we must move quickly on.

What is on offer to the two thirds of children for whom places at universities are not reserved? They can work hard at relatively low wages in what since 1997 have come to be called lousy jobs (in which they are lucky to receive a special minimum wage), but they have no "fifth option" to be out of work and not work to find work. It was mainly for their age group that Job Seeker's Allowance (JSA) was created – the next column of our table. When next considering JSA/IS (Income Support) benefit recipients, those in areas of highest uptake have been targeted most into low paid work under various initiatives, but as David Webster clearly explained in an earlier issue of the journal this chapter originally appeared in – current government policy on worklessness is also predicated on a 'blame the victim' approach where the government is "very confident that the problem lies entirely on the supply side of the labour market. In other words it is caused by the characteristics or motivation of workless people and not by any shortage of demand for labour" (Webster, 2006, p 107). It is the shortage of demand for labour that keeps many cities in their places down the bottom of Table 1, not the fecklessness of those who still live there.

On the fourth column of the table – poverty – there are no signs of a reduction in the overall national level when measured by expenditure (Brewer et al. 2006) or by Breadline methods (Pantazis et al, 2006) and, by 2005, Britain still had the 25th highest level of child poverty before transfers out of some 26 other European countries that were recently compared by Eurostat using data from 2005. The only country to perform worse was the Slovak Republic (Hirsch, 2006, p 16). A great deal of boasting is done by government over having not quite hit the first (and easiest) of the four targets on the way to abolishing child poverty. Again, things could be far worse, and again, just as with dying infants, government does not yet blame the children. It is also true that over this same time period, in the United States, there have been absolute increases in infant mortality on average for all, led by increases in the number of Black American babies dying due to rising absolute poverty levels. But compare ourselves to another twenty five countries in Europe as Hirsch did and we are still doing very badly, especially considering we are among the richest of European countries.

Finally, among these trends in geographical inequalities our fifth column, trends in housing prices and housing wealth, and wealth when more widely measured – all such measures have seen inequities rise since 1997 (Dorling et al, 2005). However, when it comes to wealth, this time the victims are being blamed in advance for factoring in the future effects of this polarisation, and so for the subsequent truculence of the young who appear not to want to save because they do not place much trust in financial institutions, nor in the advice of their government: [3]

"Millions of workers in their twenties and thirties risk turning into the 'live fast, die poor' generation unless they start saving for retirement, a Labour minister said yesterday. James Purnell, the pension reform minister, said today's affluent young would live longer than their parents but were facing poverty in old age because they were living for today rather than saving for tomorrow. In a bleak assessment, Mr Purnell warned that in the space of just five years the proportion of those in their twenties paying into a private pension had fallen from one in three to one in four." (Wilson and Webster, 2006).

As we in Britain approach the ten-year mark of this Labour administration – we ought to remember – we were warned at the start that it would be a long haul. The words were ringing in our ears, subliminally entering our thinking. The words were repeated endlessly in the run-up to the election of 1st of May 1997. The words, for those readers who were not in Britain during those days were "things can only get better if we see it through".

As victory in 1997 was celebrated the campaign theme tune began with:

> "You can walk my path, you can wear my shoes
> Learn to talk like me and be an angel too
> But maybe you ain't never gonna feel this way
> You ain't never gonna know me, but I know you

[3] Editorial note: It turns out they may have been right not to trust. The crash came later in the year this paper was published. Had their savings been in the wrong place, or had the bail out of banks failed, they could have lost all. As things stand, being told to save for a rainy day requires today an even greater leap of faith to believe that banks will be safe places for money, and that future governments will always be able to bail them out.

I'm singing it now–
Things can only get better
They can only get better if we see it through–
that means me and I mean you too
So teach me now that things can only get better,
They can only get, they only get, take it on from here
You know I know that things can only get better......"

On May 5th 2005 the third successful election campaign theme tune ended with the words:

"Touch me
Take me to that other place
Reach me
I know I'm not a hopeless case

What you don't have you don't need it now
What you don't know you can feel it somehow
What you don't have you don't need it now
Don't need it now
Was a beautiful day"

Presumably the search is now on for the fourth campaign theme tune. Clearly any budding lyricists who wish their words to be used by a new and even more bright and shiny Labour Party in 2008, 9 or 10 should be trying to rhyme – "you've only got yourselves to blame" with… "people's lives – its only a game".

## References

Brewer, M., Goodman, A. and Leicester, A. (2006) *Household spending in Britain: What can it teach us about poverty?*, Institute for Fiscal Studies Report, (www.ifs.org.uk/publications.php?publication_id=3620).

Dorling, D. (2006) 'Class alignment renewal', *The Journal of Labour Politics*, vol 14, no 1, pp 8–19

Dorling, D., Ford, J., Holmans, A., Sharp, C., Thomas, B. and Wilcox, S. (2005) *The great divide: An analysis of housing inequality*, London: Shelter.

Dorling, D., Eyre, H., Johnston, R. and Pattie, C. (2002) 'A good place to bury bad news? Hiding the detail in the Geography on the Labour Party's website, Reports and surveys', *The Political Quarterly*, vol 73, no 4, pp 476–92.

Giles, C. (2006) 'Forgotten Britain: how Labour has presided over a deepening divide', *Financial Times*, 20 March.

Hirsch, D. (2006) 'Why we are failing our children', *New Statesman*, pp 14–17, 10 July.

Jowell, T. (1997) *Public Health strategy launched to tackle the root causes of ill health*, Department of Health Press release 7 July 1997 (see DoH website).

Pantazis, C., Gordon, D. and Levitas, R. (eds) (2006) *Poverty and social exclusion in Britain*, Bristol: The Policy Press.

Parkinson, M. et al. (2006) *The state of the English cities, volumes 1 and 2*, London: ODPM.

SASI, (2006) Social and Spatial Inequalities Group, University of Sheffield, For *State of the city* data see: www.sasi.group.shef.ac.uk/socr/

Webster, D. (2006) 'Welfare reform: facing up to the geographies of worklessness', *Local Economy*, vol 21, no 2, pp 107–16.

Wilson, G. and Webster, H. (2006) '"Live fast, die poor" fate of pension-shy young', quoted in *The Daily Telegraph* by Graeme Wilson and Hannah Webster on 13 July 2007 (www.telegraph.co.uk/news/main.jhtml?xml=/news/2006/07/13/npens13.xml&sSheet=/news/2006/07/13/ixuknews.htm).

# 3

# The soul searching within New Labour[1]

*Local Economy* (2007) vol 22, no 4, pp 317–24

I am extremely grateful to the Durham University Professor and the

Member of Parliament for the City of Durham (Tim Blackman and Roberta Blackman-Woods, 2007) for their response to my viewpoint on 'Inequalities in Britain 1997-2006: the dream that turned pear-shaped' (Dorling, 2006). Far too little has been written from those still inside of the government, and its political party, that helps explain why this current government has acted and continues to act as it does. Tim and Roberta's words, and the passion behind them help, I think, to reveal why government does what it does, believes what it believes, especially in the face of alternative evidence, and helps explain how it can soldier on under great pressure.

Let us start with what the Labour dream was. For me it was best expressed in the 1994 report of the Commission on Social Justice. That report summarised the state of the nation at the time as being shameful in comparison to the social achievements of our European neighbours, and most importantly in terms of our aspirations, in terms of what we could be. 'It shames us all' were the words I remember and the report set the

---

[1] The paper from which these extracts were taken was written in response to a reply to the "Dream that turned pear-shaped" paper reproduced verbatim in chapter 2 above. Only a brief extract of my reply to that response is included here as you would have to read Tim Blackman and Roberta Blackman-Woods response to understand my full reply and as I don't think many people would argue today that the New Labour dream did not end badly.

terms of the debate for what could be better. That debate then underlay so many of the promises to reduce inequalities that were made by people who subsequently became Labour ministers (and Prime Ministers). It is sobering to read a copy of the report today and to think just how easy it would be to replicate it now: to write something just as damaging. The report's concerns were wide ranging, from concentrated worklessness, to miserable dental health provision and widespread child poverty. Surely we would not feature at the bottom of an OECD league table by child poverty measures a decade after Labour gained power? Sadly we did, even trailing the USA (UNICEF, 2007). What was achieved has not with hindsight begun seriously to deliver the social justice and much else that we (then, in 1994) dreamed of.[2]  [...]

Here is one example of the kind of thing Tim and Roberta thought I should have mentioned, although they suggest first that they would be happy to refute my complaints on any of an infinite number of criteria (such is their party loyalty):

> "... On any criteria this is a substantial change and it has been clearly perceived as such among the general population. In 1994, three years before the Conservatives were defeated in the 1997 general election, 21 per cent of households were finding it difficult or very difficult to manage on their income, and only 29 per cent were 'living comfortably' (ONS, 2006). By 2004, after seven years of Labour in power, only 14 per cent of households were finding it difficult or very difficult to manage, and 40 per cent now regarded themselves as living comfortably." (Blackman and Blackman-Woods, 2007, p 119)

---

[2] It is a crumb of comfort that Labour spin doctors early in 1997 did not ruin the song of this name, made famous in the 1996 film *Trainspotting*, the lyrics of which begin: 'when the taking and the giving starts to get too much'. Although cynicism in the 1990s was rife, the idea that how we were living was wrong was widespread, from high to popular culture, from the pages of Social Justice Commission Tomes to the cinema advertisements, including that for the film just mentioned, a film many more than two thirds could then afford to see: "Choose life. Choose a job. Choose a career. Choose a family. Choose a fucking big television, Choose washing machines, cars, compact disc players, and electrical tin openers. Choose good health, low cholesterol and dental insurance. Choose fixed-interest mortgage repayments. Choose a starter home. Choose your friends. Choose leisure wear and matching luggage. Choose a three piece suite on hire purchase in a range of fucking fabrics. Choose DIY and wondering who you are on a Sunday morning. Choose sitting on that couch watching mind-numbing spirit-crushing game shows, stuffing fucking junk food into your mouth. Choose rotting away at the end of it all, pishing you last in a miserable home, nothing more than an embarrassment to the selfish, fucked-up brats you have spawned to replace yourself. Choose your future. Choose life..." (http://www.generationterrorists.com/quotes/trainspotting.html).

**Table 1:** Change in poverty and wealth by political complexion of parliamentary constituency: in comparison to shadow cabinet (set at 100%)

| Constituencies grouped by the political post held by the MP elected for each seat immediately after the 1997 General Election: | Cabinet Minister | Government Minister (non-cabinet) | Government Backbench | Non-Tory Opposition (Lib Dem/PC/SNP) | Conservative Backbench | Conservative Shadow Cabinet |
|---|---|---|---|---|---|---|
| Breadline poor latest estimates (2001) | 201% | 178% | 133% | 127% | 103% | 100% |
| Breadline poor 1991 estimates | 197% | 173% | 127% | 125% | 101% | 100% |
| Asset wealthy latest estimates (2001) | 22% | 26% | 61% | 84% | 107% | 100% |
| Asset wealthy 1991 estimates | 29% | 39% | 76% | 94% | 119% | 100% |

*Source:* Derived from figures presented first in Dorling et al (2007).

*Note:* All rates are shown in relation to the life chances of the constituents of those areas represented by members of the Shadow Cabinet elected in 1997. In comparison to them, and in the latest period, voters represented by other Conservative MPs are 3 per cent more likely to be living in poverty whereas those represented by Labour Cabinet ministers are now just more than twice as likely to be living in poverty as compared to their Shadow Cabinet counterparts. Similarly the voters that elected the Members of Parliament that became Labour Cabinet ministers have seen their relative chances of being wealthy fall from 29 per cent to 22 per cent of those of Conservative Shadow Cabinet ministers. These statistics rely on census data so cannot be updated easily. However, simpler statistics showing similar results (but on an annual basis) can be derived from trends in life expectancy (rising most quickly for folk in Conservative constituencies) and for changes in housing prices and estimates of equity based on those. On average, those who already had most in 1997 have gained the most since 1997, and the more they had to begin with the more they have gained in terms of the years they can expect to live to and assets they can expect to acquire. Figures released on August 23 by the Office of National Statistics show inequalities in healthy life expectancy between small areas which are far wider than any yet reported in Britain: www.statistics.gov.uk/pdfdir/health0807.pdf

I have to admit that this was news to me, and good news at that. For a breakdown of who may have benefited most from any increase in comfort see Table 1, but also beware what is meant by 'comfort' and 'difficulty'. Fortunately the publication they refer to can be accessed free and online (ONS, 2006) so I searched it for the word 'difficulty'. The word appears 15 times in Social Trends 36. The proportions of older people who are reported to have difficulty with daily activity or mobility; of children who have difficulty in learning: specific, moderate, severe learning difficulties, or profound and multiple, behavioural, emotional and social learning difficulties; difficulties in acquiring basic literacy and numeracy skills and in understanding concepts (ONS, 2006, p 37); difficulties in accessing NHS dental care (a fifth of parents of 5–8 year olds in 2003; ONS, 2006, p 127); difficulty in taking part in activities like going to the cinema because of finding time (48 per cent) or cost (34 per cent, ONS, 2006, p 194). How could a third of people have problems with the cost of going to the cinema but not say that they were having financial difficulties in general? Almost everyone used to be able to go to the cinema.

Eventually I found the source of Tim and Roberta's optimism that things had got better in terms of 'difficulty to manage'. Compare the text in the source below with the quote above and note that all this excludes the largest group of respondents (to the British Social Attitudes Survey) who merely state that they are 'coping' in every year surveyed:

> The proportion of respondents who said that they were 'living comfortably' rose from 24 per cent in 1986 to a peak of 44 per cent in 2003, but fell back to 40 per cent in 2004. In contrast, the proportion who were finding it difficult or very difficult to manage fell from 26 per cent in 1986 to 14 per cent in 2004. This is of course not necessarily inconsistent with a widening of the distribution – as Figure 5.13 showed, the 90th, 50th (median) and 10th percentiles [of real disposable household income] have moved apart, but each has increased in real terms. (ONS, 2006, p 78)

Household income has increased in real terms even for the poorest. However, expectations of what constitutes a basic living and the occasional respite, like the price of cinema tickets, rise a little faster when inequalities grow.

The proportions of people who cannot afford holidays, or cannot afford to make regular savings are far higher than those reporting that they are 'finding it difficult or very difficult to manage' (Dorling et al, 2007). Managing is thus an existence worse than 'getting by' and having one holiday a year (not at a relative's home). Managing is: the rising debts not getting too high; living with poor and broken furniture; not spending money on yourself week on week; not inviting people in because you are ashamed; being overcrowded; finding it hard to give the kids the money for the school trip.[3] Managing is not living properly. Managing is not quite getting by: mustn't grumble – it could be worse. And it should not be beyond the imagination of a Labour Member of Parliament and a university professor to grasp this. All they need do is to imagine living on a quarter of their current income, or much less. [...]

So what has got better? Here are five things that have but which were not, to my knowledge on pledge cards:

---

[3] But still 'managing' to. Only 3 per cent of children's parents could not manage that, even in 1999. http://www.bris.ac.uk/poverty/pse/welcome.htm

(1) The suicide rate has continued to fall year on year from its peak in 1998 to a new low in 2004 (ONS, 2007). It is the case that suicides tend to fall under Labour administrations, and it is good news that this government is no exception, at least on this count. However, since I claimed that 'the dream went pear-shaped' health inequalities between areas have risen again to a new extreme (Dorling, 2007a). Health inequalities between people grouped by social class rather than area, in contrast, were reported to have fallen in new figures released from the Longitudinal Study in November 2007 by the ONS.

(2) The unemployment rate has fallen to an unprecedented low. True, and that is partly why our suicide rate has fallen, although suicide rates tend to fall under Labour administrations worldwide even allowing for unemployment (Shaw et al, 2002). However, as Labour MP and Select Committee member Natasha Engel said on the introduction of the new 'welfare' bill designed to ensure that eight out of ten of us soon work, and in a caveat after the obligatory praise[4] '. . . The whole Committee agrees that the 80 per cent [sic] target is wonderful; it was just the way to reach it that we had slight concerns about.' (Dorling, 2007b). Over half the poor are now in work (but still poor).

(3) Gross Domestic Product continues to rise quarter on quarter for longer than 'ever' recorded before and increasing our wealth in comparison to that of the rest of the world. True, and without that it is doubtful unemployment would have fallen so consistently (until recently); but that extra wealth is increasingly taken by a small proportion of the rich, while child poverty, even by the government's own measures has not fallen so consistently. Our banks (and Conservative voters) have done well, particularly well, under Labour.

(4) Some of the poorest of the poor are now better off and fewer people are simultaneously materially, subjectively and income poor (Brown, 2007). True, but we had to create a new category of poverty to construct this finding and there is growing evidence that widening wealth inequalities and growing debt are creating new inequalities and poverty. The closer we look the more division we see (Thomas and Dorling, 2007).

(5) We are killing fewer people, especially children, than we were a couple of years ago, as we withdraw from Iraq. Soon the rate at which young British men kill could fall to rates comparable at least to the most violent of other European nations. Who, by the way, do you think pays Mr Blair's wages as

---

[4] Yes she has been promoted since. She became the PPS (for the Right Hon, as they like to say) Peter Hain, now Secretary of State in the Department for Work and Pensions.

he works as Middle East Envoy for the 'Quartet'? That killing was not part of the dream in 1994.

If people in the Labour party did not care, Tony Blair would still be Prime Minister.

[...]

Do we now have two large political parties which dislike each other intensely, but which are beginning to resemble each other more and more, and no alternative of any significant electoral relevance? We have some way to go to get there yet. But the parties continue to believe that fundamentals are getting better, and the cheerleaders for our parties begin to look more and more alike, although they will believe in their hearts and souls that they are different. Tim and Roberta's response helps explain how both parties believe that we cannot aspire for more than a majority just 'coping', while a minority live comfortably and a minority find it difficult or very difficult to manage while living in poverty, in this richest of islands. [...]

## References

Blackman, T. and Blackman-Woods, R. (2007) A response to Dorling's 'Inequalities in Britain 1997–2006: the dream that turned pear-shaped', *Local Economy*, vol 22, no 2, pp 118–22.

Brown, G. (2007) Prime Minister's Questions, 18 July (www.theyworkforyou. com/debates/ ?id=2007-07-18a.268.3).

Commission on Social Justice (1994) *Social justice: Strategies for national renewal*, London: Vintage.

Dorling, D. (2006) 'Inequalities in Britain 1997–2006: the dream that turned pear-shaped', *Local Economy*, vol 21, no 4, pp 353–61 [Reprinted as Chapter 2 in this book].

Dorling, D. (2007a) 'Health', in Compass (eds) *Closer to equality? Assessing New Labour's record on equality after 10 years in government*, London: Compass, (http://clients.squareeye.com/uploads/compass/documents/closertoequality.pdf).

Dorling, D. (2007b) 'The real Mental Health Bill' (editorial), *Journal of Public Health Medicine*, vol 6, no 3, pp 6–13.

Dorling, D., Eyre, H., Johnston, R. and Pattie, C. (2002) 'A good place to bury bad news? Hiding the detail in the geography on the Labour Party's website, reports and surveys', *The Political Quarterly*, vol 73, no 4, pp 476–92.

Dorling, D., Rigby, J., Wheeler, B., Ballas, D., Thomas, B., Fahmy, E., Gordon, D. and Lupton, R. (2007) *Poverty, wealth and place in Britain, 1968 to 2005*, Bristol: The Policy Press.

ONS (Office for National Statistics) (2006) *Social trends*, vol 36, London: Palgrave.

ONS (2007) *Suicide rates in United Kingdom*, online data, (www.statistics. gov.uk/downloads/theme_health/Corrected_suicide_data_22Feb07.xls (accessed 11 September 2007).

Orwell, G. (1946) *Animal farm*, London: Penguin.

Orwell, G. (1949) *Nineteen Eighty-Four*, London: Secker and Warburg.

Shaw, M., Dorling, D. and Davey-Smith, G. (2002) 'Editorial: mortality and political climate: how suicide rates have risen during periods of Conservative government, 1901–2000', *Journal of Epidemiology and Community Health*, vol 56, no 10, pp 722–7.

Thomas, B. and Dorling, D. (2007) I*dentity in Britain: A cradle to the grave atlas*, Bristol: The Policy Press.

UNICEF (2007) *Child poverty in perspective: An overview of child well-being in rich countries*, Innocenti Report Card 7, Florence: UNICEF Innocenti Research Centre.

# 4

# Unequal Britain

*Socialist Worker* (2007) issue 2061, 28 July

A new report highlights the growing gap between rich and poor in Britain – it's a mess and it's getting worse...

The Joseph Rowntree Foundation released two reports last week. One showed that the British public says the gap between rich and poor is too large. The other, which seven colleagues and I produced, mapped how poverty and wealth have been distributed and redistributed across Britain since 1968. It shows that the gap between rich and poor is currently the highest it has been in 40 years.

We began in 1968, not because it was a year of student unrest and the time of the "summer of love", but because towards the end of that year and into 1969 the first national survey of poverty in Britain was quietly being undertaken.

A year that began with the Tet Offensive in Vietnam and ended with the earth being photographed from Apollo 8 is not remembered for the surveying of British living conditions on a national scale for the first time – a survey that revealed, among other things, that most ordinary folk did not take a holiday in those years. However, 1968 was the time we began to care in earnest – and the study of poverty stopped being the preserve of the sons of rich men and became part of public policy.

This started through the efforts of Peter Townsend and his fellow researchers at the University of Essex. Townsend's was the first national survey of poverty, and the first fully computerised census took place just a few years later. Because of this the late 1960s to early 1970s is as far back as we can go to look at the distribution of poverty using modern social science methods and modern concepts, such as social exclusion.

**Figure 1:** Poverty in Yorkshire in 1980 and 2000

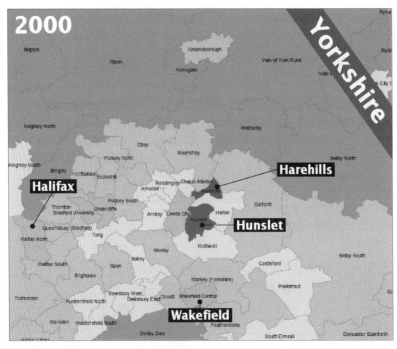

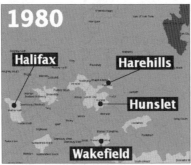

**The rise in density in the number of breadline poor in Yorkshire in 2000** (top) **as compared to 1980** (above). **Poverty in Bradford, Yorkshire, in the mid–1970s** (right).
Maps: University of Sheffield

**Figure 2:** Time Trends

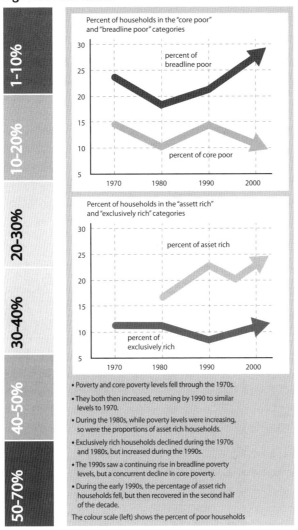

Percent of households in the "core poor" and "breadline poor" categories

percent of breadline poor

percent of core poor

Percent of households in the "assett rich" and "exclusively rich" categories

percent of asset rich

percent of exclusively rich

- Poverty and core poverty levels fell through the 1970s.
- They both then increased, returning by 1990 to similar levels to 1970.
- During the 1980s, while poverty levels were increasing, so were the proportions of asset rich households.
- Exclusively rich households declined during the 1970s and 1980s, but increased during the 1990s.
- The 1990s saw a continuing rise in breadline poverty levels, but a concurrent decline in core poverty.
- During the early 1990s, the percentage of asset rich households fell, but then recovered in the second half of the decade.

The colour scale (left) shows the percent of poor households

1-10%

10-20%

20-30%

30-40%

40-50%

50-70%

Poverty since those times has been defined as being excluded from participation in the norms of society due to lack of material resources.

### Holiday

Today, being able to afford an annual holiday that amounts to more than simply staying with your relatives is considered part of the norms of society. Not being able to afford such a holiday is a marker of poverty.

Because most people in 1968 did not take an annual holiday, lack of holidays was not a marker of poverty then. It is now. As material living standards rise, what it means to be poor changes.

**Figure 3:** Poverty in London and the South East in 1980 and 2000

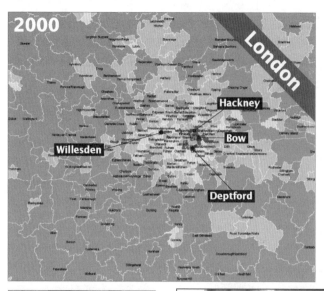

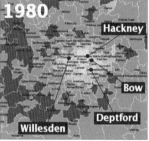

The rise in density in the number of breadline poor (top) in London in 2000 as compared to 1980 (above). Poverty in Tower Hamlets, east London last year (right).

Picture: Jess Hurd/reportdigital.co.uk

*Note:* See Figure 2 above for the key to the shades in these maps, or the first page of the colour plate section of this book.

Go back another 39 years to see how this works. Living standards in 1968 were materially far better than in 1929, and yet looking back on 1968 from today we would not say that the standards were fine.

People should be able to take a holiday at least once a year, have access to hot water in their home and so on. Yet at the time when Townsend's survey was taken many thought that poverty had been all but eradicated.

Today many would argue in just the same way that even the poorest have never had it so good.

But everyone knows that you are poor when you cannot afford an annual holiday in Britain and have problems making ends meet each month, while others jet around the world and find it hard to buy enough to spend their "spare" money. We call this "breadline poverty".

A Labour MP recently told me that in his not too affluent northern England constituency people had never had it so good. People had possessions their parents never had and although he knows there are more riches "in the south", his constituents were not that poor.

His equivalent in 1929 could have said much the same thing, and it would have been true then. But had his equivalent said that and been content with his and his constituents' lot in 1929, the Britain of 1968, let alone 2007 would have been a very different place.

The material living standards of the poorest in 1968 were only as good as they were because of the dissatisfaction of those who received the scraps in the 1920s and 1930s. This dissatisfaction was expressed through votes in that famous general election of 1945.

Without the growth of equality between 1929 and 1968, poverty in 1968 would have been far greater, and we would still have slums today.

Come forward to 2007 and think about poverty and wealth today. There are those who are less concerned with equality, including some in the current government.

### *Equality*

Most of those who in their hearts are truly unconcerned about equality – and hence poverty – sit on opposition benches in parliament. A Tory MP recently told me that his real concern was freedom, not equality. But I find it hard to see the difference between the two.

For instance, the introduction of the NHS made people more equal, and also freed many from the fear of some of the repercussions of ill health. Poverty, wealth, health, education and many other policies are all bound together. The level of poverty that we live with is a measure of the degree of freedom that we live without.

Our report maps how poverty rates declined from 1968 to the mid-late 1970s, but then rose continuously. It shows how this has been accompanied by a rise in the geographical segregation of the poor.

Geographical segregation is when groups live apart from each other. When people are moving further apart from each other, geographical segregation is said to be growing. It is a term usually used to talk about people in different ethnic or religious groups in Britain – but in general people are much more segregated by poverty and wealth than by race or religion.

We also map how many people are "asset rich" – measured primarily through housing wealth – and "exclusively rich" – those who can afford to exclude themselves from normal society. We found the former group growing slightly in number, and the latter being more stable.

The combined effect of these trends was that in 1980 two thirds of households were neither rich nor poor. By 2000 only half of households were in this "normal" category.

The overall geographical and social gaps between rich and poor narrowed over the period when Harold Wilson's Labour governments of the 1960s were in power.

Although the current government has ruled over a period when that gap has grown, there is also some good news. In the most recent period "core poverty" – the number of households with people who are simultaneously income poor, materially deprived and describe themselves as poor – fell. Such very poor households also became less geographically concentrated.

## Gap

Minimum wage and tax credits policy reduced that gap, just as government indifference, complacency or a simple lack of determination has allowed the other gaps – between very rich, rich, average and poor – to widen.

It was only in the 1980s under Margaret Thatcher's administration that everything got worse at once. That took some spectacular callousness to achieve.

The government[1] in Britain is no longer so callous, but it has not achieved what earlier Labour governments have achieved, or kept inequalities down to the lower levels that the majority of other rich capitalist countries have managed to attain. And there is growing evidence that this failure is damaging the lives of the wealthy as well as those of the poor.

Before scoffing at the idea that we should be concerned about the wealthy, stop to think for just a minute over the implications of growing inequality damaging the life chances, freedoms, and wellbeing of all.

If well paid MPs began to realise that their own lives and those of their children would be improved were inequalities in Britain to be reduced, then I suspect they might be a little more effective in their efforts to narrow various gaps than they are at present.

The most geographically segregated social group are those who are so wealthy that they can afford to exclude themselves from the schools, hospitals, cleaning, childcare, recreation and other norms for most people in society. The rich used to be more spread out but are now corralled into affluent enclaves.

---

[1] Editorial note: The 2007 Labour government as compared to the 1980s Conservative government, not the "1980's tribute" Coalition government of 2010.

**Figure 4:** Poverty in Britain in 1970, 1990 and 2000

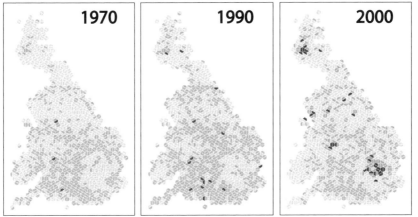

Poverty hotspots across Britain in 1970, 1990 and 2000. The maps show the growing concentration of poor areas.

*Note,* See Figure 2 above for the key to the shades in these maps

## Wealthy

I know it is hard to shed a tear for those who are so affluent. But if you are still thinking for that minute about the problems of riches, how do these rich folk have honest relationships with their husbands, wives, children, parents and friends?

All the while in the background is the issue of money – not upsetting daddy for fear of losing part of the inheritance, wondering why she asked you to sign the prenuptial agreement? I can't see how these can be especially happy lives even if largely lived in leisure.

There is, of course, more bad news for the poor. In the most recent period we surveyed, for the first time we saw large parts of many cities with over half the population becoming poor. Here in effect it is now normal to be poor. There are far fewer average households than there once were.

Get out of poverty in the south of England, become average, and there are fewer and fewer places you can afford to live! Meanwhile the affluent watch those above them become rich and feel that they are not rich enough.

Some of the affluent even think they are poor. Society in Britain has become so divided that very few people live anywhere where they can see how a representative range of folk live.

It's a mess, it's getting worse, and at the same time we have enough resources for all to live decent lives on this island.

Currently our thinking – like our levels of inequality – is back in the 1930s:"Mustn't grumble, it could be so much worse." It could – but it could be so much better than this, for everyone.[2]

## Summary

• Poverty and core poverty levels fell through the 1970s.

• They both then increased, returning by 1990 to similar levels to 1970.

• During the 1980s, while poverty levels were increasing, so were the proportions of asset rich households.

• Exclusively rich households declined during the 1970s and 1980s, but increased during the 1990s.

• The 1990s saw a continuing rise in breadline poverty levels, but a concurrent decline in core poverty.

• During the early 1990s, the percentage of asset rich households fell, but then recovered in the second half of the decade.

---

[2] *Poverty, wealth and place in Britain 1968 to 2005* by Danny Dorling, Jan Rigby, Ben Wheeler, Dimitris Ballas and Bethan Thomas from the University of Sheffield, Eldin Fahmy and David Gordon from the University of Bristol and Ruth Lupton from the University of London is published by The Policy Press. A copy of the findings can be found at www.jrf.org.uk/knowledge/findings

# 5

# Axing the child poverty measure is wrong[1]

*Guardian* (Society Section) (2010) 16 June, p 4

David Cameron says he is worried about the poorest in society but clearly does not want a redistribution of the opportunities that the rich have expropriated from the poor over the past three decades.

Frank Field, appointed by David Cameron to lead an independent review of poverty and life chances in the UK, has cast doubt on the mathematical workings and achievability of the Europe-wide poverty targets, which all aim to reduce the number of households living below three-fifths of median incomes in each country, and in Britain, to ensure that no children grow up in such households by 2020.[2]

The median net household income in Britain is £21,000, and 60% of that is £12,700 a year, or £244 a week. After housing costs, that figure falls to £206 a week for a family, or £29 a day.[3]

---

[1] Editorial note: This article is as it was published in the *Guardian* except that the sources for various statements have been reinserted as footnotes. Understandably, newspaper sub-editors don't like footnotes.

[2] Frank said "Had I been asked, I would have argued for a target that was achievable. The 2020 goal isn't. Any candidate sitting GCSE maths should be able to explain that raising everybody above a set percentage of median income is rather like asking a cat to catch its own tail. As families are raised above the target level of income, the median point itself rises. Not surprisingly, therefore, no country in the free world has managed to achieve this objective, not even those Scandinavian countries whose social models many of us admire." See: www. telegraph.co.uk/news/newstopics/politics/conservative/7803983/Poverty-is-about-much-more-than-money.html#disqus_thread

[3] Households Below Average Income (HBAI) official statistical series, See the copy available on-line at: www.poverty.org.uk/technical/hbai.shtml the latest full report (these statistics are taken from Figure 2.1 on page 15) is here: http://statistics.dwp.gov.uk/asd/hbai/hbai_2009/pdf_files/full_hbai10.pdf

In January, European Union researchers announced that 23% of children in the UK lived in a household in poverty, and that the UK ranked seventh worst out of 27 EU countries by the measure Field would like to abolish[4]. Only in poorer countries, such as Romania and Bulgaria, are a higher proportion of children living in poverty.[5]

In Denmark, Finland, the Netherlands, Germany, France and 12 other countries, the child poverty figure is as low as one in 10. One non-EU country, Norway, all but abolished child poverty by this measure as long ago as 2003.[6]

In Britain, the latest official estimates of households living in poverty – the ones Field has been charged with redefining – show that (after paying for housing) just under 2 million pensioners, almost 4 million children and almost 8 million adults of working age still live in poverty. In that year (2009), however, pensioner poverty fell by 200,000 elderly people and child poverty by 100,000 children, showing that success in reducing poverty was possible.

Field suggests that, in concentrating on money, we are not "defining poverty in the most sensible way". Yet, when you are trying to feed, clothe, wash and transport a family on pennies, your mind focuses on money.

If I were advising him on his review, I would suggest Frank Field start by looking at what George Bush enacted in his last days in office as president of the United States. George signed into law an extension of unemployment benefits[7]. Despite his political instincts for "tough love" of the poor, and despite the US's precarious financial position, full unemployment benefits were extended by another seven weeks across the country and by as much as 20 weeks in those states where unemployment rates were highest. When unemployment is high and rising, you raise benefits because it is clear there are many more people looking for work than there are jobs.

Barack Obama went further and significantly raised taxes on the rich to pay for increased benefits for what Americans call "struggling Americans",

---

[4] See page 2 of *Child poverty and child-well being in the European Union; Policy overview and policy impact analysis; A case study: UK*; Jonathan Bradshaw; University of York; Department of Social Policy and Social Work; jrb1@york.ac.uk. UK appendix of www.tarki.hu/en/research/childpoverty/index.html

[5] Ibid. Figure 1.1, page 25 of the full report to which reference 3 above is an appendix. Location, same website.

[6] *Unjust rewards*, by Polly Toynbee and David Walker; 'Solutions to inequality found on the Clapham omnibus', Review by Johann Hari, *The Independent*, 15 August 2008, www.independent.co.uk/arts-entertainment/books/reviews/unjust-rewards-by-polly-toynbee-and-david-walker-897004.html

[7] The original press reports were titled: "Bush signs law extending unemployment insurance", Reuters, 21/11/2008: www.reuters.com/article/idUSTRE4AK3UU20081121

"Americans with disabilities","American children" and "elderly Americans", to remind themselves that others are like them.[8]

Cameron says he is worried about "deep poverty", about the poorest in society. But he clearly does not want a redistribution of the money, the land, the work, the educational resources and the "opportunities" that the rich have expropriated from the poor over the past three decades.

The welfare secretary, Iain Duncan Smith, also wants to "address deep-seated poverty".[9] We are back again to Victorian concern for the poorest of all, but not for poverty in general. We are back to basics.

---

[8] See *US Office of Management and Budget: A new era of responsibility: Renewing America's promise, 2009, inheriting a legacy of misplaced priorities*, www.washingtonpost.com/wp-srv/politics/budget2010/fy10-newera.pdf

[9] www.guardian.co.uk/politics/2010/jun/05/frank-field-review-poverty-cameron

# SECTION II
# Injustice and ideology

This set of five chapters begins with reactions of shock to the Chancellor of the Exchequer George Osborne's budget of 2010 and ends with the recording of immediate disbelief over the callousness of David Cameron's government's Comprehensive Spending Review, announced towards the end of that year. In between these chapters, in Chapter 7, is a piece published in the journal *Local Economy*, written during the summer of that year, as a reminder that although the new Coalition government was particularly brutal in its actions, it can be argued that such brutality had only been made possible because of how New Labour had moved British politics to the right. This rightward shift included (as it turned out) Nick Clegg and Danny Alexander of the 'Orange Book'[1] Liberal Democrats and enough of their colleagues to ensure ineffective opposition within the Coalition to cutting immediately and cutting deep. If you also accept the argument made in Chapter 7, that in many ways New Labour was Thatcherism continued, then it is in hindsight not so hard to see how, slowly but surely, what was acceptable had shifted to make the present attack on the poor possible.

There are generations to politics. Tony Blair was born in 1953, the same year as Margaret Thatcher's twins. David Cameron was born in 1966 into what was, in effect, a new generation. Had he been an average British schoolboy, he would have been looking for work at the age of 16 in 1982, and would not have easily found it. Had he waited until he had taken

---

[1] Marshall, P. and Laws, D. (2004) *The Orange Book: Reclaiming Liberalism*, London: Profile Books. Vince Cable, Nick Clegg and Chris Hulme all wrote chapters and are all Cabinet Ministers in government as this book goes to press.

his A levels he would have entered a job market in which over a million people aged 25 and under were claiming what was then still called the dole. This was the highest ever recorded number. Shortly after 1984 Margaret Thatcher's government changed the rules so that far fewer could claim. Many hundreds of thousands ended up destitute, tens of thousands of young adults at one time or another started begging on the streets in those years. David went up to Brasenose College (Oxford) after taking a few months off to travel around the world. Just like many of the rest of Britain's elite, he had very different experiences in comparison with the vast majority of his generation. At Oxford he was taught (or 'read') philosophy, politics and economics (PPE), at roughly the same time as both Miliband brothers were taking the very same course.

Chapter 8, the third paper in this section, was published in *Public Policy Research*, in the house journal of the left-leaning think tank IPPR. It summarises the argument that inequality can be perpetuated by the wrongheaded thinking instilled early in the minds of many people in power, often by their parents, teachers or tutors. It also discusses how such a curse can be overcome. Chapter 9 tells a short story of meeting David Cameron's contemporaries when I was a 'sixth-former' growing up in Oxford, and narrowly missing having a strange-shaped glass hit my head, just after it had been thrown from a college window.

This section ends with Chapter 10 on the plan that was announced in autumn 2010 to – in effect – clear the poor from the more prosperous of southern English cities. By July 2011 it became clear that the government both knew this would be the implication and how much suffering it would cause.[2]

---

[2] Beattie, J. (2011) 'Tories lied about impact of benefit shake-up that could leave 40,000 families homeless', *Daily Mirror*, 4 July.

# 6

# Brutal budget to entrench inequality

*Socialist Review* (2010) 349, July/August, p 5

The first budget of the "progressive" coalition government saw George Osborne promise massive cuts for the poorest in society while offering tax relief for businesses...

George Osborne – flanked by two Liberal Democrats – spoke with the confidence that you would expect of a man with the pedigree of aristocracy. David Cameron had positioned himself behind Osborne so that the camera could not see him as the chancellor gave out the bad news. Thus "Dave" was nowhere to be seen as the axe was wielded across the welfare state, or when it was announced that VAT was to be increased to 20 percent, or that poor pregnant women would have the special benefits being paid to them cut. Dave's wife is pregnant.

You might think Cameron knew something about PR as he stayed out of shot. What Osborne knows about is unclear. It has been widely reported that his first job was data entry for the NHS. His only reported private sector work experience was shelf-stacking in Selfridges. After those forays into the world of work he moved into the Conservative Party's central office.

Osborne said he wanted prosperity to be shared among all of the country. He raised the spectre of national default on the country's debt as the most likely consequence of not following his advice. It was his way or no way at all. It was hard, he said, but he was the man to do it. Further back and far to his side Vince Cable, who had opposed him in the election contest so recently, literally squirmed in his seat.

To avoid national bankruptcy Osborne said (mentioning it often) he was going to bring spending into balance in just five years and he was going to achieve 77 percent of that through public sector cuts and 23 percent through tax rises. Current expenditure would have to fall by £30 billion a year to achieve this. The Queen was singled out as having her income frozen rather than reduced.[1]

This was not a budget of compromise. This was simply a brutal budget. Unprotected government departments would receive the largest cuts and these would be cuts in jobs. He did not say that explicitly: he said they would receive a 25 percent cut in four years, and a wage freeze – a cut of £17 billion in total. Given that salaries are their greatest expense (by far) that can only mean massive job losses if wages stay the same. He also froze child benefit. The only sign that the Liberal Democrats were in coalition with him was that he didn't means-test that benefit[2] and he raised basic tax allowances a little (but all of that was wiped out by other cuts to the budgets of the same families). Osborne didn't stop with taking from children, the poor, average families and almost everyone in work in the public sector. He next targeted the elderly, but only the elderly reliant on a pension, not the really rich elderly.

The overall private sector wage bill per head is much higher than the public sector wage bill because those at the top of the private sector reward themselves so excessively. There is nothing to stop them doing so even more following this budget. Osborne dropped the bosses' corporation tax to 27 percent and promised a percentage drop a year from then on to reach 24 percent in three years' time. He did say banks would be levied at £2 billion, but a similar cut would apply to people reliant on housing benefit, who are far less well-off than banks.

Osborne insisted this was a fair budget. What had he taken from the rich then? It took me some time to identify, but here it is: he promises to explore the idea of altering the air passenger levy so that, rather than operating at the level of every person flying, it becomes a charge on every plane taking off. Rich business people and celebrities might then have to pay almost as much as a charter flight bound to Ibiza. But that change was not a budget commitment, just an idea he was floating.

The commitment is to increase inequality. The rich, the "wealth creators", must be left unscathed. If you believe they create wealth what else can you do? But if such beliefs are a product of a very expensive education then I think it is time we questioned the value of such education and stopped calling it "good". There is plenty of excess wealth in this country that could have been cut to pay for the bank bailout. It all remains. It is still available.

---

[1] Editorial note: A year later it was unfrozen. Ruddick, G. (2011) 'The Queen's income to rise as Crown Estate reveals record profits', *Daily Telegraph*, 8 July.
[2] Editorial note: Within a year George Osborne had arranged for child benefit to be means tested. Families containing any single earner who paid tax at 40% would not receive any and suggestions were floated to end it when children reached age 13 http://www.timesonline.co.uk/tol/news/politics/article7147979.ece".

# 7

# New Labour and inequality: Thatcherism continued?

*Local Economy* (2010) vol 25, nos 5–6, pp 397–413

"From a political perspective, it is perhaps remarkable that it took Labour 12 years to introduce a new higher top rate of income tax. By creating a 50 per cent rate for income above £150,000, the government has effectively created a new social 'cleavage' at a point in the income spectrum that generates no political problems for it whatsoever (indeed, quite the opposite), but huge problems for its opponents. And in doing so it has transformed the politics of 'the top rate of tax'. Indeed it is astonishing that the government struggled through a whole decade with the previous highest rate kicking in right in the middle of a vocal and electorally-sensitive group (upper-middle-class earners). Nothing could better symbolise the anxiety and acquiescence to the rules of previous Conservative governments that characterised New Labour in the late 1990s than turning in on itself about what it would or wouldn't do to the existing top rate of tax, rather than realising that it didn't have to accept this dilemma, and that with a bit of strategic restructuring it could have transformed the political calculus of the problem. It isn't just the missed opportunities either, but the self-inflicted harm. Perhaps the worst way imaginable of structuring financial support for childcare was to create one system (the childcare element of the Working Tax Credit) for helping low-income households, and another (tax relief on childcare vouchers) primarily of importance to middle-income households. It's the kind of thing you might have expected a mischievous right-wing government to have done had it deliberately set out to create a conundrum for the left." (Horton & Gregory, 2009)

## New Labour – time for the autopsy

In Britain, every previous Labour and 20th century Liberal administration presided over a period when inequalities in income, wealth and health fell overall during their periods of office. It would take a deep cynicism to believe that was coincidence. Voting progressively used to bring about rapid social progress. In contrast, the overall record of the 1997–2010 Labour governments has been to preside over a period when all three of these inequalities rose. This is most clearly seen when assessed geographically across the country as a whole. To at least 2008, life expectancies, income and wealth rose most rapidly in those parliamentary constituencies that returned a Conservative MP in 1997. They hardly rose at all in the most loyal of Labour seats.[1] The 1997–2010 Labour governments had more time and more money than any of those previous Labour or Liberal administrations, but – other than in some educational outcomes – New Labour failed to achieve social progress of a kind that deserves to be placed alongside the achievements of previous non-Conservative administrations. New Labour was new. What was new was that it was not progressive. Its term of office failed to coincide with social progress but instead were more closely associated with a rapidly dividing society.

For most of the period 1997–2010 Prime Minister Blair, born in the same year as Margaret Thatcher's twins, behaved as if he was her heir. No single person is that important, neither Margaret nor Tony. But it can help to summarise periods of political history to use the surnames of people as long as we remember we are talking about the actions of a group of people, not one woman or one man. Over the 1997–2010 New Labour period of office, the majority of other rich countries in the world managed to achieve a far better record on inequality, so the problem was not 'globalisation'. In almost all OECD countries, inequalities were lower than in the UK, and

---

[1] These trends are discussed in detail, and sources of data, tabulations and formulae are all given in Chapter 5 of Dorling (2010a).

in many, when measured by income, wealth, or health, they were found not to be rising. The question we need to ask is not whether New Labour failed by why it failed.

By 2010, levels of inequality in Britain were the fourth highest amongst the 25 richest large countries in the world – income inequality was higher even than in Israel, higher than Japan and South Korea, higher than in New Zealand, Australia and Canada, higher than across all of Western Europe, other than in Portugal. During New Labour's tenure, quintile post-tax income inequalities were raised to 7.2:1. In 1997, the best-off fifth received 6.9 times more than the worst-off fifth. The increase in inequality took the country almost quarter of the way towards the inequalities experienced in the most unequal large country in the world: a quarter of the way to British society becoming as unequal as that of the United States of America.[2]

There is now overwhelming evidence that in affluent countries where income inequalities are higher, overall well-being is harmed. The mental and physical health of the population deteriorates under sustained conditions of high inequality. High rates of drug and alcohol abuse are maintained and more of the most harmful illegal drugs are consumed in more unequal countries. Rates of depression tend to be higher, especially among adolescents who rightly hold great fears for their future when the possible outcomes for them are so variable under greater inequality. Addictive behaviour is, in general, higher under conditions of greater inequality and uncertainty. This includes eating disorders and so rates of obesity are far higher in more unequal affluent countries.[3]

There is more violence, more crime, more people are imprisoned, and fewer live long into retirement – far more are discontent with their lot all the way up and down a grossly stretched out income distribution. Almost all look up and see those above them moving away from them. People look down in fear when there is great inequality. Abroad, the greatest failure of New Labour was to conduct illegal wars. At home, maintaining the high rates of income inequality brought in under Margaret Thatcher, and even allowing there to be increases in those rates towards the end of their period of office, is what the last government should be remembered for above all their achievements (of which the most notable were in education). Why

---

[2] For data sources see: Dorling (2010b).

[3] See Wilkinson and Pickett (2009). A revised edition of their book was published in 2010, since then the book has been under concerted attack by the far-right, which helps illustrate just how powerful this book is. None of the criticisms made by any of the detractors to *The Spirit Level* survive under even the most cursory of inspections of their complaints. What that shows us is that it is the very idea that 'greater equality is good' that a few people on the far right deeply – and without any justifiable basis – hate.

did New Labour do this? I would argue it was because the renewed party was partly a product of inequality, not a bulwark against it.[4]

Given the lack of social achievement it is likely that the New Labour record will largely be characterised in future as 'Thatcherism continued' or, more cruelly, as some kind of political boil on the backside of Thatcherism, a consolidation and the end results of the worse symptoms of the infection of mass selfishness – rather than any cure. The verdict of the Fabians published even during its last year of office, and shown in the long quote that begins this chapter, is indicative of what is to come from the general autopsy we should expect.[5] New Labour itself was the worse symptom of Thatcherism's success because it demonstrated how the infection of selfishness had spread into the body politic – and across the political spectrum – out from under the rock where once only free-market lunacy sheltered. History is unlikely to be kind to those who clearly helped continue a political mistake under the name of the party that once represented those who laboured hardest.

## For the remaining doubters – the record on inequality

New Labour's record in income inequality was not as good as John Major's. Figure 1 shows the trend using the most commonly graphed measure. Income inequalities were measured by other means before the 1960s but it is widely accepted that they attained historic lows around then. There was a surplus of Labour votes and a shortage of labour to be exploited in the 1960s, at least among men. You could tell your boss to shove it if you did not enjoy your work and take another job. That is what keeps wages at the bottom up. Income inequality then fell even further under the 1964–1970 Labour administration, by a whisker, and was then at an historical low. It rose under Heath's 1970–74 government, only falling at the end as the oil shock hit and unemployment rose. Inequality rates fell to the *lowest ever recorded values* next under the 1974–1979 Labour government, despite rising joblessness again. Thus income inequalities reached their lowest point ever recorded at the end of the last period of Labour government.

Figure 1 shows very clearly how the abysmal and relentless rise in income inequalities took place from 1979 right through to 1990. It highlights the mid 1980s slowdown and later acceleration. That rise in inequality ended almost exactly when Margaret Thatcher was forced out of office by her own party. Inequalities then remained stable up until the 1992 election, and fell slightly thereafter, until 1997 after which they rose, up to 2001, but then fell

---

[4] On the argument of how living under high levels of social inequality can corrupt our thinking and make us all more stupid – something of which New Labour may be an example – see: Dorling (2010c), which is reproduced as Chapter 44 within this book.

[5] One of the most acerbic early critics was: Wood (2010).

for a few years following some budgets that were, at last, truly (if only ever so slightly) redistributive. However, from 2005 onwards, income inequalities were allowed to rise again, as fast as they had in the early 1980s, and so, by 2008, the United Kingdom was as unequal in terms of income as it had last been over 80 years earlier. The last Labour government (1974–1979) left office with the population enjoying the lowest ever recorded inequalities in income. New Labour approached the year 2010 looking as if it would leave office having secured the highest rate of income inequality recorded by this Gini measure.

**Figure 1:** Income inequality in Great Britain and the United Kingdom, 1961–2008

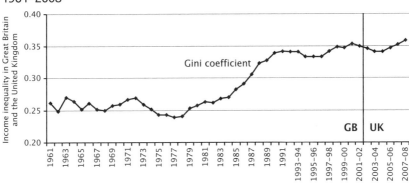

*Source:* Gini coefficient of equivalised post-tax income inequality before housing costs, 1961 to 2007–2008. Note that the data are for GB prior to 2002–2003 and for the UK subsequently (Institute for Fiscal Studies series).

In case you might think this account churlish, it is worth taking a longer view. Although we cannot calculate a Gini coefficient with much accuracy for income before 1961, we do know what share the best-off 1 per cent of the population received in income from at least 1918 onward. Figure 2 shows the time series differentiating between pre-tax and post-tax incomes so that it is possible to see what efforts successive governments were making to narrow the gap through their application of progressive taxation.

## The longer-term record and those at the top

The income share of the super-rich fell almost continuously from around 1922 until 1979. Governments in the 1920s and 1930s did not do a great deal to encourage the growing equality. Unions, strikes, social solidarity and a weakening of the aristocracy did the job instead, all with the helpful threat of mass Labour votes. Nevertheless, the gap between the two lines in Figure 2 narrows during these decades as taxation failed to become more progressive. That was all ended by the incoming 1945 Labour government, which made semi-permanent large war-time tax rises for the rich and which widened the gap between pre-and post-tax inequality (using taxation ever more progressively). This in turn led to an acceleration in income equality, with equality growing from 1945 until 1951. Rates of equality increase then slowed abruptly under the 13 years of 1951–1963 Conservative rule, before the movement towards greater equality increased in speed again from 1964 right through to 1979 – after which inequalities rose relentlessly.

It is not possible to discern the Labour landslide victory of 1997 from Figure 2. It is as if it never happened, which, in a way, is true. The income shares of the richest 1 per cent rose just as quickly after 1997 as before. The graph ends in 2008, but we know from the House of Commons Economic Bulletin[6] that, after that, average income fell overall, but rose if bankers' bonuses from 2009 were included. Bankers constitute a very large proportion of the richest 1 per cent of the population of Britain. It is very likely that statistics released in the coming months will reveal that the richest 1 per cent of the population again received 18 per cent of all income by May 2010, a proportion as high as that they last enjoyed in the decadent 1920s.

**Figure 2:** Income share of the richest 1 per cent in Great Britain 1918–2008

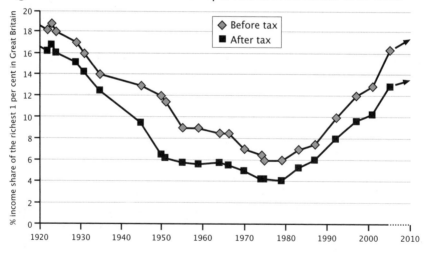

*Source:* Estimates made by Tony Atkinson and the Institute for Fiscal Studies, reconstructed by general election dates in Dorling (2010a). The lower line is post-tax income share, higher line is pre-tax.

---

[6] House of Commons Library, Economic Indicators, March 2010, Research Paper 10/20 02 March 2010, www.parliament.uk/commons/lib/research/rp2010/rp10-020.pdf

## Health inequalities – the consequences of complacency

The growing share of the overall incomes received by the best-off 1 per cent also included a growing rent they received simply for being rich in the first place. By 2010 the Hills enquiry into inequalities undertaken by the National Equality Panel was reporting that the best-off tenth of Londoners each had recourse to nearly £1 million of wealth, much of which was locked up in pensions and equity, but it was real wealth that they would (each on average) get to enjoy. This wealth was some 270 times that of the poorest tenth of Londoners! The Hills enquiry revealed that income and wealth divides were the greatest they had been in Britain for at least 40 years. If they had had the records shown in Figure 2 they could have changed that estimate to be "over 80 years". It was last true in 1997 that inequalities were the highest they had been for 40 years. New Labour doubled that statistic and brought inequality rates back up to the dizzy heights of the 1920s from their previous 1950s levels in 1997.

What happens when you preside over growing inequalities in income and in wealth? One answer is that most other aspects of life polarise too. Figure 3 shows the trend in the simple measure of life-expectancy gap in Britain between the extreme local authority districts. The gap is shown for men and women separately from when this particular ONS series begins

**Figure 3:** Inequalities in life expectancy between areas in Great Britain 1999–2008

Difference between best and worst districts by life expectancy (years):

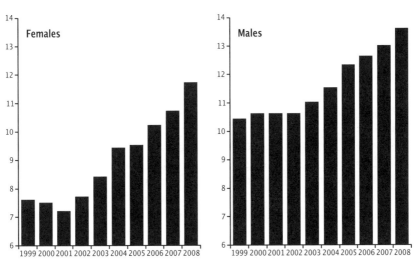

*Source:* Difference measured in years of life between the best and worst-off districts, 1999–2008 (ONS).

(1999). The key point is that New Labour inherited a high but not rapidly rising rate of inequality between areas and managed somehow to allow what had been a small increase to later become a rapidly rising gap with the rise actually accelerating in the latest period shown. Inequalities in health between areas as measured by premature death rates were not just simply rising in 2008–2009, they were growing even faster than a year before. They rose so quickly that life expectancy and premature mortality inequalities between areas grew in the last years of New Labour to be as great as any that can be measured in the 1920s and 1930s when we were last as unequal.[7]

By 2008, in Britain, men in the best-off district (Kensington and Chelsea) were living, on average, 14 years longer than men in the worse-off (Glasgow). For women, the gap was now approaching 12 years and the increase in that gap had grown more quickly (from just 7 years in 2001). Much more sophisticated measures of inequalities reveal the same pattern as these simple measures. Life expectancy gaps react far more rapidly to political changes than many commentators understand, partly because they are still disproportionately influenced by infant mortality rates, but partly because growing in importance among leading causes of premature death are diseases of despair: violence, alcohol, drugs, overdoses and accidental deaths. The rise since 2001 in health inequalities for women and the rapid acceleration since 2002 for men are not some throwback effect of Thatcherism, but the consequence of a corruption of Labour politics, belief and understanding – Thatcherism's worse and most wide ranging effect of all.

Not everything went wrong for New Labour. In education there were gains, not so much the GCSE gains (which were not so hard to secure once almost all upper-middle class children were being awarded their 5 or 7 GCSE grades A to C). The real gains that were made were those between 2005 and 2009. Then, for the first time ever as far as I and others with an interest in these things can estimate, the majority of extra university places made available went to young people from the poor half of all Britain's neighbourhoods.[8] This was not achieved at the expense of upper-middle class or even lower-middle class children and young adults – their proportions continued to rise, only more slowly, the most affluent already having reached saturation point. What appears to have happened is a fortuitous combination of events that even took science and education ministers by surprise. Lord Mandelson announced the largest ever cut to higher education budgets just a few days after the January 2010 release by HEFCE of these education statistics. The combination of fortuitous events was a declining middle class birth cohort, a near doubling of spending per pupil in state secondary schools, (which was due largely to New Labour), the introduction of educational

---

[7] Dorling (2010a)

[8] On Labour's education record see Dorling (2010d), Chapter 18 in this book, page 147.

maintenance allowances, and the expansion of the post-92 sector. However, when this one great achievement was reported it was greeted with ridicule and disbelief by readers of the newspaper that reported it – who no longer believed positive stories about the governments' record. That newspaper being: *The Guardian*.

## Why did the dream go pear-shaped?

The key question is not whether New Labour failed in most of its aspirations but why it failed. Were the 'key players' just not that bothered? 'Seriously relaxed' about what mattered most became the persistent accusation thrown at these supposed 'guilty men'. Was the task just too hard? Or were the aims of New Labour different to those publicly espoused by the party? I opt for the last of these explanations, not due to a belief in conspiracy, but from the suggestions of many writers now that a kind of mental infection occurs in affluent countries which undergo great inequality.[9] Public debate is itself corrupted by living in times that are hugely unequal and this corruption allows people to believe they are acting in the common purpose when they are, in fact, acting selfishly. To see how that could have occurred rather than the task of New Labour being viewed as too hard, or the real aims being different under some kind of conspiracy, you need to go back just a few years. Try to take your mind back almost a decade to see the still fresh-faced new prime minister requesting on television a right to a second term in office despite his party's abysmal record during its first term.

It is well worth reading again a key part of Tony Blair's infamous interview with Jeremy Paxman as broadcast on Monday 4 June 2001 (see extract in Figure 4). Even by 2001 it had become evident that Tony Blair was not as 'bothered' as previous Labour leaders had been about the widening of gaps within British society. A former life-long Labour supporter recently told me that at Tony's first Labour party conference as leader he partly mouthed the words to the 'Red Flag' as the conference drew to a close. He was a little more convincing than was John Redwood in singing the Welsh national anthem when Welsh secretary, but not much. At his second party conference as leader he did not even bother to do that, but stood waving and smiling beside his carefully positioned and apparently adoring wife. Careful observers prior to 1997 had their doubts that Tony contained a scintilla of genuine sincerity when he used the word 'socialism', or whether he understood what sincerity meant, let alone socialism. But he could act. He was very assured. He wore cuff-links and had that grin. He was charismatic.

---

[9] On wider sources see Dufour (2008), Kelsey (1997), James (2008), Irvin (2008) and Lawson (2009).

Jeremy Paxman began the interview: 'Prime Minister, there aren't enough doctors or nurses. There aren't enough teachers. There are more cars on the road than when you came to power. The train service doesn't work. Violent crime is rising. Is that what you meant by the new Britain?' It turned out that what Tony meant by 'the new Britain' was a Britain in awe of and reliant on the largesse of the super-wealthy.

In March 2010, tributes were published in the magazine *Tribune* (12 March, p. 10) to the recently deceased former Labour leader Michael Foot. Amongst the shortest was the one written by Tony Blair. It was just 13 sentences long, and roughly half of these were about Tony, not Michael Foot. In this

**Figure 4:** Tony Blair's infamous Beckham-trickle-down 'Newsnight' interview

BLAIR: When you say where is the justice in that, the justice for me is concentrated on lifting incomes of those that don't have a decent income. It's not a burning ambition for me to make sure that David Beckham earns less money.

PAXMAN: But Prime Minister, the gap between rich and poor has been widened while you have been in office.

BLAIR: A lot of those figures are based on a couple of years ago before many of the measures we took came into effect. But the lowest income families in this country are benefiting from the government. Their incomes are rising. The fact is that you have some people at the top end earning more¿

PAXMAN: ..Benefiting more!

BLAIR: If they are earning more, fine, they pay their taxes.

PAXMAN: But is it acceptable for gap between rich and poor to widen?

BLAIR: It is acceptable for those people on lower incomes to have their incomes raised. It is unacceptable that they are not given the chances. To me, the key thing is not whether the gap between those who, between the person who earns the most in the country and the person that earns the least, whether that gap is¿

PAXMAN: So it is acceptable for gap to widen between rich and poor?

BLAIR: It is not acceptable for poor people not to be given the chances they need in life.

PAXMAN: That is not my question.

BLAIR: I know it's not your question but it's the way I choose to answer it. If you end up going after those people who are the most wealthy in society, what you actually end up doing is in fact not even helping those at the bottom end.

PAXMAN: So the answer to the straight question is it acceptable for the gap between rich and poor to get wider, the answer you are saying is yes.

BLAIR: No it's not what I am saying. What I am saying is that my task is¿

PAXMAN: You are not saying no.

BLAIR: But I don't think that is the issue¿

PAXMAN: You may not think it is the issue, but it is the question. Is it OK for the gap to get wider?

BLAIR: It may be the question. The way I choose to answer it is to say the job of the government is to make sure those at the bottom get the chances.

PAXMAN: With respect, people see you are asked a straightforward question and they see you not answering it.

BLAIR: Because I choose to answer it in the way I'm answering it.

PAXMAN: But you are not answering it.

BLAIR: I am answering it. What I am saying is the most important thing is to level up, not level down.

PAXMAN: Is it acceptable for gap between rich and poor to get bigger?

BLAIR: What I am saying is the issue isn't in fact whether the very richest person ends up becoming richer. The issue is whether the poorest person is given the chance that they don't otherwise have.

PAXMAN: I understand what you are saying. The question is about the gap.

BLAIR: Yes, I know what your question is. I am choosing to answer it my way rather than yours.

PAXMAN: But you're not answering it.

BLAIR: I am.

--------------

Source: http://news.bbc.co.uk/1/hi/events/newsnight/1372220.stm

4th of June 2001

it differed from most of the other tributes. Tony Blair was (and is) a very odd man. I do not think he would understand these criticisms of him. If you think of yourself as being a gift, maybe from above, to others, how can you understand when they appear so ungrateful? However, I (and millions of others) am not at all grateful to Tony and his friends. It is helpful to say this to help others who might be thinking of trying to become political leaders now to think a bit more carefully about what they are doing and why. If you are seeking office because you think you are particularly able and gifted you are likely to cause harm. Alternatively if you seek office because you are prepared to work hard and are driven by personal experiences that have taught you about unfairness at first hand – you are much less of a potential liability.

Although the accusation of being seriously relaxed about rising income and wealth inequalities is often attributed to Tony Blair's suggestion that he was not concerned with what David Beckham received in tribute (or earning if you can call it that), it was put more succinctly by Peter Mandelson when he said he was seriously relaxed about these inequalities. Both men had added the caveat 'as long as they pay their taxes', but this is a view of taxation rather like charity. Taxation under this way of thinking about it is something you accept so as to give money to the poor, as if someone like you (David Beckham, Peter Mandelson or Tony Blair) are the magical creator of that wealth in the first place. You magically create it as it appears in your bank account – via subscriptions to satellite TV paying for football rights, or in your income from private business grateful for your acquiescence.

Towards the end of New Labour's reign, Lord Peter Mandelson appeared to particularly enjoy annoying members of his own political party by making statements about favouring inequality. In 2009 he suggested that 'anti-elitism of some parts of the left on education policy has often been a dead end'. This was presumably designed to cause more annoyance as almost everyone is anti-elitist today. On the same day a key government advisor, Sir Jonathon Porritt, working on a completely different area of policy, resigned citing Peter as the problem. What he said was: 'Lord Mandelson had been particularly hostile to the concept of sustainable development.' One week later it was revealed that Peter was trying to find a job for a friend of his (Trevor Phillips) who might otherwise become a Conservative party advisor given how easy it was to switch sides by 2009.[10] Neither Lord Peter, nor Sir Jonathon, nor Mr Phillips held any elected post, but all were in government in one way or another, and this series of spats typified the dying days of New Labour. Around Tony other men were gathered who had also come to believe that a little spoonful of extra inequality did not do too much harm.

---

[10] All the sources for these quotes are given in Dorling (2010a, p 371).

New Labour was born between the elections of 1992 and 1997. It was a time of despair on the left. To many it appeared that without a change in the voting system, the electorate, or the party, Labour could not win a working majority again.[11] Rather than galvanise the electorate to demand a viable change, Tony and his friends changed the Labour party to make it inoffensive to marginal voters whose views had been shifted so far to the right. They did this with enthusiasm because they too believed that the transformation of Britain was moving it in the right direction, that growing inequalities were okay as long as they were coupled with a little more charity for the poor, that what mattered most was economic growth and Britain's place in the world; making the country great again.

## Inequality and the struggle to keep a clear mind

Growing inequality reduces our capacity to think clearly. The best current example of this is the debate in the United States over the supposed evils of a 'socialised' health service. It is extremely hard to have a reasoned public debate in the United States given how unequal that country has become, how few people control so much of the media, and given how poor educational provision is for everyone in a society that is so divided. Those at the top are given high GPA scores and so don't realise that they often sound like dopes when talking abroad. George Bush junior had degrees from both Harvard and Yale! Britain is the closest large affluent country to the United States in terms of income inequality. As touched on in the introduction to this chapter, but worth repeating again and again, of the 25 richest countries in the world the UK is the fourth most unequal – having the fourth highest 90:10 income ratio as reported by the United Nations Development Programme in its annual World Report of 2009.

If you exclude the smaller states of Portugal and Singapore, then the UK is the second most unequal large affluent country in the world. Among the largest rich countries of the world, only in the USA are higher rates of income inequality found than in Britain.

We in Britain can easily come over as dopes to most people in most of the rest of the affluent world. We are little different, sadly, from ignorant North Americans. We are lucky to have had a National Health Service introduced at a time when we were more equal. There is a reason why Brits are called whinging Poms; they whinge because they are not happy about where they come from and the inequities there. Pom may originally have been a

---

[11] With colleagues I was guilty of helping to propagate this myth by not making it clearer that other futures were possible, in particular by not looking further back in the past. See Cornford et al. (1995, pp 123–42). We helped make it look as if Labour could not win in 1997 without it becoming a different political party.

contraction of pomegranate, but ask folk abroad now what it is short for and they more often tell you 'pompous'.

Growing inequality can, however, also focus the mind. Like proverbial frogs in the kettle, people can become used to the temperature of the water being raised up until the point that they boil, we can all fail to jump out, and we become attuned, desensitised – mush. However, if suddenly you turn the temperature up, even the slowest of frogs notice that things are suddenly worse. Inequality rates are currently escalating with the economic crash and that escalation is being coupled with falls in standards of living for the majority of the population as GDP falls. This transition occurred a few years earlier in the United States. Real median wages were falling in the years before Barack Obama was elected.

People were already getting angry. By accelerating the processes we associate with Thatcherism, New Labour has helped bring about a greater crisis of inequality and larger banking fiasco in Britain than is seen anywhere else in Europe. Iceland's banks went bust, but its society had and has a much greater degree of social solidarity than that remaining in Britain. Similarly in Ireland, despite all its troubles, there is no supposedly great financial district of Dublin in need of massive bail-outs. The Irish banks are in a mess – but they were not that country's key profit-making sector. Even Greece still has its beaches and islands to attract the Germans and their euros. What does Britain have? What is the legacy of New Labour?

Figure 5 shows the UK situated within a mass of countries trying to emulate the way that those who think of growth and wealth and prestige as all important might think. The axes of Figure 5 are both drawn on log scales. On the x-axis is shown the rising number of dollar billionaires per person in most countries in this group (for which Forbes magazine released data). It is not just that the richest countries are home to more billionaires, it is that the more unequal are too. This graph could have been used as an early warning of trouble to come in Iceland and the UAE. The y-axis shows oil consumption changing far more slowly, but note that as oil prices rise in relation to the pound, consumption fell in the UK (unlike in many other countries).

Oil consumption also fell slightly in the USA. Falling oil consumption is partly a sign that times are becoming harder for people on average incomes when they fill up the car less often. China and India might have seen some of the fastest increases in dollar billionaires amongst these countries, but they are still home to at least ten times fewer per head and a tenth of the oil consumption of people in the UK. Mr Blair, when Prime Minister, used to talk of the danger of slipping behind in some global race. The greatest danger to all of us it that we burn too much oil and tolerate the existence of billionaires. The circles in Figure 5 are mostly travelling in the wrong direction.

**Figure 5:** Oil consumption and dollar billionaires 2004–2007

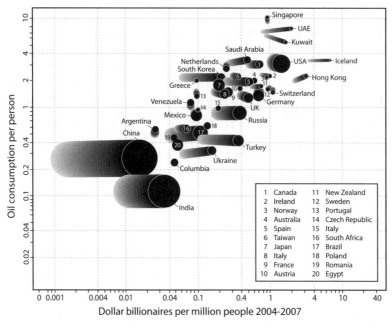

Editorial note: Between 2010 and 2011 the number of UK billionaires increased by 3 (10.4%) and oil consumption continued to decline as prices rose, and as the average person became poorer

*Source:* Gapminder (2010) Google sponsored Interactive graphing package: www. gapminder.org/data/

## A story from Airstrip One

This chapter ends with a local story, as it was first written for the journal *Local Economy*. It is the story of an airport. With the Thatcher government's help and encouragement, and after her three election victories, London City Airport began operations. Located right next to the financial heart of London, its first full year of operation was in 1988. Some 130,000 people flew in and out. Passenger numbers doubled within five years. They doubled again in the next two years of operations to reach half a million people flying per year by 1995. Next they tripled to 1.5 million by the year 2000, rose to 2.3 million by 2006, and then transatlantic flights began in autumn 2009.

When London City Airport opened there were only flights to Plymouth, Paris, Amsterdam and Rotterdam. By spring 2010 there were flights to some 30 destinations. Too many to list so they are shown in Figure 6, which is based on a re-drawing of a diagram from the Airport's own promotional material. Plymouth still features in the list, as does the surfing destination of Newquay, but no other area of England is included in destinations from the banker's favourite airport. Why go there? However, in spring 2010, the party islands of Ibiza and Mallorca were added to the outbound list. It takes

14 minutes to get to City airport from Canary Wharf, and 22 minutes from the Bank of England's tube stop. A little quantitative easing has kept the banker's favourite aircraft afloat.

**Figure 6:** Destinations you can fly from London City Airport as of May 2010

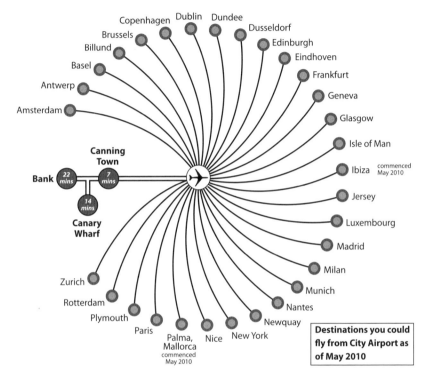

*Source:* redrawn from original source: www.londoncityairport.com/FlightInformation/ DestinationsAndAirlines.aspx [Connecting Tube and light rail stops are also shown]

In early 2010, City airport was in the news for reasons other than the opening of its new routes to Mallorca and Ibiza. Local residents had been complaining about the noise and increased frequency of flights. There is something about being flown over repeatedly by a group of very rich people that includes so many bankers that does appear to get on people's nerves more than normal airport noise can. Figure 7 shows over which areas of London the new routes from and to City airport are proposed to run.

The vast majority of the expansion of City Airport in London occurred while New Labour was in power, from 1997 onwards. Many flights now come in over Dartford and Lewisham, they bank clockwise around Lambeth, descend over Poplar before landing north east of Greenwich. These are the areas that mostly loyally voted for Labour, but from which very few people can afford to fly, let alone fly out of London City Airport. Flights leaving the airport circle out over Stratford, Ilford and Romford, or out over Barking and Dagenham, engines full throttle to gain height. There was once a time when the East End was poor because it suffered most from the pollution of smog and grime distributed by prevailing winds. Now, a major source of the noise pollution over the poorer parts of London is bankers flying to Basel, Edinburgh, Geneva, Jersey, Milan, New York, Paris and Zurich, and another 22 destinations.

**Figure 7:** New inward and outward flight paths from London City Airport, proposed 2010

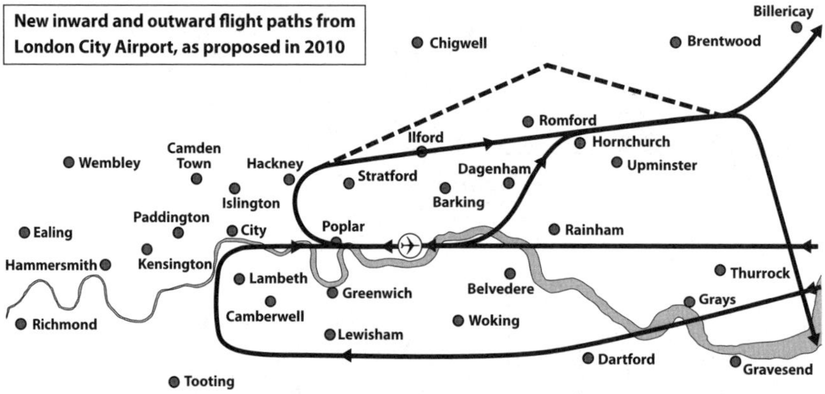

*Source:* Numerous sources including from the campaigns against the extension of the airport.

Ten times as many people are flying in and out of London City Airport, as New Labour's period of power comes to an end, as compared to when it began in May 1997. Whether this is a measure of success or failure depends on from where you are looking and what else you know.

The full story has yet to be written – I haven't mentioned Gordon Brown's part as he was still playing it when this chapter was first drafted (as I made corrections in July 2010 Gordon appeared to be looking for work in Africa). The others I have mentioned I think have largely finished their turns on stage. However, some have been written off several times before so you can never be too careful.

I'll just finish with 'some messages' from the website of the office of Mr Tony Blair (Figure 8). I think the website speaks for itself about New Labour, but that says a lot about where I'm coming from too. You might have thought of Tony: 'he's just trying to help' or 'what a nice man or 'he's got my vote'. Or, if you knew who partly funded his office, you might just think: 'banker'.

**Figure 8:** 'What we do.' From the website of the office of Tony Blair, 15 March 2010

*Source:* http://www.tonyblairoffice.org/pages/what-we-do2/ (figure redrawn from a version accessed 16 March 2010).

## References

Cornford, J., Dorling, D. and Tether, B. (1995) 'Historical precedent and British electoral prospects', *Electoral Studies*, vol 14, no 2, pp 123–42.

Dorling, D. (2010a) *Injustice: Why social inequalities persist*, Bristol: The Policy Press.

Dorling, D. (2010b) Mind the gap: New Labour's legacy on child poverty', *Poverty, Journal of the Child Poverty Action Group*, forthcoming. Copy available here: www.sasi.group.shef.ac.uk/publications/2010/Dorling_2010_Poverty.pdf

Dorling, D. (2010c) 'Mean machine: structural inequality makes social inequality seem natural', *New Internationalist*, no 433, pp 20–21, available from www.sasi.group.shef.ac.uk/publications/2010/ Dorling_2010_New_Internationalist_2010.pdf [see Chapter 44 of this book, page 347.]

Dorling, D. (2010d) 'One of Labour's great successes', *The Guardian*, 28 January, www.guardian.co.uk/education/mortarboard/2010/jan/28/labours-great-successes-university-access-danny-dorling [see Chapter 18 of this book, page 147.

Dufour, D.-R. (2008) *The art of shrinking heads: On the new servitude of the liberated in the age of total capitalism* (translation) Cambridge: Polity Press.

Horton, T. and Gregory, J. (2009) *The solidarity society*, London: Fabian Society.

Irvin, G. (2008) *Super rich: The rise of inequality in Britain and the United States*, Cambridge: Polity Press.

James, O. (2008) *The selfish capitalist: Origins of affluenza*, London: Vermilion.

Kelsey, J. (1997) *The New Zealand experiment: A world model for structural adjustment?*, Auckland: Auckland University Press.

Lawson, N. (2009) *All consuming*, London: Penguin.

Thomas, B., Dorling, D. and Davey Smith, G. (2010) 'Inequalities in premature mortality in Britain: observational study from 1921 to 2007', *BMJ*, Friday 23 July.

Wilkinson, R. and Pickett, K. (2009) *The spirit level: Why more equal societies almost always do better*, London: Allen Lane.

Wood, T. (2010) 'Good riddance to New Labour', *New Left Review*, no 62, March, April, available from www.newleftreview.org/?page=article&view=2830

# 8

# All in the mind? Why social inequalities persist

*Public Policy Research* (2010) vol 16, no 4, pp 226–31

> … as old 'social evils' have largely been overcome in affluent nations, in one of the most unequal of those countries – Britain – they have transformed into five new tenets of injustice. A continued belief in those tenets both maintains and helps to exacerbate social inequality…

## All in the mind

My maternal grandfather was born in 1916, in an era so different from today that women were not permitted to vote. Last year I asked him about the 1929 crash and what life was like for a teenager growing up in Yorkshire in the 1930s. I talked to him about jobs and he said, "You'd know if it were as bad again because – almost no matter what your qualifications – you'd be grateful to take any job."

For many people in Britain today, especially young adults not living with children, their current experiences and my grandfather's recollections are not so far apart. However, in other ways social evils today have changed almost beyond recognition. Yet there are some uncanny echoes with the prejudices of the past in how we now think and in how we stall at progress.

In 1942, when my grandfather was 26 years old, William Beveridge labelled the great social evils as ignorance, want, idleness, squalor and disease. I would claim that now those five evils have been fought and largely vanquished, to be replaced by five new evils: elitism, exclusion, prejudice, greed and despair.

These result today in one in seven children being labelled the equivalent of 'delinquent' and a sixth of households being excluded from modern social norms. These norms include being able to afford a holiday once a year: poverty surveys now find that a sixth of households say they cannot afford to take a holiday and are living on low income.

One in five adults now routinely report, when asked about their circumstances, that they are finding it 'difficult or very difficult' to get by. This was the proportion reported before the economic crash. Similarly, a quarter report not having the essentials, such as a car if you have young children, even though (if resources were just a little better shared out) there is enough for all. A third now live in families where someone is suffering from mental ill health. The fraction that ends this series of statistics concerns people's ability to choose alternative ways of living and how limited those choices are: half are sufficiently disenfranchised that they choose not to vote at most elections.

In the United States almost half of all those old enough to vote either choose not to or are barred from doing so. Local elections have been held in Britain in recent years where, at the extreme, less than a tenth of the electorate chose to vote.

The greatest indictment of unequal affluent societies is for their people to be, in effect, disenfranchised, to think they can make no difference, to feel that they are powerless in the face of an apparent conspiracy of the rich or what might simply be called 'circumstance'. Apathy has increased as we all become distracted by trying to make a living, lulled into a false sense of comfort through consuming to maintain modern lives. In the space of under 100 years we have gone from successfully fighting for the right for women to vote, to around half the population in the most unequal of affluent countries not exercising that right.

## No conspiracy of the rich

There has not been any great, well-orchestrated, conspiracy of the rich to support the endurance of inequality, just a few schools of free-market thought, a few think tanks preaching stories about how efficient free market mechanisms are, how we must allow the few 'tall poppies' to grow and suggesting that a minority of 'wealth creators' exists and it is they who somehow 'create' wealth.

That there is no great conspiracy was first realised in the aftermath of the First World War, when it became clear that no one '... planned for this sort of an abattoir, for a mutual massacre four years long' (Bauman, 2008, p 6). The men they called the 'donkeys', the generals, planned for a short, sharp, war.

Today, those who recently thought that they ran the economy, from Thatcher to Brown, all believed that growth accompanied by trickle-down economics, variously aided, would reduce inequality. There is no well or poorly orchestrated conspiracy to prolong injustice. If there were, injustice would be easier to identify and defeat.

In June 2009 the Joseph Rowntree Foundation published the results of its major consultation 'What are today's social evils?' This produced lists that included greed, consumerism and individualism as new evils, and talked about the erosion of trust and the growth of fear (Joseph Rowntree Foundation, 2009), but the consultation did not delve into the factors that might underly these changes.

I think it is clearer today (even clearer than it was just one year ago) that unjust thoughts and ideologies of inequality have seeped into everyday thinking from the practices that make the most profit. Once only a few argued that hunger should be used as a weapon against the poor. Now many grumble when inconvenienced by a strike, label those requiring state benefits 'scroungers', but hope to inherit money or to win fame.

## The evolution of injustice

It is not just that greed and individualism have risen: the nature of injustice appears to have evolved from the former five giant evils to five quite different looking modern evils. I would suggest we call these: elitism, exclusion, prejudice, greed and despair. They all reflect the way that today too many people favour arguments that actually bolster contemporary injustices in rich nations because they do not recognise the transformed injustice for what it is. But humans are far from being simply the pliant recipients of the seeds of whatever social change they sow. Hardly any foresaw what they would reap as the harmful side effects of affluence, and great numbers are now working optimistically in concert to try to counteract those effects.

My contention is that in their modern form social evils suggest that elitism is efficient, exclusion is necessary, prejudice is natural, greed is good and despair is inevitable. These tenets are most strongly adhered to by those on the right, but many weaker forms underlie much thinking in the centre and left, among parts of the green movement and are found within other (otherwise progressive) forces. It is belief in these new tenets that leads those in power to talk of people only being able to achieve up to their 'potential' (resulting in elitism).

Unjust beliefs that others are different, have different needs and deserts, can result in relative benefit payment levels being kept low. As compared to median wages, benefit levels of people not living with children have been lower under Gordon Brown than even under Thatcher (resulting in growing social exclusion for poor childless adults). A quiet tolerance of racist ideas of inherited difference has re-emerged (a new prejudice). There is a desperate continued clinging to the coat tails of greedy bankers, despite all we have seen during the financial crisis (resulting from greed, the new squalor). And a generally unquestioning acceptance of rising levels of mental illness, where the symptoms rather than the causes are addressed ('despair' rather than 'disease').

There is widespread and growing opposition to these five key unjust principles and the over-arching belief that so many should now be 'losers'. Most advocating injustice are now very careful with their words. However, it appears to me from reading a sample of their words that the majority of those in power in almost all rich countries do still believe in most of these tenets. This is despite the fact that since late 2008 majorities among half a billion people in some of the richest countries in the world have successfully voted for more radical governments than have been seen in a generation. Elections in the US, Japan, Greece and Iceland have put politicians in power who were recently thought unelectable by a majority. It would be foolish to believe that further progressive lurches are not possible.

However, in Britain it would take change at the top of each of the main three political parties to make any of them progressive enough to begin to reverse the 31 year legacy of Thatcherism. What was full-blooded in the early 1980s is now muted in 2010, but, I argue, is still Thatcherism. What other word best encapsulates the public sector cuts currently being planned by all three main parties and the refrain being sung in concert that 'there is no alternative'? Why not make pay cuts across the board, even progressive pay cuts, in place of layoffs? Such things happened in the early 1930s to teachers, other public servants, and even to the police in Britain. They are happening in Ireland and Greece and have occurred in recent years in Japan. Britain probably has to become poorer. It is far less harmful to combine becoming poorer with becoming more equal than to distribute most of the pain of falling GDP onto those with the least and the rest of the burden on those living average lifestyles.

The central argument I am trying to make here is that unjust hegemonic beliefs are still held by enough of us for them to underlie injustice and to cloud our thinking so that what are seen as reasonable suggestions in other places or at other times are often not even made in Britain today. To ask what we do after we dispel enough of these beliefs to overcome injustice is rather like asking how to run plantations after abolishing slavery, or society after giving women the vote, or factories without child labour. The answers have tended to be: not very differently than before in most ways, but vitally different in others.

Dispelling the untruths that underlie the injustices we currently live with will not suddenly usher in utopia. A world in which far more people genuinely disapprove of elitism will still have elitism and something else will surely arise in place of what we currently assume is normal, as that 'normality' starts to look like crude, old-fashioned snobbery, as has happened so often before. Almost no one in an affluent country today bows and scrapes or otherwise tugs their forelock in the presence of their 'betters'.

What I have come to understand from others is that it is in our minds that injustice continues most strongly, in what we think is permissible, in how we think we exist, in whether we think we can use others in ways we would not wish to be used ourselves.

## Rawls was wrong: inequality harms us all

All five faces of social inequality that currently contribute to injustice are clearly and closely linked. Elitism suggests that educational divisions are natural. Educational divisions are reflected in both children being excluded from life choices for being seen as not having enough qualifications, and in those able to exclude themselves, often by opting into private education. Elitism is the incubation chamber within which prejudice is fostered. Elitism provides a defence for greed. It increases anxiety and despair as endless examinations are undergone, as people are ranked, ordered and sorted. It perpetuates an enforced and inefficient hierarchy in our societies.

Just as elitism is integral to all the other forms of injustice, so is exclusion. The exclusion that rises with elitism makes the poor appear different, exacerbates inequalities between ethnic groups and, literally, causes racial differences. Rising greed could not be satisfied without the exclusion of so many, and so many would not be excluded now were it not for greed. But the consequences affect even those who appear most successfully greedy. The most excluded might be most likely to experience despair, but even the wealthy in rich countries are now more prone to such symptoms, as are their children (Dorling, 2009). A growth in the incidence of depression and anxiety has become symptomatic of living in our more unequal affluent societies.

The prejudice that rises with exclusion allows the most greedy to try to justify their greed and makes others near the top think they deserve a lot more than most. The ostracism that such prejudice engenders further raises depression and anxiety in those made to look different. As elitism incubates exclusion, exclusion exacerbates prejudice, prejudice fosters greed, and greed — because wealth is simultaneously no ultimate reward and makes many without wealth feel more worthless — causes despair. In turn, despair prevents us from effectively tackling injustice.

Removing one symptom of the disease of inequality is no cure, but recognising inequality as the disease behind injustice, and seeing how all the forms of injustice that it creates, and that continuously recreate it, are intertwined is the first step that is so often advocated in the search for finding a solution (Wilkinson and Pickett, 2009). The status quo is not improved 'by introducing an inequality that renders one or more persons better off and no one [apparently] worse off' (Arneson, 2009, p 25). The awarding of more elite qualifications to an already well titled minority reduces the social standing of the majority. Allowing those with more to have yet more raises social norms and reduces more people on the margins of those norms to poverty through exclusion. To imagine that others are, apparently, no worse off due to inequality rising requires a prejudicial view of others, to see them as 'not like you'. This argument legitimises greed.

There is a danger that if Britain keeps its benefits so low (Job Seeker's Allowance is just £9 a day) and allows unemployment to rise rather than reducing wages at the top, the country may start to look more like a backwater of social progress. Where social security is concerned, rights are already being rapidly curtailed: starting later in 2010, 'clients' will be compelled to undertake 'meaningful activity' after spending 12 months on Jobseeker's Allowance. However, in other areas the outlook is more positive. For instance, a move away from elitism can be observed. The government's Children's Plan (published in 2007 before the economic crash made change so obviously imperative) suggested that schools in England should aim for children to understand others, value diversity, apply and defend human rights and for staff to be skilled in ensuring participation for all: '[there should be] no barriers to access and participation in learning and to wider activities, and no variation between outcomes for different groups. [Children should] have real and positive relationships with people from different backgrounds, and feel part of a community, at a local, national and international level' (Department for Children, Schools and Families, 2007, pp 73-4).

Less bound by elitism, the Welsh government's advice to schools in 2006 was that they should encourage more play, as learning is about play and imagination. In Wales it is now officially recognised that children can be stretched rather than being seen as having a fixed potential; the Welsh government says that if children play just within their capabilities, they feel their capabilities extend as a result.

In Scotland the educational curriculum is similarly being redesigned, for learning to ensure the development of '… wisdom, justice, compassion and integrity' (Shuayb and O'Donnell, 2008, p 22). All this for Britain is very new, and for England much of it is yet to come; but it may be a tipping point in the long-term trend of what people are willing to tolerate for their children's futures.

## Conclusion: those to whom evil is done

In the British Government's Budget of spring 2009 taxes were raised so the rich would, if they earned over a certain limit, again pay half their surplus gains as tax.[1] The House of Lords proposed an amendment that all companies should, by law, publish the ratio of the wages of their highest paid director or executive to the wages of the lowest paid tenth of their workforce. In the same year the new Equality Bill was introduced to Parliament, with Equalities Minister Harriet Harman stating that it was now the British government's understanding that inequality hurt everyone.

At the start of this century wage inequalities were 'higher than at any point since the Second World War and probably since representative statistics were first collected at the end of the nineteenth century…' (Machin, 2003, p 191). People in Britain thought little of this before the economic crash; they were told it did not matter; 'growth' would improve everyone's life. Big inequalities were viewed as natural. Key members of the government said they were 'seriously relaxed' about the situation; inequality was not an issue for them. Religious leaders concerned themselves with the plight of the poor, not the size of the equality gap. The British had forgotten that for most of their recent history they had not lived like this.

Despair grew, greed spiralled, prejudice seeped in, more were excluded. The elite preached that there was no alternative, that their experts were so very able, that the 'little people' were safe in their hands, and that greed really was good. Even when the economic crash came they said recovery would follow quickly and things would soon be back to normal. Many are still saying that as I write these words in March 2010. There is a general strike in Greece today. There have been small runs on the pound and even the Euro! In Ireland the unfair distribution of the struggle has resulted in more public protests. In Iceland over a quarter of the population signed a petition demanding to not pay the newly created national debt (to the UK and the Netherlands). Outside Sheffield Town Hall hundreds of people have just rallied against 1,000 job cuts announced by the local council.

In some ways we have been here before. In 1929 the stock market rallied several times, followed by massive unemployment in the US, and real falls in prices in Britain, which occurred again in 2009. The government cut wages across the public sector by 10 per cent in the 1930s. Although we began to become more equal in wealth during that decade, inequalities in health peaked as those dying young were found disproportionately among

---

[1] Editorial note: This tax increase was maintained in both the budgets of 2010, but later that year VAT was raised which penalises the poor far more, especially those without earnings. This is because the poor spend a higher proportion of what little income they have on necessities and many necessities are not exempt from VAT.

the poorest. In many other newly rich countries, especially Germany, it was far worse. In his poem September 1, 1939, W.H. Auden wrote:

> *'I and the public know*
> *What all schoolchildren learn*
> *Those to whom evil is done*
> *Do evil in return.'*

The most unequal of rich countries were those most willing to go to war overseas 64 years on from 1939. More equitable nations are more likely to find it easier to refuse to join any supposed 'coalition of the willing', or make only paltry contributions to it. When injustice is promoted at home to maintain inequality, it also becomes easier to contemplate perpetrating wrongs abroad. In the richer countries social wounds caused by inequality have been plastered over by building more prisons, hiring more police and prescribing more drugs. But by 2007 it was becoming more widely recognised that rich countries could not simply allocate money to ease the symptoms of extreme inequality. There was much agreement that: 'Extreme social inequality is associated with higher levels of mental ill health, drugs use, crime and family breakdown. Even high levels of public service investment, alone, cannot cope with the strain that places on our social fabric' (O'Grady, 2007, pp 62-3).

Inequality cannot keep on growing. But it will not end without the millions of tiny acts required in order that we no longer tolerate the greed, prejudice, exclusion and elitism that foster inequality and despair. Above all else these acts will require teaching and understanding, not forgetting once again what it is to be human: 'The human condition is fundamentally social — every aspect of human function and behaviour is rooted in social life. The modern preoccupation with individuality — individual expression, individual achievement and individual freedom — is really just a fantasy, a form of self-delusion...' (Burns, 2007, p 182). We need to realise that, and accept that none of us — including and especially our political leaders – is superhuman, but also that none is without significance. Everything it takes to defeat injustice lies in the mind. So what matters most is how we think.[2]

---

[2] Editorial note: The end of this chapter borrows a great deal from the ending of *Injustice: Why social inequalitiy persists* in a good example of self-plagiarism.

## References

Arneson, R.J. (2009) 'Justice is not equality', in B. Feltham (ed) *Justice, equality and constructivism: Essays on G.A. Cohen's 'Rescuing justice and equality'*, Chichester: Wiley-Blackwell, pp 5-25

Bauman, Z. (2008) *The art of life*, Cambridge: Polity Press

Burns, J. (2007) *The descent of madness: Evolutionary origins of psychosis and the social brain*, Hove: Routledge.

Department for Children, Schools and Families (2007) *The Children's Plan: Building brighter futures*, Norwich: The Stationery Office.

Dorling, D. (2009) 'The age of anxiety: why we should live in fear for our children's mental health', *Journal of Public Mental Health*, vol 8, no 4, pp 4–10.

Dorling, D. (2010) *Injustice: Why social inequality persists*, Bristol: The Policy Press

Haydon, D. and Scraton, P. (2008) 'Conflict, regulation and marginalisation in the North of Ireland: the experiences of children and young people', *Current Issues in Criminal Justice*, vol 20, no 1, pp 59–78.

Joseph Rowntree Foundation (2009) *Contemporary social evils*, Bristol: The Policy Press.

Machin, S. (2003) 'Wage inequality since 1975', in R. Dickens, P. Gregg and J. Wadsworth (eds) *The labour market under New Labour: The state of working Britain 2003*, Basingstoke: Palgrave Macmillan, Chapter 12.

O'Grady, F. (2007) 'Economic citizenship and the new capitalism', *Renewal: A Journal of Social Democracy*, vol 15, nos 2/3, pp 58–66.

Peston, R. (2008) *Who runs Britain? How the super-rich are changing our lives*, London: Hodder & Stoughton.

Rutherford, J. and Shah, H. (2006) *The good society: Compass programme for renewal*, London: Lawrence & Wishart.

Shuayb, M. and O'Donnell, S. (2008) *Aims and values in primary education: England and other countries* (Primary Review Research Survey 1/2), Cambridge: University of Cambridge Faculty of Education.

Stephens, L., Ryan-Collins, J. and Boyle, D. (2008) *Co-Production: A manifesto for growing the core economy*, London: new economics foundation.

Wilkinson, R.G. and Pickett, K. (2009) *The spirit level: Why more equal societies almost always do better*, London: Allen Lane.

# 9

# Glass conflict: David Cameron's claim to understand poverty[1]

*Roof Magazine* (2010) vol 35, no 1, p 10

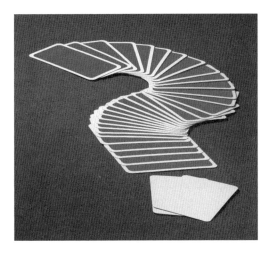

For two years at Oxford, I overlapped with prominent Bullingdon club Conservatives. I was not in their set and didn't see Boris Johnson hiding in the bushes at the botanical gardens in his attempt to evade arrest, nor the very young-looking George Osborne in his tailcoat.

I did once get hit by a champagne glass thrown from what I think was a Brasenose College window, but I have no evidence that it was David Cameron who threw it. Like Jeffrey Archer, I wasn't studying at the university. I was at secondary school, and it came as a shock that there were people who happily threw glasses at schoolchildren out of college windows.

Recently, I heard Mr Cameron say 'Don't dare lecture us on poverty,' and it reminded me of that strange-shaped glass that broke as it bounced off my head.

Many children growing up in Oxford could not name the city's colleges or identify types of wine glasses, but they do know what it is like to live in a city and a country where the powerful look down on the less well off and appear to see straight through them.

---

[1] Original title ended "... and his wish to 'eradicate dependency' seem wide of the mark".

In November, Mr Cameron announced that his party would reduce state intervention to 'eradicate dependency' and bring back the 'natural bonds of duty and responsibility'.

The government responded to Cameron's speech saying, 'David Cameron is calling for the state to withdraw, leaving people to fend for themselves and charities and community groups to pick up the pieces. This is a return to Thatcherism, or even 19th century liberalism – cutting back on government action on poverty, yet still backing tax cuts for the wealthiest estates.'

Strong words, yet this was the same government that cut taxes for the wealthy when it doubled the inheritance tax threshold at the end of 2007, the same government that brought in private contractors to insult people on the dole in a futile attempt to get the growing ranks of unemployed to compete harder for jobs.

This was the government that had brought markets into health, education and housing to the detriment of people's expectations to be treated fairly, regardless of where they came from or how well they could play the market.

Cameron's policies are just a stronger brand of what we have been forced to accept already. Earlier this year, he outlined his plans for housing. He would abolish 'all regional planning and housing powers exercised by regional government, returning powers and discretion back to local communities', he would reduce funding of poorer areas (what he calls 'equalising away by Whitehall').

He would allow citizens to veto council tax rises, but says nothing about allowing them to object to the affluent being taxed less. He would give local authorities the discretion to reduce business rates for businesses they favoured.

His party says that it will 'permit local authorities to devolve unlimited funding to ward councillors'. Try to imagine arranging social service, education and housing where for every appointment or decision, council officers have to go cap in hand for funding to a councillor.[2]

Regional development agencies are also to be abolished because they 'demonstrated insufficient empathy with the needs of business'. But all the Conservatives will be doing is increasing the sums transferred from the North to the South – this amounted to £150 million in 2009 when monies were cut from the regional development budgets to fund the housing market rescue packages.

Conservative policy on housing, education, health, social security and employment is just a more callous version of New Labour. Some assistance may be given by those architects of New Labour policy who have already

---

[2] Editorial note: By summer 2011 it became clear that this devolution meant the wholesale contracting out of entire council services where a majority of councillors voted for that. Butler, P. (2011) 'Every council scandal puts town hall outsourcing reforms in spotlight', *The Guardian*, 17 June

shifted across to the Conservative benches or 'networks'. Blair advisers Sally Morgan and Julian le Grand are to help with the 'new schools network'. David Freud, once a welfare tsar, has entered the Lords and now appears in Conservative party broadcasts.

If the *Daily Mail* is to be believed, Trevor Phillips, head of the Equalities and Human Rights Commission, has apparently been persuaded by his friend, Peter Mandelson, not to shift sides. However, according to the *Telegraph*, the chief executive of the charity Tomorrow's People, Debbie Scott, has jumped in with Cameron. Many more will follow.

I left Oxford, and my chances of bumping into the Bullingdon boys, to go to university in Newcastle in 1986. I live in Sheffield now.

When Cameron was young he apparently used to visit Sheffield. Wikipedia, a source as reliable as our major newspapers, says he 'spent much of his early life in Totley, Sheffield'. But in the late 1970s and 1980s, Totley was nowhere like the parts of South Yorkshire featured in the film *Brassed Off* where 'Coco the Scab' (Stephen Tompkinson) gave his speech about how God made Tories: 'We've got all these bodies left, but we're right out of brains and we're right out of hearts and we're right out of vocal cords…'

The Social and Spatial Inequalities group, of which I am a part, recently published a report,[3] funded by a Sheffield MP, which shows the big differences in wealth that still exist on opposite sides of the city. Cameron

---

[3] Thomas, B., Pritchard, J., Ballas, D., Vickers, D. and Dorling, D. (2009) *A tale of two cities: The Sheffield project*, Sheffield: SASI. Copy available here: www.sasi.group.shef.ac.uk/research/sheffield/index.html

may have seen one side – the affluent bit in Totley[4] – but he is not in a position to judge the other.

During his student days at Brasenose, he probably had a few lectures on poverty. But that gap in his knowledge needs to be addressed before he is equipped to take on the role of leading us all – rich and poor.

---

[4] Editorial note: The reference to David Cameron possibly having spent some time in Sheffield is dubious, but found here "The son of a stockbroker, Cameron grew up in Sheffield's quaintest little village, Totley, before going to a preparatory school in Berkshire and onto Eton, Oxford and the notorious Bullingdon Club." See the website: www.asylum.co.uk/2009/11/17/posh-or-not-how-do-you-like-your-prime-ministers/. It is possible some confusion arose over the maiden name of his wife, Samantha Gwendoline Sheffield. The more reliable source, when it comes to famous figures, Wikipedia, makes no mention of any Totley connection to Dave and says Sam is the daughter of Sir Reginald Adrian Berkeley Sheffield, a Baronet, landowner, thrice descendant of King Charles II of England and at one point husband of Samantha's mother, Annabel Lucy Veronica Jones. Similarly, David William Donald Cameron is a direct descendant of King William IV and his mistress Dorothea Jordan.

# 10

# Clearing the poor away[1]

*Socialist Review* (2010) November

The comprehensive spending review announced the start of a new era of engineered social polarisation: a further separation of the lives, hopes, homes and chances of rich and poor.

One of the first announcements was that new tenants of council and other social housing will now have to pay at least 80 percent of market prices in rent. At a stroke millions of low paid families are to be excluded from living in hundreds of towns, cities and villages where they no longer earn enough to "deserve" to be.

At age 60, shadow chancellor Alan Johnson[2] is adept at dealing with callousness. His immediate reaction to the cheering that greeted the government announcements was that for many coalition MPs it was now

---

[1] Editorial note: Under the by-line "…With the poorest set to suffer most from cuts, this frontline article looks at the damage the spending review will do to the lives of millions…" this article was published in response to the greatest tranche of spending cuts announced towards the end of 2010.

[2] Editorial note: Replaced by Ed Balls in early 2011. And now writing his memoirs.

obvious that "this is what they came into politics for". George Osborne (39), who became an MP in 2001, ended his speech saying he had brought sanity to our public finances and civility to our economy. The printed version of his speech suggests the word was "stability", not "civility", but George was mumbling at that point and I think he thinks he is civilised.

Osborne announced that housing benefit will not be paid for people under the age of 35 who live alone – this previously applied only to those under 25. There would be a 10 percent cut in council tax benefit for those who cannot afford to live in certain areas. The few remaining people living on modest incomes near affluent suburbs or in economically successful towns and villages are to be cleansed away.

We now know that the spending review is at least as regressive as the June budget, as were the cuts announced for local council core funding. The best-off fifth of society will lose just 1 percent of their entitlements to public services and spending, the lowest losses of any group. Furthermore, a million people currently on employment and support allowance due to ill health will each lose £2000 a year if they cannot find a job. Osborne announced further privatisation of pensions, with the state pension age rising rapidly to 66 years. Only those with private provision can now retire at the normal age. Public sector pensioners will have £1.8 billion removed from them by 2014-15. This will further impoverish many of that group. Pension credits will be frozen for three years.

No family on benefits is to receive more than the income of an average family in work, no matter what the circumstances of their children. If you are poor – or are made poor when you lose your job or have a pay cut forced on you – and have three or more children, you may need to leave your town for a new life in a cheaper area, away from where the remaining well paid work is.

Understanding demographic trends is crucial to understanding the review. Provision for the NHS does not include the extra costs of the post-war baby boomers retiring, or the cost of new privatisations being introduced there (which were not even in the Tory manifesto). Provision for education does not maintain current rates of spending per child once the new privatised "free" school costs are added in. University places will be slashed, but 75,000 more apprenticeships are to be created for the children of the more-deserving, better-behaved poor – those who know their place. The educational maintenance allowance for less well-off children will be phased out, another significant cut to children's finances which, when combined with all the chancellor's other measures, means that child poverty will rise – despite what he suggested in this speech.

But not everyone loses out. More affluent savers who lost money they invested in Equitable Life and the Presbyterian Mutual Society will soon receive £1.7 billion from taxpayers - mostly from taxpayers poorer than them. Thus money is being redistributed towards the affluent. And there will be more property for the affluent to buy with these windfalls in and around London, in villages and in market towns, as the poor vacate their homes for cheaper places to live.[3]

Raising the cap on train fares will mean that those who do move out to make ends meet will end up paying even more to get into London and other cities for work. Local government will be allowed to borrow more in richer areas, against expected business rates, instead of Westminster borrowing, so that the places where business makes a lot of money can be spruced up. Local government in poorer areas cannot make such newly permitted borrowing.

Osborne is younger than me, and I am still a relatively young university professor. His work experience has been limited to shelf-stacking and a few weeks of filing in the NHS. Danny Alexander, the chief secretary to the treasury, is even younger (38). For a year he had a job outside of politics, doing PR for a national park. Between them, these inexperienced young men - who as far as I know have never been on the dole - announced a huge raft of cuts which their own figures say will directly make half a million public servants redundant.

The former Tory chancellor, and current secretary of state for justice, Ken Clarke (69), had warned of a double-dip recession if cuts were savage. On 21 October, Teresa Perchard, director of policy at the Citizens Advice Bureau, warned that housing benefit changes would "create a group of nomads... maybe not where the jobs are". On the same BBC radio programme, Alan Johnson said that Osborne's speech was "unfair, unwise and untruthful in some of the statistics" and that the chancellor was "asking children to make a bigger contribution than the banks".

There were a huge number of alternatives to what took place on Wednesday 20 October, but few of those alternatives would have resulted in the cleansing and clearing out of so many poorer people (and people made newly poor) from more prosperous areas of the country. Many younger people will now go abroad to find work or a university place. Many of them will never return. Poorer families will struggle the most, but fewer will be visible through the windows of ministerial cars. This is how you break a society.

---

[3] Editorial note: The first 'compensation payments' to affluent Equitable Life policy holders were made on 30 June 2011.

# SECTION III
# Race and identity

We guard our identities, are cautious over what we say to others. All of us who are sane worry about how we are perceived. We fear being ostracised. You can see all of this in how people behave when they are being filmed. One day in 2008 I read in a newspaper that:

> *Danny Dorling, Professor of Human Geography at Sheffield University, was an adviser on the Cutting Edge documentary, 'Rich Kid, Poor Kid', which will be broadcast on Channel 4 at 9pm on November 13*

I hadn't formally been an advisor to the film, but I had talked a lot to the people involved while they made the film, which concerned a poor mixed-race girl and a rich white girl growing up as very near neighbours in London. They only met because of the film. The film was all about their different identities, how wealth and poverty separated them, and, indirectly, about race.

Race separates us because poverty and wealth separate us. Where people live in households not so strictly segregated from other households by income gulfs, racial distinctions are less frequently made. In very equal affluent societies people are often said to look more alike or even to be of a fictional homogeneous race. In 2005 Trevor Phillips, the former Chair of the Commission for Racial Equality, recognised none of these points when he first wrote about Britain 'sleepwalking into segregation'. I wrote my first article on race as a response to Trevor's claims. This section begins, in Chapter 11, with the previously unpublished original version as sent to the *Observer* newspaper, complete with numerous tables. The newspaper was kind enough to print a shorter version of it despite my deluging them with figures!

My reply to Trevor is followed below by another newspaper article on the film of the lives of the rich girl and the poor girl in 'Rich Kid, Poor Kid', followed in turn, in Chapter 13, by a previously unpublished commentary on the linking of race and crime (this time an invited response to a discussion paper concerned with why people from ethnic minorities are so over-represented both in prisons and as victims of crime).

The next contribution, Chapter 14, was first published with two colleagues in the *British Medical Journal* and shows how equally remarkable statistics can be found demonstrating the unevenness of access to medical school on examination of students' ethnicity interacting with social class. The final chapter of the section, Chapter 15, is a comment on race and the implications of the recession, published in the newsletter of the independent race equality think tank, the Runnymede Trust.

# 11

# Ghettos in the sky[1]

*The Observer* (2005) 25 September, pp 14–15

"Ghettos in English cities almost equal to Chicago" ran the headlines by the end of last week. "Sleepwalking to segregation" began an editorial in the *Times*. All this as a result of one speech made in Manchester, but made by the Chair of the Commission for Racial Equality, Trevor Phillips. Mr Phillips had some interesting points to make on Thursday night. However, his central claim – that we are drifting toward racial segregation - is wrong. Residential racial segregation is not increasing as he claimed. There are no neighbourhood ghetto communities in Britain – and the "new" research he referenced, to try to support his claims, is neither new nor authoritative. The source for the central claim was a speech given a couple of weeks earlier by an academic based in Australia. The carefully considered conclusion of academics in Britain is that there are no ghettos here. In short, Trevor Phillips has been ill informed or has simply not understood what his organisation

---

[1] This is the original version of the article, with the original title 'Ghettos in the sky', as submitted to the *Observer* newspaper with 6 tables of evidence. A much shorter edited version with no tables was published under the more provocative (but still accurate) title "Why Trevor is wrong about race ghettos". This is the full version as submitted to the newspaper.

has been telling him. Racism is rife in Britain but it is not being expressed through rising levels of neighbourhood segregation. Nor are any ghettos likely to be formed in the near future. If ignorance of these trends extends as far as the Chair of the Commission then debate on segregation in Britain will be all the poorer for it and we will neglect the segregation that really is occurring: by poverty and wealth.

Had Trevor Phillips read the work of the academic who has studied segregation in most detail in Britain over recent years he might have thought a little more carefully before making his claims. In fact if he had only read the first two sentences of Dr Ludi Simpson's most recent paper he would have learnt that "Racial self-segregation and increased racial segregation are myths for Britain. The repetition of these myths send unhelpful messages to policy makers." Dr Simpson, who works at the University of Manchester, also spoke on the BBC from that city on Thursday night, and explained why Trevor's central message was wrong. But, by the time he spoke, the Friday papers were already being printed and Trevor's message was spreading uncorrected.

The most up-to-date segregation indices for different ethnic and religious groups were published over a year ago. They were calculated from the latest census and are comparable with figures published a decade earlier. For all ethnic minority groups identified by the census the indices of segregation fell between 1991 and 2001. These are the indices to which Trevor Phillips referred in his speech – also called the indices of dissimilarity. They fell fastest for those of Black and Other Asian origin.

For no ethnic minority group have these indices risen. In contrast, segregation rose over the same period in Northern Ireland for many religious groups. The local pattern in particular cities will vary slightly, but, nationally – ethnic minority neighbourhood segregation in Britain is falling – and there are no ghettos, no neighbourhoods where a majority of residents belong to a particular minority group. Even if there were there is no reason to see that as a problem, but before proposing opinions, it is important to get the simple facts right.

What may have confused Trevor Phillips is the work reported by an Australia-based academic at a conference over the summer. That work referred to the extent to which different groups in Britain may be becoming more isolated rather than more segregated. It is not hard to see why the indices that academics use to measure these things could so easily confuse. The segregation index is a measure of the proportion of people who would have to move home for a group to be evenly spread across the country. The higher that index for a particular group the more people from the particular group would have to move - were that group to be evenly distributed between neighbourhoods. It is falling for all minority groups. In contrast, the isolation index is a measure of how often individuals from a particular group are likely to meet other individuals from their group. The two are related but do not measure the same thing. Most crucially, if disproportionate numbers of people in a particular group are of child bearing age, have children, and so the group grows in size (similarly in all neighbourhoods), the index of segregation remains the same while the so-called index of isolation rises.

The idea that a group becomes more isolated is farcical if the index rises simply because the group contains large numbers of young adults starting families. Most young adults have children; adults of ethnic or religious minority groups are no different. This normal demographic change accounts for much that concerns Trevor. In the cities that he lists as having particularly high concentrations there are simply more young adults of particular ethnic groups of child bearing age – and they are having children. They are having children in much the same numbers that young adults of their age of all other ethnic and religious groups are having children. Having children is not some decision to self segregate – it is normal. Where young adults are clustered the numbers of people in a particular minority group will tend to rise when they have children. Similarly, in these neighbourhoods few people in the young groups are dying from old age (because they are not old). So the group size is not declining due to natural mortality. Again this is simple demographics – not segregation. The rise in the index of isolation mainly reflects demographic changes not any tendency to segregate by ethnicity in Britain.

The index of isolation is thus not necessarily a good measure to use, but it might be useful for the Chair of the Commission for Racial Equality to know (if he does refer to it), it is highest in Britain for people of Christian faiths and then for those who state they have no religion. These are the most geographically isolated groups in Britain. The most segregated religious groups in England and Wales are people of Jewish and Sikh faiths, not Muslims as is often supposed; while the levels of geographical isolation of people of Catholic faith in Scotland exceed those of any minority religious or ethnic group in England. All these facts are taken from just a couple of pages of a 2001 Census atlas of the UK that was published in 2004 (see Statistical Appendix below), but by now there are many other sources of this data that can be called upon to see that no neighbourhood ghettos are being formed in Britain. Trevor simply failed to check his facts.

There are shocking statistics concerning segregation directly by the state that the Chair of the Commission does need to address. In some areas African-Caribbean boys are up to 15 times more likely to be excluded from school than are white boys, and when it was last measured, up to 12 times more likely to be incarcerated in prison in Britain. Children and young people are being segregated out of classrooms and disproportionately into prisons by ethnicity in this country. The Commission has enough real work to do that it need not create fictitious evils to remedy. In terms of education

Trevor is right to say that children are more segregated by school than by neighbourhood, but this is only slightly so and has only been measured at one point in time. He is wrong to imply in his speech that schools are increasing the trend towards spatial racial segregation – a spatial trend that we know is decreasing – when we do not know how the intake of schools by ethnicity and religion is changing over time. Our schools and universities are becoming more unequal in their intake, but not necessarily by religion nor by ethnicity.

What is most unfortunate about this misunderstanding is that it detracts from the neighbourhood segregation that is most clearly occurring in Britain but which is about poverty and wealth, not race nor religion. Neighbourhoods are becoming more segregated by rates of illness and premature mortality.

Depending on when and to whom a baby is born – inequalities in their chances of reaching their first birthday have widened since 1997. Neighbourhoods are rapidly becoming more segregated by wealth – most clearly by housing equity through which the best-off tenth of children should already each expect to each inherit £80,000 simply because of where they were born, plus interest – a sum which makes baby bonds obsolete in future effect. Neighbourhoods are segregating by the availability of work, particularly good jobs. They are segregating in terms of educational opportunities as the majority of extra university places have been taken up by the children from the streets where most went to university to begin with.[2] The fortunes of Britain's ethnic and religious minorities depend at least as much on where they live as on how they are perceived by the colour of their skins or the faiths they profess. There are independent ethnic penalties to gaining good employment (in lay terms - racism) and that can be proved with census data, but there is no increased neighbourhood racial segregation. That, though, is not to say that other racial concentrations cannot be found – especially of children.

The ghettos referred to in Trevor's speech do not exist. Britain has no neighbourhood ghettos that correspond to the situation in the United States. However, had his researchers looked at the census more carefully then they would begin to see much else that should concern them. Cut Britain up horizontally rather than by neighbourhood and you do find minority-majority areas. For example above the fifth floor of all housing in England and Wales only a minority of children are white. The majority of children growing up in the tower blocks of London and Birmingham - the majority

---

[2] Editorial note: This was the case in 2005; it was no longer the case by 2010 as New Labour's education policies did manage to see the very last batch of extra university places being awarded in slightly higher numbers to those who were previously least likely to go to university. See section IV below on Education and Hierarchy, especially Chapter 18 on page 147. However, the new government of 2010 then abolished baby bonds.

of children "living in the sky" in Britain – are black. From the level of the street you cannot see the colour of the skin of the faces of the children at the windows above the fifth floor. The Chair of the Commission needs the census to tell him what is happening as much as any of the rest of us do. Our gut feelings are not good enough, our own lives too isolated for us to extrapolate from experience. The evidence comes mainly from social statistics. Britain is increasingly segregated by inequality, poverty, wealth and opportunity, not by race by area. The only racial ghettos in Britain are ghettos in the sky in neighbourhoods which are, at ground level, amongst the most racially mixed in Britain, but where the children of the poorest are – more often than not – black. We have not been sleepwalking into segregation by race, but towards ever greater segregation by wealth and poverty. That is what matters most to the life chances of people in Britain.

## Statistical appendix

All the tables below show two indices of dispersal by district for each religious group in England and Wales. The first (1) is the index of segregation, the proportion of people who would have to move districts to be evenly spread; the second is the index of isolation (2), the chance of a person of a particular religion meeting another person of their religion, at random within the district they live. Religious affiliation in Britain was not asked before 2001 (except in 1851) and so religious segregation and isolation in Britain can only be measured for one point in time (it was asked in Northern Ireland prior to 2001):

**Table 1:** Religious segregation in England and Wales in 2001 by district showing two measures

| Index (%) | Christian | Buddhist | Hindu | Jewish | Muslim | Sikh | Other | None | Not stated |
|---|---|---|---|---|---|---|---|---|---|
| 1 | 4.8 | 29.8 | 56.2 | 62.1 | 54.2 | 62.5 | 19.5 | 10.2 | 4.7 |
| 2 | 72.9 | 0.5 | 6.4 | 5.1 | 10.3 | 3.9 | 0.4 | 15.8 | 7.8 |

The source of this table and those that follow below in this appendix: pages 56 and 57 of Dorling, D. and Thomas, B. (2004) *People and Places: A 2001 Census atlas of the UK*, Bristol: The Policy Press.

*Note:* Index 1 is the traditional segregation index (proportion of the group that would have to move to have an even spread) and Index 2 is the index of isolation (how often neighbours are of the same group).

The two statistics of dispersal calculated for the English and Welsh religious groups can also be calculated for the six Northern Irish religious groups identified by the census and are shown in Table 2 below, but for both the 1991 and the 2001 censuses.

**Table 2:** Religious segregation in Northern Ireland in 1991 and 2001 by district showing two measures

| Index (%) | Catholic | Presbyterian | Church of Ireland | Methodist | Other | None | All Protestant |
|---|---|---|---|---|---|---|---|
| 1 (2001) | 20.75 | 20.85 | 14.01 | 30.13 | 16.90 | 15.96 | 10.49 |
| 2 (2001) | 50.20 | 25.69 | 17.03 | 5.18 | 7.40 | 15.77 | 30.09 |
| | | | | | | | |
| 1 (1991) | 21.37 | 20.77 | 13.43 | 30.50 | 15.60 | 13.64 | 9.93 |
| 2 (1991) | 48.61 | 26.45 | 19.71 | 5.63 | 8.90 | 12.12 | 31.70 |

*Note:* The Protestant column at the end provides the results for the three main Protestant religions combined. Index 1 is the traditional segregation index (proportion of the group that would have to move to have an even spread) and Index 2 is the index of isolation (how often neighbours are of the same group).

The most isolated group in 2001 were Catholics and that level of isolation has risen by 1.92% as compared to the measure taken in 1991 (using the same geographical areas). However, at the district level, Catholics are becoming slightly less segregated and Protestants slightly less isolated.

Outside of Northern Ireland the only area of the UK where Christian denomination was asked for was in Scotland. The table for Scotland below can thus be compared to that for the Province:

**Table 3:** Religious segregation in Scotland in 2001 by district showing two measures

| Index (%) | Church of Scotland | Catholic | Other Christian | Buddhist | Hindu | Jewish | Muslim | Sikh | Other | None | Not stated |
|---|---|---|---|---|---|---|---|---|---|---|---|
| 1 | 6.56 | 25.99 | 17.01 | 21.24 | 40.34 | 55.56 | 43.78 | 44.82 | 18.38 | 8.43 | 8.78 |
| 2 | 49.68 | 24.43 | 9.21 | 0.12 | 0.16 | 1.37 | 1.40 | 0.25 | 0.47 | 20.84 | 4.28 |

*Note:* Index 1 is the traditional segregation index (proportion of the group that would have to move to have an even spread) and Index 2 is the index of isolation (how often neighbours are of the same group).

In 2001, by district, Catholics were more segregated in Scotland than in Northern Ireland, the Church of Scotland was more isolated than the Church of Ireland, and other Christian religions were more separated from the rest of the population than were Methodists in the Northern Irish Province. Hindus, religious Jews, Muslims and Sikhs were all more segregated in Scotland than were the Christian religions in Northern Ireland. They are even more segregated in England and Wales than in Scotland. Only those with no religion were more segregated in Northern Ireland than elsewhere and even they were less isolated.

The table below shows the two indices of dispersal by district for each ethnic minority group in England and Wales. Again, they are the index of segregation (1), the index of isolation (2). These statistics reveal that just over sixty percent of people of Caribbean origin, Africans, Pakistanis and

Bangladeshis would have to move district to be evenly spread. The other groups are less segregated. The White group is by far the most isolated and is also more separated from the rest than is any other group, followed by Bangladeshis then Indians. Black Others, along with the Chinese, Asian Others and Other Others are the least separated of all the ethnic groups in England and Wales, having allowed for their sizes.

**Table 4:** Segregation by Ethnicity in England and Wales in 2001 by district, two measures

| Index (%) | White | Caribbean | African | Black-Other | Indian | Pakistani | Bangladeshi | Chinese | Asian-Other | Other-Other |
|---|---|---|---|---|---|---|---|---|---|---|
| 1 | 5 | 62 | 62 | 42 | 55 | 61 | 61 | 32 | 39 | 39 |
| 2 | 93 | 5 | 7 | 2 | 9 | 6 | 10 | 1 | 2 | 2 |

Index 1 is the traditional segregation index (proportion of the group that would have to move to have an even spread) and Index 2 is the index of isolation (how often neighbours are of the same group).

The table below shows the changes in the two indices of dispersal for England and Wales by ethnic group between 1991 and 2001. The only groups which have become more segregated, ever so slightly, are White and Other-Other. However, the White group is the only group to have become less isolated (isolation tends to increase as groups grow in size mainly where they were before).

**Table 5:** Change in segregation by ethnicity in England and Wales by district, two measures

| Change 1991-2001 | White | Caribbean | African | Black-Other | Indian | Pakistani | Bangladeshi | Chinese | Asian-Other | Other-Other |
|---|---|---|---|---|---|---|---|---|---|---|
| 1 | 1% | 0% | −4% | −6% | −2% | 0% | 0% | −1% | −11% | 1% |
| 2 | −2% | 0% | 3% | 0% | 1% | 2% | 3% | 0% | 1% | 0% |

Index 1 is the traditional segregation index (proportion of the group that would have to move to have an even spread) and Index 2 is the index of isolation (how often neighbours are of the same group).

The table below shows the 2001 levels of the two indices of dispersal for Scotland by ethnic group. The only change that has occurred since 1991, when decimal points are not shown, is that there has been a single percentage point drop in the degree of separation experienced by Pakistani people in Scotland. Scotland is treated here separately from England and Wales because slightly different questions on ethnicity were asked in Scotland. Again the most isolated group is White, but their levels of isolation are now near the maximum of 100%. The most segregated group is Pakistani, followed by the other Asian groups. Lowest amongst these Asian groups in Scotland is the level for people identifying as Chinese, a lower rate again is only found for the Scottish Caribbean and Other–Other ethnic groups. In comparison, in England and Wales, the Chinese are the least segregated after White. The smallest groups are not necessarily the most segregated.

**Table 6:** Segregation by ethnicity in Scotland in 2001 by district, two measures

| 2001 | White | Caribbean | African | Black-Other | Indian | Pakistani | Bangladeshi | Chinese | Asian-Other | Other-Other |
|---|---|---|---|---|---|---|---|---|---|---|
| 1 | 0% | 25% | 38% | 24% | 41% | 49% | 47% | 30% | 34% | 26% |
| 2 | 99% | 0% | 0% | 0% | 0% | 1% | 0% | 0% | 0% | 0% |

Index 1 is the traditional segregation index (proportion of the group that would have to move to have an even spread) and Index 2 is the index of isolation (how often neighbours are of the same group).

# 12

# Worlds apart: how inequality breeds fear and prejudice in Britain

*The Guardian* (2008) 12 November

A new documentary lays bare how inequality breeds fear and prejudice in Britain through the eyes of two very different teenage girls (the 'Cutting Edge' documentary, 'Rich Kid, Poor Kid', was broadcast the day after this article was published, on Channel 4 at 9pm on November 13). […]

Britain has changed. A generation ago, our children knew more about each other. They were more likely to go to the same school if they lived on the same street, and they were more likely to know of the lives of others around them, even where there was great difference between their families' incomes.

Today, children in Britain live in more fear and ignorance of each other. The well-off are ferried around by car, told not to walk down the wrong street – and, if they do walk, told that other children are dangerous and not to be mixed with. Poorer children are told they are worth less in comparison with others. They are labelled as failures in a country where we avidly count academic qualifications. Poor children are told that they are poor due to the fault, failure and the lack of "responsibility" of their parent(s).

These changes and the impact they have on individual lives are explored in tomorrow night's Channel 4 'Cutting Edge' documentary, 'Rich Kid, Poor Kid', as it follows two teenagers in London from different ends of the social scale meeting for the first time.

Alice, 15, lives in a six-bed townhouse. She says she lives in an oasis of safety surrounded by "dangerous" areas that are not "upper-middle class" like her enclave. Her only connection with the children who live in the council flats nearby is that "they nick our bikes ... apart from that, we never had any reason to connect with them at all".

Alice doesn't think of herself as rich. You have to have many millions to be rich, she says. Her mother, Fiona, doesn't like where she lives. She says it's too near to the scary estates where "people get murdered, where people aren't British. You don't see any white people round here, they are all blacks. I don't think you should say that ... but it's true."

At the opposite end of the same street lives 17-year-old Natalie, in a two-bed council flat with her mother and brother. The family lives on £165 a week. Natalie, who left school at 15, is the one who phones up the council to try to find a school place for her five-year-old brother, who missed out on getting a place in reception. She's the one in charge of her family. Her mother gets depressed and can't cope, and her brother sleeps on the floor, although his family bought him a bed and assembled it while filming. It takes all Natalie's determination to get him a place in a school.

Note: the girls pictured in each other's homes
Photograph: Phil Fisk

## Loan shark

Natalie's mother is finding living hard enough itself, but she knows what matters. She knows the point when you realise that you can never have a childhood birthday again. When her mother borrows £100 to pay for Natalie's birthday, she does so at a 55% interest rate from a loan shark.

Alice's father works in finance; Natalie's father died when she was six. Although these two girls live within a stone's throw of each other, they live at the social extremes of life in Britain.

However, for the purposes of the C4 programme, they get to meet. But first they are to be shown photographs of each other. "She'll be a chav," Alice predicts. And Alice will be "white and she has blond hair and she wears a lot of foundation", Natalie says. When they eventually meet, they look, they stare, they talk, and they listen. Natalie explains how her family ended up on benefits. They hug.

"I made a comment about how people who don't work don't deserve to have benefits," Alice says. "I have to kind of take in that other people have issues … She thinks we're posh. I've been brought up on fear, haven't I?"

When they meet again, Natalie suggests they "can go round the estate or through the estate". Alice has never been through. "This is my block; it's a shithole, but I like it," explains Natalie. They visit each other's homes. They compare holidays – Butlins and skiing. Alice's mum apologises for how small her garden is; Alice explains that their piano is "only" a baby grand. Natalie doesn't appear to feel out of place in Alice's home. Indeed, it is Alice who seems to feel out of place, questioning her own views. Natalie is taking her little brother to school, having got him a place, and that is how we leave these two teenagers. Neither is likely to have their lives fundamentally altered by having spent a day with the other.

Inequalities in income and wealth breed fear, distrust, angst, anger and poverty. Rising inequalities amplify all of this, make the poor suffer more, and make so many of the well-off sound ignorant when they try to justify these inequalities and their wealth. The two girls in this documentary had no choice about what they were born into. They did not choose to be educated separately. But they, and so many of the others like them, will be the ones who have to sort out the mess our society has put them in.

# 13

# How much evidence do you need?
# Ethnicity, harm and crime[1]

CCJS online commentary (2008)

## How much evidence do you need?

Racism permeates societies in ways that make it hard for most of us most of the time to recognise how omnipotent it is. Racism is also in the ether in a much wider sense than is usually recognised. Thinking that is in itself racist in origin, in underlying argument, is used in much talk by affluent people when they try to justify why others are poor. Others are often assumed to be of different 'stock', not to have the supposedly inherent and superior abilities of those in power.

It is often suggested, if not that often directly, that many people are not well-off because they 'have not got what it takes'. In essence such an argument is no more or less racist than those arguments that people with darker skin pigments are somehow inferior to those with lighter skins.

Overt racism in 21st century Britain works on the basis of skin colour first and religion second. In the past religion ranked higher as a marker of who were to be discriminated against (Catholics, Jews and Huguenots for instance). The signs and labels change even though the underlying ways in which groups are stigmatized and devalued remain very similar over time.

---

[1] This commentary was published on-line by the Centre for Crime and Justice Studies (CCJS) and can be found at www.crimeandjustice.org.uk/ehcresponses.html where the article to which it is a response can also be sourced (which is also the single reference at the end of this short piece, all other references are given in the footnotes).

Racism occurs when it is suggested that some peoples are less valuable, less needed than others, have less of a right to be and to things – than others.

This is how it is put in reports of surveys by academics:

> "The Fourth National Survey of Ethnic Health (Nazroo, 2001) finds there is also 'a sense of being a devalued member of a devalued low status group' and the 'stress of being a victim of racial harassment.' and 'suggests a relationship between experiences of racial harassment, perceptions of racial discrimination and a range of health outcomes across different groups' which are independent of socio-economic effects." (Roberts and McMahon 2008, p 42)

And how many people experience being victims of racial harassment? "Over *a third* of minority groups reported experiencing overt racism in Britain in 2005 and at least five times as many racially motivated crimes occurred as were reported."[2]

And how racist is the population at large? That you can discover through numerous surveys depending on what you think a racist attitude might be. You might think racism is more common among the working class, however *thirty percent* of the supposedly most influential movers and shakers of London surveyed in late 2007 said they would not vote for a London Mayor if the candidate were Muslim.[3]

And, when a senior police officer in the London Metropolitan Police Force complained of racist discrimination, it was repeatedly suggested in the press that because he was on a high salary, he should not complain.[4] There is great ignorance.

On ignorance, education policy "itself remains unaddressed, as a source or carrier of racism…"[5] many more black pupils are excluded from schools due to "systematic, racial discrimination in the application of disciplinary and exclusions policy …[and in 2006 we learnt that] Black pupils were '*five times* less likely to be registered as 'gifted and talented'".[6] Those who are most vocal and confident in their criticism show how (on race) New Labour's education policy has been assessed overall as being in its effect:

---

[2] Lewis, M. and N. Newman (2007) *Challenging attitudes, perceptions and myths*, Report for the Commission on Integration and Cohesion, London: The Commission on Integration and Cohesion, p 6.

[3] *Evening Standard*, London: Tuesday 13 November, 2007, pp 8-9.

[4] In the last few days of August 2008, on Radio 4's 'Today' programme, including on 1 September.

[5] Ball, S. J. (2008) *The education debate*, Bristol: The Policy Press, p 172.

[6] *Ibid*, p 173, quoting in turn from the *Independent on Sunday*'s release of an unpublished Department for Education and Schools report in December 2006.

"actively involved in the defence, legitimation and extension of White supremacy".[7] This is through the choices that are being made over what is taught, how ideas of inherent difference are propagated, and whose version of history and geography, literature and science is presented in our national curriculum. But the wider face of racism in education is IQism – the idea that inherited 'talent' exists and hence diverges between different social groups including people grouped by race/ethnicities.

Ignorance was one of the five great social evils identified over 60 years ago. Another was Want, and the most acute want in Britain tends to affect those which are most often the target of racists. In the year 2000 mothers labelled as asylum seekers had to beg if, for their newborn children, they "ran out of milk mid-week, having spent their single £25 [food] voucher".[8] In 1943 Winston Churchill had written that "…there is no finer investment for any community than putting milk into babies."[9]

Over a thousand refugees were recorded as having died or been killed due to government control on migration in just a three year period in the late 1990s. Two brothers from India tried to get to Britain holding on within the undercarriage of a plane. One survived. Just after the end of this three-year period another two boys aged 15 and 16 were found dead in the landing gear of a plane that had arrived in Brussels from Mali. One had written a letter. It was later found on his body:

> "Excellencies, gentlemen – members and those responsible in Europe, it is to your solidarity and generosity that we appeal for your help in Africa. If you see that we have sacrificed ourselves and lost our lives, it is because we suffer too much in Africa and need your help to struggle against poverty and war … Please excuse us very much for daring to write a letter." [10]

If it were white children dying in the undercarriage of a plane you would have heard of their stories, the letters, lives, wishes, hopes and fears.

The Labour government of the millennium introduced new laws in Britain to fine lorry drivers if stowaways were found in their vehicles, with no exceptions: "…the Conservatives asked if drivers would be fined if the asylum-seeker on board was a baby? They would. What if the baby had died en route? The police would have to investigate whether he or she had died

---

[7] *Ibid*, p 172, quoting in turn David Gillborn from 2005.

[8] Hayter, T. (2004) *Open borders: The case against immigration controls*, London: Pluto Press, pp 108–09.

[9] Timmins, N. (2001) *The five giants: A biography of the welfare state*, new edition, London: HarperCollins, p 47.

[10] The quotation can be found on page 103 of Hayter 2004 (*Ibid*) – also see pages 108–09 for how those who survive are then treated.

in British territory before deciding if a fine was necessary."[11] As long as the baby is long dead you would not be fined for accidentally bringing it into the country, but – by implication – even if you were to kill the baby… ?

They were not thinking of a white baby when they said that. They were not thinking that much at all.

After Ignorance and Want, amongst the five evils next came Idleness. The years of life people suffer from being unemployed or underemployed can be estimated given data on their ethnicities, qualification, residence and occupation.[12] Years of life are lost from being more likely to be convicted to a prison sentence, or a longer sentence for committing a crime if you are black rather than white. In 1991 the census revealed that in crude terms a man was *seven times* more likely to be in prison if he were black.[13] By "…2005, BME people accounted for approximately 24% of the male prison population and 28% of the female prison population (Home Office, 2006a). Between 1995 and 2003 the numbers of BME prisoners doubled from 8,797 to 17,775 (Home Office, 2006c) [when the] Home Office changed the recording method and began using new census categories." (Roberts and McMahon, 2008).

The fourth evil was Disease. Most people in Britain who are too ill to work due to ill health now suffer from mental illnesses rather than physical ones. It is worth again simply repeating the evidence:

> "The 2007 census (Commission for Healthcare Audit, 2007) further highlights higher rates of admission, detention under the Mental Health Act, seclusion (being locked in a room) and referrals from criminal justice agencies. For men and women, the rates of admission for BME groups were over three times higher than average (*ibid*). In the 'other Black' group, admission rates were ten times higher than average. For detentions under the Mental Health Act on admission, there was an increase from 39% in 2005 to 43% in 2007 with overall rates of detention higher than average among Black Caribbean, Black African, Other Black and White/Black Caribbean Mixed Groups. Seclusions were also higher than average among Black Caribbean, Other Black men and among Other white in both genders. Black Caribbean, Black African and White/Black Caribbean Mixed groups had higher than average rates by 56%, 33% and 33% respectively (*ibid*)." (Roberts and McMahon, 2008, p 33).

---

[11] Cohen, N. (2004) *Pretty straight guys*, London: Faber and Faber, p 74.

[12] Simpson, L. et al (2009) 'Jobs deficits, neighbourhood effects, and ethnic penalties: the geography of ethnic-labour-market inequality', *Environment and Planning A*, vol 41, no 4, pp 946–63.

[13] Dorling, D. (1995) *A new social atlas of Britain*, Chichester: Wiley, p 12.

The fifth and final evil was Squalor. Slums in Britain have almost all been cleared. Overcrowding for most has been rapidly declining – but by 1998-2006 – in the UK "…over an eight year period the number of statutory homeless households fell by slightly over 8%; yet, in the same period the number of non-white BME homeless households increased by 14.5%. There was a striking increase in the number of homeless African/Caribbean households of between 25% and 42%" (Roberts and McMahon, 2008, pages 17 and 18). The unequal distribution of squalor continues: "33% of Pakistanis and Bangladeshis living in unfit dwellings compared to 6% White" *(ibid)*.

British society, like many other societies, is a very racist society. A society bound together partly through ideas of racial intolerance, of inherent inability, a society in which a majority of people are willing to accept (or at least easily ignore) gross inequalities based partly on the racist views of others (and their own). This racism is most obviously manifest in attitudes to people who try to flee here (as it was before for the Huguenots, Catholics and Jews). It is least overt in official talk about the inherent abilities of some groups over others. But once you accept racism of any kind, other kinds seep into the consciousness and they all then become more acceptable.

From the senior (Black) police officer being paid in excess of £100,000 a year to the boy from Mali found dead with a letter in his pocket, to the class of poor mainly white school children written off because they supposedly come from the 'wrong stock', racism is a crime that causes both gross harm and which partly constructs ethnicity. The Huguenots, Jews and Catholics partly have their places in British ethnic history recorded because of the crimes committed against them that formed them as groups and had huge impact on their lives. Without such crime, without such discrimination, ethnicity and race fade and disappear.

**Main reference**

Roberts, R. and W. McMahon (2008) *Debating race, ethnicity, harm and crime*, London: Centre for Crime and Justice Studies (www.crimeandjustice.org. uk/opus1603/EHC_Apr_web_version.pdf).

# 14

# UK medical school admissions by ethnicity, socioeconomic status, and sex[1]

*BMJ* (2004) 328, pp 1545–46

Ethnic minorities and women are no longer underrepresented in UK medical schools, but lower socioeconomic groups still are.[2] Given the strong political pressure on higher education institutions to develop "widening participation" programmes[3,4], a valid quantitative index of the impact of such programmes is needed urgently. Such an index should be derived from robust and accessible primary data, reflect the impact of multiple independent variables in different population subgroups, allow comparisons across institutions and over time, and be readily understandable by non-statisticians. Statistics on the entry profile of UK medical schools are usually expressed as the selection ratio (the proportion of admissions to applications).[5] We propose that the standardised admission ratio (see box), which expresses the number of pupils admitted to medical school as a proportion of the

---

[1] Authors: Kieran Seyan, Trisha Greenhalgh and Danny Dorling. Note that the social class being referred to is that of the medical school students' families, not of the social class to which such students may be joining. Original title began "The standardised admission ratio for measuring widening participation in medical schools: analysis of ..."

[2] Secretary of State for Education (2004) *Medical schools: Delivering the doctors of the future*, London: Department for Education and Skills.

[3] Universities UK (2003) *Fair enough: Wider access to university by identifying potential to succeed*, London: Universities UK.

[4] Higher Education Funding Council (2003) *Social class and participation: Good practice in widening access to education* (follow-up to 'From elitism to inclusion'), London: Higher Education Funding Council.

[5] McManus IC. (2002) 'Medical school applications – a critical situation', *BMJ*, no 325, pp 786–7.

number who would do so if places were allocated equitably across all socioeconomic and ethnic groups and equally by sex, should become the standard measure of widening participation. It would not, of course, be an index of discrimination at selection stage.

| Definition of the standardised admission ratio for applicants to medical school |
| --- |
| Number of admissions from a particular population subgroup as a proportion of all admissions |
| Proportion of the general population that belongs to that subgroup |

See extra table at end of this chapter for the detailed results of applying this formula to 82 population subgroups in the UK.

## Methods and results

Figure 1: Standardised admission ratios by social class and ethnicity for UK medical school admissions 1996–2000 (log scale)

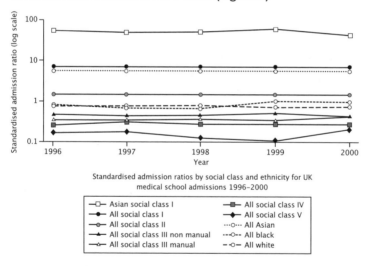

Standardised admission ratios by social class and ethnicity for UK medical school admissions 1996–2000

—□— Asian social class I    —■— All social class IV
—●— All social class I    —◆— All social class V
—○— All social class II    ···○··· All Asian
—▲— All social class III non manual    ---○-- All black
—△— All social class III manual    -○- All white

We calculated standardised admission ratios using data from the Universities' Central Admissions Service database (www.ucas.ac.uk/figures) on UK medical school admissions from 1996 to 2000 (the last year for which full figures are so far available, and the last year in which socioeconomic status was measured in traditional social class bands) as a numerator and the labour force survey (www.statistics.gov.uk) as a denominator (see Figure 1 above). Using the values for 2000, we found that standardised admission ratios varied around 10-fold by ethnicity – from 6.07 in Asians (over-represented) to

0.73 in white people (under-represented) – and around 30-fold by social class – from 6.76 in social class I to 0.20 in class V (see table appended to the end of this chapter). But when we calculated the ratios by ethnicity and social class they varied 600-fold from the most over-represented group with a significant denominator (Asians from social class I, 41.73) to the most under-represented group with fewest admissions (black people from social class IV, 0.07; note that no black people from social class V were admitted to medical school from 1996 to 2000).

White and black pupils from social class I were around 100 times more likely to gain a place at medical school than those from classes IV or V. Asian pupils seemed to compensate better for poor origins, but those from social class I were still 6–10 times more likely to gain a place than those from classes IV or V. The standardised admission ratio for women increased from 1.08 in 1996 to 1.15 in 2000, and that for men fell correspondingly. Sex specific standardised admission ratios did not vary significantly by socioeconomic status, but they did vary by ethnicity, with Asians having similar ratios for men and women but black and white men being significantly under-represented compared with women.

## Comment

We found massive inequalities in medical school admissions by social class. Although the confidence intervals around individual values are likely to be high, especially in subgroups with small denominators, the overall picture is valid. It should not be assumed that the ideal situation is for the standardised admission ratio for all population subgroups to be 1.0, since this would imply that all contain equal proportions of pupils who are suitable for a medical career – an implausible hypothesis.[6] The standardised admission ratio is a composite index – being derived from both the proportion of people who apply to medical school in any subgroup and the proportion of applicants who get accepted – and hence should be interpreted with caution.

With these caveats, we believe the standardised admission ratio will be a useful "bottom line" index for quantifying the inequalities in medical school entry (and entry to any higher education course) between subgroups as widening participation initiatives are implemented and evaluated. In a companion paper, the reasons for the wide differences in admission by social class are explored.[7]

---

[6] Editorial note: This does not necessarily mean that more from higher social classes might be better 'suited' academically. It is very possible that more from lower classes might be better suited practically to working in the medical profession given the average differences in life experience and experience of ill health by social class.

[7] Greenhalgh, T., Seyan, K. and Boynton, P. (2004) '"Not a university type": focus group study of social class, ethnic, and sex differences in school pupils' perceptions about medical school', *BMJ*, no 328, pp 1541–4.

## Acknowledgements

We thank Janet Grant for advice on medical admissions datasets, George Davey Smith for advice on the measurement of social class, and three referees for helpful comments on earlier drafts of this paper.

**Funding**: None. This project was part of a BSc dissertation by Kieran Seyan.

## Extra table

The standardised admission ratio for measuring widening participation in medical schools: analysis of UK medical school admissions by ethnicity, socioeconomic status, and sex.

### Standardised admission ratios for UK medical schools 2000

| Ethnic group | % of UK population | % of all medical school admissions | Selection ratio* | % of admissions from social classes I and II | Standardised admission ratio by social class† | | | | | | |
|---|---|---|---|---|---|---|---|---|---|---|---|
| | | | | | Overall | — | = | III non-manual | III manual | ≥ | > |
| Asian: | 4.2 | 25.5 | 0.55 | 60.5 | 6.07 | 41.73 | 5.41 | 3.83 | 3.29 | 3.56 | 5.15 |
| Bangladeshi | 0.5 | 0.9 | 0.40 | 48.0 | 1.80 | 9.82 | 1.27 | 1.89 | NC | 1.93 | 6.00 |
| Indian | 1.7 | 13.8 | 0.63 | 74.0 | 8.12 | 72.32 | 7.96 | 3.17 | 4.68 | 2.78 | 0.18 |
| Pakistani | 1.3 | 4.5 | 0.62 | 39.0 | 3.46 | NC | 5.29 | 3.71 | 2.71 | 2.25 | 3.08 |
| Chinese | 0.3 | 2 | 0.45 | 68.0 | 6.67 | 54.55 | 6.01 | NC | 9.02 | 2.86 | NC |
| Other | 0.4 | 4.3 | 0.51 | 73.6 | 10.75 | 127.05 | 3.63 | 6.96 | NC | 4.76 | NC |
| Black: | 2.0 | 1.9 | 0.36 | 82.8 | 0.95 | 6.20 | 1.75 | 0.16 | 0.64 | 0.07 | NC |
| African | 0.9 | 1.4 | 0.34 | 70.0 | 1.56 | 12.25 | 1.63 | 0.24 | 1.83 | 0.37 | NC |
| Caribbean | 1.0 | 0.3 | 0.44 | 78.3 | 0.30 | 0.78 | 0.75 | 0.10 | 0.25 | NC | NC |
| Other | 0.1 | 0.2 | 0.39 | 100 | 2.00 | 18.18 | 3.92 | NC | NC | NC | NC |
| White | 92.2 | 67.6 | 0.70 | 79.5 | 0.73 | 4.93 | 1.22 | 0.27 | 0.32 | 0.13 | 0.05 |
| Other | 0.6 | 3 | 0.52 | 72.6 | 5.00 | 53.64 | 2.67 | 2.38 | 4.71 | 1.21 | NC |
| Not known | 0.2 | 2 | 0.40 | NA | 10.00 | 9.82 | 1.27 | 1.89 | NC | 1.93 | 6.00 |
| Total | 100 | 100 | 0.63 | 72.5 | 1.00 | 6.76 | 1.38 | 0.41 | 0.42 | 0.28 | 0.20 |

*Selection ratio=admissions as a proportion of applications.
†Some ratios are high as the ratios are based on very small denominators.
NA=Data not available. NC=Not calculable because there were no pupils in this subgroup.

# 15

# Race and the repercussions of recession[1]

*Runnymede Trust Bulletin 360* (2009) December, pp 1–3

The greater the crash the longer it takes to take stock of the implications. The 1929 financial crisis was so great that in the immediate aftermath bankers and politicians assumed that the only thing that was possible was a quick recovery, because they had not known different times; many false dawns were predicted before it was finally realised, by around 1933, that much had changed forever.

The repercussions varied around the world. In the United States charismatic leaders ensured the slow ushering in of new equalities, as the assets of the affluent crumbled, and the lives of the children of slaves and of slave owners moved slightly closer together. In Berlin the repercussions were used by equally charismatic leaders to build up racial division. Great financial crashes are rarely wasted, but they can be used in many different ways. Charismatic leaders do not emerge out of the ether. What is possible

---

[1] Editorial note: This chapter was written as an editorial looking at the inequalities emanating from the recession, comparing the fortunes of black and minority ethnic groups with those of the white population, analysing the statistics on employment, education and housing and making the claim that: Race is as much made by contemporary inequality as by circumstances of history.

in the art of politics in times of change is determined by a million tiny actions. Here are a few examples.

## Employment

The job losses that came with the onset of the current crash hit black and ethnic minorities harder than the national average worker. Although almost everywhere a majority of the population is white, and even though we often lack recent data subdivided by ethnicity, geographical place names can be used as a shorthand for what has so far occurred.

By August 2009 – the month in which the official claimant rate returned to levels last seen when Tony Blair became Prime Minister in May 1997 – official unemployment rates were highest in the Ladywood, Sparkbrook and Small Heath areas of Birmingham, in the West of Belfast (a white minority area often ignored), in Liverpool Riverside (aka Toxteth), in the constituencies named 'central' in Leeds and Manchester, and in the Bethnal Green, Bow, Hackney and Shoreditch neighbourhoods of London. Rates of official unemployment in the places in this list varied between 12% and 20%.[2] Real rates will have been much higher.

By contrast, rates were lowest in West and North Dorset, Henley, Witney, Woodspring, Buckingham, Skipton[3] and Ripon, and in places such as the constituency of Runnymede and Weybridge. Unemployment rates in these places varied between 2.0 and 2.5 per cent. Thus the banking bailout successfully secured the jobs of those living in these leafy Home Counties, in north Somerset near the Bristol banking back-offices, and in North Yorkshire retreats (close to those Leeds banks).

The job losses are set to rise far higher. They will rise highest in the poorest areas and amongst the poorest groups. Within those groups it will be those who have been least well served by the education system who will suffer most, and then those who employers decide not to favour because, in hard times, employers might be tempted more to 'look after their own'. Racism was required to ensure that a majority of young Black Caribbean, 'other' Asian, and Black African men were either unemployed or on a government scheme even as long as a decade after the 1981 recession hit, as were a majority of Bangladeshi and Black African women in 1991.[4]

---

[2] All figures from www.parliament.uk/commons/lib/research/rp2009/rp09-072.pdf Unemployment by Constituency, August 2009, Research Paper 09/72 16 September 2009.
[3] If you doubt that Skipton is part of the London banking world, ask yourself why a direct train runs from that small town to King's Cross, timed to arrive for ten to ten in the capital each morning?
[4] Here 'young' means aged 16 to 24 as a proportion of those in the workforce. Figures from the 1991 census were given on page 92 of Dorling, D. (1995) *A new social atlas of Britain*, Chichester, John Wiley & sons. Open access copy at: http://sasi.group.shef.ac.uk/publications/new_social_atlas/index.html

## Education

High priest among those in power in Britain who see salvation in market mechanism is Peter Mandelson.[5] Throughout early 2009 Baron Mandelson came under sustained pressure to alleviate the worst effects of the recession, including increasing university places in line with official aspirations and the huge increase in demand that came with recession (applications up 11 per cent). Much of the flack was deflected to the more junior Higher Education Minister, David Lammy.[6] Lammy had to field the complaints, but it was Mandelson who got to decide what to do. In the end, Mandelson offered an extra 1 per cent of places, not fully-funded, to allow universities to take a tenth of those extra applicants. Given the profile of who gets to go to university, and the ethnic make-up of the majority of additional applicants, youngsters from non-traditional backgrounds, it is not hard to work out who loses out most directly from Mandelson's penny-pinching. It is a little harder to see the knock-on effects of not taking more young people into universities in a time of recession.[7]

The 10,000 extra students who were allowed to attend university in 2009 have been given a chance not just to study, but to duck out of one of the worst youth labour markets seen since at least the 1930s. However, the alternative is unlikely to have been the dole; these are mainly highly qualified young people. The places were reserved for students to study science, technology, engineering and maths. Had they not become students, almost all of them would have found work. That is what happens to most highly qualified young people, even in recession.[8]

The curtailing of university funding will not greatly hurt the old and ancient universities – the ones where freshers' fairs tend to mean a sea of white faces, with the odd exception from minority groups that reoccurs every year with remarkable predictability (as to which groups are the exceptions). The slashing of funding will greatly affect places such as London Metropolitan University, one of the most ethnically diverse higher education

[5] [At the time of writing] First Secretary of State, Secretary of State for Business, Innovation and Skills, President of the Board of Trade and Lord President of the Council, former member of Parliament for Hartlepool (within his constituency there were 3,872 claimants of unemployment benefits as of August 2009, up 1204 in the year).

[6] Member for Tottenham (5,685 claimants of unemployment benefit as of August 2009, up 1544 in the year).

[7] Editorial note: It is worth remembering that the very first, albeit very small, cuts to university places were announced by New Labour in 2009 to take place in 2010. Few people will remember those in the light of the huge cuts to state funding of higher education announced by the Coalition during 2010.

[8] Editorial note: However, by early 2011 we learnt that as many as a fifth of the graduates of 2010 were signing on to receive unemployment benefits. The latest recession was unusually detrimental to the young.

institutions in the country, where about 550 staff are facing the threat of redundancy because of errors not of their making.

There is a particular irony in that the most pressing problem that will cross Mr Lammy's desk in his last few months as the first black Minister for Higher Education will be trying to decide what to do about London Met when his boss tells him there is no cash. He should ask a question, as they did in the United States 75 years ago: is there really no cash? Next year, with the backlog created by this year, with fewer opportunities abroad, there may well be as many as 100,000 extra young people who would rather be studying, than competing in the job market. These are made up not just of the 40,000 who did not manage to get in this year, and a similar 40,000 we can expect next year, but also some slightly older young people who have found that going straight into work from age 17 or 18 was not so great for them, and returning gap year people who will not be replaced by so many going on gap years in future.[9]

## Housing

In the same week that the paltry 10,000 extra university places were taken up, Vince Cable suggested a tax on those properties worth more than £1 million pounds.[10] He did this to explain how it was possible to ensure that no one earning less than £10,000 need pay tax, but still take as much in taxes. This was the first time a mainstream politician in Britain in the current crisis had made the suggestion to replicate part of how the British coped with the last great financial crash. In the 1920s and especially the 1930s various costs, including death duties, led to many of the great families 'donating' their homes to the National Trust and finding something a little cosier to live in, a place without a household of forty servants, say. Most of the land in Britain is still owned by the descendants of those immigrants who took it by force after 1066. If you are short of about £175 billion (and counting), there are things you can do other than slash public spending with savage cuts.

---

[9] Editorial note: Many are now considering emigrating during 2011, although like most emigrants the majority are not planning to be abroad for long. A huge amount has changed for the worse for university students and recent graduates since the end of 2009 when this article was published, especially for those who are neither white nor 'privileged' by wealth.
[10] Vince Cable also said that Britain's £158 billion public sector pay bill should be frozen by reducing the highest incomes in the public sector. This too was partly done before in the 1930s. In contrast, on the same day the 'bosses union', the Confederation of British Industry, said tuition fees should be raised, students should pay higher interest rates on their loans, and maintenance grants should be scaled back. They have not yet suggested putting small children back up chimneys but they too are acting much like their predecessors after that last financial crash, being the last to see the light showing that the way out is not endless cuts.

A land-tax, of the kind such as that tiny half a percent over a million flat-rate tax Mr Cable suggests, is hard to avoid. If you can't pay the tax, you sell a little of your land to pay it. Farms don't go out of production, if anything the land is used more efficiently. Divided by the 24 million hectares of land in Britain, £175bn is only £7265 per hectare, or 73p a square metre. I (nearly) own a house and would happily pay my share. I've got a garden too, but 73p a year for having each square metre of that is cheap.

Obviously it wouldn't be that fair to charge the same amount for every square metre. The Duke of Westminster's land holding could be worth a tad more per square metre than the crofters of Sutherland, more even than my garden in Sheffield, but the money's there. Live in a tower block on the other hand, and (to get back to race, although we never really left it) remember that half the children who live above the fifth floor in England are not white, and their parents' tax would be paltry. In fact the combined land value tax of all the families of all those children who live in tower blocks could be less than that Duke might have to pay. Property owners like Madonna would complain. Others might quite like the idea of buying up the Duke's property so he could pay his fair share of the new national debt, given how much of the nation he owns.

## Conclusion

What would happen to race relations in Britain if there was such a redistribution as happened before in America and here in the 1930s, and as happened in Germany and Japan following the Second World War? What happens when people are less divided by differences in the wealth they inherit and how their life-chances are so much determined by the wider resources of wealth held by their families, by the places they grow up in, through the schools they can go to? What happens in countries where inequalities in wealth are so much lower than those which have re-emerged in places such as Britain and America over the course of the last few decades? Race is as much made by contemporary inequality as by circumstances of history. Great financial crashes are rarely wasted, but when it comes to race, they have been used either to greatly reduce division or to greatly increase it. This last occurred in different places but all at the same times. There is no reason to believe it will be different this time.

# SECTION IV
# Education and hierarchy

The eight chapters that have been squeezed into this section cover a range of issues in various ways. All were originally written for very different audiences. This section begins with a piece written for secondary school children ostensibly on the price of fish but highlighting world inequalities and hierarchies. That is followed by two papers concerning who is permitted to access tertiary education, one previously unpublished, the other published in *The Guardian*. Then come two chapters on social mobility (first in Britain and then comparing Britain to Germany) and two (for the *Fabian Review* and *The Observer*) on class and pay divides. However, if you wished to select just one chapter from this section, the last one, 'Raising equality in access to higher education', summarises much from the other chapters. It is also interesting in that it appears only in print here. As explained in the initial footnote to that chapter, it was rejected at the very last moment for publication in the journal from which I had received a request to write it during 2010. I had been asked for a summary based on a conference presentation, of which the paper is a faithful, if somewhat sanitised, account.[1]

This chapter is included here not simply because I think it provides a good summary of the issues of the section, but also because I think its rejection for publication at the final hurdle helps a little more in explaining elitism. If

---

[1] The original presentation, including slides and even a video recording of what I said, was entitled 'Spatial inequalities in access to university, jobs and 'good' schools' and can be found towards the bottom of this web page: http://sasi.group.shef.ac.uk/presentations/

you want to know why some academics are so elitist, you need to know that they do not get to read arguments such as that in Chapter 23 of this book in the journals that they read, often because those arguments are rejected before publication. You can decide for yourself about the quality of the final chapter in this section, but you are only able to do that because I am able to print it here. Of course, many papers are rejected for good reason. However, more orthodox economics journals tend to abound in papers containing bad propositions.

I think the final chapter of this section provides a typical example of censorship within parts of British academia today, but also of the time-wasting of others' efforts. The chapter was invited for publication, with a particular remit: to write up a conference presentation. It was then substantially revised to better fit the editorial slant of the journal, despite fitting the original remit. And it was then rejected regardless of this because someone further up the hierarchy than the editor who commissioned it made that decision. True elitists do not greatly value the lives or time of others who think differently.

# 16

# What's it to do with the price of fish?[1]

*GCSE Geography Review* (2009) vol 19, no 3, pp 6–8

"What's it to do with the price of fish?" is another way of saying "why is it relevant?" Price – how much money something is sold for – in this saying is used as another word for "important". This might seem strange; why would the price of fish be used in place (as a metaphor) for whether something matters? Especially given that prices vary so much over time, and between places. Prices vary because they are based on a combination of costs of making, growing or catching (production), availability, need, and how much people are willing to pay (demand). Each of these things varies.

Now consider the price of fish or of food more generally. Food is a basic human need. However, most of us in Britain do not produce our own food. We live in a money-based economy where people are paid in tokens (coins and notes, or electronically into their bank account), which can then be exchanged for other goods or services of their choice. If the price of food increases then we can buy less of it. If the price increases too much it is possible that we could starve because we couldn't access enough food. This is happening now in some parts of the world. This is why the prices of fish, and other food stuffs, matter very much.

Prices are important parts of the trade relationships that exist around the world. Much of our food comes from thousands of kilometres away. Our daily intake can easily include apples from New Zealand, rice from the

---

[1] Editorial note: Written with Anna Barford who was the principal author of the paper this chapter is based on.

United States, chocolate from the Côte d'Ivoire and coffee from Ethiopia. Between producers and consumers there stand various people: traders who buy and sell goods, people processing and packing goods, people actually moving goods, advertisers marketing goods and shop owners selling goods. Also involved are governments and international bodies who usually try to protect the financial interests of one group at the expense of another. Thus one person's "goods" can be another person's "bads".

It need not be that way but it usually is.

It really is the case that one person need not suffer because another gets what they want. There really is enough for everyone, and often too much for the rich which is one reason why we are getting fatter in Britain!

The question of how to share out properly is one of distribution. As it can be hard to understand how things are shared out around the world, here are some maps that simplify our complex and dynamic world. Map 1 shows that the highest value of fish imports are to the richest parts of the world (particularly Japan, Western Europe, North America). Map 2 shows where most undernourished people lived in 2002; they lived in very different parts of the world from where major fish imports were received (many undernourished people live in China, South Asia, and Sub-Saharan Africa). Of course fish prices are not driving this, but ability to buy fish has much the same pattern as where people with most money in the world live (see Map 3).

**Map 1:** Fish imports. Territory size shows the proportion of worldwide imports of fish (in US$) that are received there

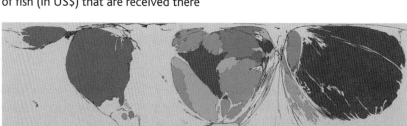

Note: The area of each country is proportional in size to the subject being mapped on this map and the four that follow.

**Map 2:** Undernourishment in 2000. Territory size shows the proportion of all undernourished people worldwide, who live there

**Map 3:** Gross Domestic Product in 2002. Territory size shows the proportion of worldwide wealth, that is Gross Domestic Product based on contemporary exchange rates with the US$, that is found there

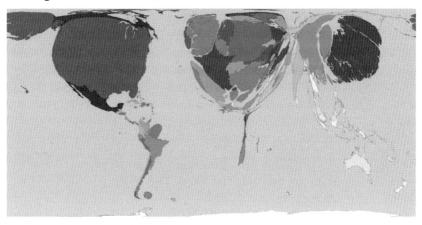

The CAFOD (Catholic Agency for Overseas Development) website suggests that "just because we can't change the world all in one go, we can still give a man a fishing net. Then he can earn a living, feed his family, and send his children to school." From looking at the maps above, what do you think of this approach? We think it has the benefit of providing the tools to start a small business. However, if the prices that can be charged for fish are driven down it could be that the woman or man with the fishing net cannot earn enough to feed their family and send their children to school. The price of fish determines not just who can buy it, but also how much money is made from fish sales. The fisherman/woman could be caught in a position of selling their catch for less money than they need to feed themselves. And finally, what is the point of a net if there are almost no fish to be caught? The pollution and drying out of lakes and over fishing in the sea have dramatically reduced fish stocks worldwide (see Map 4). It is not fish that we get fat on in Britain. Although there is currently enough for everyone, if we carry on like this other things as well as fish will begin to run out. Shoals of fish, though, can grow in number again, but only if we learn how to share better.

**Map 4:** Fish At Risk. Territory size shows the proportion of fish species assessed as locally at risk of extinction, found there

Currently far more global efforts go into global aid than in trying to work out how better to share our finite resources. There is a clear role for foreign aid from both non-governmental organisations and governments, particularly when it is addressing a humanitarian crisis. The quick provision of food, shelter and medicines can save many lives. However, many aid projects do not address the underlying causes of such crises, that may make a future crisis even worse. Most people killed by disasters are in poorer parts of the world (Map 5) partly because there are generally fewer hazard warning systems, communications systems, durable buildings, medical facilities, and other resources which would help deal with any disaster.

The reason for some places lacking basic infrastructure is partly poverty, which is linked to international trade relationships, including the price of fish. When your mum or dad next asks you "what's that got to do with the price of fish?", why not reply "a lot!"?

**Map 5:** Killed by Disasters. Territory size shows the proportion of all deaths caused by disasters, which overwhelm local resources, for people who died there 1975–2004. It includes outbreaks of infectious diseases not normally found there

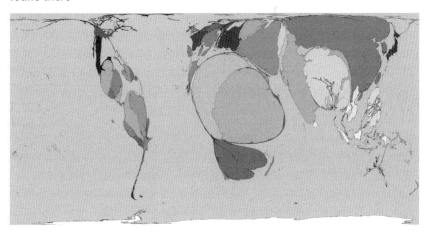

## The worldmapper project

We have produced 366 world maps,[2] that distort countries based on many topics, for example the proportion of children living there, fruit exports from there, or people with malaria living there.

Data is used to shrink and expand territories: the more of something that is found there, the bigger the country.

The data used are mainly from United Nations agencies, including the World Health Organisation, United Nations Development Programme and the United Nations Environment Programme. The maths behind these maps was developed by the physicist Mark Newman, following work by the geographer Waldo Tobler. This website is run by researchers at the Universities of Sheffield (UK) and Michigan (USA). The maps, posters, frequently asked questions, data, and other articles are all available at: www. worldmapper.org

---

[2] Editorial note: There are now over 1,000 maps on the Worldmapper website including new maps of every country in the world drawn by Ben Hennig showing where most people in each country live.

# 17

# Little progress towards a fairer education system[1]

Unpublished commentary on universities (2005)

HEFCE's 'Young participation in higher education' report was published this week and, as Sir Howard Newby makes clear in his forward, it is the first to have results accurate enough to chart the changing participation chances of those from different backgrounds. The results might come as something of a shock for those who have assumed that university intakes have been widening socially in the recent years.

Instead the worst inequalities are found to be deep and persistent. On the way to reaching this conclusion interesting results crop up that are quite unexpected. Remember the surge in participation in 1997 to avoid the introduction of tuition fees? (it never was). Think that the participation of the poor fell when maintenance grants were abolished? (it didn't). Or that the rich have responded to 'mass higher education' by securing postgraduate study for the new elite? (not yet). The first use of accurate participation rates makes this report essential reading for anyone interested in the debate on university funding and student fees as, to put it simply, your preconceptions of the facts are likely to be wrong.

In fact the results are so accurate that it is now possible to chart the changing chances of young people going to university given just the month

---

[1] Commentary written jointly with Mark Corver and intended for publication in the *Times Higher Education Supplement* but not cleared by HEFCE (Mark's employers) in time for publication, so put up on the web instead, and now printed here for the first time. It should be read in the context of Chapter 18 which immediately follows it and shows how much changed between 2005, when we wrote this, and 2010.

of their birth. For example, a boy born in September is now 15 per cent more likely to go to university than one born in August. That is the magnitude of the effect of being one of the youngest in your school year in England.

Sex inequality has grown to a similar level: in just six years young women have risen from a 6 per cent advantage in 1994 to being 18 per cent more likely than men to participate in higher education (HE) by the year 2000. The bad news for young men doesn't stop there: tracking them through their time in HE shows that they are two-thirds more likely to drop-out than their female friends. This, together with a simple extrapolation of participation trends, suggests that we might well see 50 per cent more young graduate women than young graduate men from the children who started secondary school last September.

However, for those of you now worried about your summer-born boys, or who are reassured over the chances of your autumn-born girls – all this is irrelevant in the light of what this report really shows matters for children's chances. What matters is where our children grow up, as the chances of going to university between areas doesn't vary by percentage points, but by 5 or 10 fold between substantial groups of young people divided by where they live.

There are widening differences between the regions. Young people in London are now nearly 60 per cent more likely to go to university when compared to those living in the North East – at a stroke inequalities greater than the combined effects of sex and birth month. But to concentrate on these differences is an over-simplification and hides the real geographical divides that exist throughout the country.

For example, looking at parliamentary constituencies shows that in some areas going to university is a matter of course for young people, with more than two thirds doing so. And these areas are not always where you might think. The four highest participating constituencies in Britain have two representatives in the north – Hallam in Sheffield and Eastwood in Scotland – with the other two, more predictably, being Kensington and Chelsea, and Westminster. Any child growing up in these four parliamentary constituencies is at least six times more likely to get to university than are the children represented by the members of parliament for Sheffield Brightside, Nottingham North, Leeds Central or Bristol South. In these areas going to university makes you the odd one out, only one in ten, or less, currently go.

## Neighbourhood inequalities in access to higher education

Zoom into the maps of participation further and the inequality progressively deepens. The 30,000 or so young people living in the most advantaged wards are more than ten times as likely to go to university than the matching 30,000 in the least advantaged wards. Feel it is unfair that the older girls in your summer-born son's class are now over 30 per cent more likely to go to university than he is? Spare a thought then for what the children living in some areas, through a (similar but now geographical) accident of birth, might make of their more advantaged peers being *around 1000% more likely* to have the opportunity to enjoy the benefits of higher education.

Over the cohorts considered by this report (those reaching 18 between 1994 and 2000) these huge geographical inequalities have hardly altered. A number of groupings are used to track these inequalities and they all give the same message: little has changed. There is, of course, interesting detail. Generally, the most disadvantaged areas have shown the highest growth rates when measured proportionally, which has reduced the relative participation inequality slightly. But this growth is from such a low base that, in absolute percentage point terms, it is very much smaller than that of most advantaged groups. This means that the majority of 'extra' young HE places have gone to children from already advantaged areas and so the participation gap between the groups has increased.[2]

A surprise to some will be that the participation for the poorest areas has steadily increased over the period: no obvious 'deterrent' effect from tuition fees or the abolition of grants can be seen. Young people, in contrast to what many commentators on higher education assumed they would do, have apparently acted as if they have ignored the fee and grant changes. This finding occurs several times in the report.[3] The small perturbations seen in overall participation rates seem to be explained by year-on-year population changes and GCSE improvements. Even when some young people had a choice to avoid fees, by bringing forward their plans or changing where they study, they seem not to have taken it.

What has made these area inequalities in young participation so deep and persistent? Finding the true causes for 'why' is notoriously difficult, and the report steers clear of claiming this, but some clues are to be found in its description of what high and low participation areas are like. This shows that these areas differ not just in participation rates but in almost every respect,

---

[2] Chapter 18 which follows this chapter details how that gap then decreased very substantially between 2005 and 2010. The majority of 'extra' education towards the end of those years going to those from much less advantaged backgrounds.
[3] Editorial note: It is even possible that the rise in standard fees to £9,000 a year in some cases from 2012 onwards would see no great fall in participation in elite (and some less elite) institutions as young people, both desperate for a future and optimistic that they will do well despite saddling themselves with huge future debts, continue to apply. Repayment rates are around 3% plus whatever the annual rate of inflation might be in future years for all but the least well-off of future graduates. Coupled with the loans most students will take out to cover their rent and to allow them to eat and buy the odd book, estimates are being made of average debts of £70,000 in today's money. If fees rise in the future at the rate they have been rising in recent years, then this is an underestimate.

to the extent that different parts of Britain are now so educationally distinct that they could be different countries.

Through both statistics and visiting these areas it is clear that low participation areas are disadvantaged in many ways. Indeed these areas face so many disadvantages that it is hard not to feel that access to higher education is unlikely to be the most pressing concern of people living there. One relationship that is particularly striking for small areas is the association between the level of young participation and the proportion of adults holding a higher education qualification. The near five-fold difference in the proportion of graduate adults between the highest and lowest participating 20 per cent of areas very closely mirrors the difference in young participation.

Clearly, geographical inequalities in access to higher education reflect wider geographical inequalities in society, in schools, in young people's home environments in the aspirations and expectations of themselves and their parents. These represent embedded disadvantage that will take a generation of measures like Sure Start, and much more besides, to reduce substantially. Interventions at the HE application stage, such as taking into consideration the circumstances under which A-levels were gained, are welcome and might help to even-up the institutional distribution of those entering HE slightly. But they are not going to have any material impact on the deep participation inequalities between neighbourhoods shown so clearly in the report.

Inequality is most evident in the detailed maps of participation, released as a supplement to the report on HEFCE's website. These show that there is a line which snakes its way around the country separating groups of young people into those with good chances and those with poor chances of participation (and much more besides). This line runs through the core of our cities with many cities split internally by social cliffs separating young people living within a few hundred yards of each other but in educationally opposed worlds. If you have ever wondered where the wrong and right side of the tracks lay in Britain, HEFCE have now mapped them in detail (www.hefce.ac.uk/polar, see Figure 1 for the national map).

In looking at the experiences of entrants from different backgrounds the report delivers a final statistical surprise. It finds that if you make it into higher education and stay the course to get a degree, then whether you are from advantaged or disadvantaged backgrounds you have pretty much the same chance of going on to postgraduate study. Indeed, young qualifiers who originally came from low participation areas are, thanks mainly to postgraduate teaching qualifications, slightly more likely to carry on to postgraduate study. Of course, this encouraging finding needs to be tempered by the fact that so few young people from disadvantaged areas get a degree that, in terms of numbers, those from advantaged areas utterly dominate the postgraduate population as they do the undergraduate population.

**Figure 1:** Young participation by Learning and Skill Council areas: England only*

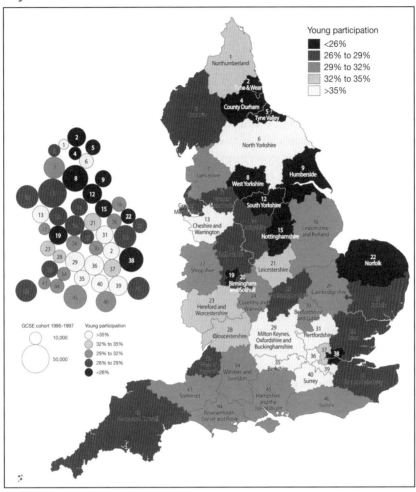

* The rates shown are of young people gaining access to university. This map and inset cartogram was not included in the original article but it does highlight what is seen on the polar website, which also included many far more detailed maps and their more useful population cartogram counterparts. See: www.hefce.ac.uk/widen/polar/nat/map/lsc_GB.pdf

## Social inequalities in access to study for all and postgraduate study

The postgraduate finding is particularly interesting since all the preceding educational stages have a common theme of low achievement by those from disadvantaged backgrounds leading to a high level of attrition on the progression to the next educational level. In contrast, at this rarefied transition we have an unexpected jewel of apparently equal progression. We do not know what it is about the mix of support we currently provide for young postgraduate students that has allowed this relative equality – largely unmeasured and untended – to flourish. Finding out might help us preserve it, saving the next generation from having access to postgraduate study as its widening participation battleground.

The history of debates on educational participation in Britain – on the introduction of elementary education, on secondary education, on comprehensive schooling – shows a common path. In response to the first concerns raised, an argument is put forward that not all young people need to have access to the same educational opportunities as others. Then this argument is always eventually lost, and participation widens in the long term. The argument then moves on from participation to inequality in provision, such as the disparity in school GCSE results.

If young participation in higher education were to follow this pattern, then it is clear that we have barely started on this path: it is difficult to find social statistics more polarised than our measures of young participation.

The government's aspiration of 50 per cent participation refers to a wider age group than the 18 and 19 year olds covered by this report, but reaching it would translate to at the very most an extra 7 percentage points or so on our measures. Suppose each group of young people enjoyed this same percentage point rise in participation: this is optimistic since the report finds that young people living in the most advantaged areas get more than their fair share of extra participation. Currently the most advantaged 20 per cent of young people have around 4.7 times the participation of the least disadvantaged, even this near-impossibly of optimistically equally distributed growth would, on average, reduce this advantage to 3.3 times.[4]

Is that enough? If not then we have some difficult choices. We could propose changing our HE admission system to deny places to well qualified applicants from advantaged backgrounds to reduce inequalities. This would be unpalatable, especially to the influential people who live in high participation areas and, besides, it is not the fault of these children that they were born into advantaged families and so penalising them for that may well appear unfair. This leaves the alternative of providing enough extra young HE places to accommodate both the expectations of the advantaged and our hopes for the disadvantaged.

Over half the young people living in the most advantaged 20 per cent of areas go to university and, by and large, they seem to benefit from the experience and go on to graduate jobs afterwards. So, unless you believe that children born in some areas are somehow inherently less able to benefit from higher education than others, then there seems to be no reason why

---

[4] Editorial note: This "near impossibility" is in fact what then occurred for 5 years. See footnote 5.

all children should not enjoy this level of opportunity, regardless of where they live.

To raise all English young people to the current participation level of autumn-born young women in the most advantaged areas would need a doubling of the number of young people going to university.

You can blame the parents, the schools, the social environment for the divides we see in young participation; but unless there are significant increases in higher education places in future these divides simply cannot materially diminish. To raise the participation rate of all English young people to that of the current participation level of autumn-born young women in the most advantaged 20 per cent of areas would need a doubling of the number of young people going to university. There will come a time when very many extra university places will be needed in the course of a fairer education system in this country, but as yet we are far from that point.[5]

---

[5] Editorial note: As the next chapter shows, from 2005 to 2010 we moved with remarkable rapidity towards the point of actually seeing real improvements following the results of the report which this chapter summarised, but sadly then, under the new 2010 Coalition government, in the face of huge rises in the numbers wanting to go to university, we saw a most severe curtailing of funding for university education which will take us back to before even the small progress reported here was realised. These current regressive policies are set to be coupled with a great deal of vacuous and largely fake concern being raised to (it will be repeatedly said) widen participation in a supposedly new way, by allowing through a very tiny number of children from very poor backgrounds to go to the most elite institutions and parading them, and this, as some kind of accomplishment. See the footnote 4 of Chapter 23 below on how this approach failed in the 1930s (p 175 of this volume).

# 18

# One of Labour's great successes[1]

*The Guardian* newspaper (2010) 28 January

Today's Higher Education Funding Council report on who is getting into universities shows that after years of effort children from poorer areas are going in growing numbers to university. Many more university places have been provided in the last few years.

For the first time ever recorded, the majority of those additional places have been taken up by children living in the poorer half of British neighbourhoods. This will probably be seen in future years as the greatest positive social achievement of the 1997–2010 governments.

The success was achieved not at the expense of upper- and middle class children, who have also seen their chances improve. It occurred because of the way the education system as a whole has expanded and, most importantly, as a result of massive increases in funding per child in state secondary schools in recent years.

Save the Children this week report that more children are living in the worst of poverty in Britain today as compared to 2005. The life expectancy

---

[1] Editorial note: This is the *Guardian* on-line version of an article on how much changed in widening participation between the situation described in the Chapter above in 2005, and 2010. A shorter version of this text appeared in the *Guardian* newspaper (28th January, p 10). Note how both this chapter and the previous chapter begin by referring to the work of the Higher Education Funding Council which allows us to monitor widening participation in universities in a constant way over time. That may well not be possible soon. The Coalition government appears to wish to redefine widening participation as allowing just a tiny number of children from very poor backgrounds to go to the most prestigious universities, while some of the universities that cater for the largest numbers of students from the poorest backgrounds in Britain may be shut down.

gap between areas continues to widen alarmingly, faster in recent years than before. The wealth gap is growing despite the crash. But here is one unprecedented success.

Participation at universities has been widened in such a way that no one lost out and those who had been most badly served in the past saw their chances improved the most. Education turns out to have been a priority as evidenced by the increased equality of outcomes now being reported.

The funding council's report is one of the most accurate pieces of work that has ever been undertaken in the monitoring of social policy across the United Kingdom. The fortunes of every child in Britain are now carefully tracked over time and between institutions so that the trends can be plotted with uncanny accuracy.

By the end of 2009 some 36% of people in Britain were studying at a university by the age of 20. The increase almost perfectly matches the earlier improvements there have been in GCSE results which in turn almost perfectly match the earlier increases in spending per child in state schools. All this was made much more affordable by the decline in the size of the birth cohorts involved. Spending and places have been increased as the numbers of young people coming through have been decreasing.

The introduction of education maintenance allowances provided a huge boost to school staying on rates in the poorest areas. Government did help and can take a lot of the credit, but it also helps that so many more affluent children were already going to university that they were not crowding out the rest. In contrast, the 1960s expansion was an almost exclusively middle class expansion in university places.

Britain still allows fewer of its adults to go to university than the majority of people in other affluent nations are able to. Given this, few will credibly argue that 36% entering by age 20 is too many. The target was 50% by age 30 by 2010. That will still be missed. However, given the gains in GCSEs still coming through, barring draconian restrictions on entry to university in the future, we should expect the participation rate to continue rising for many years to come.

Britain remains a hugely divided country; the prospects for the 20% of young people who do not even think of going to university are bleak. The current prospects for all school and university leavers are bleak, and going to university is not the be all and end all. But something has changed. Probably forever. Universities are no longer just for the likes of them.

# 19

# Do three points make a trend?[1]

Compass website (2008) 4 November

Newspaper articles have to have short, snappy titles. Like this *Guardian* one:

"Social mobility on the rise at last, says report"[2]

Whereas the following is a bit too long:

"Social mobility possibly on the rise at last, suggests a graph on page 36 of a report which included only three data points and measured something that may not be strictly comparable"

Well, the second sound-bite is certainly a bit more of a mouthful!

---

[1] Editorial note: This chapter is a short commentary which had been placed on the web pages of the political group Compass. It was written because at the time I was a member of the Academic Reference Group advising ministers on the Social Mobility White Paper. I'd received a very nice letter from the Prime Minister's Private Secretary. In the end my most significant contribution was probably to write this short piece!

[2] Watt, N. (2008) 'Social mobility on the rise at last', says report, *The Guardian*, 3 November, www.guardian.co.uk/society/2008/nov/03/socialexclusion-gordonbrown-social-mobility-labour (Nicholas Watt was the newspaper's chief political correspondent. Social mobility is more about politics than education or employment).

Here is the graph on page 36 of that report which was the basis for all this fuss:

**Figure 1:** Three points that were claimed to make a trend

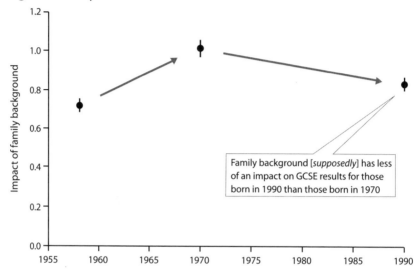

Pretty isn't it?

It's useful too. But it represents just a fraction of a tenth of a percentage of the information in the government report that the headline was based on. The headline was based on this fraction because this was one of the very few parts of the entire report that could be drawn upon to suggest that there had been an improvement in social mobility during the first years of this current century. It is argued that this is because those children who were born in 1990 studied for their GCSEs in a country that had been changed by a Labour government. The argument made by government ministers and reflected in that *Guardian* headline was that that graph, in particular, demonstrated success.

Here is the graph's original title:

> "The importance of family background to GCSE attainment appears to have declined for children that recently sat them★
>
> ★Relationship between family income and GCSE attainment, line shows standard errors (1)"

The key thing it says is that because those little vertical lines through the dots don't overlap on the Y axis – the dot to the far right really is a little lower than the dot in the middle.

It is what they like to call "statistically significantly" lower. It is not just by chance that it is there. It is time to celebrate. Social mobility – if you believe this graph and ignore most other key evidence, including the evidence in that same report – has increased.

And here are the claims made as a result of the drawing of that graph. The claims that appear on the same page of that report – released to the public later that day (Monday 3 November 2008):

> "– Data are available on the GCSE attainment of a group of children born in 1990/91 who took their exams in 2006 (1)
>
> – These suggest a statistically significant decline in the importance of family background on educational attainment compared to children born in 1970 (2)
>
> – These findings, therefore, suggest that family background will have less of an impact on the income of these children when they reach adulthood than those born in 1970, they are likely to experience higher social mobility (3)"

And here is the reference on that famous "page 36" that explains what those little, (1)s, (2)s and (3)s are at the end of all three quotations shown immediately above.

> "This study also includes data on children born in the 1980s, but the samples are too small to reveal any statistically significant changes in the relationship between family background and attainment (1), (2), (3) Gregg and Macmillan (2008) Intergenerational Mobility and Education in the Next Generation, mimeo"

This note does make you wonder whether the little dot for the 1980s might have been a bit higher than the little dot for 1990, albeit with a long vertical line through it, but that is by the by.

What matters most is that these three little dots do not imply any increase in social mobility because they are measuring three very different things.

The dot for 1958 measures the O level achievements of children around the year 1974. These children's futures were not decided by those achievements, but largely by how they did in an examination most took around 1969: the eleven plus. It was a different world. Family background had a little less effect because what determined your O level results was largely whether you got into a grammar school to be able to take O levels.

The dot for 1970 measured the O level or CSE achievements of children born in that year in exams taken around 1986. The large majority of children went to comprehensive schools then, and stayed on to 16. Very large numbers took these exams, in comparison to those born twelve years earlier, and the exams mattered. The key date for determining future life chances had moved on to how you did in these exams and studied (or not) at ages 15 and 16. A CSE grade 1 was said to be equivalent to an O level grade C, and getting 5 C's or above was very good, and quite unusual in a normal school. Get that and you could be a bank clerk rather than a labourer. It mattered. The poorest of children still did not take these exams.

The dot of 1990 measured the GCSE achievements of children born in that year in exams undertaken around the year 2006. By 2006 GCSE's were no longer the life-chances-determining-examination that O levels and CSE's had been. Children on average did far better in them. The grammar school in-a-school apartheid of those old examinations had been partly removed, although huge numbers of children are entered for GCSE's where the maximum grade available is still a C. But life trajectory came to be determined later, at A level and equivalent stage, in retaking exams, and then in whether you were one of the one third of 18 or 19 year olds to get to university by 2008. The battle had moved on from getting into grammars at age 11 to getting to university by 19; age 16 was no longer where it most mattered.

The various GCSE gaps can only narrow. That is because affluent children now routinely receive more GCSEs of high grades than is good for any child. When the vast majority of the children of social class one get seven good grades or more, they cannot do much better without it becoming silly. From that point on any improvement below is seen as a narrowing of the gap. That little dot should carry on bouncing down and down. Hopefully, though, we won't have to see it again, just on its own, as we will have learnt that GCSE gaps are not where the battle for social mobility is being fought any more. That battle is now over who gets apprenticeships; are they any good; and it is over who gets into university; and increasingly what university.

In fact it is reported in the *Financial Times* today that Paul Gregg, who is partly responsible for the data the graph in question comes from, says the GCSE results "are encouraging". But he adds: "GCSEs are only the beginning of the story of life chances and earnings".

"If more and more people are getting good GCSEs – and they are – then GCSEs may be less important than they were as the key to future life chances. People may need A-levels, or a degree or even a masters to really get on. It is a little like literacy, which was a huge advantage 200 years ago but became less so as more and more people could read." The clutch of policies Labour has introduced may indeed have a lasting impact on social mobility for children born after 2000, he says. But it will be years before the evidence is clear. And right now, he says, "it is a bit premature to claim a big success".[3]

The three dots in the graph, which the story of increasing social mobility relies on, are significantly different from each other. But that does not mean that a significant change has occurred in social mobility. In health, in wealth, in poverty, in university entry or the gaining of no qualifications (in the latest Institute for Fiscal Studies reports) even in income, we are continuing to polarise.[4] For a few years at the start of the century income inequalities dipped slightly, which was picked up by a recent OECD report, but sadly they are now rising again. The overall reduction in social mobility is seen mostly clearly between areas of the country – in terms of life expectancy rates, debt levels, and university access rates.

Had the Conservatives won the 1997, 2001 or 2005 elections I am convinced the situation would be worse now than it is. But it could be so much better. It is much better in most other affluent countries. But it will not get better if we delude ourselves by looking at just three dots on a graph.

---

[3] Nicholas Timmins (2008) 'Can do better in the social mobility class', *Financial Times*, 4 November.
[4] Editorial note: It is telling to note that less than two years after writing these words I was penning the preceding chapter on university entry no longer polarising. It might be tempting to imagine that this reflected increased social mobility at GCSE level, first identified in the 1990 birth cohort. Maybe these three points did, after all, point to that development, if not a longer-term trend. We will eventually find out.

# 20

# Educational mobility, England and Germany[1]

## *Social Europe* (2010)

Good politics has always seen well-funded, public provision of education as a vital pathway to delivering the Good Society. This article draws on recent evidence from Germany and the UK to show that even in more equal societies, such as Germany, attention still needs to be paid by progressive politicians to education – in particular, the importance of non-elitist, comprehensive education systems for all, regardless of means.

Educational systems in England and Germany affect social inequalities in different ways. Social inequalities are narrower in Germany, but not thanks to German education systems. The English education system is highly discriminatory too, but it would be a mistake to believe that the German model is much better.

Germany follows an elite model of higher education.[2] From the age of 10, children are allocated into different types of secondary schools. Admission to the *Gymnasium* (grammar school) leads to a qualification that allows

---

[1] Editorial note: First published in 2010 on the website of the Journal *Social Europe* jointly with Benjamin Hennig. original title began "Angles, Saxons, inequality, and ..."

[2] Ben Ansell developed a formal model for the role of politics in higher education reform in which he emphasised the trilemma between mass enrolment, public subsidisation, and total public spending for political parties. (Ansell, B. (2008) 'University challenges: explaining institutional change in higher education', *World Politics*, no 60, pp 189–230). Ansell argues that left-wing policy is not targeted at tertiary education for the masses as they receive their main electoral support from the working class which rarely takes part in tertiary education and thus is not in favour of increased spending in higher education.

university access after age 17. *Hauptschule* (secondary modern schools) are nowadays considered a dead-end path leading to limited chances in a highly competitive society. The latest statistics suggest that there is a very limited mobility between the different secondary school tracks – most of it leading "down" from *Gymnasiums* to the other tracks. The figures reveal growing inequalities, characterised by 8% of the 15-17 year olds leaving the educational system without any qualifications, and only 72% of 18-25 year olds gaining an upper secondary school qualification, which is now considered to be the minimum qualification for success in the labour market.[3]

In Germany gross enrolment in tertiary education remains at a level of approximately one third (graduation figures are considerably lower at 22%), being far lower than in other European countries. Federal governments[4] never seriously attempt to change this, and even left-wing governments focused more on increasing education mobility by subsidising access to universities for the poor rather than enabling a higher university attendance rate overall. What appears to create more equal opportunities for all turns out to be ineffective. Exclusion from better education predominantly takes place when entering secondary school.

By 2007 public loans or grants only accounted for 13% of university students' funding in Germany, some 53% of the support came from parents (or families). The rest was raised by the students themselves, loans and other sources. Thus support for the poor fails even for the few who gain a higher secondary qualification. In addition, political attempts to establish comprehensive schools to separate children at a later stage have taken off very slowly, not least because of the decentralised structure of education policy. Income inequality in Germany may be lower than in England but the gap between rich and poor there has been widening in recent years. Social status counts as much again now as it last did before the Second World War.[5]

England, achieved its most recent and (in contrast to Germany) quite radical changes in higher education under the New Labour government, which moved the country towards a partially private system, changing the

---

[3] Figures derived from *Education in the Federal Republic of Germany 2008*, published by the Federal Ministry of Education and Research.

[4] It must be said that national federal governments have limited power in educational policy in Germany. The federal states (*Bundeslaender*) control this field of politics, while the national government can only set certain frameworks. Changes thus require the consent of 16 state administrations with a very heterogeneous political structure, consisting of different coalitions with parties from the whole political spectrum, all following their own political agendas and ideologies. The Germany educational landscape thus remains a patchwork of 16 different educational policies, all competing to be better than the others. Financing education, however, is dependent on the national government, as the federal states have no power to levy taxes.

[5] Not discussed here is another dimension of inequality which affects the second generation of migrants that were recruited in the 1960s. Children from migrant families (*citizens with migrant backgrounds* as they are called in Germany) are more likely to be in lower qualification school types, even those of an otherwise equal social status.

funding structures considerably and greatly reducing the public subsidisation per student. Unexpectedly, the new policy proved to be successful in increasing the gross enrolment up towards 36% of those aged under 20, and probably 50% of those aged under 30 if these trends continue (which is a big *if*). As a result, educational mobility is considered to be above average in Britain as compared to other affluent countries (higher ranking on educational mobility were Finland, New Zealand and Denmark).[6] A huge and largely unrecognised part of this success is the beneficial legacy of mass secondary comprehensive education. Education proves to be one of the few factors that reduce inequalities in England, although it fails to reduce inequality in general. Private education is important for the wealthy to distance themselves from the rest of the educational system.[7] Of all the OECD countries the UK spends more than any other[8] on private secondary education, almost all of that spending being in England.

Comprehensive secondary education helps partly wipe out the disadvantage the English suffer from concentrating almost a quarter of their resources on just 7% of children in private schools, children selected because their parents are rich. The most telling statistic that reveals this is that more children from the city of Sheffield attend university than from the city of Bristol. Sheffield is poorer but has the great advantage of very few private schools (unlike Bristol).[9] Scotland and Wales do even better in different ways. Northern Ireland still has its own problems with educational segregation, but by class more than religion (hence above we have mainly talked about England).

The graph below shows how it is possible for Germany, a country with high social equality and mobility to also have *below* average educational mobility. Radical changes in education happen seldom, but they do exist, such as the 1970s comprehensivation of British schools. More recently Sweden, for example, targeted educational inequality in the 1990s and went from a highly selective educational system towards comprehensive tertiary education provision now aimed at more than 80% of young people. However, the Swedes also experimented with parent–led schools which worked well at first but are currently causing problems.

High social mobility (represented by low 'income immobility' on the graph above) tends to reflect low social inequality. That is why all the circles

---

[6] Pfeffer, F. T. (2008) 'Persistent inequality in educational attainment and its institutional context', *European Sociological Review*, vol 24, no 5, pp 543–65, doi:10.1093/esr/jcn026.

[7] Private education is a phenomenon with (still) little importance in Germany: As 'better' state education remains more elitist, there is hardly any demand for it. With an increasing number of comprehensive schools and growing inequalities, this may change in the near future.

[8] And at 25% of the combined state and private budget for 7% of children this remains more, proportionately, than any other OECD country apart from Chile.

[9] See: Dorling, D. (2010) *Injustice: Why social inequality persists*, Bristol: The Policy Press.

**Figure 1:** Social/educational mobility and inequality – international comparisons

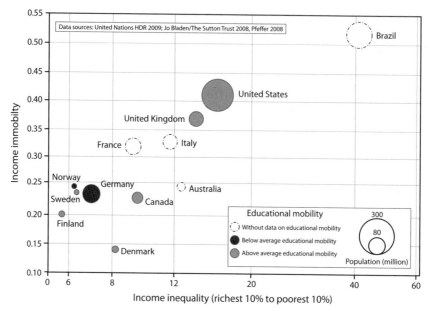

line up so well in the graph above. However, the position of a country on this graph does not reveal whether its system of education is in general progressive or regressive. There are better places for good politicians to look than both Germany and England for how best to teach young people and thereby promote the Good Society.

# 21

# Cash and the not so classless society[1]

*Fabian Review* (2008) vol 120, no 2

There was once an age when class came with breeding. One's parents gave one one's position. One might stray a little above or below (a perfect marital match is never possible), but one knew one's place. Then, for much of the last century, class was about occupation – you only had to ask someone his or her job and you felt you knew almost everything you needed to know about them. But in 2008 that is no longer true. The 50 per cent of the British people who can just about pay the bills, but who should not even imagine paying inheritance tax, have a huge range of occupations. Just as those above and below them do. These middle class families tend to have two jobs (the British norm), two cars (the norm), a small semi-detached or large terraced house, a combined income that pays the mortgage, food, fuel and a couple of holidays a year, (one of them somewhere warm). Nowadays, class is all about money.

In the 19th century, accent, clothing, title and behaviour reflected our origins. There were schools for all classes: the Great Schools for those destined for greatness, and a multitude of not-so-great schools – mostly created or expanded under Victoria's reign – catering for the children of different strata of the new middle classes. You could tell whether a family was upper-middle, middle-middle, or lower-middle class from the school their children attended.

The working classes had their day schools, Sunday schools, church schools and elementary schools. You could also tell their class from the street they inhabited. Charles Booth had maps of London beautifully coloured – you could see the subtle differentiation between all the areas not shaded golden

---

[1] Also reprinted in the *New Statesman*'s magazine as "Cash and the class system", 24 June 2008

yellow, the colour of the servant-keeping classes. You could also see those areas shaded black and labelled 'vicious, semi-criminal, poor'.

Mrs Beeton wrote a book on household management that sold well in those days. It turns out she only had one servant, but she did a good job of pretending to have more. Her book sold well because of a popular demand for information on how to act up to the class you wished to be. Just like Nigella Lawson today, she provided the fantasy that you too could appear to be of better stock and be more respectable.

We used to have popular guides to the British class system that told you how to appear just a slight cut above. But in 2008 those at the top have to try to appear like the rest, chummy and normal. This year women had to be told they must wear knickers to enter the Royal Enclosure at Royal Ascot. How did we get here from there? [2]

It was a slow change through the 20th century. The decimation of the sons of the Great Schools in the 1914–1918 war, the 'gifting' of stately homes to what is now the National Trust, the collapse of the financial might of the upper class through the 1920s and 1930s, and a progressive tax regime that lasted from the end of the Second World War until the beginning of Thatcherism – all these things changed what class meant. Whereas, under Victoria, secondary schools had been designed to segregate the middle class, the 1944 Education Act split up the working class. It had the side effect of creating a one-off generation selected at 11 by what was called an ability test, a few of whose 'winners' later got good jobs in universities and mused about class. They were almost all boys as the 11-plus tests had been made easier for boys.

Unsurprisingly, these Grammar School boys, with occupations their fathers had often not heard of, came to think of occupation and job title as very important. They designed class systems based on men's occupations. Occupation was seen as a proxy for behaviour, for leisure pursuits, for taste, for class. Under this system the university lecturer from humble origins was equal to the don who did not need to draw his salary. Women fitted awkwardly into such schema.

Unfortunately, classification based on occupation came to predict some behaviour less well over time. Almost from the moment when the occupations were grouped, people started voting less and less reliably by occupational class. They took longer to stop behaving so predictably in lifestyle, partly because health outcomes have long antecedents, but premature mortality too has become recently a little less predictable by class.

Have we become a more classless society?

_____

[2] Editorial note: Coincidentally, but giving away something of my class status, Isabella Beeton was probably my great-great-something aunt, her step-father being Henry Dorling (the first clerk of Epsom race course). I wonder what Victorian Henry would have thought of young women being told to wear knickers to enter the Royal Enclosure. Could he have imagined it at Epsom, or of his descendants writing it off as a joke?

It doesn't feel quite like that to me.

What I think has shifted is how we know what class we are in.

Give someone a fancy job title today and it may not mean quite as much as it did a few decades ago. You know what 'general manager for the horizontal arrangement of goods for sale' means, and what is being stacked where. Similarly two jobs can have the same title but be very different things. Different Members of Parliament, for instance, have very different lifestyles and differing levels of income and wealth.

Now there are better ways to gauge class. Tell me where you went to school, what your father's job was then, and your home postcode now, and I'll quite happily put you in a pigeon hole. It still helps to know your job title, but I'm not that bothered about it. I'd be much more interested in your financial situation and that of your wider family. How many millions do you and your siblings, cousins, parents, grandparents and offspring collectively have recourse to if it were pooled? I know you'd never pool it. But it is access to just a little bit of that pool which often makes the difference between what happens to families when folk get divorced, lose a job, become sick, need a deposit or some other underwriting.

Your class is your family wealth. For many people that wealth is zero or less. If you cannot save £10 a month and take an annual holiday you are most probably poor. If you cannot do those things, and know you are poor, and you have a low income, then you are approaching another class below. Not an underclass – there really is no such thing as a group destined for the bottom due to some fallibilities they have. The very poor are, instead, those whose dream of a life where their greatest worry is that they cannot save £10 a month or take a holiday once a year. Roughly a quarter of people are poor, they cannot save or afford to take even a very cheap holiday each year. A tenth of the population are very poor, poor no matter how poverty is defined.

Above the poor in Britain are a group who have been squeezed in number in recent years: those who are neither wealthy nor poor. These are people who are socially included. They can partake in the norms of society. They are normal. If you are normal you can pay for the schools trips, and a holiday, but not for the holiday in Mauritius. You are getting by, but not comfortably. You are in a shrinking middle group, and any time (right about now) you will be in a minority. Today you make up 50 per cent of UK households. Across Britain – outside of London – most people are still normal but that normality ranges itself from living a whisker above poverty to a whisker below the wealthy (see Figure 1).

The wealthy are the 25 per cent of the population who do have some (little) cause to worry about paying inheritance tax. Only a third of this group ends up paying it, but they almost all worry about it. You are in this group if your estate were to be liable for that tax should you and your spouse

**Figure 1:** British society divided into social classes by poverty and wealth status (%)

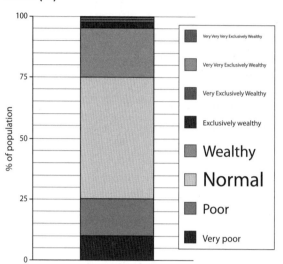

simultaneously drop dead today. Don't forget to count those life insurance policies, or the writing off of the mortgage, or that death-in-service lump sum. But don't worry: most people like you will manage to spend your wealth in old age long before you have a chance to pass much of it on. The odds are that you are also partaking in most of the norms of society. Most people in this group choose not to use private health and education provision. If they did, other luxuries would have to be forgone.

However, within the wealthy are a group who routinely do exclude themselves from the norms of society: for ease of remembering we'll call them the exclusive rich. They make up just around 5 per cent of us.

What sets the exclusive rich apart from the rest is not their use of private provision, but their large properties, multiple foreign holidays, both often coupled with the outright purchase of new cars. You need to be doing about two out of three of those things, while preferably also having a six-figure household income, to be up with these Joneses.

There is a national fixation with this group, and enough written on them to sell a month of Sunday newspapers. So all I'll say here is that they are fractal in nature. Within the best-off 5 per cent of households in Britain half are so much better-off than the rest that they make the other half feel poor. Within that better-off half, half are so much better-off that... it's a recursive definition. It ends with the poor sods at the top – paranoid about being kidnapped and knowing that their children and lovers lie to them for their wealth and suspecting their servants of pilfering. This is our wealth-based British class system today.

It is a 25-50-25 division, the edges of which can be shaved off to almost infinite layers of abstraction. It may sound crude, but money is. Airs and graces no longer matter. In fact it's crucial to try to avoid them regardless of which end of the scale you are from. Dress down if you might otherwise look like a 'toff', take off that tie, unclip that accent. Dress up if you come from more dour stock: sensible suits, a neat hair cut, hold your knife and fork right. All the old markers of class fade as, for men, a ubiquitous 'bloke' is created; women have to look 'smart'.

We can all still see the signs, though. Those brown leather shoes that only men from certain (great) schools still wear, that fake handbag that only women not quite *au fait* would carry … but the signs matter less and less. Those whose occupations are labelled 'working class' still have a predilection to vote Labour more than their generally lower incomes would suggest. This means, in effect, we will not be asking with much accuracy about class in the next census. An income question is asked in the United States census, it is asked in censuses and surveys across Europe, it may even be asked in the 2011 census in Scotland,[3] but it is not set to be asked in 2011 in England and Wales. There must be a civil servant living in a 1950s fantasy land somewhere who thinks that it is of some great use to know that a person's job label is 'manager'. We're only getting useful information when we know that they are a manager and that the annual income of their household is roughly £40k, and that only one adult in their family works. Income is not being asked about in the 2011 census not because of any real fears of asking the question or because some folk might complain. It is not being asked about because we are afraid of what we will be told, and of what kind of a segregated country we will see. Sometime soon, the proposed 2011 census questionnaires will be laid before Parliament. Parliament decides whether to accept what the civil servants propose. Parliament altered the 2001 form – Parliament could alter it again. Don't you want to know what Charles Booth's maps would look like if redrawn today?[4]

---

[3] Editorial note: In the end the Scots lost their battle to ask about income in their own census. They will be asking if households have access to 4 or more cars as a new and extremely indirect measure of wealth and as a tiny improvement on the 2001 Census (which did not go above 3 or more cars as a category!). The form can be found here: www.gro-scotland. gov.uk/files2/the-census/scotlands-census-2011-specimen-questionnaire.pdf

[4] Editorial note: The British parliament didn't want to know. In fact, they were so adamant that they didn't want to know that the government didn't just not ask about income in the 2011 census, next the then new Coalition government announced that there would be no census for 2021, no questions on any subject, let alone on income or wealth. We can use other sources to try to estimate what Charles Booth type maps might look like if redrawn today, but official bodies will not release tax and benefit data at a fine enough scale to do this accurately. A census question would be one of the best ways of ensuring that we knew whether we were divided again street by street as we were towards the end of the Victorian era, but first we require a campaign to reinstate the census! Alternatively, the aftermath of the English riots of August 2011 might increase Parliament's interest in knowing just how segregated every small area has become.

# 22

# Britain must close the great pay divide[1]

*Observer* newspaper (2010) 28 November

...UK wage inequality is approaching levels not seen since the end of the first world war. A cap on bosses' pay is vital if Britain is to become a fairer place...

Do you know how well you are rewarded and how you compare with your colleagues? Here's a simple way to work it out. First, calculate how much you are paid an hour, without subtracting tax and national insurance.

At £5.93 an hour, the minimum wage for those aged 21 and over, you are almost perfectly representative of the poorest fifth of employees. Moving up the income ladder, if you receive just over £7 an hour, you are in the next bracket, the "modest" fifth. At £10 an hour, you are now, more or less, the median worker – while £14 an hour takes you into the more "affluent" fifth of employees.

---

[1] Editorial note: The statistics with which this chapter begins were the most up-to-date concerning the median incomes of each quintile group of earners in Britain at the time of writing.

At close to £21 an hour, which translates to an annual salary of just over £40,000, you are bang in the middle of the best rewarded fifth of all employees. You earn getting on to twice the national average. In short, you are, in relative terms, rich.

But here's the thing. If you are in that top income bracket, you may not feel rich. In fact, although you are heading towards double the median income, you might well feel part of the "squeezed middle".

This vague term – deliberately vague, perhaps, when used by Ed Miliband, determined as he is to reach out to as many potential voters as possible – seems, at times, to capture all of us who are neither poor nor rich.

However, the exact details of what we are paid – in particular the gap between the best and worst paid, which is wider in Britain than in much of the developed world – is an urgent political topic. Earlier this year, Will Hutton, executive vice-chairman of the Work Foundation and an *Observer* columnist, was appointed by the government to head a review into creating fairer public sector pay – and to determine to what extent a multiple between top and bottom public sector pay, say 20 to 1, could help shape norms of private sector pay. This week, Hutton will rehearse his first thoughts in the review's interim report.[2]

Vince Cable, the business secretary, has also launched a review of British business which includes an analysis of executive pay. In addition, the think-tank Compass, in collaboration with the Joseph Rowntree Charitable Trust, has set up its own "high pay commission" after failing to convince the coalition that it should set up one of its own.

A recent poll by Compass and the Joseph Rowntree trust showed that only 1% of people think that top executives should be paid as much as they are. Another striking figure revealed that 64% believe that a chief executive should take home an annual salary of less than £500,000. This contrasts sharply with the actual pay figures. Research by Income Data Services found that the average FTSE 100 chief executive was paid £4.9m, a figure that had risen more than 50% in a year. This equates to 200 times the average wage.

The previous year – between June 2008 and 2009 – the earnings of the FTSE 100 chief executives had fallen 1%, in the wake of the financial crash. Examining this year's figures, it seems that restraint at the top was short-lived, and it's back to business as usual.

---

[2] The interim report can be downloaded from the Treasury's website. It was placed there on 1 December 2010 and is titled "Hutton Review of Fair Pay in the Public Sector". See: www. hm-treasury.gov.uk/indreview_willhutton_fairpay.htm Hutton bases his review on Rawls flawed " 'difference principle', the notion that inequality is permissible only to the extent that those at the bottom can be said to benefit from arrangements which allow others to be very much richer." (page 13 of the interim review). It is flawed because growing inequality itself is now known to disbenefit society, especially the poor. See page 87 of this book and section entitled "Rawls was wrong: inequality harms us all".

This week, it is widely expected that Hutton will support the concept of a pay multiple. It will be hard, given the terms of his review, not to imagine that he will also advocate the principle being extended to the private sector.

Why do pay differentials matter? Plenty of recent research – best detailed in Richard Wilkinson and Kate Pickett's book – *The spirit level* – suggests that a wide range of statistical indicators, from mental health to social mobility, are better in more equal societies. These societies tend to have narrower income distributions.

One consequence of wide pay differentials is a more atomised society. We do not mix as much as we used to in the 1950s. Now we tend to stick much more with our "own"; we read the newspapers written for people like us, we buy food sold for people like us, our children go to schools for children like them.

Across much of western Europe the income inequality ratio is lower than in Britain. It is lower in Australia, New Zealand and Canada too. Japan's ratio is half Britain's.

What's more, in Britain high-paid work is concentrated in particular families. So while in a prosperous home you might find two high incomes, in a poorer home one low income might be supplemented by a convoluted mix of benefits – a pattern found far less often abroad.

For much of the 20th century, the income gap in Britain narrowed steadily as we gradually became a more equal society. In 1918 the richest 1% of earners was rewarded with 19% of all income, receiving about 19 times more than the average earner. By 1935 the top 1%'s share of income had fallen to 14%; by 1950, 12%; by 1960, 9%; by 1970, 7%; and by 1980, 6% (and only 4% after taxes).

This was all achieved without stipulating a ratio from top to bottom – but it was much lower than 20:1. And, in fact this process towards a more equal society seemed inexorable, an almost natural consequence of an advanced democracy. During these years – the three decades or so after the end of the Second World War – this trend was part of the political consensus.

However, in the late 1970s a few of us got greedy; the rest of us failed to stop the greedy, and they spread their ideas around (if not their money). By 1983 the income share of the best-off percentile was back up to 7%; by 1992 it was 10%; by 1997, 12%; by 2001, 13%; by 2005, 16%.

Today, with the return of big City bonuses, I very much suspect it will be back up to 18%. We should have a national day of mourning when we return to a level of inequality last experienced at about the time of armistice day in November 1918.

New Labour did not do as much as it might, perhaps, in checking the trend. In 1997 the hourly pay rates for each fifth of earners were all lower than they are now, but so were the gaps between our earnings. And income cannot, of course, be divorced from other factors. The cost of housing rose even faster than average earnings, for instance, and it can be argued that the poorest ended up with even less choice over where they lived at the end of New Labour's time in office.

Though Alistair Darling's final budget could be deemed progressive, with the introduction of a new top rate of tax for those earning more than £150,000, during New Labour's reign, as a whole, the income ratio of the richest to the poorest earners rose from to 3.6 to 3.9.[3] Hence the poor became relatively poorer despite receiving on average an extra £2 an hour for their labour.

In Tory chancellor George Osborne's first budget, the effects of the unevenly distributed £6bn of local authority cuts and the punitive £81bn cuts of the comprehensive spending review were all designed to be regressive. I say designed because you don't introduce a regressive policy by accident. So the gap will have grown again since narrowing slightly at the start of this year.

In the 1970s, the earnings ratio between the richest and poorest fifth of UK earners used to be nearly 3 to 1. It approaches 4 to 1 today. In recent decades, the greater part of the increase in inequality occurred during Margaret Thatcher's premiership, but Tony Blair added a little extra dollop of unfairness on top, and Gordon Brown – his own sliver.

When we consider families as a whole, and not just the family's central breadwinner, the inequality ratio is found to be even greater. The richest fifth of families by income in 1997 each received 6.9 times the income of the poorest fifth in 1997. By the time of the election the Liberal Democrats were loudly complaining that the ratio had risen to 7.2 to 1. In other words, from 1997 to 2009, we moved a quarter of the way to becoming as unequal in income distribution as people experience in the United States.

Will Hutton's predicted proposal of suggesting a maximum full-time pay ratio of 20:1 may help this situation, but we need to take the principle seriously and apply it to the private as well as to the public sector with whatever necessary adjustments need to be made. Otherwise high-earning public sector employees will simply carry on comparing their salaries with those earned by private-sector employees.

On the minimum wage, someone working 38 hours a week now earns £11,700 a year. Twenty times that is an annual salary of £234,000 (or £118 an hour). Ask the British people their views, and you find that the

---

[3] Editorial note: This is the ratio for the *median* income of the best-off and worse-off fifths, which amounts to just over half the rise in inequality that can be measured between the *mean* levels of household incomes by quintile (which rose form 6.9 to 7.2). This ratio for individuals is lower because it is the ratio of median, not mean incomes, and because inequalities between households tend to be greater than between individuals. Well paid individuals are often married to other well paid individuals. This exacerbates social inequalities overall.

overwhelming majority consider this more than ample. It is approaching twice what the prime minister is paid, for instance.

However, there are a handful of public-sector workers receiving more than £100 an hour. I predict a rapid adoption of the £7.85-an-hour London living wage in their organisations to raise the permissible take-home pay at the top to £310,000 a year (or £157 an hour).

I may be a cynic, but I would prefer that approach to not seeing wages rise at the bottom. However, I think almost everyone would be better off if wage rises at the bottom were coupled with wage reductions at the top.

Hutton's proposals could begin to change how we think. It is assumed that constraint at the top results in a contraction of the whole income distribution – one reason is that top earners, so research suggests, do not like those just beneath them in earning power getting too close to them. Couple that with wider adoption of the living wage and you have more rises at the bottom, stagnation in the middle, and maybe even a few cuts at the peaks.

This, though, can only happen if the effects are spread across all occupations, not just the public sector. Why should an excellent brain surgeon receive "only" 0.5% of a top banker's income? At the peak of excess a top banking boss can receive £40m a year in remuneration. 0.5% of that income is a salary of £200,000 a year, which is just about in the possible range of top surgeons' salaries. You can have 200 excellent brain surgeons, and quite a few more average ones, all for the cost of a single man in a suit running a large bank in Britain.

If the chief executive's pay fell, the surgeon could soon be earning a far higher proportion of that top banker's income without anyone having to spend a penny. And all the rest of us would be richer, as we would not be being charged so much by our banks to allow them to pay those exorbitant salaries and bonuses.

The good news is we can change – and any public sector reform should be accompanied by private sector change. I would suggest that, just as many parts of the public sector have begun not to work with private sector companies that do not pay the living wage, a new clause is simply added to those ethical contracts. This clause would demand that for any new public sector work where the private sector is contracted in, no one should be paid more than 20 times that living wage. And why? Because helping to support such profligacy is a waste of public money.[4]

---

[4] Editorial note: As it happened, in his final report to government Will Hutton did not even recommend a 20 to 1 inequality limit for pay differentials in the public sector. Maybe he and those advising him could see where it might lead and how they might personally lose out? The lists of those whose advice he sought are given in appendices in both reviews, but not the incomes of a single advisor.

# 23

# Raising equality in access to higher education[1]

## Original article (2011)

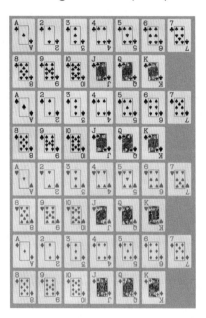

---

[1] In summer 2010 I was invited to write this paper for probable publication within a forthcoming special issue of the *National Institute Economic Review* which is published quarterly by the National Institute of Economic and Social Research in London. I had received that invitation to write the paper based on a conference presentation and was told at the time that "This is an influential journal which targets policy-makers in the UK and other European countries as well as an academic audience and aims to do so in a timely and topical manner. The articles are assured of quick turnarounds by referees so that issues of immediate policy interest can be addressed." I submitted the paper in November. The turnaround was quick. In December the editor of the special issue suggested many changes, all of which I accepted (I have reinserted a few of the more interesting deletions in the footnotes which follow so you can see what was excluded). The paper was accepted subject to final review. In January the paper was rejected for publication because a single anonymous referee did not agree with its tone, including my suggestion that the raising of state retirement age was being "forced through". Apparently I was being "very loaded and inaccurate". I offered to make changes but to no avail. I've included the paper here so you can decide for yourself. I am grateful to the editor of the special issue, Geoff Mason, for all the changes he has made to the copy you can read here and to professors Andy Green and Lorna Unwin who originally asked me to write it. The footnotes to this paper are illustrative of some of the more interesting asides that are often removed from academic papers. The original title of the previously unpublished article ended "... and the prospects for the future."

## Abstract

The Higher Education Funding Council Report of January 2010 on who is getting into universities in Britain revealed that, after years of effort, children from poorer areas were finally going in growing numbers to university. Many more university places have been provided in the last few years and, for the first time ever recorded, the majority of those most recent additional places have been taken up by children living in the poorer half of British neighbourhoods.

This change may well be seen in future years as the greatest positive social achievement of the 1997–2010 government. This was achieved not at the expense of upper- and middle class children, who have also seen their chances improve. It occurred because of the way the education system as a whole has expanded and, most importantly, as a result of massive increases in funding per child in state secondary schools in recent years.

This improvement might well have been reversed in autumn 2010 as unprecedented numbers of applicants were turned away from universities, and it will almost certainly be reversed in future following the Comprehensive Spending Review of October 2010. However, even before the cuts to come, access to good schools, universities and jobs remained far more socially determined by class and place of birth in Britain, than in almost any other affluent nation. Now the young adult job market is rapidly changing as work becomes both more scarce and changes in its nature. The secrets to young people's futures are not in their genes but are largely captured by their postcodes and dates of birth: just a dozen letters and numbers in total.

**Key words:**[2] higher education • secondary education • social class • geographical inequality • United Kingdom • England

## Introduction

"The danger that has settled in upon us since the shock administered by the events of the last year is that the clamouring throng who find the gates of higher education barred against them may turn against the social order by which they feel themselves condemned" (Young, 1958, p 13).

---

[2] Editorial note: As you can see, the article was at the point of having had its key words assigned and diagrams reformatted into the house style of the journal which had invited me to write it before its last minute rejection.

Over half a century ago Michael Young warned us of what might happen were a government to attempt to make savings by curtailing access to higher education. He was writing about a fictitious 2034 economic catastrophe. He could have been writing about today.

This paper argues that the way in which we currently allocate university places will, in a few decades time, come to appear as perverse and haphazard as was entry to elementary education prior to the 1880s, and as secondary education places were allocated prior to the 1960s. Perverse here means harmful to almost all, from the poorest to the richest. What is needed is to reconsider what is a good education, a good university and a good job. That need is especially urgent as a result of the spending cuts announced in October 2010 being greater for the higher education teaching budget than for almost any other sector of government spending.

Michael Young was writing in a period of austerity in the 1950s. The early 1950s was the last time that the National Health Service financial settlement was as low in constant price terms as that announced on October 20th 2010 (Emmerson, 2010). It was also the last time that for a couple of years the proportion of adults being admitted to universities in Britain fell (Timmins, 2001). We have to turn back to the early 1950s to know what austerity feels like and to get a sense of the grievances it can cause if it is coupled with rising inequalities, with not being "all in it together". This was the essence of Michael Young's 1958 book.

From the 1870s onwards the school leaving age has steadily risen, firstly in leaps and bounds during the more progressive early years of the last

**Figure 1:** School-leaving age (years) and university entry (%), Britain, 1876–2013

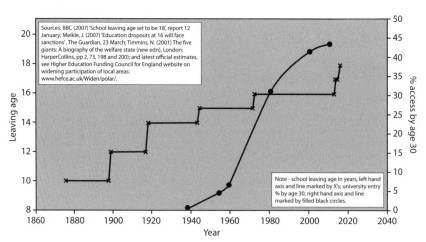

*Note:* Leaving age is the stepped line whose scale is shown on the left hand axis. The proportion attending universities is the smooth line, shown as the percentage of 30 year olds who have attended university (scale shown on the right hand axis). *Source:* Dorling (2010).

century and then more slowly, until very recently (see the stepped line in Figure 1). In contrast, the proportion of young people gaining access to university education has followed an S shaped curve, rising most quickly in the progressive 1960s, and then in the late 1980s and early 1990s, but slowing down more recently, and possibly being about to fall significantly depending on the decisions made over the coming year (see the smooth line in Figure 1).

## University access in 2005

Figure 1 shows that around 43% of 30 year olds had attended university at some point by the year 2005. Of those, around two thirds had attended by the time they were aged 19. However, students from different parts of the country tend to have very different chances of attending university and, if they do attend, very different chances as to which university they will gain admittance to.

To study these inequalities Britain can be divided up into 1282 'tracts', each with roughly equal numbers of people living in them. The proportion of young adults from each tract attending university has been calculated with the assistance of Mark Corver[3] from the Higher Education Funding Council for England (where the "access" data is held). All the tracts have been divided into ten groups of equal population size, ranging from those where young people were most likely to enter university (51% attending by age 19), to those where they were least likely (13% attending). Each tract represents about half a parliamentary constituency. Table 1 shows the results.

**Table 1:** Access to higher education by neighbourhood of residence

| Decile | Chance of going (%) | All (%) | Elite (%) | Least popular (%) |
|---|---|---|---|---|
| 1 | 13 | 4 | 3 | 18 |
| 2 | 18 | 6 | 6 | 13 |
| 3 | 22 | 7 | 6 | 12 |
| 4 | 24 | 8 | 7 | 11 |
| 5 | 27 | 9 | 9 | 9 |
| 6 | 30 | 10 | 10 | 9 |
| 7 | 33 | 11 | 11 | 9 |
| 8 | 37 | 13 | 14 | 7 |
| 9 | 42 | 14 | 14 | 7 |
| 10 | 51 | 17 | 20 | 5 |
| Britain | 30 | 100 | 100 | 100 |

*Source:* Thomas and Dorling (2007) pp 100–03.

---

[3] Editorial note: See Chapter 17, page 139, for an earlier paper Mark and I wrote on these issues.

Table 1 shows, for each geographically defined decile group of children, from least *advantaged* by neighbourhood (decile 1) to most (decile 10), what proportion of all university students in 2005 came from each set of areas as a proportion of all young people who could have gone. It also shows those same numbers, but scaled to 100 to show from where an 'average' university admits its students, what proportion of students studying in elite universities came from such areas, and what proportion of students studying in the least popular universities came from such areas.

The elite universities are the tenth of institutions which tend to draw from the most well-to-do areas. They equate roughly to what have been called, the most selective universities: Birmingham, Bristol, Cambridge, Durham, Edinburgh, Imperial College, London School of Economics, Nottingham, Oxford, St Andrews, University College London, Warwick and York (Sutton Trust, 2007). The 'least popular' universities are those institutions which are least competitive in entry and which include much of the higher education that is taught in further education establishments, and the 'worse performing' of what are often referred to as 'recruiting' universities.

As Table 1 makes clear, the majority of students attending 'recruiting' universities (usually former polytechnics) have been drawn in recent years from the areas in which young people are least likely to attend university. In contrast, young people are most likely to attend elite ('selecting') universities if they have grown up in the most affluent of neighbourhoods.

The table shows that by 2005 there were four students from the best-off tenth of neighbourhoods studying in an elite institution for every one then studying in a least popular university (20/5=4). Conversely, there was only one student from the least advantaged tenth of areas attending an elite university, for every six who attend one of the least popular universities. Only 4% of young people attending university were from the least advantaged tenth of large neighbourhoods, Only 0.66% of young people from those least advantaged areas attended an elite university in 2005.

There is great current concern that, with funding cuts, the potential closing of some 'recruiting' higher education institutions may have a massively disproportionate impact on young people from poorer neighbourhoods and be highly socially regressive in effect. Any changes to university funding which deter even more young people from the least advantaged areas from seeking access to an elite university could see that tiny 0.66% figure fall. Rather than just 1 in 150 young people from the worst-off tenth of large neighbourhoods attending an elite university in Britain, that fraction could revert back to the numbers more common in the 1930s. Michael Young wrote about just that situation in his book in 1958, noting that students from poorer areas often had to work much harder than upper class youngsters in order to get to university.[4]

Figure 2 shows that disparities in higher education participation are greatest at each end of the distribution. The proportion of young people in the worst-off decile of areas who attended university was five percentage points lower than in the second-lowest decile, while the participation rate in the highest decile was some nine percentage points above that in the next highest decile. This is the pattern of inequality of access by area in 2005.

**Figure 2:** Inequality in university access, 2005 by area

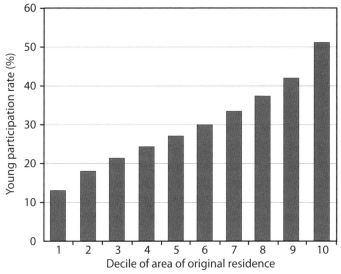

*Source:* Table 1 above

---

[4] Or, as he put it, for every hard working student from a poorer area, how many more extremely lazy youngsters from the upper classes then 'studied' at university, Michael Young was basing his assertions on reports produced in the 1930s that showed this to be the case. [Added editorial note: In particular see Chapter 10 by David V Glass and J. L. Gray entitled 'Opportunity and the older universities: a study of the Oxford and Cambridge scholarship system', within J. Hogben (1938) *Political arithmetic: A symposium of population studies*, London: George Allen and Unwin. Reprinted by Routledge in 2010. On page 439 of that volume details are given concerning how the majority (52.7%) of 'scholarships' and 'exhibitions', designed supposedly to widen participation slightly – even in those times – were being awarded to pupils from "Public and Private Schools" (note also that the word 'Public" here is the bizarre title given to the most private of private schools, those whose head is invited to a particular annual conference): "The conclusion to be drawn from this last table is that the bulk of State scholarships, in relation to school populations, is going to boys from wealthier families or from families of higher social status than was intended by the authors of the scheme" (page 442).]

The geography of variation in access reveals far more than the aspatial statistics above can do. Figure 3 shades each of the census tracts in England and Wales (south of Middlesbrough) by which combination of higher education institutions the young adults from that place were most likely to attend if they went to university in 2005. The map is a population cartogram in which every parliamentary constituency is represented by a hexagon. Each hexagon is cut in half as the large neighbourhoods we have statistics for are half constituencies. A key to the regions is provided and Sheffield Hallam constituency is labelled as an example of a locality youngsters grow up in with significantly greater chances of attending university than in any of the other Sheffield constituencies that surround it.[5]

Figure 3 shows that only in one half of one constituency in North London (Hampstead to be precise)[6] are young people who attend university most likely to attend an elite university. The half constituency is shaded dark red

**Figure 3:** Which type of university people aged 18–19 are most likely to attend by area of residence at age 15

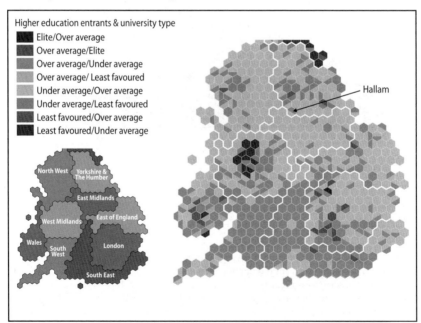

*Source:* Thomas and Dorling (2007) pp 100–03.

[5] In 2010 Sheffield Hallam was the seat of the Deputy Prime Minister, within the 'six constituency area' that is Sheffield city.

[6] This part of Hampstead is a neighbourhood where, if a youngster tells you they have been offered a place at university, you should not be surprised to hear that it is one of those institutions whose names are best known.

(see the colour plate of Figure 3) to indicate that of those who are not in that majority (attending an elite university), the majority of the rest go on to attend an 'over average' university which is usually a Russell Group or other red brick establishment.

The light red half hexagons in Figure 3 are the next most educationally fortunate set of neighbourhoods where attendance at university is most likely to be in one of those 'over average' establishments, and if not that then in an even higher 'elite' place (a place you tend to go 'up' to). Both Oxford and Cambridge have a quarter of their cities coloured light red, and these are the most expensive quarters to live in. The more affluent half of Sheffield Hallam constituency is the only large neighbourhood in a city like Sheffield where this is the most likely set of destinations of those who go to university (and more go to university from here than from anywhere else in Sheffield).

In the other half of the Hallam constituency, coloured lightest grey, and across almost all of the North of England, much of East Anglia and also a large part of London, the most likely university a young person will attend, if they go to university, will be a former polytechnic. In contrast, west of London, and south of Oxfordshire, the map is coloured darker pink and there is a great block of areas where, if university access is obtained, it is usually to an older institution, often based in the North of England, such as in Leeds, Liverpool, Manchester, Newcastle or Sheffield. Thus southern accents tend to predominate in northern campuses and student areas during term time.

The lightest pink colour in the key indicates those half-constituencies where attendance at an 'over-average' institution is most likely, but if not that, then the most likely destination of those going to university is an 'under-average' institution in terms of popularity, many of which are post-1992 universities.

The light grey, of which there is a particularly distinctive spatial block in Birmingham, represents those areas where young adults are most likely to go to an under-averagely popular institution and, if not that, to an even less popular 'least-favoured' one. The two dark grey shades on the map are areas where, for the few that do gain access, it is most often to the institutions which are least favoured. These neighbourhoods are found in places between Birmingham and Stoke, and in the North East of England just above North Yorkshire. Interestingly, it is here that we have the only examples of 'split' neighbourhoods. For example in some parts of South Wales most who go to university go to a local 'least favoured' institution, but the majority of the rest attend an over-averagely popular institution.

## Changes since 2005

In all the changes that occurred in government, to government funding and then to government spending plans over the course of the year 2010, it is easy to forget that in terms of educational statistics the year began with the revelation that the geographical and social gaps just described had recently narrowed and narrowed greatly. In January 2010 the Higher Education Council for England published its report on trends in access to universities over time (HEFCE, 2010). The report found that when quintiles are considered, the worst-off fifth had a 15% chance of university participation in 2005. That rose to 19% by 2010. This was a huge increase for young people (aged 18 and 19) in the worst-off fifth of areas in terms of their chances of attending university, representing an extra one in twenty five going in just five years.

The quintiles being considered here are groups of wards sorted by participation rate and so the range of outcomes are slightly wider than those reported for the deciles above (calculated by larger census tract), despite the population being split into five groups rather than ten. However, the sources of data are nearly identical.

The narrowing in life chances by area which has occurred since 2005 does not look dramatic if shown on a graph giving all rates over time for each quintile group as in Figure 4 below. But note here that, even though the absolute gap between quintile groups one and five fell between 2005 and 2010, it had risen between 1995 and 2005.[7]

**Figure 4:** Young people's chances of attending university by ward quintile

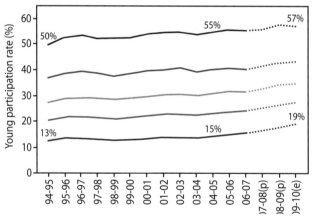

*Source:* HEFCE (2010) Figure 2, page 5, including projections (p) and estimates (e), methodology explained in full in the original source

---

[7] The small drop in access for the best-off quintile is thought to be partly due to slightly more pupils from the most elite of public schools aiming for Harvard or the Sorbonne in recent years (Corver, 2010), and also a little lack of imagination over having suitable 'insurance offers' amongst some of these children who are then shocked when they don't necessarily secure a place in the university of their dreams (see the story of Florence on page 181).

The improvement in just 15% of young adults in the worst-off areas participating in university in 2005 rising to an estimated proportion of 19% by 2010, based on early application data and other sources, is the fastest improvement ever recorded in absolute terms, an extra child in 25, one extra child per class, 5 children going rather than 4 from every class in every school in a poorer area of the country in just 5 years.[8]

The HEFCE report made various attempts to explain why participation had risen so quickly in the worst-off fifth of areas and one predictor stood out as being far more important than any other. The numbers and grades of GCSE's being achieved by these young people around age 16 was improving at exactly the rate required, several years earlier, to result in the improvement to university participation later observed in their lives (Figure 5).[9]

**Figure 5:** Actual (1994–2010) and GCSE-predicted participation rate (2004–2010) in the poorest areas of England

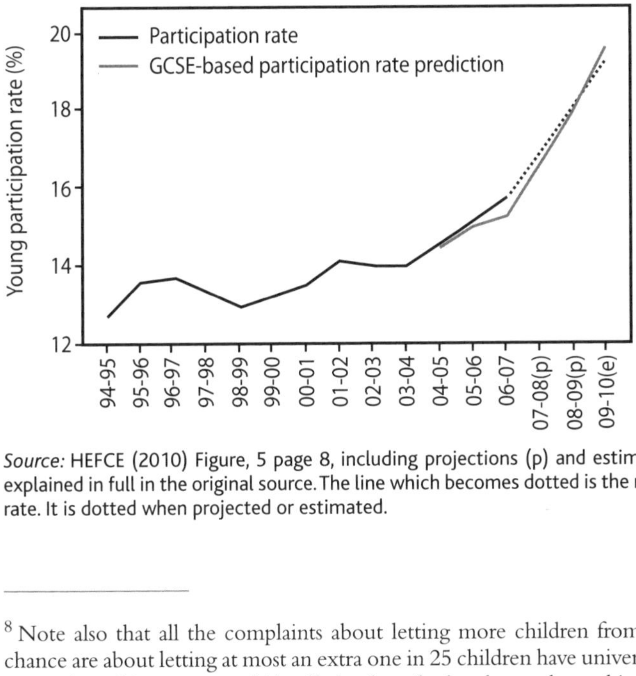

*Source:* HEFCE (2010) Figure, 5 page 8, including projections (p) and estimates (e), methodology explained in full in the original source. The line which becomes dotted is the measured participation rate. It is dotted when projected or estimated.

---

[8] Note also that all the complaints about letting more children from poorer areas have a chance are about letting at most an extra one in 25 children have university access from these areas. This achievement could hardly be described as the workers taking over the parapets of power. It is not as if they are being allowed in for any reason other than that they are finally being allowed to get the grades that give a young person a chance at access to university.

[9] At this point the editor suggested that I insert the following sentence and I agreed as a compromise although I have never read Chowdry et al's paper and was not entirely happy with the implications of including this: "This confirms previous findings by Chowdry *et al* (2008) that poor attainment in secondary schools is the biggest single barrier to young people from poorer neighbourhoods attending university". If you are interested in the study that I was asked to add a reference to (although I had not read it), see: Chowdry, H., Crawford, C., Dearden, L., Goodman, A. and Vignoles, A. (2008) *Widening participation in higher education: Analysis using linked administrative data*, Report R69, Institute for Fiscal Studies: London, UK.

And what caused the rise in GCSE passes amongst this cohort of children studied by HEFCE? In fact, it seems to be largely explained by rises in average funding for secondary school pupils over the period which (with the appropriate lag) in turn almost perfectly predicts the GCSE rises and hence the later upturn in admissions to higher education from the poorest areas of England (see Figure 6).

**Figure 6:** Actual (1994-2010) and spending-predicted participation rate (1999–2010) in the poorest areas of England

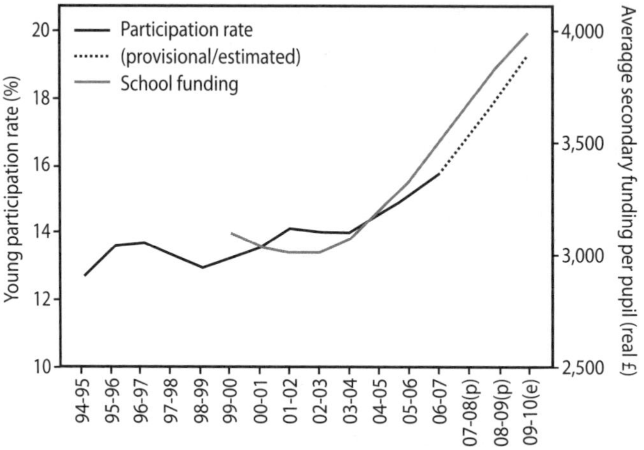

*Source:* HEFCE (2010) Figure, 25 page 35, including projections (p) and estimates (e), methodology explained in full in the original source [Participation rate is the line which becomes dotted].

The implications appear to be that: spend more per child and they will gain better GCSE results, they will then, at least in this period, go on to attend university in greater numbers in almost direct proportion to that spending. It should hardly be surprising that this is the case. The same mechanism operates to ensure that higher numbers of children attending private schools, especially expensive private schools, obtain many GCSE's and then A levels and go to universities in large numbers. Their parents would not pay if this were not the case.

There were two other factors that helped university admission rates from poorer areas to increase, one of which was mentioned in the HEFCE report, the other which was not (at least not explicitly). Educational Maintenance Allowances were mentioned explicitly (paragraph 32, page 8), the introduction of which enabled many young people from poorer areas to be able to afford to stay on at school. These allowances are to be phased out following the Spending Review of October 2010.

The other factor is government funding of university places which is the ultimate determinant of what young people's chances are. If the places are not funded, they cannot be won. The spending review of October 2010 resulted in cuts of up to 75% in government funding of teaching within higher education being announced, with unknown compensation from higher fees being introduced.

## The situation in 2010

Some critics of rising university participation appear to believe that young people from more disadvantaged backgrounds and areas would often be better suited to 'learn a trade' rather than be the fifth child out of a class of twenty five to go to university (Dorling, 2010). It has to be put as bluntly as that because it is very obvious that this sentiment is held as strongly as that.

In recent months some newspaper stories have implied that upper class and upper-middle class families were losing out to the children of working class parents for whom exceptions were being made to ease them into universities to which they apparently did not belong. For example, *The Times* newspaper on April 10th reported on Florence MacKenzie, who they described as "upset and angry". Their report continued:

> 'Universities would have fought over Florence MacKenzie, 18, in previous years. On course to achieve A and A★ grades in her A levels, she has straight A★s in her nine GCSEs, plays hockey for her school, and is Grade 8 at piano and violin. She and her parents were baffled when she was rejected by three of her five chosen universities. Florence, from Banbury, is happy with her place studying English at University College London, but was turned down by Edinburgh, St Andrews and Durham. All are popular universities, hugely oversubscribed for her chosen subject, allowing them to be extremely picky. Edinburgh allocated 70 per cent of places on a points system that favoured teenagers from poor schools, those whose parents did not go to university, or those from Scotland or northern England. Florence goes to an independent girls' school in Warwick so did not qualify. It set a hurdle of 11 GCSEs at A★ to qualify for the remaining 30 per cent of places, but many schools (including Florence's) do not set this many. She said: "I was very keen on Edinburgh and upset when rejected by them − angry as well after I found out the reasons why. I don't think it's a fair way of doing it, they should interview like other universities." As many as 25 candidates are pursuing each place on popular courses at leading universities.' (Woolcock, 2010)[10]

---

[10] Anyone familiar with university applications will note the totemic "grade 8" at various musical instruments (a function of parental financial support), the place in the school sports team (mainly a function of how small the school is and how many teams it has) and the A★s (largely a function of the kind of school you attend).

But what are the job prospects for those youngsters not lucky enough to manage to gain access to a university place? The latest ONS figures from the Labour Force Survey show that, when scaled up to the population as a whole, there were some 156,000 fewer young adults and older children working in 2009 as compared to 2008, despite the age cohort still expanding slightly due to more births to this group some 16 to 24 years earlier.

Table 2 shows that the largest falls in employment amongst young adults (and 16 and 17 year olds) were in Sales jobs[11]. Next, general office assistant and clerk jobs fell by almost 20,000 nationally amongst this age range. All this was almost entirely due to 24 years olds turning 25 and almost no new younger adults and older children being hired. The next largest falls were in warehousing and box-shifting: "Other goods handling & storage occupations".

Retail, that sector that employs a tenth of the population of Britain was slowing down rapidly and the workforce in it which was, in effect, being shed – simply by not recruiting - was the young. For example it was the young who were the bulk of the people who could no longer work at Woolworths when those stores closed on 800 high streets in December 2008 and January 2009.[12]

Work opportunities for youngsters also fell in painting and decorating and joinery and building in general as fewer people moved home, while in sales it was "Telephone salespersons and call centre agents & operators" who were not being taken on. In a number of other occupations, such as "marketing associate professionals", "retail cashiers/check-out operators", "conveyor belt assemblers (of electrical products)", young people were simply not being taken on in large numbers anymore and so employment rates within young age groups fell rapidly.

---

[11] Fewer young people were being paid to stand in shops asking if you wanted "help with anything". This is, in itself not a bad outcome, but even those jobs are much more worthwhile and much less boring for many young adults when compared with the alternative of sitting at home and watching television.

[12] With the loss of 27,000 jobs around Christmas 2008. See: http://news.bbc.co.uk/1/hi/7811187.stm

**Table 2:** Jobs in which youth employment fell the most, 2008–09
Change in jobs (numbers) – and job title

| | |
|---|---|
| -33,762 | Sales and retail assistants |
| -19,722 | General office assistants or clerks |
| -13,264 | Other goods handling and storage occupations |
| -12,747 | Customer care occupations |
| -8,247 | Painters and decorators |
| -7,961 | Labourers, build and woodwork trades |
| -7,714 | Telephone salespersons |
| -6,976 | Marketing associate professionals |
| -6,506 | Carpenters and joiners |
| -6,126 | Personnel and industrial relations officers |
| -6,107 | Bricklayers, masons |
| -5,989 | Retail cashiers/check-out operators |
| -5,969 | Assemblers (electrical products) |
| -5,169 | Civil Service admin officers and assistants |
| -5,099 | Fishing and agriculture related occupations |
| -5,073 | Call centre agents and operators |

*Source:* ONS, Labour Force Survey for 16-24 years olds, change 2008-2009 kindly supplied by the Prince's Trust. [showing exact number estimates but only accurate to nearest 1000]

Although Table 2 shows that employment fell in sixteen categories of work for young adults and older children between 2008 and 2009 by over 5000 jobs in each category (at most by over 30,000 jobs in one), it did rise by over 5000 jobs in six areas of employment. The smallest rise was in teaching, as government was still spending on increasing employment in the public sector at this time to try to ward off the worst effects of the recession. That rise in spending per child shown in Figure 6 above was still resulting in more jobs for new young secondary school teachers in 2009 as compared to 2008 (see Table 3 below).

All the rest of the few recent new jobs have been in the entertainment sectors, mainly because of increases in overseas tourism to Britain as the pound fell and also, perhaps, as government liberalised both the domestic betting and online betting industries. Note also that leisure and theme park attendant positions saw a rise in youth employment equating to 5,700 posts nationally. Receptionists, restaurant and catering managers and – above all else – waiters and waitresses saw increased employment opportunities, especially in London, but these job gains were massively outweighed by the overall loss in posts available to the young (shown in Table 2), and the absence of long-term career paths in many of the poorly-paid service jobs where young people did find employment.

**Table 3:** Jobs in which youth employment rose most, 2008–09
Change in jobs (numbers) - and job title

| | |
|---|---|
| 5,193 | Secondary education teaching professionals |
| 5,731 | Leisure and theme park attendants |
| 5,733 | Receptionists |
| 5,800 | Restaurant and catering managers |
| 7,083 | Accounts wages clerks, bookkeepers |
| 8,164 | Waiters, waitresses |

*Source:* ONS, Labour Force Survey for 16-24 years olds, change 2008-2009 kindly supplied by the Prince's Trust. [showing exact number estimates, but only accurate to the nearest 1000]

In aggregate these extra jobs totalled only 37,700. Overall some 222,000 fewer people aged 16-24 were employed in jobs for which figures were available for both years, and this was when places in higher education were still expanding.

## Conclusion

Unprecedented numbers of young people are set to leave British universities and schools in autumn 2011. Unprecedented numbers will apply and fail to gain a place in higher education this coming academic year. Political leaders and policy-makers need to be asked if it makes sense to have millions of unemployed and poorly trained youngsters, while at the same time forcing through an increase in the retirement age. It is worth recalling that, during the Great Depression in the 1930s, when it would have been very hard to imagine the world of near full employment, we actually planned for and created that in Britain by the 1950s, 1960s and 1970s.

Why not now try to imagine a better future, with many more young people going to university, people able to retire at an age they can enjoy, and near full employment for all who want it in between? What is needed is hope, imagination and faith in the ability of other people, especially the young. Many higher education analysts and policy makers harbour the views that the present system is a meritocracy, and that meritocracy is desirable. Michael Young's masterpiece of 1958 is worth returning to in order to understand the disadvantages of limiting entry to higher education.

**Figure 7:** They way we used to think[13]

*Source:* Ernest Bevin 1933

---

[13] This figure was removed by the editor as unsuitable for publication before the paper was rejected entirely. It has been a long time since it was asked what the economy could do for us, rather than what we could do for the economy. It has been a very long time since we were in as dire straits as we are in now. It is worth looking back at what we did the last time. It is worth worrying why some economists are so keen to censor such consideration. I did ask if it would be possible to know who the anonymous member of the editorial board of the journal was who said this piece could not be published, but they chose to remain in the shadows.

Looking back at Figure 7 and at the conclusion above, I am still forced to ask, apart from including women as well as men, brown faces as well as white, and not having everyone wearing a cap, how else would you redraw the cartoon shown above for today?

## References

Corver, M. (2010) Personal communication to the author.

Dorling, D. (2010) *Injustice: Why social inequality persists*, Bristol: The Policy Press.

Emmerson, C. (2010) Speech at the annual conference of the *Royal Statistical Society's Statistics User Forum*, London, 27 October 2010; personal communication.

HEFCE (2010) *Trends in young participation in higher education: Core results for England, Report 2010/03*, Bristol: Higher Education Funding Council for England, www.hefce.ac.uk/pubs/hefce/2010/10_03/10_03.pdf

Sutton Trust (2007) 'University admissions by individual schools', Report posted on *The Guardian* newspaper website (see footnote 4 page 10 of that report): http://image.guardian.co.uk/sys-files/Education/documents/2007/09/20/Strust.pdf

Thomas, B. and D. Dorling (2007) *Identity in Britain: A cradle-to-grave atlas*, Bristol: The Policy Press.

Timmins, N. (2001) *The Five Giants: A biography of the welfare state*, new edition, London: HarperCollins.

Woolcock, N. (2010) 'Bright pupils are rejected in scramble for university', *The Sunday Times*, April 10, www.timesonline.co.uk/tol/life_and_style/education/article7093817.ece

Young, M. (1958, 1961) *The rise of the meritocracy 1870–2033: An essay on education and equality*, London: Thames and Hudson.

# SECTION V
# Elitism and geneticism

The first short chapter in this section was written at the end of a debate among male academic geographers concerning geography's exclusion from the celebration of the 150-year anniversary of the publication of Charles Darwin's *On the origins of species*. A great deal of geographical work had been required to write that book, not least many expeditions, the most significant of which may not have been undertaken by Charles himself. However, geographers – like many other academics – have often forgotten that Charles Darwin was simply a cog in much greater wheels of thinking. It was that thinking that resulted in the discoveries later attributed uniquely to him.

We often now fail to remember that not all the Victorian discoveries about our origins and about how we are currently biologically ordained (our supposed genetic propensities to harbour greatness) are necessarily still seen as valid. We also tend to forget that unsung women and other men, such as Alfred Wallace (who wrote about the geography of animals), also played a hugely important part in inching our knowledge forward. In Alfred's case he was simply not rich enough, and perhaps not vain enough, to be able to afford to take the bulk of the credit, as is implied below (page 190).

From their very inception, genetic theories as applied to theories of natural selection concerning crude evolutionary ideas of the 'descent of man' have tended to result in unfortunate outcomes because writers confuse the very long-term processes that result in the creation of species with the short-term implications of random variation within species. The long *Fabian essay* which follows the Darwin editorial elaborates on this and includes a summary of some new arguments now being made. These arguments suggest that we are almost all now born as near equal in intellectual potential as makes no material difference.

Sadly, very few of the elite have heard of the recent discoveries concerning how inherently equal in capacity we might well be, and they tend not to believe in those findings and arguments when they do hear them. The penultimate chapter in this section is a *Soundings* article which tells of the contemporary repercussions of so many people still seeing other human beings within the society they live in as being of different 'stock'. This, as the final chapter in this section (from *New Statesman*) highlights, culminates in the super-rich being able to justify their soaraway wealth as supposedly being just reward for almost belonging to a separate species from the rest of humanity. How can great inequalities in wealth and opportunity otherwise be justified? And how else is it possible for those, with most, to be able to tolerate the suffering of billions in poverty? A final table and graph has been added to the end of that chapter showing the simple consequences of inequalities either continuing to soar to new heights, or reducing rapidly. Neither is likely, although either (or anything in between) is conceivably possible.

# 24

# The Darwins and the Cecils are only empty vessels

*Environment and Planning A* (2010) 42, pp 1023–25

If we men with our fascination for the big man are going to remember Darwin, we should not forget that his thinking was also an example of a very particular evolution (Castree, 2009). Darwin came to and modified an idea already formed by others (Summerfield, 2010). Part of what was special about him, why he is now remembered, was because of how wealthy a man he was before he began to think his thoughts (Finnegan, 2010). The kernel of his big idea had already been described to him by a poorer man: Alfred Wallace (Davies, 2008). This part of the story only entered into public debate over Darwin's legacy late in that supposed anniversary year of 2009, and only after a few fellows of the Royal Geographical Society started a campaign named after his ship, the Beagle (Driver, 2010). The allegations are worth repeating:

"In 1855, Wallace's first paper on evolution prompted Charles Lyell to warn Darwin that Wallace seemed close to solving the 'species problem' and to urge him to publish his own theory. Three years later, while studying the fauna of the Malayan archipelago, Wallace completed his theory and sent it to Darwin from the island of Ternate on 9 March 1858. Sent to England on the same boat was a letter to Frederick Bates, who received it on 3 June. It seems that Darwin wrote to Joseph Hooker on 8 June, saying he had found the 'missing keystone' that enabled the completion of his evolution theory, while on 18 June, he wrote that he had just received a letter from Wallace proposing a theory of evolution identical to his own – a very suspicious chronology! Although it initially became known as the Darwin-Wallace theory, Darwin took the glory and Wallace was largely forgotten. Lacking Darwin's establishment connections, Wallace was shabbily treated" (Venables et al, 2009).

In responding to Darwin's anniversary it has already been noted by geographers that: "With the thinnest veneer of qualification, environmental determinism is back in vogue" (Kearns, 2010). So too again in vogue is eugenics, in this case with the veneer of appearing in crypto-form. 'Crypto' meaning the name 'eugenics' is no longer openly used, although the concepts are, again, now more and more frequently mentioned (Connelly, 2008). In the most unequal of affluent countries, such as the United States and United Kingdom, it appears to be becoming acceptable again to talk of there being genetically inherited differences in the mental abilities of different groups of people (Dorling, 2010a). Geographers could be doing more to counter this current regressive trend, given their advantage of being well placed to remember the dismal imperialist past of their own discipline.

The idea that different people are made of different mental 'material' was most commonly espoused in the era of 1920s and 1930s when those who advocated the inheritability of intelligence wrote that it "... is seen with especial clearness in these numerous cases – like the Cecils, or the Darwins – where intellectual ability runs in families" (Wells et al, 1931, p 823). That the offspring of such families do not now dominate intellectual life provides an extra spoonful of evidence to add to the great pile built up since the 1930s that now discredits eugenics and other such:

> "foolish analogies between biology and society [whereby the world's richest man] ... Rockefeller was acclaimed the highest form of human being that evolution had produced, a use denounced even by William Graham Sumner, the great 'Social Darwinist'" (Flynn, 2007, pp 147–8).

Today again a few 'great men' are very rich and inequalities in income, health, voting, and wealth are as wide as they were at their 1920s heights (Dorling, 2010b). Our fascination has been rekindled for myths of chaps with maps sailing across oceans in vacuums of scientific imaginative purity discovering truths just waiting to be uncovered. The big men with beards are again being venerated. We too easily forget the strangeness of the Victorian English arrogance that fuelled beliefs in the supposedly great insights of these few. The danger Hannah Arendt highlighted in the 1960s is re-emerging: an "absence of thinking ... the refusal to read, to think critically or deeply, the rejection of all but one or one kind of book" (Goldberg, 2009, p 373). We even usually now forget to mention the full title of Darwin's work: *The origin of species by means of natural selection, or The preservation of favoured races in the struggle for life* (Dorling, 2010c). And because we forget, we labour in danger of failing to notice the return (in a new form) of old evil ideas about ability and evolution.

The Charles Darwin who paced up and down the path at Down House, who collected beetles in the hills of Barmouth (where he later struggled over revisions of his text) has long ceased to exist. His name is now as much an empty vessel to be filled with the arguments of others as was his mind in the 1850s. We now keep him alive as a monster, not as he was but as how we choose him to be, and only if we choose him to be. His bushy visage adorns the reverse of the £10 note because his mythical might is valued slightly below that of Adam Smith (whose bug-eyed face is etched on every new £20 note in circulation).

**Figure 1:** Alfred Russel Wallace (1823–1913)

Author of *The geographical distribution of animals* (1876) and many other fine works. Social activist, land reformer, early opposer of social Darwinism and eugenics, supporter of women's suffrage and opponent of militarism. Recipient of the Royal Geographical Society's Founder's Medal in 1892. Oh – and early proposer of a theory of evolution due to natural selection...

Other people we choose to forget (Kundera, 1999). The circumstances might be none of our making, but our choice concerning which version of those circumstances we are to remember will alter all our futures. Venerate Darwin as anything more than he was and you help to condemn many others to be dismissed as inadequate in a world being nastily reconstructed anew to pit the 'favoured few' against the 'unfavoured masses'.

And who were the Cecils?

Exactly!

## References

Castree, N. (2009) 'Charles Darwin and the geographers', *Environment and Planning A*, no 41, pp 2293–8.

Connelly, M. (2008) *Fatal misconception: The struggle to control world population*, Cambridge, MA: Harvard University Press.

Davies, R. (2008) *The Darwin conspiracy: Origins of a scientific crime*, London: Golden Square Books, www.darwin-conspiracy.co.uk/book/chapters/The Darwin Conspiracy.pdf

Dorling. D. (2010a) 'The Fabian essay: the myth of inherited inequality,' *Fabian Review*, vol 122, no 1, pp 19-21. [see Chapter 25 of this volume]

Dorling, D. (2010b) *Injustice: Why social inequality persists*, Bristol: The Policy Press.

Dorling, D. (2010c) 'The return to elitism in education', *Soundings spring*, issue 44, March. [see Chapter 26 of this volume]

Driver, F. (2010) 'Charles Darwin and the geographers: unnatural selection', *Environment and Planning A*, no 42, pp 1–4.

Finnegan, D. (2010) 'Darwin, dead and buried?', *Environment and Planning A*, no 42, pp 259–61.

Flynn, J.R. (2007) *What is intelligence? Beyond the Flynn effect*, Cambridge: Cambridge University Press.

Goldberg, D.T. (2009) *The threat of race: Reflections on racial neoliberalism*, Oxford: Blackwell.

Kearns, G. (2010) 'The descent of Darwin', *Environment and Planning A*, no 42, pp 257–8.

Kundera, M. (1999) *The book of laughter and forgetting*, London: Harper Collins.

Summerfield, M. (2010) 'Observations on Darwin and geography', *Environment and Planning A*, no 42, pp 262–4.

Venables, A., Wimpenny, J. and Lloyd, D. (2009) 'Evolution of the Darwin conspiracy', *The Guardian*, Letters, 3 December.

Wallace, A.R. (1876) *The geographical distribution of animals*, London: Macmillan.

Wells, H.G., Huxley, J. and Wells, G.P. (1931) *The science of life*, London: Cassell and Company Limited.

# 25

# The Fabian essay: the myth of inherited inequality

*Fabian Review* (2010) vol 122, no 1, pp 19–21

...The science is clear: intelligence isn't inherited. So it's not just wrong for politicians to talk about potential, it's bad for equality...

John Hills's National Equality Panel report of January 2010 revealed that our social divisions are even wider than we thought. In London today the best-off tenth of citizens have recourse to 273 times more wealth each than do the worst-off tenth. Never before has so much been held by so few; and such great inequalities in wealth can dull our thinking by creating a pernicious assumption that people are inherently different.

If most people in affluent nations believed that all human beings were alike – were of the same kind, the same species – then it would be much harder to justify the exclusion of so many people from so many social norms. It is only because the majority of people in many affluent societies have come to be taught that a few are especially able, and others particularly undeserving, that current inequalities can be maintained. It seems inequalities are not being reduced partly because enough people have come – falsely – to understand inequalities to be natural, and a few to even think inequalities are beneficial.

The code word used to talk of inequality as natural is to talk of children having differing 'potentials'. This belief in inherited intelligence – geneticism – is dangerous and remains uncritically challenged at the heart of much policy making in Britain. But recent evidence can help dispel the myth that children from different social backgrounds are born with differing potential.

It was only in the course of the last century that theories of inherent differences amongst the whole population became widespread. Before then it was largely believed that the gods ordained only the chosen few to be inherently different and therefore favoured – the monarchs and the priests. Back then mass deprivation was a fact of life, as there simply could not be enough produced to enable the vast majority to live anything other than a life of frequent want.

It was only when more widespread inequalities in income and wealth began to grow under nineteenth century industrialisation that theories attempting to justify these new inequalities as natural were widely propagated. Out of evolutionary theory came the idea that there were a few great families which passed on superior abilities to their offspring and, in contrast, a residuum of inferior but similarly interbreeding humans who were much greater in number. Often these people, the residuum, came to rely on various poor laws for their survival and were labelled paupers. Between these two extremes were the mass of humanity in the newly industrialising countries, these were people labelled as capable of hard working but incapable of great thinking.

These early geneticist beliefs gave rise to eugenics. Eugenics had become almost a religion by the 1920s; one that famously gripped many prominent Fabians at the time. It was an article of faith to believe that some were more able than others and that those differences were strongly influenced by some form of inherited acumen. However, after the horror of the genocide of the Second World War, where men of all classes fought and died together, and after the later realisation of the importance of generation and environment to achievement, eugenics was shunned. Contemporary work on epigenetics – the study of heritable changes in gene expression that do not involve changes to the DNA sequence – explicitly steers away from saying genetic makeup determines the social destiny of humans along an ability continuum. But, in contrast to modern scientific understanding, geneticism is the current version of the belief that not only do people differ in their inherent abilities, but that our consequent 'ability' (and other psychological differences) are to a large part inherited from our parents.

There are sceptics, but the overwhelming weight of progressive scientific opinion now suggests that, if there is any inherited influence on acumen, the effects are tiny. Recently I have brought together the evidence and have been convinced that there is no general, even slight, inherited inequality.[1] Sadly, many political commentators are unaware that the debate as to whether inherited acumen is minuscule or non-existent has moved on. For instance

---

[1] Dorling, D. (2010) *Injustice: Why social inequality persists*, Bristol: The Policy Press (Chapter 3, footnote 28, page 326 – should you want the details).

even the *Guardian* newspaper recently published an article which suggested that "common sense tells us that inherited inequality is in part the result of economic injustice and in part the results of disparities of intelligence."[2]

As Professors of Psychiatry and Psychology at the University of Minnesota (and international authorities on genetics and twin-studies) Irving Gottesman and Daniel Hanson, pointed out five years ago: "questions of nature versus nurture are meaningless." They explain that depending on the circumstances into which we are born and given how malleable and unformed our brains are at birth, none of us are destined regardless of circumstance to be either great thinkers or great imbeciles.

Intelligence is not like wealth. Wealth is mostly passed on rather than amassed. Wealth is inherited. Intelligence, in contrast, is held in common. James Flynn's work has shown how successive generations of children appear to out-perform their parents when their apparent intelligence is measured. Unlike monetary wealth, what matters most when it comes to appearing to be clever is the generation you are born into, then where and to whom you are born.

The similar outcomes of identical twins are often held up as evidence of genetic influence on IQ. If identical twins are separated at birth and then adopted by different families, they will appear to perform in a way that is correlated. This is, however, unconvincing as proof of inherited intelligence. Firstly, as Flynn explains, they perform similarly because they are of the same generation. Secondly, there is a great deal of evidence to suggest that teachers and other key individuals treat children slightly differently according to their appearance, leading to differential attainment. And, of course, the one thing we know about identical twins is that they tend to look very much like each other.[3]

Studies of how Afro-Caribbean children did badly in school in the 1960s when taught by white teachers in London, or of what happens when you suddenly decide in an experiment to treat all the blue eyed children in a classroom with disrespect, show how much it matters how children are treated when they are learning. The correlations between the measured test performances of identical twins separated at birth are slight; slight enough to easily be explained, not by genes, but by how different sets of teachers are treating them in similar ways because of their similar physical appearance. Tall,

---

[2] Blond, P. and Milbank, J. (2010) 'No equality of opportunity', *The Guardian*, 28 January 2010, p 28.

[3] For one of the most insightful discussions, which does not discount the genetic possibilities, but which says they are so tiny that by implicit implication appearance could be as important, see the open access copy of the summary of James Flynn's December 2006 lecture which was given at Trinity College Cambridge: www.psychometrics.sps.cam.ac.uk/page/109/beyond-the-flynn-effect.htm (accessed 9/7/2009), the full length version of the argument is: Flynn, J. R. (2007) *What is intelligence? Beyond the Flynn effect*, Cambridge: Cambridge University Press.

good looking, white children receive (on average) more praise in societies where the bias is toward height, certain perceptions of beauty and being white – and get correspondingly better results.

The current scientific consensus is that intelligence – the capacity to acquire and apply knowledge – is not an individual attribute that people come with, but rather it is built through learning. No single individual has the capacity to read more than a miniscule fraction of the books in a modern library, and no single individual has the capacity to acquire and apply much more than a tiny fraction of what we have collectively come to understand. We act and behave as if there are a few great men with encyclopaedic minds able to comprehend the cosmos; we assume that most of us are of lower intelligence and we presume that many humans are of much lower ability than us. In truth the great men are just as fallible as the lower orders; there are no discernable innate differences in people's capacity to learn, other than those caused by failing to develop basic cognitive functions. Take, for example, Margaret Thatcher's 'tall poppies' speech:

> "I would say, let our children grow tall and some taller than others if they have the ability in them to do so. Because we must build a society in which each citizen can develop his full potential, both for his own benefit and for the community as a whole, a society in which originality, skill, energy and thrift are rewarded, in which we encourage rather than restrict the variety and richness of human nature."

The 'full potential' idea presumes some great variety in potential. That variety is not found when looked for – except by those who wish to find it. There is variety in outcome, but not in opportunity, if unhindered. Human intellectual ability is rather like our ability to have opposable thumbs or binocular vision or to sing: we evolved to have it. There are cases where children are born with potential fixed low – but these are the results of just a few conditions, such as oxygen depletion at birth, chromosomes causing Downs Syndrome, malnutrition problems and severe lack of attention. It is much more an either/or, for those unlikely to do like others regardless of subsequent circumstance, than the commonly perceived continuum of intelligence. Our problem today is that 100 years of intelligence testing strengthens the idea of there being a curve of ability potential.

Britons spend proportionately more money than any country other than Chile on private education – more even than the USA (below higher education level). Half of all 'A' grades at A-level go to the 7 per cent of children privately educated. It's very sad for the English – but a great natural experiment for the world to show that you can simply take a set of children and throw money at them and they will appear to do well at tests. That does not mean there is a continuum and these children are near the top end of it – what it does mean is that you could take 7 per cent of almost any set of children and put them in an environment that means they appear to learn more than the other 93 per cent. If there were a continuum to ability potential then the private schools – and especially the top public schools – would have found it far harder than they did to monopolise the A grades.

Learning for all is far from easy, which is why some educators confuse a high correlation between test results of parents and their offspring with evidence of inherited biological limits. Human beings cannot be divided into groups with similar inherent abilities and motivations; there is no biological distinction between those destined to be paupers and those set to rule them.

In academia today, perhaps unsurprisingly, those whose arguments more often suggest possible heritability are disproportionately found in the most elite institutions, and especially among many of those who advise some of the most powerful governments of the world. Eugenicism has risen again, but now goes by a different name and appears in a new form and is now hiding behind a vastly more complex biological cloak. For example, it was recently stated in a textbook supposed to be concerned with 'fairness' and including amongst its editors people near the very heart of government, that "there is a significant correlation between the measured intelligence of parents and their children … Equality of opportunity does not aim to defeat biology, but to ensure equal chances for those with similar ability and motivation."[4] This quote was written by a professor based in the city of Oxford. It is disproportionately from places such as Oxford University that possible excuses for exclusion are more often preached. To give another example from the same institution: "children of different class backgrounds tend to do better or worse in school – on account, one may suppose, of a complex interplay of socio-cultural and genetic factors."[5] Outside of Oxford, researchers are so much more careful with their words when it comes to suggesting such things. Why?

There are many advantages – but also disadvantages – to working in a place like the University of Oxford when it comes to studying human societies. It is there and in similar places – like Harvard and Heidelberg – that misconceptions about the nature of society and of other humans can so easily form. This is due, Pierre Bourdieu has claimed, to the staggering and strange social, geographical and economic separation of the supposed

---

[4] Miller, D. (2005) What is social justice. Social Justice: Building a Fairer Britain. N. Pearce and W. Paxton. London, Politicos: 3-20. (pages 14-15).

[5] Goldthorpe, J. and M. Jackson. (2007) 'Education-based meritocracy: the barriers to its realisation', *Economic change, quality of life and social cohesion 6th framework network*, from www.equalsoc.org/paper_fetcher.aspx?type=2&id=11. (page S3).

*crème de la crème* of society into such enclaves.[6] During the time these Oxford academics were writing, the British Prime Minister had clearly come to believe in a kind of geneticism, as revealed in his speeches.

Tony Blair disguised his geneticist beliefs by talking of them as the "God-given potential" of children, but it is clear from both the policies he promoted, his 'scientific Christianity', and the way he talked about what he thought of his own children's special potential, that his God dealt out potential through genes.[7]

A strand of eugenics thinking hung on in the way many left-wing policy-makers in Britain treat and describe inequality and the poor. We need to exorcise these past ghosts before we can get out of some of the ruts in our current collective thinking. We need to understand that the modern forms of crypto-eugenic belief – geneticism – lead to an implicit acceptance of social segregation, to enclaves, escapism, excuses for huge wealth gaps and an argument being made which promotes inequality as good.[8]

---

[6] Bourdieu, P. (2007) *Sketch for a self-analysis* (English language edition), Cambridge: Polity Press.

[7] For the full wording of his text about children's abilities delivered in 2005, see: Ball, S.J. (2008) *The education debate*, Bristol, The Policy Press, p 12. Tony's comments about the work which would be beneath his children are recorded in Steel, M. (2008) *What's going on*, London: Simon and Schuster, p 8.

[8] Editorial note: In Britain most recently it has been the Australian writer Peter Saunders (not to be confused with the Australian academic of the same name) who has been at the forefront of such arguments, including making the argument that we need to create more servile simple jobs for people he labels as stupid. Whenever someone comes along with such arguments look for their track record and for where they have been dismissed before. Usefully on his website Peter provides examples of how best to deal with him:

> "In recent days, some politicians and commentators in New Zealand have attacked me for suggesting that, on average, people in higher occupational classes are brighter than people in lower class positions. I have been labelled 'extreme right wing' and a 'nut job' for pointing out the link between social class and intelligence. …The problem is that one-sixth of the population has an IQ under 85. At this level, people struggle with tasks like reading and understanding official documents, or working out a budget. These are the people who used to do the unskilled jobs that have now disappeared, and many of them are now long-term welfare dependent."

However, given that most people who are unemployed are young, for Peter's argument to work we must have very recently become more stupid. I think we can become more stupid, but this is more the case when it comes to arguments such as Peter's which are themselves good evidence that progress is not inevitable and of how poor argument can be promoted. The quote is from his website: www.petersaunders.org.uk/social_class__intelligence.html (accessed in February 2011).

# 26

# The return to elitism in education

*Soundings* (2010) Issue 44, March, pp 35–46

> …A society's attitudes to innate intelligence are closely correlated with its levels of inequality…

As inequality becomes ever more deeply entrenched into contemporary everyday life, there has been a creeping return to the idea of innate ability. At the same time, priorities in education have become increasingly determined by a utilitarian concern for the needs of the economy, rather than for developing the thinking of each child. One place where the effects of these interconnected trends can be seen is in the OECD's reports on learning skills (for it is now part of the business of the OECD – an organisation of economists – to tell countries how well educated their children are). Its comparative report on learning skills among 15-year-olds is therefore a good starting point for a reflection on the connections between elitism, neoliberal ideas of competitiveness and concepts of innate ability.[1]

The Netherlands is the country which best approximates to the OECD economists' favoured 1:1:2:2:1 distribution of children according to categories of ability (which are, respectively: limited, barely adequate, simple, effective and developed – corresponding to the OECD's international testing levels of 1 to 5 – see Figure 1). It may surprise you to learn that the Netherlands – with 51 per cent of its children classified as 'simple' or worse – fares particularly well on comparisons of this kind. Only half a dozen

---

[1] See *Programme for international student assessment*, OECD, Paris 2007.

countries, out of more than fifty surveyed, did significantly better when last compared (in 2006):[2] an even larger percentage of children were awarded the damning labels of 'limited', 'barely adequate' and 'simple' in both the United Kingdom and the United States.

According to the OECD, in Finland and New Zealand the top level 'genius strand' is reached by 4 per cent; in the United Kingdom and Australia it is 3 per cent; in Germany and the Netherlands 2 per cent; in the United States and Sweden 1 per cent; and in Portugal and Italy nearer to 0 per cent. These are the children who, according to the educational economists, show real promise. These are the children who have been trained in techniques such that they answer exam questions in the ways that the examiners – operating in the light of OECD economic beliefs – would most like them to be answered. The way this small group of children behave, they could one day even become educational economists themselves.

As it turns out, however, the proportions of such children are so low in these comparisons because the international tests are set in a way that seeks to arrange the distribution of results around a 'bell curve', whose smoothly tapering tails are cut off precisely to produce results that label 1.3 per cent as geniuses and 5.2 per cent as know-nothings.

The OECD report does not actually include any statistics shown as bell curves, perhaps because its authors know that such representations would arouse suspicion. But if you read the report's technical manual (released three years after the survey), you will find hidden after 144 pages of equations and procedures the statement that, in calibrating the results (adjusting the scores before release): 'those releasing this data … assumed that students have been sampled from a multivariate normal distribution'.[3] Given this assumption, almost regardless of how the students had 'performed', the statistical curves produced would have been bell shaped. The data was made to fit the curve. It is not hard to devise a set of questions and a marking scheme that results in those you test appearing to be distributed along a bell curve. But to do this you must first have it in your mind to construct the world as being like this. It is not revealed as such by observation.

---

[2] Editorial note: The 2009 PISA results were released after the original article (which this chapter was based on) was written: OECD (2010), PISA 2009 at a Glance, OECD Publishing. http://dx.doi.org/10.1787/9789264095298-en. They suggested that amongst a larger pool of countries the Netherlands remained towards the top. That country ranked 11th out of 65 countries surveyed and was significantly above the OECD average in the Mathematical proficiency of its children (*Ibid*, Figure 1.5, page 21); 11 out of 65 in Science (*Ibid*, Figure 1.8, page 27) and 10th out of 65 in Reading (*Ibid* Figure 1.2, page 15). The UK ranked 28th, 16th and 25th respectively. The PISA results remain a useful source of information on educational outcomes, just as early experiments on making humans smoke remain a useful source of information on health outcomes. That does not mean that either kind of study is necessarily something we should wish to see repeated.

[3] OECD, PISA 2006 Technical Report, Paris 2009.

**Figure 1:** Distribution of children by ability (per cent) according to the OECD, 2006

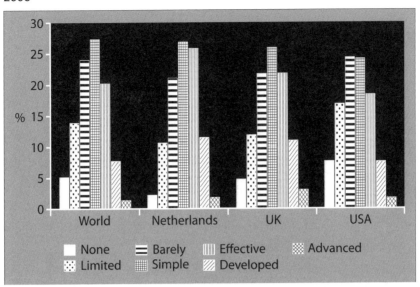

*Editorial note:* The shortening of the labels is my work. See debate in 2010 in the journal *Radical Statistics* on that.

*Source:* Data given in OECD PISA Report 2007 (derived from figures in table 1, page 20 of that report)

It goes without saying, of course, that there is very little room within a bell curve to be at the top.

The knowledge base that the OECD refers to is a particular kind of knowledge that comes from a particular way of valuing people, of seeing the world, a way that came to dominate the thinking of those appointed to high office in the rich world at the start of the twenty-first century. For example, the OECD uses the results of its international comparative exercises for the purpose of making claims that 'having a larger number of schools that compete for students was associated with better results'. Indeed, many of the people who work for organisations such as the OECD feel they have a duty to suggest that competition between countries, schools and pupils is good, and a duty to encourage it as much as they can. They appear to be appointed largely on the basis that they share this belief, and that – in the case of the education section – they can produce tables showing how many children are doing badly, how few are doing well, and, by inference, how much better prepared the large majority need to be to achieve such things as 'Science Competencies for Tomorrow's World'. Their imagined tomorrow's world is a utopia where all will benefit from increased competition, from being labelled by their apparent competencies. This is a place where it is imagined that the good of the many is most enhanced by promoting the ability of the few.

Another way of understanding the cultural embeddedness of concepts of intelligence and intelligence testing is to observe that ever since we have been trying to measure 'intelligence' we have found its levels to have been rising dramatically. This is true across almost all countries in which we have tried to measure it.[4] The average child in 1900 measured by today's standards would appear to be an imbecile, mentally retarded, a 'virtual automaton'. Our intelligence when measured is so much greater than that of our parents that you would think they might have wondered at the extraordinary subtlety of their children's conversations. All that actually happened, of course, was that in affluent countries over the course of the last century most people became better fed, and were better educated in the kinds of scientific thinking which score highly under intelligence tests.

## IQism: the underlying rationale for the growth of elitism

The merits of thinking of intelligence as something of which each individual has an allotted quotient (i.e. the concept of IQ), through having its origin in earlier theories of innate ability, was pushed forward fastest in Britain in the 1950s, when almost all eleven year olds were subjected to testing to determine which kind of secondary school they would be sent to. In the later 1960s and 1970s this brutal sorting of children into camps was challenged, and the comprehensive system was widely introduced. But today the beliefs which lead to this discrimination against the many have once more become the mainstream beliefs of those who make recommendations over how an affluent economy should be run.

The assumption underpinning the concept of IQ is that intellectual ability is limited physically, like height. (Most people who were initially told of the idea were also told that their IQ was high; while the people who propagated the idea thought that their own IQs were even higher.) But thinking is as much like height as singing is like weight. You can think on your own, but you best learn to think with others. Education does not unfold from within but is almost all 'induction from without'.[5] There are no real 'know-nothings'. We are all occasionally stupid, especially when we have not had

---

[4] See for example Tuddenham, R. D. (1948) 'Soldier intelligence in World Wars I and II', *American Psychologist*, 3; Flynn, J.R. (1984) 'The mean IQ of Americans: massive gains 1932 to 1978', *Psychological Bulletin*, 95; Flynn, J.R. (1987) 'Massive IQ gains in 14 nations', *Psychological Bulletin* 101.

[5] White, J. (2002) *The child's mind*, Falmer: Routledge, p 76.

enough sleep, or feel anxious and 'don't think'. We are similarly all capable of singing or not singing, singing better or worse, singing in groups or alone.

What is seen as good singing is remarkably culturally specific, varying greatly by time and place. Work hard at your singing in a particular time and place and people will say you sing well if you sing as you are supposed to. It is possible to rank singing, to grade it, and to believe that some singing is truly awful while some is exquisite, but the truth of this is as much in the culture and ear of the listener as it is from the vocal cords of the performer. Someone has almost certainly been silly enough to propose that human beings have singing limits which are distributed along a bell-shaped curve. After all is said, we are all capable of being stupid. But the bell-curve-of-singing idea did not catch on. We are not as vain about how good we are at yodelling in the shower as we are about being told we are especially clever.

The misconception of the existence of 'gifted' people grew out of beliefs that talents were bestowed by the gods, who each originally had their own special gifts (of speed, art, or drinking, say). The misconception was useful for explaining away the odd serf who could not be suppressed in ancient times, or the few poor boys who rose in rank a century ago. But then ideas about intelligence changed, and such a distribution of "a few with talent" was abandoned in favour of a distribution reshaped as bell-curved: the bell curve as a general description of the population became popular as more people were required to fulfil social functions that had not existed in such abundance before: engine operator, teacher, tester. This led to the creation of tests that could produce a bell-curved set of statistics.

If you apply an IQ test to a population that the test was not designed specifically for, most people will either do very badly or very well; they will not perform in a way that produces a bell-curve distribution. Tests have to be designed and calibrated to result in such an outcome. In a more equal society, the aim would be to move the rising bars of the curve to those found rightwards, and attempts were made in this direction during the 1970s. However, in the neoliberal era we have returned to a more restricted view of the distribution of talents.

Although in the affluent west we are now almost all fed well enough not to have our cognitive capabilities limited physically through the effects of malnutrition (on the brain), and more and more children are better nurtured and cared for as infants, and although we are now rich enough to afford for almost all to be allowed to learn in ways our parents and grandparents were mostly not allowed, we still hold back from giving all children that encouragement and, instead, tell most from a very early age that they are not up to the level of 'the best in the class'. And never can be – by definition.

Within our families all our children are special, but outside those cocoons they are quickly ranked, told that to sing they need to enter talent shows that only a tiny proportion can win, told that to learn they need to work harder than the rest and – more importantly – need to be 'gifted'.

Children need to be 'gifted', it is now commonly said, to attain the level of a well developed 'level 5' child (see Figure 1). They need to be 'especially gifted' to be that seventh of a seventh that reach 'level 6', and it is harder still to win a rung on the places endlessly stacked above that scale. Most are told that even if they work hard they can at best only expect to rise one or two levels, to hope to be simple rather than no-knowing; or to have effective knowledge, to be a useful cog in a machine, rather than just be a simpleton (if you do particularly well). Aspiring to reach more than one grade above your lot in life is seen as fanciful.

Arguing that there is not a mass of largely limited children out there is portrayed as misguided fancy by the elitists. Most of the elitists say this quietly, but occasionally a few say what they think in public, and I have collected some of these musings in the book from which this article is drawn[6]. Such public outbursts are not the isolated musings of a few discredited former schools' inspectors or other mavericks. They reveal what is generally believed by the kinds of people that run the governments that appoint such people to be schools' inspectors. It is just that elitist politicians tend to have more sense than to tell their electorate that they believe most of them to be so limited in ability.

You might think that what the OECD educationalists are doing is trying to move societies from extreme inequality in education, to a world of much greater equality. However, the distribution of 'ability' is not progressively changing shape from left-skewed to right-skewed. As the figures show, in countries such as the Netherlands, Finland, Japan and Canada, the system teaches more children what they need to know to reach the higher levels. In those countries it is less common to present a story of children having innate differences. But in other countries, such as the United Kingdom, Portugal, Mexico and the United States, where more are allowed to learn very little, children are more often talked about as coming from 'different stock'.[7] The position of each country on the scale of how elitist their education systems are also varies over time. In fact, ways in which different groups are treated differently within countries at different times can be monitored by looking at changes in IQ test results. This evidence clearly demonstrates that the tests measure how well children have been taught to pass them. That is

---

[6] See Dorling, D. (2010) *Injustice: Why social inequality persists*, Bristol: The Policy Press. For one example see Clark, L. (2009) 'Middle-class children have better genes, says former schools chief … and we just have to accept it', *Daily Mail*, 13 May.

[7] See Chapter 8 (on education) in: Wilkinson, R. and Pickett, K. (2009) *The spirit level: Why more equal societies almost always do better*, London: Allen Lane.

why the generation you are born into matters so much in determining IQ. Intelligence tests have nothing to do with anything innate.[8]

## The return to elitism

In the United States the 'IQ gap' between black and white Americans fell between the 1940s and the 1970s, but by the start of the twenty-first century inequality had risen back to 1940s levels. The move away from, and then back to, elitism occurred in tandem with changes in the social position and relative deprivation of black versus white Americans.[9] From the 1940s to the 1970s black Americans won progressively higher status; they won the right to be integrated more into what had become normal economic expectations; and wages equalised a little between black and white. Then, from the 1970s to 2009 the wage gap grew; segregation increased again; and civil rights victories were rolled back by the mass incarceration of young black men. Measured levels of ability decreased in relative terms at around the same rate.

Treating a few people as especially able inevitably entails treating others as especially unable. And if you treat people like dirt you can watch them become more stupid before your eyes – or at least through their answers to your multiple choice questions in public examinations, and in their restricted options in life thereafter. From the 1970s onwards poor Americans, and especially poor black Americans, were progressively treated more and more like dirt. To a lesser extent similar trends occurred in many other parts of the affluent world, in all the rich countries where income inequalities grew. And they grew most where IQism became most accepted.

IQism can be a self-fulfilling prophesy. If you believe that only a few children are especially able, then you concentrate your resources on them and subsequently they will tend to appear to do well. They will certainly pass your tests, as the tests are designed to pass a certain number, and the children you selected will have been chosen and then taught to pass the tests. Young people respond well to praise to learn, and get smarter when they learn as a result. The young respond badly to disrespect; it reduces their motivation to learn: they perform badly in tests when they are taught with

---

[8] There is not space here to go into all the research on IQ and genetics. But see, for example, footnote 3 on page 195 above on J.R. Flynn's insightful discussion on identical twins, which argues that it is possible to take his logic one step further and propose that similar appearance could be key to explaining away apparently innate ability. Teachers and other adults tend to treat and teach children differently according partly to their physical appearance. For the tiny differences that would need to be explained by this see: *What is intelligence? Beyond the Flynn effect*, Cambridge University Press, 2007. See also his open access lecture www. psychometrics.sps.cam.ac.uk/page/109/beyond-the-flynn-effect.htm.
[9] M. Gladwell, (2007) 'What I.Q. doesn't tell you about race', *New Yorker*, 17 December.

little respect. Telling children they rank lowly in a class is a way of telling them that they have not earned respect.

Children are not particularly discerning about what they are taught. They will try to do well at IQ tests if you train them to try to do well at IQ tests. Almost all people want to fit in, to be praised, not to rank towards the bottom, not to be seen as a liability. Indeed it was recognition of these effects that helped drive educationists' campaigns for an end to the 11-plus system in the 1970s.

Unfortunately, greater equality of opportunity is almost always seen as a threat to the relatively privileged. And, although the start of the 1970s was a great time to be ordinary in affluent countries, and not a bad time to be poor, it was a disconcerting time if you were affluent. Inflation was high; if you were well off enough to have savings, those savings were being eroded. You began to realise that your children were not going to be as cushioned as you were by so much relative wealth, by going to different schools from most children. When politicians said that they were going to eradicate the evil of ignorance by educating all in Britain, or that they were going to have a 'Great Society' in America, they did not mention that this would reduce the apparent advantages that your children had. Equal rights for black children, a level playing field for poor children – these were seen as threats in a race in which only a few can win. And as the economy deteriorated in the late 1970s, this fear of equality grew, and so did the backlash against the progressive changes of the 1960s and 1970s.

It is not hard for most people to know that they are not very special. Even affluent people, if not delusional, know in their heart of hearts that they are not very special; most know that they were members of what some call the 'lucky sperm club', born to the right parents, or just lucky – or perhaps both lucky and a little ruthless. It is only those with the strongest of narcissistic tendencies who think they became affluent because they were more able. Those who couple such tendencies with eugenicist beliefs think their children are likely to inherit their supposed acumen. The rest – the vast majority of the rich, who are not so stupid – had a choice when greater equality appeared on the horizon. They codriveuld throw in their lot with the masses, send their children to the local school, see their comparative wealth evaporate with inflation and join the party, or they could try to defend their corner, pay for their children to be segregated from others, and look for ways to maintain their advantages, in particular by voting into power politicians who shared their concerns. They managed to convince enough voters that politicians of the centre left – who were responsible for this levelling of the playing field – had been a shambles. They did this in both the United States and United Kingdom. In Britain in 1979, and in the United States in 1980, the right won office.

As segregation of children in different state secondary schools in Britain was being (to a large extent) abolished, a boom began in the private sector, in newly segregated 'independent' schooling. At the same time changes were gradually introduced into the state sector that allowed increasing levels of competition within an allegedly comprehensive system. By 2007 the English school system had become a market system, in which schools competed for money and children. The expansion of private schools was accompanied by the introduction of 57 varieties of state school. Privately educated children (7 per cent of the total) took one quarter of all advanced level examinations and gained over half the places in 'top' universities.[10] The better funded of the 57 varieties of state school accounted for most of the rest of elite places (supplemented by those who had some other advantage at home). Elitist systems claim to be meritocracies, but in such systems almost no-one gets to the top without substantially benefiting from the unequal distribution of educational opportunities.

To believe that your children are in the top fifth requires first to believe that there *is* a top fifth. At any one time you can subject a group of children to testing and a fifth can be singled out as doing best. That fifth will be slightly more likely than their peers to rank in the top fifth in any other related test, but that does not mean that there is an actual top fifth that is waiting to be identified. The higher the correlations between different tests, the more the same children come to be selected as being in that top fifth under different test regimes. The more this happens, the more they will have been coached to perform well, and the more likely they are to live in a society that takes the idea of such testing seriously – a society, from government to classroom, that implicitly accepts the idea of inherent differences in ability, in intelligence quotas (or quotients), even when not explicitly admitting that they do. It is the smallest of steps from that position to accept that what you think is inherent is inherited.

From putting prize winners on pedestals to putting whole populations in prisons, how we treat each other reveals how we see each other. This IQism has become the current dominant unquestioned underlying belief of most educational policy-makers in the more unequal of affluent nations.[11]

People who have taught the children of the affluent classes at the universities they go to have seen the result of this growth in elitism. These children have been educationally force-fed enough facts to obtain strings of A grades, but they are no more geniuses than anyone else. There is a tragedy in making young people pretend to have super-human mental abilities which neither they nor anyone else possess. To justify their situation they have to

---

[10] Tomlinson, S. (2007) 'Learning to compete', *Renewal*, vol 15, nos 2/3, p 120.
[11] Gillborn, D. and Youdell, D. (2000) *Rationing education: Policy practice, reform and equity*, Buckingham: Open University Press.

swallow and repeat the lie being told more and more often; that only a few are especially able and that those few are disproportionately found amongst the higher social classes.

In the more unequal affluent countries, such as Britain and the United States, it has become a little more common in recent years for the elite to suggest amongst themselves that children born to working class or black parents simply have less natural ability than those born to higher class or white parents.[12] The people who say such things are merely a little more bold in uttering the claims made commonly, if discreetly, by the class they are in or have joined. They often go on to quietly suggest that children of different class backgrounds tend to do better or worse in school on account of some 'complex interplay of sociocultural and genetic factors'.[13] It may sound more nuanced to include words such as 'complex', and 'sociocultural' in your educational parlance, but once 'genetic factors' are brought into the equation all nuance is lost. 'Genetic factors' can be used to defend arguments that any category of less privileged people – women, black people, working class people – is (it is often claimed) inherently less able. Slip 'genetic factors' into your argument and you cross a line.

Sadly, it is belief in mumbo jumbo like the IQ gene that results in teachers being asked around the rich world to *identify* children who may become especially 'gifted and talented', with all the consequences that that implies. At times these assumptions are made explicit, such as in the official proposals to change English Education Law in 2005 in which it was claimed that: 'we must make sure that every pupil – gifted and talented, struggling or just average – reaches the *limits* of their capability'.[14] In England the idea that different children have different limits has for so long been part of the social landscape that, despite the best efforts and advice, it still underlies key thinking.

Yet we all become more able through learning. We learn collectively. And it is through learning together that we will eventually come to understand.

---

[12] In Britain in 1997, the then head of the nation's Economic and Social Research Council and his colleagues suggested that there was the possibility: '… that children born to working-class parents simply have less natural ability than those born to higher-class parents'. Documented in White, S. (2007) *Equality*, Cambridge: Polity Press, p 66.

[13] '…children of different class backgrounds tend to do better or worse in school - on account, one may suppose, of a complex interplay of sociocultural and genetic factors.' Goldthorpe, J. and Jackson, M. (2007) 'Education-based meritocracy: the barriers to its realisation', *Economic change, quality of life and social cohesion 6th framework network*; see www.equalsoc.org/uploaded_files/regular/goldthorpe_jackson.pdf.

[14] Cited in Ball, S.J. (2008) *The education debate*, Bristol: The Policy Press, p 180, quoting from the 2005 DfES White Paper on 'Higher standards: Better schools for all', p 20, paragraph 1.28 (emphasis added).

# 27

# The super-rich are still soaring away[1]

*New Statesman* (2010) April

> …It is not sustainable for social inequality to continue to rise
> at its current rate…

Has anyone noticed that this week we entered the end of times? You know, when the impossible begins to happen: all that is solid turns into dust - that kind of thing? There had been signs for some time. Things began to happen that simply could not continue.

Take immortality for a start. The most recent figures for life expectancy in the Royal Borough of Kensington and Chelsea saw life expectancy rise by more than a year in a year last year. Randeep Ramesh, writing in *The Guardian* on Wednesday[2] noted that in 2008, a female born in London's exclusive Kensington and Chelsea could expect to live until 88.9 – a year earlier she would have reached 87.8. That's an increase of one year (and just

---

[1] Editorial note: References have been inserted back into this chapter from the draft article. They were not included when it was first published. I have also added a few more notes to these footnotes as the changes in just a year have been remarkable.

[2] Ramesh, R. (2010) 'London's richest people worth 273 times more than the poorest', *The Guardian*, 21 April, www.guardian.co.uk/uk/2010/apr/21/wealth-social-divide-health-inequality

a tad more than one month) in life expectancy of women across that entire area. What's strange about that you might ask? Well, what would happen if it were to continue? People in the Royal Borough, women at least, would never die! Are the residents of Kensington and Chelsea becoming immortal or are we currently living in the strangest of times? I opt for the latter.

In Glasgow, over the same period, life expectancy rose by less than one month, from 77.1 to 77.2 years for women in the three years ending 2007 to the three ending 2008. These are the latest figures that ONS have released. That same estimate fell from 70.8 to 70.7 for men living in Glasgow although such a small fall might be due to chance.[3] Britain has yet to experience what is already happening in the USA: absolute falls in life expectancy in certain areas, children just beginning to live shorter lives than their parents in the poorest of places – while the rich and super-rich still pull away and see their lives stretch out ever further ahead of them.

It is not so much the stalling of improvements to living standards in the poorest of areas that is pointing towards an end to times as we have known them, but what is happening in the richest of areas. In talks in recent weeks I have been commenting on house prices in Central West London and saying how remarkable it was that while housing prices across many parts of Britain are falling, they have been rising, by as much as £200,000 for a two-bed flat a year, again in that Royal Borough of Kensington and Chelsea (from around £500,000 a flat in 2008 to well over £700,000 a flat in 2009). Then this weekend *The Observer* published a map showing those flats standing at an average price of £821,496 as of January 2010. What?! Another £100,000 pound a piece for even average pieces of property in that part of London? What's going on?[4]

The *Sunday Times* finally gave us a clue in its publication of the annual Rich List (also this weekend). The wealth of the super-rich in Britain had risen by 29.9 per cent in the year to 2010. It is now said to stand at £335.5bn for the best-off 1,000 people combined (or £335 million each if shared

---

[3] Editorial note: A year later rises of several months were reported in life expectancy in Glasgow for both men and women so it would appear unlikely, as yet that a real fall had begun in 2008. However, even by the start of 2011 most of the public sector cuts to hit Glasgow and the lowering of living standards there were only just beginning.

[4] Editorial note: By the end of 2010 the BBC was reporting that the *average* price of a home in the Royal Borough of Kensington and Chelsea had risen by 12.1% to stand at £1,272,398. The mean price for a detached house rose to £7.1 million, a semi or terraced house was now priced at £3 million, and a flat at £814,000. The increase recorded in that last quarter alone had been 17.7%. See: BBC (2010) *UK house prices: July-September 2010*, 17 November, http://news.bbc.co.uk/1/shared/spl/hi/in_depth/uk_house_prices/html/aw.stm

**Chapter 4:** Figure 1: Poverty in Yorkshire in 1980 and 2000 [see page 50]

The rise in density in the number of breadline poor in Yorkshire in 2000 (top) as compared to 1980 (above). Poverty in Bradford, Yorkshire, in the mid-1970s (right).
Maps: University of Sheffield

**Chapter 4:** Figure 2: Time Trends [see page 51]

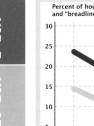

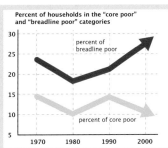

Percent of households in the "core poor" and "breadline poor" categories

percent of breadline poor

percent of core poor

Percent of households in the "assett rich" and "exclusively rich" categories

percent of asset rich

percent of exclusively rich

- Poverty and core poverty levels fell through the 1970s.
- They both then increased, returning by 1990 to similar levels to 1970.
- During the 1980s, while poverty levels were increasing, so were the proportions of asset rich households.
- Exclusively rich households declined during the 1970s and 1980s, but increased during the 1990s.
- The 1990s saw a continuing rise in breadline poverty levels, with a concurrent decline in core poverty.
- During the early 1990s, the percentage of asset rich households fell, but then recovered in the second half of the decade.

The colour scale (left) shows the percent of poor households

**Chapter 4:** Figure 3: Poverty in London and the South East in 1980 and 2000 [see page 52]

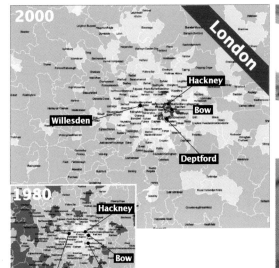

The rise in density in the number of breadline poor (top) in London in 2000 as compared to 1980 (above). Poverty in Tower Hamlets, east London last year (right).

Picture: Jess Hurd/reportdigital.co.uk

**Chapter 4:** Figure 4: Poverty in Britain in 1970, 1990 and 2000 [see page 55]

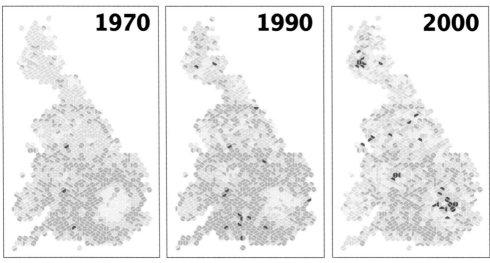

**Poverty hotspots across Britain in 1970, 1990 and 2000. The maps show the growing concentration of poor areas.**
The proportion of households in each area who are poor is indicated by colour (key below).
Every half-hexagon is half a parliamentary constituency.

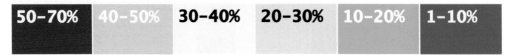

| 50–70% | 40–50% | 30–40% | 20–30% | 10–20% | 1–10% |

**Chapter 23:** Figure 3: Which type of university people aged 18–19 are most likely to attend by area of residence at age 15 [see page 176]

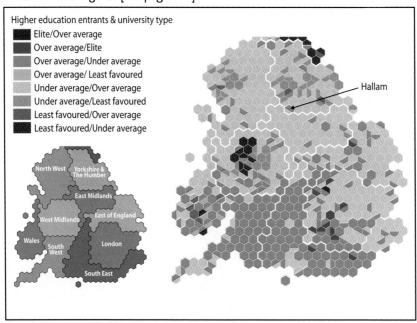

Source: Thomas and Dorling (2007) pp 100–03.

**Chapter 29:** Figure 1: Most disadvantaged to most advantaged neighbourhoods: normalcy score [see page 223]

*Note:* This is a cartogram showing every parliamentary constituency in Britain as a hexagon with roughly similar populations and hence sizes. The divisions within each constituency are also shown.

**Chapter 36:** Figure 2: A fragment of Booth's descriptive map of London poverty [see page 266]

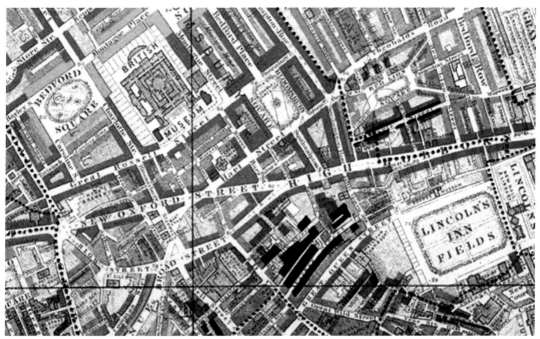

*Source:* Dorling et al (2000) Figure 1. Detail: Booth's maps. Key: Yellow: Upper-middle and Upper classes. Wealthy, Red: Well-to-do. Middle-class, Pink: Fairly comfortable. Good ordinary earning, Purple: Mixed. Some comfortable, others poor, Pale Blue: Poor. 18s. to 21s. a week for moderate family, Dark blue: Very poor, casual. Chronic want, Black: Lowest class. Vicious, semi-criminal.

**Chapter 36:** Figure 3: Plan of the city of York – slum areas to servant keeping classes [see page 267]

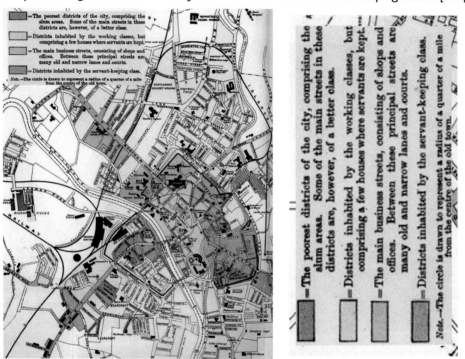

*Source:* Seebohm Rowntree, B. (2000 [1901]) *Poverty: A study of town life*, Bristol: The Policy Press.

**Chapter 36:** Figure 6: Vickers map: York 2001 [see page 274]

*Key:* Blue: "Idyllic Countryside"; Orange: "Comfortable Estates"; Light Green: "Typical Traits"; Brown: Inner City Multi Cultural (not found in York); Dark Green: "Blue Collar"; Red: "Melting Pot"; Purple: "Constrained by Circumstances". Source: Map supplied by Dan Vickers, when PhD student, University of Leeds. Based on analysis of the 2001 census jointly with the Office for National Statistics, unpublished at that time.

**Chapter 36:** Figure 8: Highest poverty neighbourhoods in Detroit, 1970–2000 [see page 276]

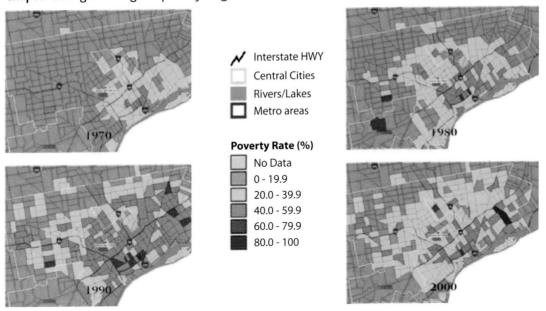

*Source:* Jargowsky (2003) Figure 5.

**Chapter 36:** Figure 9: Breadline poor households across the Liverpool/Manchester area, 1970 to 2000 [see page 277]

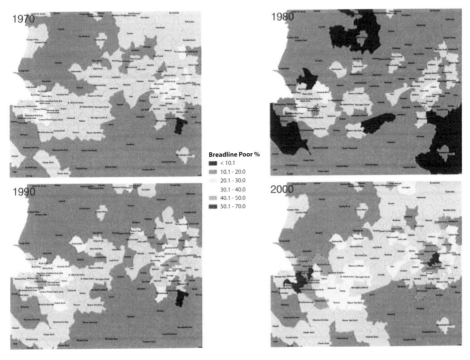

*Source:* Figure 2. Dorling et al (2007)

**Chapter 36:** Figure 10: Breadline poor households across the Home Counties (including London), 1970 to 2000 [see page 278]

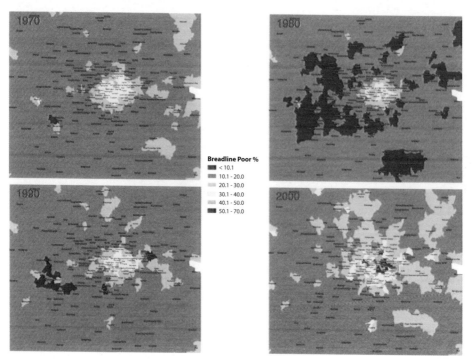

*Source:* As above.

**Chapter 36:** Figure 11: Asset wealthy households across the Home Counties (including London), 1980 to 2000 [see page 279]

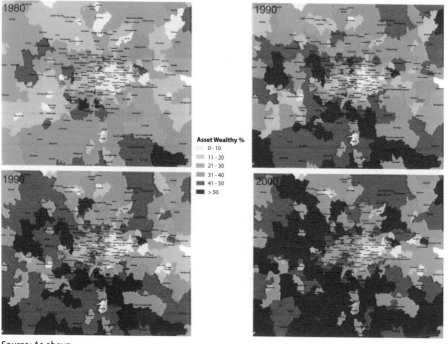

*Source:* As above.

**Chapter 36:** Figure 12: Distributions of the breadline poor in 2001 and the change in their numbers 1991–2001 by constituency [see page 280]

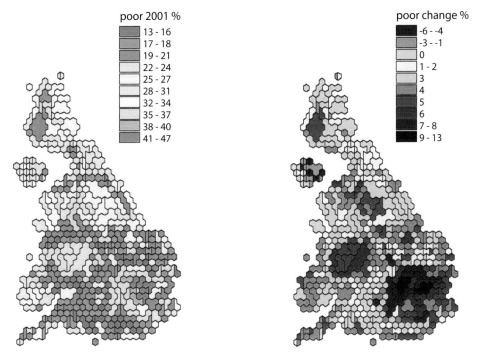

*Source:* Dorling, D and Thomas, B. (2004) *People and places: A 2001 census atlas*, Bristol: The Policy Press.

**Chapter 36:** Figure 13: Distributions of the 6% exclusive wealthy and the 11% core poor around the year 2000 [see page 280]

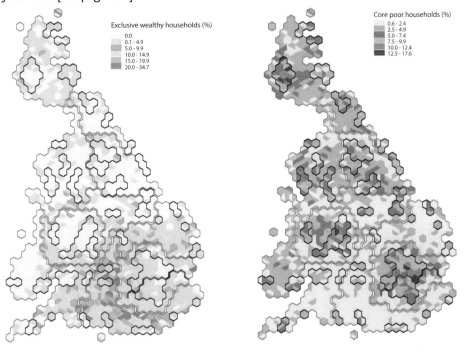

*Source:* Thomas, B. and Dorling, D. (2007) *Identity in Britain: A cradle-to-grave atlas*, Bristol: The Policy Press.

**Chapter 36:** Figure 16: Worldmapper maps of the lowest and highest incomes living on under 1$ a day:...over 200$ a day [see page 283]

*living on under 1$ a day:*

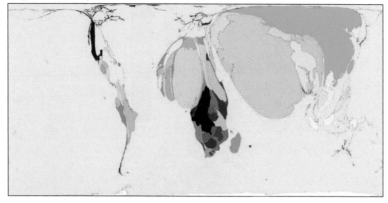

*...over 200$ a day*

*Note:* All in Purchasing Power Parity (PPP) $'s
*Source:* www.worldmapper.org

**Chapter 36:** Figure 17: Visualisations of world income, a and b [see page 286]

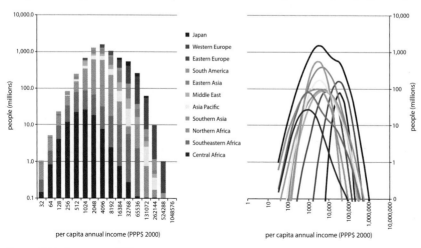

*Source :* Table 1 - see page 285

**Chapter 40:** Figure 1a: Rich world female mortality rates 1850–2000 (per year per 1,000) [see page 312]

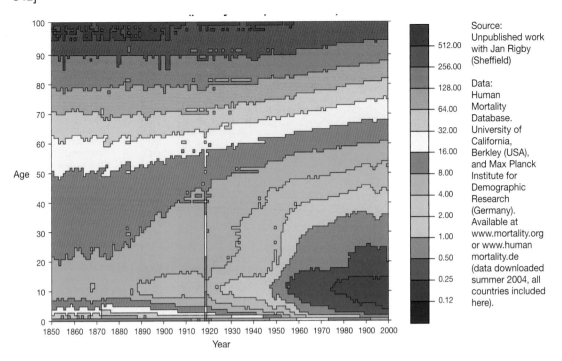

**Chapter 40:** Figure 1b: Rich world male/female mortality rates 1850–2000 (per year per cohort) [see page 312]

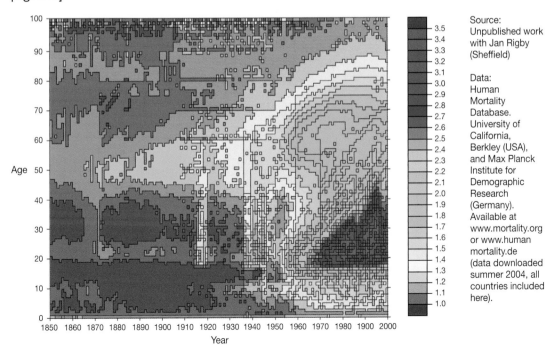

**Chapter 40:** Figure 2a: USA male/female mortality ratios 1900–2071 (per year per cohort) [see page 313]

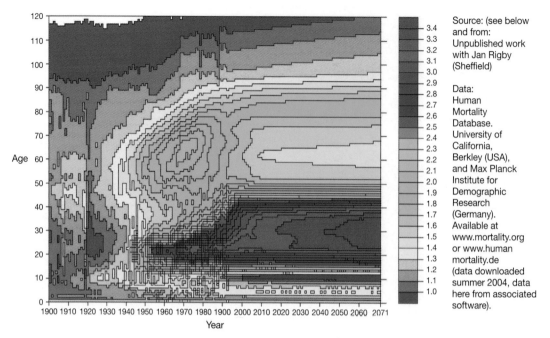

Source: Life Tables for the United States Social Security Area 1900-2080 by Felicitie C. Bell *et al*.

**Chapter 40:** Figure 2b: England–Wales male/female mortality ratios 1840–2050 (year/cohort) [see page 314]

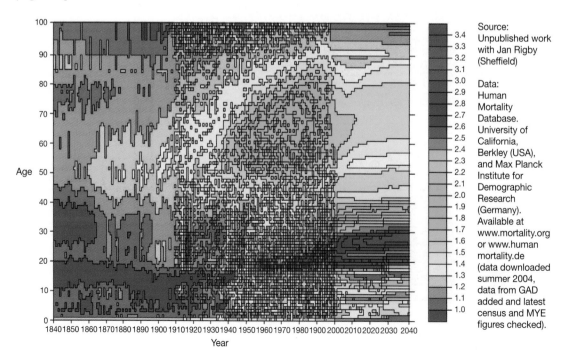

**Chapter 40:** Figure 3a: Sickness and disability in the Uk in 2001 and change from 1991 [see page 315]

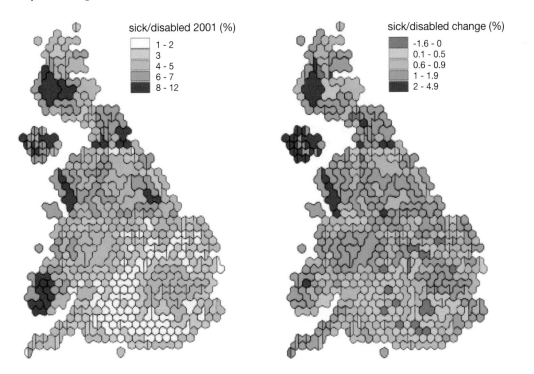

**Chapter 40:** Figure 3b: Limiting long term illness in the UK in 2001 and change from 1991 [see page 315]

## Chapter 40: Figure 4a: Key to the human geography of the UK [see page 317]

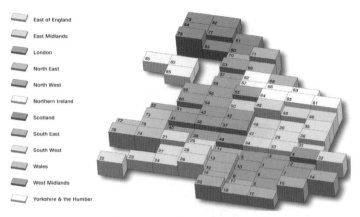

- East of England
- East Midlands
- London
- North East
- North West
- Northern Ireland
- Scotland
- South East
- South West
- Wales
- West Midlands
- Yorkshire & the Humber

Key to the Human Geography
of the UK

1 London Central
2 London East
3 London North
4 London North East
5 London North West
6 London South & Surrey East
7 London South East
8 London South Inner
9 London South West
10 London West
11 Buckinghamshire & Oxfordshire East
12 East Sussex & Kent South
13 Hampshire North & Oxford
14 Kent East
15 Kent West
16 South Downs West
17 Surrey
18 Sussex West
19 Thames Valley
20 Wight & Hampshire South
21 Bristol
22 Cornwall & West Plymouth
23 Devon & East Plymouth
24 Dorset & East Devon
25 Gloucestershire
26 Itchen, Test & Avon
27 Somerset & North Devon
28 Wiltshire North & Bath
29 Bedfordshire & Milton Keynes
30 Cambridgeshire
31 Essex North & Suffolk South
32 Essex South
33 Essex West & Hertfordshire East
34 Hertfordshire
35 Norfolk
36 Suffolk & South West Norfolk
37 Birmingham East
38 Birmingham West
39 Coventry & North Warwickshire
40 Herefordshire & Shropshire
41 Midlands West
42 Staffordshire East & Derby
43 Staffordshire West & Congleton
44 Worcestershire & South Warwickshire
45 Leicester
46 Lincolnshire
47 Northamptonshire & Blaby
48 Nottingham & Leicestershire North West
49 Nottinghamshire North & Chesterfield
50 Peak District
51 Cheshire East
52 Cheshire West & Wirral
53 Cumbria & Lancashire North
54 Greater Manchester Central
55 Greater Manchester East
56 Greater Manchester West
57 Lancashire Central
58 Lancashire South
59 Merseyside East & Wigan
60 Merseyside West
61 East Yorkshire & North Lincolnshire
62 Leeds
63 North Yorkshire
64 Sheffield
65 Yorkshire South
66 Yorkshire South West
67 Yorkshire West
68 Cleveland & Richmond
69 Durham
70 Northumbria
71 Tyne & Wear
72 Mid & West Wales
73 North Wales
74 South Wales Central
75 South Wales East
76 South Wales West
77 Central Scotland
78 Glasgow
79 Highlands & Islands
80 Lothian
81 Mid Scotland & Fife
82 North East Scotland
83 South of Scotland
84 West of Scotland
85 Northen Ireland: (3 seats)

## Chapter 40: Figure 4b: The geography becomes simpler over time [see page 317]

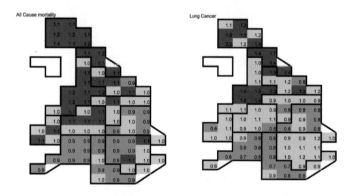

Source: Mortality records and population estimates, calculated for *The Human Geography of the UK* book

## Chapter 40: Figure 4c: Trends in UK inequalities – life expectancy and income [see page 317]

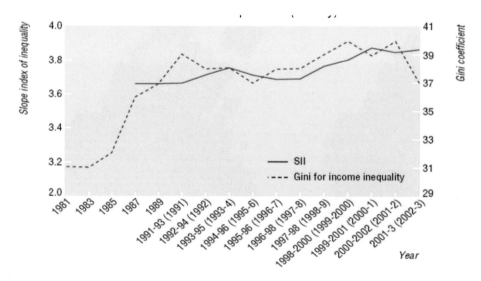

**Chapter 40:** Figure 5a: Demand for the health industry [see page 319]

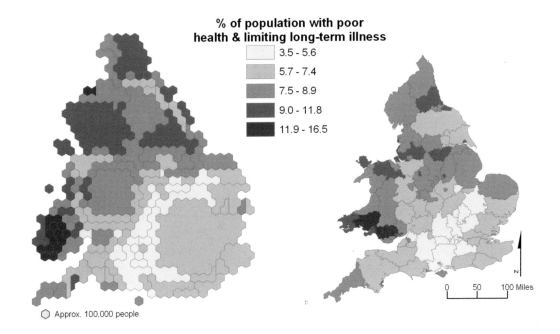

**Chapter 40:** Figure 5b: Supply for the health industry [see page 319]

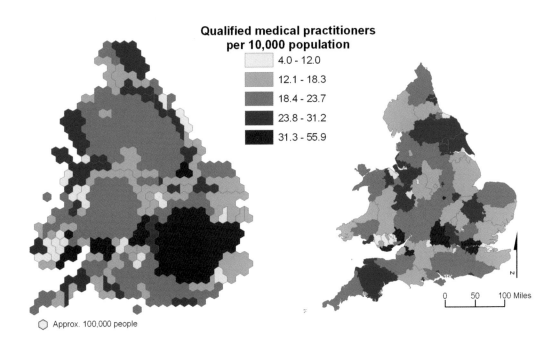

## Chapter 40: Figures 7a-7e: Population, life expectancy, health spending [see page 321]

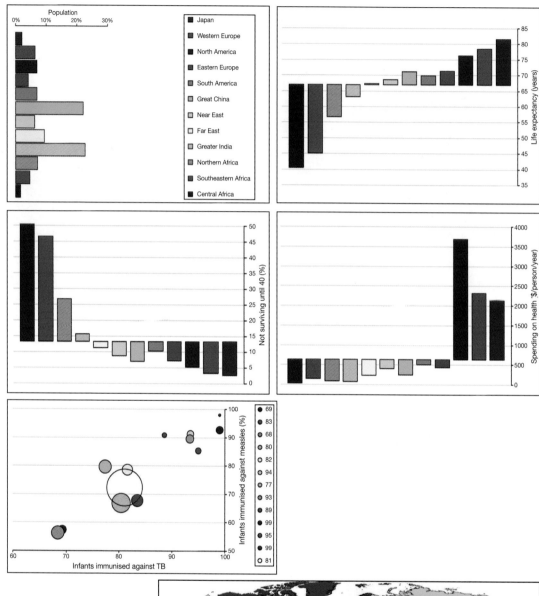

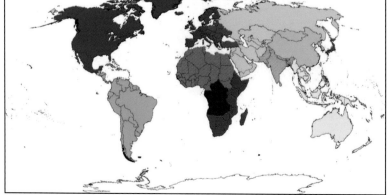

**Chapter 40:** Figures 8a-8f: HIV, GDP, infant mortality, life expectancy, income [see page 323]

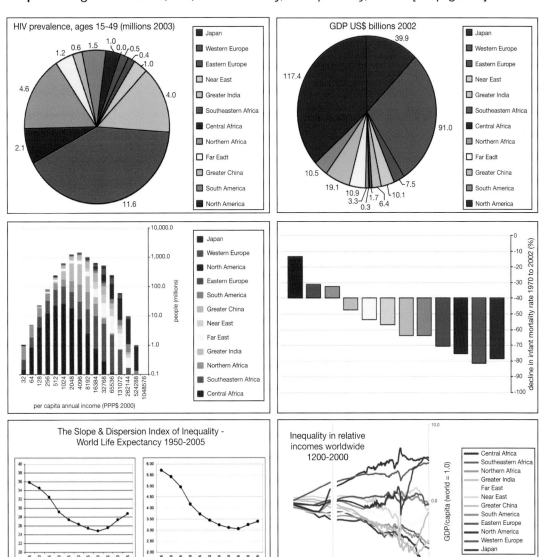

**Chapter 51:** Figure 1: Worldmapper population cartogram [see page 381]

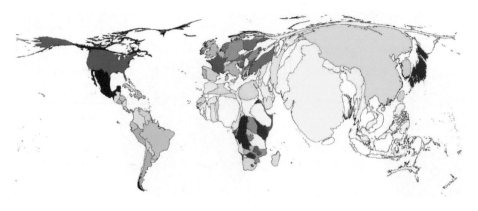

**Chapter 51:** Figure 2: Grid-based world population cartogram (2000) [see page 381]

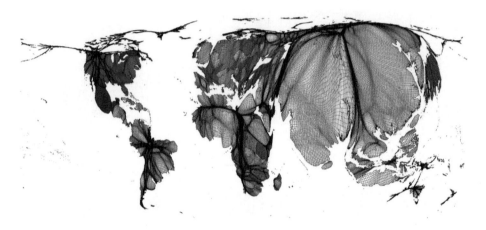

**Chapter 51:** Figure 3: Grid-based population cartogram of the contiguous United States (2000) [see page 382]

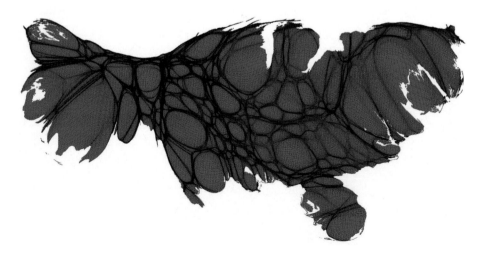

out 'fairly').[5] The *Daily Telegraph* nicely summarised what the *Sunday Times* was reporting.[6]

OK – how sustainable is that? Take a 29.9 per cent annual rise in wealth and apply it again to the super-rich. Within four years, their wealth would double to £955bn in total. In just 22 years they would hold some £106trillion between the 1,000 of them. You start running out of planets at this point. Short of extra-terrestrials coming down from space delivering pallets of gold to the most wealthy people in Britain there is no way in which the current excesses of the rich can be continued. Even for only a few years. The best-off 1,000 people each picked up an extra £77m last year - that's £77m a piece (net of all outgoings). Next year that will be an extra £100m each for the 1,000 people at the top of the rich list unless this acceleration in inequality abates.

It will end because it has to – because it is not physically, not humanly, not even biologically possible for our current rates of inequality to continue to rise as they are rising. The rich are profiting by lending money to struggling governments at exorbitant rates. Prices are rising so quickly in Kensington because the pound has fallen so overseas super-rich are moving in ("investing" from abroad). Life expectancy is rocketing in the most affluent of places because anyone who is not hitting all the jackpots there now has to leave, they cannot afford to stay. But soon the very rich will have to move home too, to make room for the new super-super-rich.

Oh – vested interest – I've written a book about it: *Injustice: Why social inequality persists*. It came out last week. It was printed just a few weeks earlier and all the facts checked out fine then – but, already, it looks conservative in what it was describing. I don't think the super-rich had the accuracy of my data at heart when they strove to become so much more affluent in such a short amount of time.

When the BBC reported the super-rich seeing their wealth rise more than it has ever been recorded to before, at 10.29pm as the last story on the Sunday night news,[7] they suggested that this was good news – a sign that the economy recovery was happening. It makes you wonder how they would report a plague of frogs falling from the sky, or an ash cloud, say. Do we need to start wandering around and saying the end is nigh? Or should we start looking at where the solution to some of our problems of national debt might lie – very close to home?

---

[5] Editorial note: There was an error in the original article which read "or £3.3bn each if shared out 'fairly'". Although many people commented on the article nobody noticed my inability to divide by 1,000.

[6] Coping, J. (2010) *Sunday Times Rich List 2010: Britain's richest see wealth rise by one third*, 24 April, www.telegraph.co.uk/finance/personalfinance/7624159/Sunday-Times-Rich-List-2010-Britains-richest-see-wealth-rise-by-one-third.html

[7] BBC news at 10, 24 April 2010.

**Table 1: Additional** Table – The wealth of the superrich under two scenarios[8]

| Year | Rises (£bn) | Falls (£bn) | Year | Rises (£bn) | Falls (£bn) |
|------|-------------|-------------|------|-------------|-------------|
| 2009 | 258 | 258 | 2021 | 5,962 | 5.9 |
| 2010 | 336 | 189 | 2022 | 7,745 | 4.3 |
| 2011 | 436 | 138 | 2023 | 10,060 | 3.1 |
| 2012 | 566 | 100 | 2024 | 13,068 | 2.3 |
| 2013 | 735 | 73 | 2025 | 16,976 | 1.7 |
| 2014 | 955 | 54 | 2026 | 22,052 | 1.2 |
| 2015 | 1,241 | 39 | 2027 | 28,645 | 0.9 |
| 2016 | 1,612 | 29 | 2028 | 37,210 | 0.7 |
| 2017 | 2,094 | 21 | 2029 | 48,336 | 0.5 |
| 2018 | 2,720 | 15 | 2030 | 62,788 | 0.3 |
| 2019 | 3,533 | 11 | 2031 | 81,561 | 0.3 |
| 2020 | 4,590 | 8.1 | 2032 | 105,948 | 0.2 |

*Note:* Scenario 1 is that the increases in their wealth as measured between 2009 and 2010 were to continue, leaving each with a mean wealth of £106 billion by 2032. Scenario 2 is if the 37% falls of 2008 to 2009 had continued, rather than reversed, which would leave each with 'just' £200,000 a piece by 2032. As of August 2011 we are closer to scenario 1 (a 25% rise 2010–2011).

---

[8] Editorial note: This table was not included in the original article. The numbers can either be read as the total wealth of the 1,000 richest in £billions, or their mean average holdings in £millions. The fall in their wealth was reported by Nikkhah, R. (2009) Sunday Times Rich List 2009 – Analysis: The Sunday Times Rich List 2009 reveals that Britain's wealthiest individuals have lost £155 billion in the last year, April 25, www.telegraph.co.uk/finance/5220243/Sunday-Times-Rich-List-2009-Analysis.html. The subsequent rise is given in the article referenced in footnote 6.

**Figure 1:** Additional graph – The change in the mean average individual wealth of the 1,000 richest people in Britain under two scenarios (£ millions)

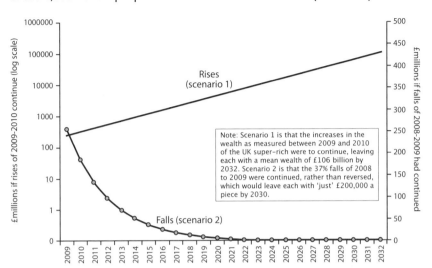

Note: Scenario 1 is that the increases in the wealth as measured between 2009 and 2010 of the UK super–rich were to continue, leaving each with a mean wealth of £106 billion by 2032. Scenario 2 is that the 37% falls of 2008 to 2009 were continued, rather than reversed, which would leave each with 'just' £200,000 a piece by 2030.

*Note:* A log scale is used on the left-hand axis under the scenario of continued rapid increases, such as those of 2009–10, in the wealth of those 1,000 people who were most wealthy to begin with. The right-hand scale simply uses an arithmetic scale to show how the wealth of those richest people would have diminished had the falls in their holdings of riches in 2008–09 continued unabated. The source of the data for this figure is in Table 1.

# SECTION VI
## Mobility and employment

This section concerns social class, movement between classes over time (social mobility) and the ways in which people still largely come to have their class assigned (employment). The story begins with a chapter from a *Guardian* article that summarises how people are increasingly members of 'poor', 'average', or 'rich' classes, and demonstrates how, in many areas, there has been a substantial decline in the proportions that fall into the 'average' categories. In 'old money' these were 'upper-working class' or 'lower-middle class'. Within this chapter it is suggested that, if current trends continue, soon only a minority of people will be 'normal' in their social position; only a minority will fit within the centre of the income range. Instead a majority will be either rich or poor.

The second chapter in this section, taken from a trade union magazine (*Rapport*), continues the theme of suggesting that soon it really will no longer be normal to be normal. Geographical residential location for many is being increasingly determined by monies that have to be inherited or gifted from relatives. Ever more differentiated incomes from employment (and interest on unearned wealth) result over time in gross inequalities in the financial endowments gifted to different groups in society. However, many affluent Britons, especially some who have retired overseas (with the help of their wealth), see the problems as caused by influxes of immigrants, not by increasing inequality. An extract from an academic paper first printed in the French language geography journal *Géocarrefour* is included next to highlight this. Its primary concern is to report on the growing dominance of London over British society and British human geography; or how the key determinant of the economic and social fortunes of major towns and cities in Britain in recent years has simply been how far they are located away from London. Its secondary concern is to highlight xenophobia among so many of the elite of England regarding their fellow citizens.

The story in this section is brought to a close with a chapter that reproduces an article originally written for the magazine *New London Review*, which was sold in only one small part of London. It reports on the extent of the divides inside London itself, on the extent of poverty, inequality, excess and suffering there. London contains both the greatest excesses of wealth and one of the largest spatial concentrations of unemployment in Western Europe. This is followed by an article from the *British Medical Journal* on the evidence for adverse health consequences from enforced labour programmes for the unemployed, and exploring what the alternatives were to mass youth unemployment in earlier periods. Those alternatives were ignored following the general election of May 2010.

# 28

# The trouble with moving upmarket

*The Guardian* (2007) 17 July

Poverty rates in Britain declined from 1968 to the late 1970s, but since then have risen continuously. Our report for the Joseph Rowntree Foundation[1] shows how this trend has been accompanied by a rise in the geographical segregation of the poor from the rich – where the two groups live physically apart.

There is some good news, though. In the most recent period, the number of households with people who are the poorest – income poor, materially deprived and subjectively poor – fell, and such very poor households also became less geographically concentrated. It has become evident that government policy can reduce that gap.

The people in the most geographically segregated social group are those who were so wealthy that they could afford to exclude themselves from the schools, hospitals, cleaning, childcare, recreation and other norms for most people in society. As they grew wealthier, however, the richest did not grow greatly in number, but became corralled in fewer and fewer parts of the country.

---

[1] *Poverty, wealth and place in Britain 1968 to 2005* by Danny Dorling and others is published by Policy Press, copy available here: http://image.guardian.co.uk/sys-files/Society/documents/2007/07/17/JRFfullreport.pdf

**Table 1:** The most divided constituencies in Britain 1980-2000

| 1980 %'s | | | 2000 %'s | | | Rank | Parliamentary Constituency |
|---|---|---|---|---|---|---|---|
| Poor | Average | Rich | Poor | Average | Rich | Out of 641 areas | |
| 9 | 67 | 24 | 15 | 24 | 61 | 1 | Chesham and Amersham |
| 10 | 77 | 13 | 15 | 36 | 50 | 2 | Surrey Heath |
| 10 | 72 | 18 | 16 | 31 | 53 | 3 | Maidenhead |
| 16 | 75 | 9 | 26 | 38 | 36 | 4 | Meriden |
| 13 | 68 | 19 | 19 | 31 | 50 | 5 | Winchester |
| 10 | 69 | 21 | 19 | 32 | 49 | 6 | Orpington |
| 12 | 72 | 17 | 18 | 35 | 47 | 7 | Windsor |
| 30 | 66 | 3 | 46 | 30 | 23 | 8 | Regent's Park and Kensington North |
| 12 | 71 | 17 | 16 | 35 | 48 | 9 | Buckingham |
| 11 | 69 | 19 | 18 | 34 | 48 | 10 | Hitchin and Harpenden |
| 30 | 68 | 2 | 48 | 32 | 19 | 11 | Islington South and Finsbury |
| 10 | 67 | 22 | 15 | 33 | 52 | 12 | North East Hampshire |
| 12 | 62 | 27 | 18 | 28 | 54 | 13 | South West Hertfordshire |
| 31 | 66 | 3 | 50 | 33 | 18 | 14 | Holborn and St Pancras |
| 12 | 65 | 23 | 18 | 32 | 50 | 15 | Tatton |

*Note:* The proportions in the three 1980s and three 2000 columns each sum to 100% (other than due to rounding). These are the 15 Constituencies with the greatest loss of households living in average circumstances in Britain 1980–2000.

At the extreme end are the most affluent parts of, for example, the Mole Valley in Surrey, and Chesham and Amersham, in Buckinghamshire. In 1980, a majority of the population in these places were neither rich nor poor. Now only a quarter of households there are non-poor, non-wealthy, while more than a third in these areas are counted in our most exclusively wealthy category. Today, the majority of people living in the most expensive areas will have moved there over the last few decades, making such places unaffordable to almost everyone else. In a more unequal society, everyone is less free to choose where they live.

In the most recent period, we saw for the first time large parts of many cities with more than half the population becoming poor. In these places, it is, in effect, now normal to be poor.

This is hardly surprising, given that just over a quarter of households nationally are poor and that there has been a rise in geographical segregation both of rich and poor over time. You would have to spread the poor very evenly in fictional mixed communities to hide concentrations with such a high national poverty rate – high both by international and historic standards.

It took a long time to pull together information from four surveys of poverty and four censuses, to collect other data on consumption and the assets of the rich, and to merge them to produce a picture of Britain that allows our changing geography of wealth and poverty to be mapped over thousands of communities in comparable ways for the first time in such detail.

The most obvious result is that you cannot expect to reduce poverty and the spatial concentration of poverty while wealth becomes more concentrated, both socially and spatially.

Poverty was at its minimum in the last 40 years when fewest people were so much wealthier than the average. Poor and wealthy were less geographically segregated from the rest. Given current trends, only a minority of people may soon live in "normal" households. The majority will either not be able to afford to live a normal life – to avoid debt and take a holiday, or, at the other end of the scale, they will be concerned about inheritance tax, buying their way out of state provision, and how many holidays a year they can take.

That future has already arrived in London, where rich and poor jostle together most closely. And if the long-term trends we have identified continue, then socially much of the rest of the country will start to look that way. So why let things carry on polarising when we can see that we are heading in the wrong direction?

### Exclusive enclaves

- Chesham and Amersham in Buckinghamshire has seen the greatest polarisation between rich and poor in England and Wales since 1980. Then, 67% of its households were living in "normal" circumstances (neither rich nor poor). By 2000, that figure had plummeted to 24%. A quarter of households were rich in 1980, but this had soared to 61% by 2000. Meanwhile, the proportion of poor households went from 9% to 15%.

- Other areas with dramatic recent concentrations of wealth include Surrey Heath (13% rich in 1980 to 50% by 2000) and Maidenhead (18% to 53%).

- Few exclusive enclaves are found in the North. One area which makes it into the top 15 constituencies of areas to have lost the greatest number of average households since 1980 is Tatton in Greater Manchester where half the population were rich by the year 2000. Two decades earlier less than a quarter had been so well off.[2]

---

[2] Editorial note: This last point was added to this version of the article as Tatton was George Osborne's constituency and by 2010 he had become Chancellor of the Exchequer.

# 29

# Britain – split and divided by inequality

*Rapport: Journal of the Youth Worker's Union* (2007) October, pp 4-5

Next time you are talking to someone from the other side of town don't assume they know what you are talking about – what is normal in Britain is slowly being split in two.

Much about life in Britain is getting better. We are slowly and surely becoming more tolerant of others, for instance, although we still harbour great racism. We may not be becoming happier on aggregate, but for those most distressed, rates of suicide have been falling in recent years. And again at the extremes, our youngest children are safer now than they have ever been, from disease (and from violence from us). However, at the heart of British society something is slowly pulling us apart. This pressure has different effects at different stages in our lives and it is *not* a pressure that will be well revealed by government statistics.

Indices of multiple deprivation really don't say much about a place. They are inhuman things, not unlike most social statistics. The map shown here (Figure 1) comes from an atlas which is a little different. In it, for over one thousand areas, we have tried to work out what is normal in each place.

In many large neighbourhoods it is normal for the parents of children aged under five not to have a car. Most under fives live in homes with no access to a car in these areas. Their mums or dads walk everywhere with them, carry the shopping and take it on the bus. And that is normal.

Elsewhere in a huge number of neighbourhoods most under fives live in households with access to two or more cars. When they are taken to the shops the issue is whether to go in mum's or dad's car, or the people carrier, not how many bags can be carried under the buggy. We have more than enough cars to give some up and, simultaneously, for every family with children that needs one to have one. Instead, in those places that had most cars to begin with, more have appeared in the last decade. Some children in Britain still die young despite falls in the amount of deliberate forms of violence and disease afflicting them. Car drivers are the most effective killers of our children in Britain. More cars driven by parents who need a car – and far fewer driven by most other groups – would make us all safer.

## No more normality

In childhood lives are now so split by neighbourhood that inequalities in the wealth children can expect to inherit simply by being born where they were now dwarf those compared to any time since the upper classes began to lose their country estates over a century ago. Older children's and young adults' chances of going to a university now divide areas between places where it is almost inconceivable to go to university, as compared to those neighbourhoods where soon, to not go will be an achievement. For people of my age, growing up in the late 1960s and 1970s in Britain we lived in far more comparable places than today; more drab, worse material circumstances; more overt everyday violent racism for some; but a much more common experience of childhood than any child can experience today. There are no longer many normal places.

For adults of working age the country is now split into suburbs, villages and estates by the housing that folk can afford. This split is greater now than at any time we have data for. Monies you may or may not inherit, fewer used to, and the social grade of your occupation determines your place of residence. Access to millions of cars has allowed people to live much further from where they work and further from those they fear. Location, location, location is all about the neighbours, not about the views.

In some places a majority of adults will always rent, or have a mortgage but never own. In others the second largest group, even by ages 40 to 59 (after mortgagees) now own property outright. The numbers owning multiple homes are rising, while there has been no fall in those households who own no property. In some places it is now normal to be in poor health between the ages of 60 and 74. A majority of the age group living there are ill. In other places the majority of people of these ages are in good health. The number of neighbourhoods where people are average, for instance being of fair health at these ages, is almost certainly still falling. Life expectancies are already rising fastest where they were highest to begin with and most slowly where they were lowest a decade ago. More people are well off. But more are also poor. Fewer live in areas where a majority are neither rich nor poor.

## How we map out…

The map shown in Figure 1 takes what is normal at each of seven ages of life and gives a score of −1 to it if people are disadvantaged, +1 if they are advantaged, and 0 in between. The seven scores are summed to then shade the map. Figure 1 only makes sense in colour; see plate section.

At the one extreme of normalcy in Britain is where it is normal to be advantaged no matter who are you are or how hard you try (or don't try). Live in that part of Britain and you are unlikely to appreciate you are advantaged because, after all, doesn't almost everyone have cars, money, go to college, get a good job, get to own their home, enjoy a healthy retirement, and die old? If you lived in any of these neighbourhoods you would find it quite difficult to appreciate just how advantaged you mostly are, because you don't differ that much from your neighbours.

At the other extreme of normalcy are the areas where most children will have recourse to no wealth; almost no young adults will go to university; many will not work and almost all who do work are in the worst paid jobs; average age of death will be much lower than 80; and so on – and all of this in these neighbourhoods is normal.

**Figure 1:** Most disadvantaged to most advantaged neighbourhoods: normalcy score

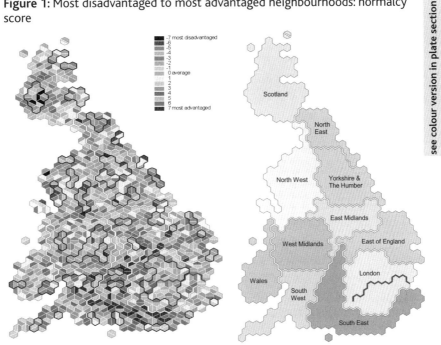

see colour version in plate section

*Note:* This is a cartogram showing every parliamentary constituency in Britain as a hexagon with roughly similar populations and hence sizes. The divisions within each constituency are also shown.

## Is employment freedom?

Most people think they are average when asked. In most respects most are not. Most say they are normal, but what is normal alters rapidly as you travel across Britain. What is locally normal ranges from a crescent west of London of 'advantage', where to succeed is to do nothing out of the ordinary, to the 'peaks of despair', where to just get by is extraordinary.

In the poorest parts of Britain rates of violence are rising, especially for young men, and the murder rates nationally have only been rising over the last two decades because of the huge rise in deaths due to killing in these areas. Across most of Britain your chances of being killed due to such violence have fallen and continue to fall.[1] Murder is still incredibly rare in this country, if not as rare as in most of our more equitable neighbours. Instead it is the low level everyday violence of being seen as surplus to requirements in a country made rich by international banking that causes the most damage to young people in Britain today. Half the poor are now in work. Employment is not freedom. The rich are increasingly constrained in where they feel it is safe to live and are much more spatially segregated than they were a decade, or two, or even three ago. There is much more to achieve than being the richest of small islands in the world. Economic growth coupled with rising inequalities does not make a good society. Neither do government policies designed simply to alleviate some of the worst miseries of the worse-off. These are akin to charity.

The dominant reaction to the slow splitting of society by government is to deny it is happening. The opposition fall on the symptoms of the divide as supposed evidence that their 'no such thing as society' party has something positive to offer.[2] Minor political parties whistle in the wind. As a country we've spent so long trying to get rich that now we are rich (at least on average), we are finding it hard to work out what to do next. The richest countries in the world no longer need to get richer, but they desperately need to become fairer.[3]

---

[1] Editorial note: See Chapter 1 of this volume, page 13, for more details of changing murder rates. In 2010 the United Nations Development Programme *Human Development* report was published. It included in its appendix a statistic suggesting that the homicide rate in the UK was amongst the highest in the affluent world, at 48 per million per year. It is probably lower, but we should be wary of thinking our murder rate is so low.

[2] Editorial note: The supposedly positive thing, later being labelled 'Big Society'.

[3] Editorial note: The need to become fairer becomes more acute once the country as a whole stops becoming richer.

# 30

# London and the English desert: the grain of truth in a stereotype[1]

*Géocarrefour* (2008) vol 83, no 2

## A nation at ease with itself?

> "Economically we live on borrowed money, and environmentally on borrowed time." (Walden, 2007, p 122).

[Some of what the archetypal Englishman, George Walden,[2] says is very apposite, but much else] that Walden says is easily refuted with or without a university education. People in England are not so polite that they do not express their most bigoted of views both often and loudly, most prominently as offensive newspaper headlines concerning immigrants. Despite this, no part of England is seeing the lines of ethnic mini-states forming. Rural villages are no more threatened in (or about to be relieved from) their ethnic homogeneity now than they have ever been. If not a single illegal

---

[1] Editorial note: See the original article for where the first 5,989 words of this article and seven figures not shown here can be found. The article concludes with the section reproduced here.
[2] George Walden (MP for Buckingham from 1983 to 1997, and briefly Minister for Higher Education)

immigrant or counterfeit asylum seeker enters the UK in the future then the population will rapidly fall rather than swell to extraordinary size, as George suggests above.[3] And if you lived in Paris, might you not be put off choosing to spend a weekend in Lyon, Bordeaux or Marseilles by all the English tourists and ex-pats coming into town with a grievance complaining over whatever became of the home country?

A fairer summary of our English human geography is given with the use of a little more data than can be collected by one man's eyes and ears. For instance, what do we find if we aggregate the five key variables described so far to create a very simple overall index of the state of the English cities combining the five traditional measures of quality of life as seen through lack of disease, ignorance, idleness, want and squalor as reflected through their modern day equivalents of high life expectancy, good qualifications, low work-related benefit claims, low rates of poverty and high house prices? These key state-of-the-city indicators are summarised in Table 1 (p 288). As can be seen, the indicators are sorted by an overall score (and a change over time measure is given). This overall index confirms the general impression given by the more than one hundred maps and cartograms contained in the full report I have been relying on.[4] The impression is that, in general, English cities are clearly divided between those in the South-East of the country and those situated towards the North-West. And the South East is increasingly dominated by London.[5]

There is little sign of that North-South divide narrowing and many indications that, again in general, it is widening. The same few exceptions to this generalisation are repeatedly mentioned in the full report; most notably York ranks within southern cities (7th overall and the only northern city in the top dozen). All 22 cities at the bottom of Table 1 are in the North, as defined in the research project[6] this data was originally put together for (it is 23 cities if Wakefield is included, which ranks equally with Peterborough). The next four are all southern, but those four are socially and/or spatially at the greatest distance from the capital: Hastings, Plymouth, Luton and

---

[3] Editorial note: For more detail of George's suggestions over the terrible effect he thought immigration was having in Britain see the full version of this paper. George wrote of his thoughts on immigrants while living as a very English ex-pat retiree in France. He appeared to think nothing of the follies of hypocrisy.

[4] Editorial note: That full report, the *State of the English cities* technical report, was never published, even on-line. It was written for the government department ODPM (Office of the Deputy Prime Minister). They preferred glossy reports over more down-beat ones.

[5] Editorial note – this is exactly the same table as shown in chapter two of this volume, but sorted by a different column in the version reproduced here. Here the cities are ranked by average score in 2003, in Chapter 2, Table 1 of this volume they are ranked by the change column but the data, columns and cities are otherwise identical (see pp 33-4).

[6] Editorial note: It became "The Places Database" to be found here: www.places.communities. gov.uk/ as of March 2011, having begun life in cyberspace here: www.sasi.group.shef.ac.uk/ socr/ (where an original copy can still be found).

Peterborough. There is no southern city which, overall on all five indicators, compares badly or even equally to any of the worst-off twenty northern cities. In general, the better off a city was on these scores in the recent past, the more it has improved in the period to 2003 (see Figure 1).

**Figure 1:** Change in city 'performance' score to 2003, versus average prior score

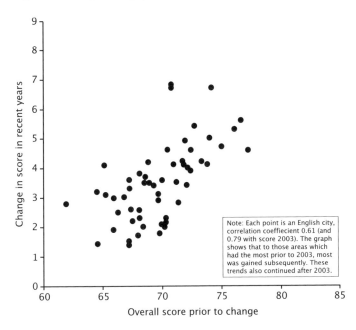

Note: Each point is an English city, correlation coeffiecient 0.61 (and 0.79 with score 2003). The graph shows that to those areas which had the most prior to 2003, most was gained subsequently. These trends also continued after 2003.

*Note:* Each point is an English city located by change in score in recent years (y axis) and overall score prior to that change (x axis), correlation coefficient 0.61 (and 0.79 with score in 2003).

A simpler way to put this is to state what it would take for Liverpool, at the bottom of the table, to become like Leeds, midway, and for Leeds to become like Cambridge (at the top). For Liverpool to be like Leeds, its people's life expectancy would have to rise by 2.5 years more than that of Leeds in the future, 5% more of its adult population would need to gain a degree, 9% of the working age population would have to come off IS or JSA benefits (and none off such benefits in Leeds), overall poverty would have to fall by 4% and average housing prices rise by £31,650.

For Leeds to be like Cambridge life expectancy in Leeds would have to increase by 1.3 years more than in Cambridge in the near future, an extra 22% of the population would need to gain a degree, 4% fewer people would need to be on work-related benefits, poverty rates would need to fall by 3% and house prices would have to rise by an average of £125,600 per home.

English cities can appear in a series of leagues when the data in table 1 is considered in the round. A "premier league" of four cities with high average

**Table 1:** Key state of the city indicators, sorted by an overall score (and change measure provided in final column) divided into six leagues

| Division | City | Life expectancy 2001-2003 | 2001 % of adults with a degree | % working age claiming JSA/IS 2003 | % of poverty by PSE 1999–2001 | Average housing price '03 | Average score 2003 | Change in score over time |
|---|---|---|---|---|---|---|---|---|
| Premiership | Cambridge | 79.5 | 41 | 5.1 | 29 | 244,862 | 82.3 | 5.6 |
| | Aldershot | 79.0 | 22 | 3.7 | 17 | 238,991 | 81.9 | 4.6 |
| | Reading | 79.6 | 26 | 4.7 | 20 | 211,794 | 81.5 | 5.3 |
| | Oxford | 79.2 | 37 | 6.1 | 30 | 255,181 | 80.9 | 6.7 |
| | Crawley | 79.6 | 19 | 4.8 | 22 | 205,506 | 79.8 | 4.7 |
| | Bournemouth | 79.7 | 17 | 7.1 | 21 | 214,296 | 79.1 | 5.0 |
| | York | 79.4 | 23 | 5.4 | 25 | 147,513 | 78.2 | 5.4 |
| 1st | Worthing | 78.8 | 16 | 6.4 | 20 | 186,992 | 78.0 | 4.1 |
| | Brighton | 78.4 | 29 | 9.3 | 27 | 212,361 | 77.6 | 6.8 |
| | Southend | 79.0 | 13 | 7.5 | 19 | 186,481 | 77.6 | 4.2 |
| | London | 78.6 | 30 | 10.3 | 33 | 283,387 | 77.5 | 6.7 |
| | Bristol | 78.9 | 23 | 7.7 | 25 | 160,708 | 77.1 | 4.6 |
| | Southampton | 78.8 | 19 | 6.9 | 25 | 172,585 | 76.9 | 4.9 |
| | Norwich | 79.8 | 18 | 7.5 | 27 | 138,187 | 76.3 | 3.9 |
| | Portsmouth | 78.8 | 16 | 6.6 | 25 | 157,145 | 76.2 | 4.0 |
| | Milton Keynes | 78.2 | 18 | 6.6 | 25 | 161,625 | 76.0 | 4.2 |
| | Swindon | 78.2 | 15 | 6.6 | 22 | 150,689 | 76.0 | 4.1 |
| | Gloucester | 78.4 | 16 | 8.5 | 22 | 141,690 | 75.5 | 3.4 |
| | Warrington | 77.9 | 17 | 6.8 | 23 | 119,668 | 75.1 | 4.6 |
| | Northampton | 78.2 | 17 | 7.8 | 24 | 135,871 | 75.1 | 4.1 |
| | Ipswich | 79.0 | 16 | 10.1 | 25 | 134,514 | 74.7 | 3.5 |
| | Chatham | 77.7 | 12 | 7.7 | 23 | 142,374 | 74.2 | 2.8 |

**Table 1:** continued

| Division | City | Life expectancy 2001–2003 | 2001 % of adults with a degree | % working age claiming JSA/IS 2003 | % of poverty by PSE 1999–2001 | Average housing price '03 | Average score 2003 | Change in score over time |
|---|---|---|---|---|---|---|---|---|
| 2nd | Preston | 77.7 | 17 | 7.2 | 26 | 97,038 | 73.6 | 3.6 |
| | Derby | 78.1 | 18 | 10.5 | 27 | 114,280 | 73.1 | 4.2 |
| | Leeds | 78.2 | 19 | 8.9 | 32 | 119,262 | 72.8 | 3.1 |
| | Nottingham | 77.5 | 18 | 9.8 | 28 | 123,663 | 72.7 | 3.4 |
| | Telford | 77.9 | 13 | 9.0 | 27 | 115,722 | 72.6 | 2.9 |
| | Leicester | 78.0 | 17 | 11.0 | 28 | 124,812 | 72.6 | 2.3 |
| | Blackpool | 77.2 | 13 | 8.9 | 24 | 103,656 | 72.5 | 2.2 |
| | Plymouth | 78.1 | 13 | 9.8 | 28 | 118,978 | 72.4 | 3.5 |
| | Hastings | 77.4 | 15 | 13.4 | 25 | 163,128 | 72.3 | 3.7 |
| | Luton | 77.2 | 14 | 9.7 | 28 | 143,698 | 72.2 | 2.0 |
| | Wakefield | 77.5 | 14 | 9.0 | 28 | 110,407 | 72.1 | 3.5 |
| | Peterborough | 77.5 | 14 | 9.5 | 28 | 123,089 | 72.1 | 2.1 |
| | Coventry | 77.8 | 16 | 10.9 | 28 | 111,165 | 72.0 | 3.8 |
| | Huddersfield | 77.2 | 15 | 8.7 | 29 | 97,815 | 71.6 | 1.8 |
| 3rd | Manchester | 76.7 | 19 | 11.6 | 30 | 119,569 | 70.9 | 3.6 |
| | Sheffield | 77.9 | 16 | 10.4 | 33 | 96,328 | 70.8 | 3.6 |
| | Wigan | 76.5 | 12 | 8.6 | 27 | 88,946 | 70.7 | 2.6 |
| | Birkenhead | 77.9 | 13 | 12.2 | 29 | 95,632 | 70.6 | 3.3 |
| | Bolton | 76.8 | 15 | 10.4 | 29 | 89,281 | 70.4 | 2.3 |
| | Mansfield | 77.1 | 9 | 9.4 | 28 | 947,49 | 70.4 | 2.0 |

# FAIR PLAY

**Table 1:** continued

| Division | City | Life expectancy 2001-2003 | 2001 % of adults with a degree | % working age claiming JSA/IS 2003 | % of poverty by PSE 1999–2001 | Average housing price '03 | Average score 2003 | Change in score over time |
|---|---|---|---|---|---|---|---|---|
| 4th | Grimsby | 77.6 | 10 | 11.5 | 28 | 77,898 | 70.0 | 2.6 |
| | Doncaster | 77.3 | 11 | 10.6 | 30 | 82,267 | 69.8 | 3.0 |
| | Birmingham | 77.4 | 14 | 12.8 | 33 | 122,794 | 69.7 | 2.2 |
| | Stoke | 76.9 | 11 | 10.3 | 29 | 78,834 | 69.7 | 1.7 |
| | Newcastle | 77.1 | 16 | 12.8 | 34 | 111,220 | 69.2 | 4.1 |
| | Barnsley | 77.2 | 10 | 10.8 | 32 | 79,492 | 68.9 | 3.0 |
| | Rochdale | 76.4 | 14 | 12.2 | 31 | 92,523 | 68.8 | 2.5 |
| | Burnley | 76.8 | 12 | 10.7 | 31 | 55,879 | 68.7 | 1.5 |
| | Bradford | 76.9 | 13 | 11.5 | 33 | 75,919 | 68.6 | 1.4 |
| | Middlesbrough | 77.1 | 12 | 13.1 | 32 | 81,760 | 68.4 | 3.1 |
| 5th | Sunderland | 76.6 | 12 | 12.4 | 34 | 91,322 | 67.8 | 3.2 |
| | Blackburn | 75.8 | 14 | 12.7 | 30 | 70,969 | 67.8 | 1.9 |
| | Hull | 76.6 | 12 | 17.1 | 33 | 72,374 | 66.0 | 1.4 |
| 6th | Liverpool | 75.7 | 14 | 18.0 | 36 | 87,607 | 64.7 | 2.8 |

*Note:* Cities in the North of England have their row shaded grey in this table

230

scores from 80.9 to 82.3 is clear (including Oxford and Cambridge), followed by 18 "first division cities" with scores from 74.2 to 79.8 (from Crawley to Chatham, including London and Bristol). There is a gap and then a "second division" of 14 cities scoring between 71.6 and 73.6 (from Preston to Huddersfield, including Leeds and Nottingham), followed by a "third division" from 70.9 to 70.4 (headed by Manchester and down to Bolton and Mansfield), and a "fourth division" from Grimsby to Middlesbrough, including Birmingham and Newcastle); next with Blackburn, Sunderland; then Hull as a fifth division; and then Liverpool following below in division six, an English city in a group of its own.[7]

Almost all southern cities are in the premier league (or at least the first division) of Table 1. Less than a half dozen are found in the second division and none below that. Division two downwards is dominated by cities of the North of England.

To borrow from the subtitle of a recent atlas of poverty produced for the United States (Glasmeier 2005) England, as viewed through the lens of its cities, is "one nation, pulling apart". Not to state this clearly would be unfair to the readers as the patterns are so clear. This is the grain of truth within George Walden's lament. Given how obvious such a conclusion is from the maps reproduced here, it is imperative that this simple truth is not lost in the study of the nuances of more subtle changes occurring in urban England as revealed by this data.

There is a final graph which is worth showing here for how well it reflects the most basic of understandings of British economic geographical divides, which this database[8] should aid. Most of what the data can tell you can be read from a train timetable. What matters above all else for the cities of England is how far each is away from London (see Figure 2).[9]

---

[7] Editorial note: If other cities in the United Kingdom were included outside of England, Liverpool might potentially be joined in a group by Swansea, Glasgow, Belfast and other similar Western ports and old industrial centres.

[8] Editorial note: The contributions to that database by the group I work can be found here: *State of the English cities* report – Sheffield Files, page: www.sasi.group.shef.ac.uk/socr/

[9] The train time data is mapped in this volume, Chapter 1, Figure 1 (page 35). It was also reproduced in the original version of this paper and the data is available at the following web address: www.sasi.group.shef.ac.uk/socr/data/SOCD52_train_times_to_london.xls. On line booking systems were used to create this dataset. Journey searches were set to 0800 to London on 10 Feb 2005. From the 5 journeys returned, the fastest journey time was chosen, rounded to nearest five minutes. Note that all these datasets and many more are available from www.sasi.group.shef.ac.uk/socr/

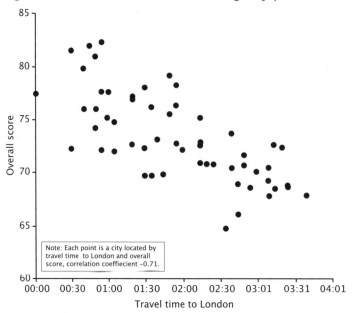

**Figure 2:** Train times to London versus average city 'performance' score 2003

Note: Each point is a city located by travel time to London and overall score, correlation coeffiecient –0.71.

## The English and their geography

So what's to become of the English and their geography?

Mr Walden has some interesting things to say – despite his strange belief that the brains of different humans are somehow differently wired in different continents (see quotation immediately below). It is often said that the historic reason for much of the population of the North of England to exist has long gone. Next time you hear that, remember the coffee houses that transformed over the course of centuries to become financial trading markets. They are no more reliant on London clay for their location than they ever were on the destination of imported coffee. Thus for the English:

> "In many ways their future isn't in their hands. It's in those of China, India and the rest, who'll soon be making many of the things they make here to the same standard at a quarter the price. Nor will the Asian business brain [sic] be content to rely on British financial services for ever, whether it's in Leeds or London. And the idea that the second coming of the North will be based on garden centres in Liverpool (Heseltine), art galleries in Gateshead or casinos everywhere (Tessa Jowell) is risible, as well as cynical.
>
> There are pleasant enough places, which a bit of global warming could brighten up, but with the best multicultural will in the world I find

it impossible to envisage a genuine rebirth of northern towns, their culture, their supremacy. Maybe I'm wrong, though I doubt it, and in any case it scarcely matters. One of the charms of the North is that, like China in the time of Marco Polo, you can say what you like about it and no one can contradict you, because apart from a trip to Durham and a holiday in the lake District they haven't been there for years, if ever, and have absolutely no intention of going." (Walden, 2007, p 99)

Reading his thoughts it becomes evident that the Englishman, George Walden, does not have a multicultural bone in his body, and so mustering his best multicultural will does not get him very far, but he does have a point about the relationship of those in power to the North of England and the precarious situation that they find themselves in, relying on a few (almost entirely American owned or run) banks to finance London. Did I mention our English subservience to America a little earlier? It's so well accepted now that we often forget to!

What the English desert lacks above all else is money. Money in England has spiralled into the South East in recent decades – sent like food, water and tribute to a centre that in reality makes nothing of much value, but which extracts a high charge from the rest of the world for the "services" it provides. And, given where it is,[10] often those in the centre feel powerless to alter course. A course that, it is becoming clearer day by day, is especially dependent on the will of a few powerful people and banks based in America.

If you ever wondered why the English kow-tow so much to the Americans, simply look at which nation of birth is most overrepresented in the heart of the capital. The largest group of immigrants (especially children) in the wealthy heart of London were born in America.[11]

And, briefly before we end, what of Wales, Scotland and Ireland? Well there is more than one story to tell, just as the story of America is needed to understand why we now have an English desert. All that I have tried to do here is to combine the very recently revealed angst of a former government minister with a few numbers produced for the appendices of the reports given to current government ministers.[12] The result, again as I said in introduction is, I think, a story of England reminiscent of one told

---

[10] The power centre is in the heart of the capital, wedged between the discrete hedge fund offices in Mayfair and the all imposing and (recently) far less profitable banking towers of Canary Wharf. Parliament is surrounded by bankers.

[11] Editorial note: see Dorling, D. (2011) *So you think you know about Britain?*, London: Constable and Robinson, for a discussion on where the most immigrants are to be found and who they are.

[12] *The state of the English cities*, published 7 March 2006 by what was the Office of the Deputy Prime Minister, ISBN 10 1-851128-45-X and to be found here:*www.communities.gov.uk/publications/regeneration/state4* (at least as of March 2011. Hardcopy is priced at £60.00 but it is free to download still).

of France some sixty years ago (Gavier, 1958). This was the last time many of us in England learnt what there was to French geography other than through holiday and retirement destinations.

However, before you think you are immune from this English desertification disease and its precursors, ask an average English school child now of what they know of the geography of France and they will probably be able to tell you the rough location of something their parents could not: that thing is Euro Disney...now – whose idea was that?

### References

Dorling, D. and Thomas, B. (2004) *People and places: A 2001 census atlas of the UK*, Bristol: The Policy Press.

Elliot, L. and Atkinson, D. (2007) *Fantasy island: Waking up to the incredible economic, political and social illusions of the Blair legacy*, London: Constable and Robinson.

Gavier, J. (1958) *Paris et le désert Français*, Paris: Editions Flammarion.

Glasmeier, A. (2005) *An atlas of poverty in America: One nation, pulling, apart, 1906–2003*, Pennsylvania: University of Pennsylvania.

Thomas, B. and Dorling, D. (2007) *Identity in Britain: A cradle-to-grave-atlas*, Bristol: The Policy Press.

Walden, G. (2007) *Time to Emigrate?* London: Gibson Square.

## Appendix: the North/South dividing line

When asked where the north/south divide is geographers in Britain have a tendency to give vague answers. Although this is understandable, I think we now have enough detailed information on life-chances, political views, health and wealth in Britain to be able to say with a little more certainty where the line lies (see Figure 3 below).

This is the line that separates upland from lowland Britain, the hills from the most fertile farmland, areas invaded by Vikings from those first colonised by Saxons. Numerous facts of life divide the North from the South – there is a missing year of life expectancy north of this line. Children south of the line are much more likely to attend Russell group universities for those that do go to university (and they often go to the North to study![13]), a house price cliff now runs along much of the line, and, on the voting map, the line still often separates red from blue voters.

In terms of life chances, the only line within another European country that is comparable to the North-South divide is that which once separated East and West Germany. This is found not just in terms of relative differences

---

[13] See the map shown in Chapter 23, page 176 of this volume, which reveals that difference – or better still, the colour version of that figure in the plate section.

in wealth either side of the line, but most importantly in terms of health where some of the extremes of Europe are now found within this one much divided island of Britain.

By county the North lies above the old counties of Gloucestershire, Warwickshire, Leicestershire and Lincolnshire and 'nips' only into parts of some of those counties. Most of each of those counties, and all the areas of England below them, are in the South. By constituency the North includes and lies above the new parliamentary constituencies of the Forest of Dean on the north bank of the Severn; it includes West and Mid Worcestershire, Redditch, Bromsgrove (and hence all of Birmingham), Meriden, Coventry South and North East, Warwickshire North, Nuneaton, Bosworth, Loughborough, Rushcliffe, Newark, Bassetlaw, Brigg and Goole, Scunthorpe,

**Figure 3:** The North-South Divide

Cleethorpes, with the dividing line ending at Great Grimsby on the south bank of the Humber.

It would be possible to go further and split some of these constituencies in half.[14] It would be possible to identify enclaves and exclaves along the border, but this would suggest too much of a rigid line, and the border does move, especially when a new motorway is built or a train line to London is improved.

Within the North are places that look and sometimes act (e.g. vote) like the south. Areas around the vale of York and Cheshire are contenders here – but they are still northern. Similarly there are parts of the south, especially within London that are very unlike much of the rest of the south, but they are still southern. Scotland and Wales are part of the North, despite having managed to eschew the Victorian attempts to label them 'North' and 'West' Britain respectively.

---

[14] Editorial note: In fact journalists working with the ITV 'Tonight' programme, as broadcast on 27th January 2011, travelled to Evesham and reported from the southern end of a constituency there which I placed, as a whole, in the North, as being out of place… See: www.itv.com/news/tonight/episodes/northversussouth/

<h1 style="text-align:center">31</h1>

# Are the times changing back?

*New London Review* (2010) no 2, pp 16–17.

There are painful similarities between life lived in London now and the unjust inequalities of Victorian times.

## London viewed from the South[1]

Tourists visiting Covent Garden are often drawn to Christopher Roger's stall at Jubilee market. Among many other eye-catching items, he sells panoramic views of London drawn from a vantage point located somewhere in the sky just south of the river. Hovering over Lambeth and looking North, London's iconic buildings are spread out: from Parliament in the west to the Gherkin in the East, from the Globe Theatre in the foreground to Hampstead Heath in the distance, all the opulence of the capital is on display.

Images such as this sell, but they cut out most of London, and of the country beyond. The south and east of London is cropped from the frame. The churches, towers and buildings of state and finance block out views of the people and their homes, of commuters, of maisonettes, of children and of markets. In images such as Roger's "London looking North" the land south of the river appears laid out to service the heart of the capital. Bridges, roads and rail cross the Thames like so many tangled arteries bringing sustenance to the city and square mile.

---

[1] Editorial note: Footnotes were not included in the original version that was printed. They have been reinstated here.

**Figure 1:** Contemporary panorama of London looking north west from the London Eye[1]

---

[1] I could not persuade Christopher to let me reproduce one of his images, so here is a more conventional photograph: www.bigstockphoto.com/image-5997958/stock-photo-vintage-london-panorama However, should you be interested in his drawings see: *London looking North* (by Christopher Rogers, 2004) as now used on a jigsaw puzzle: www.jigsawpuzzlesworld.com/jigsawpuzzle.php?refnum=G830

London is a city of contrasts, not the smooth working concert it can appear to be from the air. From high enough up you can no longer see the people and the whole appears like a machine (see Figure 1). Delve down into the lives of Londoners and it becomes clear that all is not flowing so smoothly. Using their own words Peter Hall tells a thousand tales of Londoners in his collection on *London voices, London lives: Tales from a working capital*.[2] With thousands of numbers (rather than own accounts) John Hills and his enquiry achieved the same, earlier this year.[3] It was the Hills Enquiry which released the statistics showing that London is one of the most divided of rich cities on the face of the planet.

---

[2] Hall, P. (2007) *London voices, London lives: Tales from a working capital*, Bristol: The Policy Press, 498 pages, £24.99 (paperback).

[3] Hills, J,. Brewer, M., Jenkins, S.P., Lister, R., Lupton, R., Machin, S., Mills, C., Modood, T., Rees, T. and Riddell, S. (2010) *An anatomy of economic inequality in the UK: Report of the National Equality Panel*, Centre for Analysis of Social Exclusion, London School of Economics and Political Science, London, UK, http://eprints.lse.ac.uk/28344/

Nationally, or across England at least, the richest tenth of adults have recourse to at least 96 times the wealth of the poorest tenth. In London that ratio is now 273 times. A tenth of Londoners each have wealth estimated, on average, to exceed £933,563, in contrast to the assets of the richest from the bottom tenth of Londoners, which equate to, at most, £3,420. A small part of that inequality is due to older Londoners usually being a little wealthier, but even if you just compare the citizens of the capital of the same ages, 55 to 64 year olds say, the poorest of the best-off tenth in their middle age in London (now with £1,653,191 on average) are still, on average, 126 times richer each than the richest of the poorest tenth who have recourse to (at best) assets of only £13,113 in (what for them is more likely) their old age. No wonder Londoners are so split politically.

These rich and poor people in London are of the same age. When counted in calendar years, each is aged around 60, but the rich each have more than twice as long left to live than the poor, so great are inequalities in life expectancy in London. The rich will get to vote in half a dozen more general elections on average, the poor in just a couple more if lucky. A large part of the wealth of the richest tenth of Londoners (by age 60) is tied up in pension rights and housing equity, but that is real wealth. It means that they will live into old age in comfort and can retire away from the capital should they wish, selling their home to finance the move. Equity and pensions are real wealth.

In many ways Londoners are again living lives as unequal as they last did when Dickens published *Hard times* in 1854, just as cholera was breaking out around Broad Street. The major difference today is the sewer system which makes everybody much better off materially. However, psychologically, gross inequality still harms us all. Murder rates have returned again to levels last reordered in Victorian times (when it was legal to carry arms). Violent crime might have fallen a fraction in recent years but our fear and mistrust of one another is again palpable. Panoramic views of London were as popular in Victorian times as they are today. J.H. Banks drew his famous aerial view in 1845 from somewhere just above Southwark (see Figure 2). The main visual differences between then and now are the smokestacks and great sailing ships of the past, today replaced by skyscrapers.

The greatest social difference between now and the Victorian era is that today the super-rich are so much more opulent. Of the richest 1,000 people in Britain, most live in or near London. In the year to 2010 *The Sunday Times* reported their individual wealth to have risen, on average, faster than ever recorded before, by £77 million apiece, totalling some £335.5 billion shared out amongst just 1,000 individuals. Most of the poor no longer go hungry, but they exist as far beneath the sight and understanding of the wealthy as they ever did.

**Figure 2:** A panoramic view of London. Drawn and engraved by J.H.Banks, 1845[4]

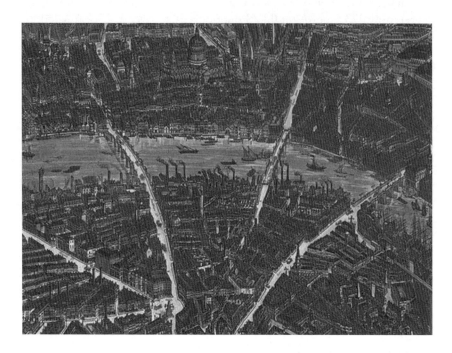

It is not just in terms of murder rates, wealth inequalities or panoramic picture popularity, that the view of London from the South again appears so similar to that shown so long ago. Just as Charles Dickens advocated change through his writing and other Londoners mapped poverty and agitated for change so successfully in the century that followed him, so too today there is growing agitation. There are again a huge number books on inequality, surveys of poverty, and newspaper columns written in anger.[5]

In 2010 the London Sustainable Development Commission commissioned Professors Richard Wilkinson and Kate Pickett to write on the modern day "Impact of income inequalities on sustainable development in London".

---

[4] Source: British Library. See: www.bl.uk/reshelp/images/maps/large14281.html

[5] Editorial note: Early on in 2010 Matthew d'Ancona wrote: "We can no longer insulate ourselves against poverty", London Evening Standard, 5 March 2010, //www.thisislondon. co.uk/standard/article-23812470-we-can-no-longer-insulate-ourselves-against-poverty.do in which it was reported that "On 12 October 1843, *The Times* ran an editorial lamenting the bitter paradox that "within the most courtly precincts of the richest city of GOD's earth, there may be found, night after night, winter after winter … FAMINE, FILTH AND DISEASE." This week's campaign in the *Evening Standard* on London's dispossessed has identified precisely the same pathology, more than 160 years later. How is it that the greatest city on the planet, this thriving republic of prosperity, culture and vitality, is still home to the most dreadful poverty?' One answer to Matthew's question is to let him know that the wealth of those 1,000 richest people each rose by an average of £60 million from 2010–2011. It is a clue as to where the money has gone (*Sunday Times Rich List*, revealed late in spring 2011).

Their report was published in March.[6] They produced an overall index of health and social problems for all London boroughs. At the head of that index were Southwark and Lambeth. What Richard and Kate then went on to do was to show how these problems might be reduced if income inequalities in London were reduced to the levels normal in an affluent country, levels experienced by countries such as France and Canada (which do not allow 1000 people to individually hold £335.5bn[7] of the national wealth).

The Report also calculated what the effects of a fairer society might be on a borough such as Lambeth. It found that rates of mental illness in Lambeth should be expected to more than halve if London were to become only as unequal as the average rich city in the world. Obesity rates should be expected to reduce by more than a third; teenage pregnancies by more than two thirds (to only be a third of their current rate). These are huge improvements to life in south London. You may well doubt they are possible, if so why not read their report? It is available for free to read here: www.londonsdc.org.uk/lsdc/research.aspx

The Report was commissioned by a body whose chair was appointed by Boris Johnson[8] – you are living in remarkable times; wealth and health inequalities are spiralling out of control and even Boris knows it and is concerned. Go back just another century and a half or so from 1854 and the view from South London was even more remarkable. In 1666 people sat on hillsides on the south and watched as the smoke from the Great Fire drifted off to the West (see Figure 3).

How we currently live never remains the same for that long. Change is sometimes rapid, but often harder to see when it is gradual. For almost four decades the lives of Londoners have been becoming more divided. That trend could be changing direction again today. Where would you look to finance a national structural deficit of £70bn or more[9] if you were looking from south of the river? What would your eyes alight on?

---

[6] Editorial note: The report can also be found here (www.equalitytrust.org.uk/londonequality) (March 2011) – *The impact of income inequalities on sustainable development in London* where it says: "This is a new report written by Richard Wilkinson and Kate Pickett, published by the London Sustainable Development Commission".

[7] Editorial note: A figure which rose by some 25% or some £60bn in the year between when this chapter was first published as an article and today.

[8] Editorial note: Mayor of London at the time of writing.

[9] Editorial note: Later that year the eyes of the agents of the wealthy would alight on public spending which they cut by £81bn in the Comprehensive Spending Review of October 2010.

**Figure 3:** The Great Fire of London viewed from South of the river, contemporary to `1666[10]

[10] http://commons.wikimedia.org/wiki/File:GreatFireOfLondon1666_VictorianEngravingAfterVisscher300dpi.jpg

# 32

# Unemployment and health[1]

*British Medical Journal* (2009) 338, b829

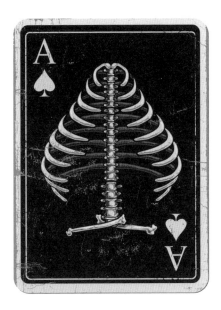

The best guides we have to the possible future effects of mass unemployment are studies of previous epidemics. In men who had been continuously employed for at least five years in the late 1970s, mortality doubled in the five years after redundancy for those aged 40-59 in 1980. Adjustment for socioeconomic variables, previous health related behaviours, and other health indicators had almost no effect on this increase.[2] The increased risk of mortality after redundancy tends to be greater in men than in women.[3] This is because men are generally affected more from a prevailing belief that when things go wrong no one will be there to help.[4]

---

[1] Editorial note: Full title is 'Unemployment and health: health benefits vary according to the method of reducing unemployment', (2009) *BMJ*, no 338, b829.

[2] Morris, J.K., Cook, D.G. and Shaper, A.G. (1994) 'Loss of employment and mortality', *BMJ*, no 308, pp 1135–9.

[3] Mathers, C.D. and Schofield, D.J. (1998) 'The health consequences of unemployment: the evidence', *Med J Aust*, no 168, pp 178–83.

[4] Kraemer, S. (2007) 'Review: textbook of men's mental health', *Br J Psychiatry*, no 161, pp 573–4.

The detrimental effects of unemployment were widely recognised after the great depression of the 1930s. However, by the early 1980s unemployment became viewed, as it was by some in the very early 1930s, as a "price worth paying." We learnt through bitter experience again that it was not. By 2009 even the leader of the British Conservative Party argued that, "Unemployment is never a price worth paying and we need to take very big, bold and radical steps to help unemployed people back to work."[5]

Research into mass unemployment during the early 1990s in the United Kingdom found that people in secure employment recovered more quickly from illness. In contrast, unemployment increased the chance of being ill, especially for those who had never worked or had had poorly paid jobs.[6] Unemployment increases rates of depression, particularly in the young – who form most of the group who have never worked and who are usually most badly hit when jobs are few. Parasuicide rates in young men who are unemployed are between 9.5 and 25 times higher than in employed young men.

In the UK, we know much about the detrimental health effects of unemployment and some of the methods used to alleviate it because the 1981 and 1991 censuses were taken during periods of mass unemployment, and because 1% of these census populations were studied longitudinally. For young people there is a continuum of health damaging states from being unemployed at one extreme to being placed on what were called youth opportunity programmes in the 1980s, to having a paid apprenticeship, to having a secure job, to being in college.

Youth opportunity-type schemes are almost as detrimental to psychological good health as is unemployment itself.[7] Temporary employment is slightly better but not as good as a properly rewarded and organised apprenticeship.[8] Secure work is better than all these options, but the best option for men and women aged 16-24 in the 1980s and 1990s was going to college, because factors associated with going to college were associated with lower suicide risks by the 1990s.[9]

---

[5] David Cameron quoted in the Wall Street Journal's online reporting from the World Economic Summit, 19 Feb 2009. http://davos.wsj.com/quote/07Ve8YI400cRt?q=David±Cameron.

[6] Bartley, M., Sacker, A. and Clarke, P. (2004) 'Employment status, employment conditions, and limiting illness: prospective evidence from the British household panel survey 1991–2001', *J Epidemiol Community Health*, no 58, pp 501–6.

[7] Morrell, S.L., Taylor, R.J. and Kerr, C.B. (1998) 'Unemployment and young people's health', *Med J Aust*, no 168, pp 236–40.

[8] Branthwaite, A. and Garcia, S. (1985) 'Depression in the young unemployed and those on youth opportunities schemes', *Br J Med Psychol*, no 58, pp 67–74.

[9] Dorling, D. and Gunnell, D. (2003) 'Suicide: the spatial and social components of despair in Britain 1980–2000', *Trans Inst Br Geographers*, no 28, pp 442–60.

The direct effect of reducing unemployment has been estimated to prevent up to 2500 premature deaths a year, but the indirect effects of being employed are thought to be far greater.[10] Without the constant presence of unemployment, income inequalities tend to fall because people simply walk out of poorly paid work when they are poorly treated.[11]

Work for the dole schemes were tried in the 1980s with detrimental effect. In recent times of mass unemployment with rising inequality, poorly paid work has become relatively more demeaning. The modern equivalent of the New Deal – the welfare programmes through which America spent its way out of depression in the 1930s – would be to offer young adults a degree of government commitment that was comparable in sentiment but updated in real terms: good quality apprenticeships, permanent public funded jobs, and more highly valued education.

The most highly valued education is university education. Figure 1 shows the year-on-year change in the proportion of 18 and 19 years olds going to university in the UK between 1995 and 2005 plotted against the year on year change of the size of the young cohort, both expressed as proportional changes (M. Corver, personal communication, 2009). The figure shows that in 1997 UK universities coped with a sudden 9% increase in potential student numbers caused by a rapid increase in demand. There was only a small 1% fall in the proportion of young people going to university despite the large increase in the population aged 18 and 19 (because of the spike in births before the early 1980s recession). In 1997 the national number of university entrants thus increased by more than 8%.

Logistically, assuming that funding is available and students attain the required academic standards, university intakes could rise again by 8% in a single year if they had to. If this rise is combined with the anticipated 2% drop in the current size of the birth cohort, the proportion of young people going to university (around 30%) could increase by up to 10% – that is, around three extra young people in every 100 could go to university in a single summer.[12] However, the figure also shows that when numbers of 18

---

[10] Mitchell, R., Dorling, D. and Shaw, M. (2000) *Inequalities in life and death. What if Britain were more equal?*, www.jrf.org.uk/sites/files/jrf/jr086-inequalities-life-death.pdf.

[11] Wilkinson, R. and Pickett, K. (2009) *The spirit level: Why more equal societies almost always do better*, London: Penguin (Allen Lane).

[12] Editorial note: These numbers were inserted to attempt to show that there was capacity for universities to increase their intake rapidly to reduce potential graduate competition for scarce jobs and so reduce youth unemployment (mainly amongst young people who had no chance of going to university at all). What occurred was the opposite. By early 2011 it looked as if university places were to be cut for the first time since the 1950s and one in five recent university graduates were reported as being out of work and looking for work, competing for jobs with other young people. Masters, and other easily variably sized courses, increased in intake dramatically, despite even higher debts being amassed. There was talk of forcing other young people into labour gangs regardless of their wishes, hopes, vocations or inclinations, or the likely long-term health consequences.

**Figure 1:** Year on year change in the proportion of 18 and 19 year olds going to university in the UK between 1995 and 2005 versus the year on year change of the size of the cohort. Derived, with permission, from figures in two reports[13,14]

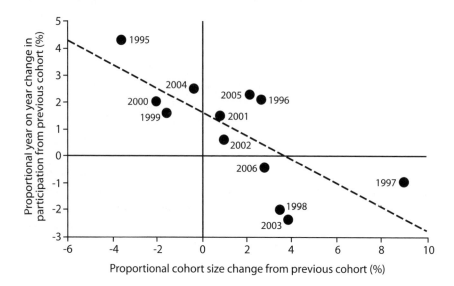

and 19 year olds decline, national university student intake is usually held constant, not increased. Just as in the 1930s, radical measures like this would face great initial opposition. It was more than four years after the 1929 crash that the New Deal began to be implemented in the United States.

If three extra young people per 100 this summer go to university and are out of the job market, another three people could fill those jobs that the first three might have taken, another three percentage points come off the dole queue and fewer youngsters compete with older workers who have recently been made redundant. More importantly, this approach recognises that unemployment is bad for health, and that the best way of alleviating it is to show faith in and respect for the young, because they are nowadays always worst hit by unemployment. More education does not need to mean more debt.[15] It is just a question of priorities and recognising when the time is right for someone to be there to help.

[13] Corver, M. (2005) *Young participation in higher education*, Higher Education Funding Council for England report 2005/3, www.hefce.ac.uk/pubs/hefce/2005/05_03/.

[14] National Audit Office (2008) Widening participation in higher education, NAO report 725 (2007-2008) www.nao.org.uk/publications/0708/widening_participation_in_high.aspx.

[15] Dorling, D. (2004) 'Top up fees and medicine, waive repayments completely if working life is spent in the NHS', [letter] *BMJ* no 328: p 712, doi:10.1136/bmj.328.7441.712.

# SECTION VII
# Bricks and mortar

This section begins with the shortest chapter in the book, written with Mary Shaw, and published when we both worked in the School of Geographical Sciences at the University of Bristol. *The Lancet* would not normally publish a paper authored by a couple of non-clinicians, but the subject – mass visible homelessness – had become of such concern that early figures on the relative death rates of different types of homeless people were of great interest then. However, the response was mostly to remove the worst of street homelessness by forcing people away from the areas in which they were begging and sleeping. Death rates among the homeless who have a roof over their head, but with no real home, may be five times lower than among those on the streets, but remain five times higher than among the population who are better housed.[1] Widespread street homelessness had hardly existed during my childhood, which had ended in 1986. A dozen years earlier and we are adding up early deaths which result from destitution. Just another dozen years later and I was writing about the lack of housing

---

[1] Shaw, M., Dorling, D. and Brimblecombe, N. (1999) 'Life chances in Britain by housing wealth and for the homeless and vulnerably housed', *Environment and Planning A*, vol 31, pp 2239-48.

for the population at large (Chapter 34). It is as if there had been a coup. A population which had been relatively well housed at the start of the 1980s experienced growing rates of homelessness in the 1990s and then more widespread housing shortages.

The magazine which traditionally championed issues of homeless was called *Roof*. It ceased publication during 2010, an early victim of people cutting back on their subscriptions and on donations to *Shelter*, the charity that published it. A year before it folded the second chapter in this section was published, detailing how there is clearly enough housing for all in Britain, but also how it has become so badly shared out. In very recent years even mildly affluent homeowners have lost out to wealthier bankers.

Next the focus turns to New Zealand where the best data on housing, smoking and health are collected. This allows us to assess how the workings of a very private housing market underlie the determinants of growing geographical inequalities in health. The paper was published in 2010 in *The Annals of the Association of American Geographers* because Americans live with the most geographically polarised of health outcomes in the rich world. The findings are just as relevant to the UK where the increasingly unfair way in which our national housing stock is shared out is closely related to how inequalities in health between areas have risen.

This section ends with two more recent studies of growing geographical polarisation in poverty and wealth as it is being visualised both in Britain and worldwide. 'Because enough is never enough' was published in *The Journal of Applied Spatial Policy* as an example of just how much detail we now know of the geographies of who has most and who has least, where they live, and how these two residential patterns are interrelated. This is followed by a short extract from a much longer paper also published in 2010, in *The Geographical Journal*, on how these housing patterns in turn are connected to how we categorise people according to their area of residence, on how those places then separate groups, including separation by race, mortality and politics, and even by patterns of when we give birth, influenced too by hopes and fears over housing.

# 33

# Mortality amongst street sleeping youth in the UK[1]

*The Lancet* (1998) 29 August, p 743

Sir – Elise Roy and colleagues (July 4, p 32)[2] report on mortality among street youth in Montreal, Canada. They found standardised mortality ratios (SMRs) among street youth aged 14–25 years (n=10) were almost 12 times that of the general population (11·67/1). As is the case in North America, while there is some evidence of the morbidity of the homeless in Britain,[3] little is known about their death rates as compared with the general population. However, a charity for the homeless, Crisis, has published details of deaths among Londoners who were classified as being of no fixed abode on their death certificates,[4] with information on age and sex. From these data it is possible to calculate SMRs for male rough sleepers in London. The number of rough sleepers is taken from the 1991 Census.[5]

---

[1] Written jointly with Mary Shaw and published as a short note of correspondence.

[2] Roy, E., Boivin, J-F., Haley, N. and Lemire, N. (1998) 'Mortality among street youth', *Lancet*, no 352, p 32.

[3] Bines, W. (1994) *The health of single homeless people*, York: Centre for Housing Policy, University of York.

[4] Grenier, P. (1996) *Still dying for a home*, London: Crisis.

[5] Shaw, M. (1998) *A place apart: the spatial polarisation of mortality in Brighton*, Bristol: University of Bristol.

**Table 1:** Mortality among rough sleepers in London and among the general population

| Age (Years) | Male rough sleepers in London (1995/96) | | | | Total male population of England and Wales (1995) | | |
|---|---|---|---|---|---|---|---|
| | Rough sleeper deaths | Rough sleepers | Death rate per 1000 people | SMR (95% CI) [Note national average was 100] | Deaths | Population | Death rate per 1000 people |
| 16-29 | 14 | 341 | 41.1 | 3,732 (2,038-6,263) | 5,759 | 5,101,800 | 1.1 |
| 30-44 | 12 | 292 | 71.9 | 3,127 (1,935-4,780) | 12,826 | 5,682,900 | 2.3 |
| 45-64 | 32 | 203 | 157.6 | 2,074 (1,418-2,928) | 44,460 | 5,830,200 | 7.6 |

There are undoubtedly many difficulties with the reliability of these data; it is impossible to calculate with great accuracy death rates for this indeterminate and mobile population. The results in the table are, however, the first to be calculated for a UK sample, and suggest that the death rates of male rough sleepers aged 16–29 years are almost 40 times those of the general population. For all men aged 16–64 years, this number is about 25 times greater (SMR=2587).

Although it is not surprising that rough sleepers have higher death rates than the general housed population, the magnitude of the difference noted here is startling. In the light of the fact that homelessness seems to be becoming a permanent feature of society, this high rate is cause for grave concern.

# 34

# Daylight robbery: there's no shortage of housing[1]

*Roof Magazine* (2009) vol 34, no 3, p 11

'Our system for regulating markets and for prosecuting market crime is completely broken. If you mug someone in the street and you are caught, the chances are that you will go to prison. In recent years mugging someone out of their savings or their pension would probably earn you a yacht.' Sir Ken Macdonald, a former Director of Public Prosecutions, *The Times*, 23 February 2009.

'Joining an investment bank was like "joining a gang of jewellery robbers just after they made the heist of the century and just before they got caught by the police."' 32-year-old mergers and acquisitions banker with an MBA quoted by Adrian Cox in the *Financial Times* 10 February 2009.

---

[1] Original article had the subtitle ..."the stock has just been shared out abysmally – and that's the fault of the market"

It would hardly be surprising if the average homeowner felt they'd been mugged during the past 12 months, and were bruised and battered from an average loss of about £25,000.

It's not so much the money. If you're philosophical, you know you never really had it anyway. But the cash's disappearance was out of your hands – and you can't help feeling that you've been taken for a ride by people who walked away with riches before the crisis hurt everyone else.

Down the average street, 40 properties are now worth an aggregate of £1 million less than last year. All those millions of lost £25,000s. If you had a mortgage it was money that was yours, not the banks.

If you are a mortgagee, wherever you live in Britain, the bank now owns a higher proportion of your home. If the government properly nationalised the banks then we would all be a little more equal, but the government is trying desperately not to take that course, even printing money to avoid it.

The last time this happened, there was hyper-inflation. That is worth remembering if you've a tracker mortgage and inflation does return.

What do the banks say? Be cheerful. Keep a stiff upper lip. Recovery will come. The latest Halifax house price index bulletin said: 'The house price to average earnings ratio has declined from a peak of 5.84 in July 2007 to an estimated 4.42 in February 2009, a fall of 24 per cent. The ratio is at its lowest level for six years (February 2003: 4.41). The long-term average is 4.0.'

The implication is that housing is now 'affordable' – we should be looking for the upturn. But back in 2003, people were not buying because housing was affordable. They were buying because they thought they had no choice, because they did not want to fail to get on the bottom rung of a ladder.

The rise in house prices at the end of the 1990s, and in the first seven years of this decade bore no relationship to increases in demand. The rate of young household formation was actually dropping in every county in the Halifax index, while house prices rose rapidly everywhere between 1997 and 1999.

The explanation was: 'A shortage of quality properties has created localised hot-spots in certain areas of the country, particularly around Greater London.' (Housing Finance, August 1999). The words 'quality properties' were shorthand for snobbery and fear, for wanting to buy homes away from the growing ranks of poorer people.

Those localised hotspots of house price growth converged and spread to make speculation a national craze. In rich countries throughout the world price escalation became an epidemic. In the United States you chose between trying to catch the last wave, taking out a mortgage you could never repay, or bringing your kids up in the trailer-park.

Ultimately it is distance from trailer-parks that determines what is a 'quality property'.

Small groups of people have walked away with ill-gotten earnings. Holiday homes they bought abroad, a bit of land held here, or there, or a child's 'trust fund', 'as insurance'. The rich hold no mortgages, they live without debt.

In 2009, if you are a normal 'homeowner', it is easier now than at any time in memory (since the 1930s) to realise that you have a lot in common with people in other tenures, people in insecure renting, council tenants who have paid for the building and upkeep of their homes many times over. You might even see you have something in common with people threatened with homelessness.

You have been robbed. That is not to say that you 'earned' the money when your home appeared to rise in value. But there were people intent on stoking up the distrust, fear and social inequality required to convince many, like you, that it was worth borrowing so much just to live a little further away from others.

You were mugged by those who peddled stories that there was a shortage of housing, when in fact we've never had so much, just never shared it out so badly. You were done over by people with £1 million bonuses who were not that sure what they were doing, or why.

The most seriously injured by this latest outrage will be those who have their homes repossessed. The ones likely to lose most will be those who bought in the cheapest areas, the areas where prices fall furthest.

But we all lose out as our cynicism grows and our mistrust of each other's motives and intentions rises. We lose out as some begin to look for 'bargains' to snap-up at auction. We lose out as those with a motive try to shock the failed market back to life lie to us. They say it is time to buy, and oppose moves to increase social renting as that would 'weaken demand'.

It was false demand, demand stoked with fear, not need or even greed. When households fall into mortgage arrears, they should be able to transfer ownership of their property from a bank to the local authority (the 'right to sell') to avoid repossession. You should demand that it is not profitable for one household to own many properties, second and holiday homes, often left empty. But insist instead that the 'right to sell' is extended. A right which means that anyone's neighbours can become council tenants. Just as council tenants have a right to buy. That way you can look up the hill and not look in awe. Most importantly, if you don't want to be robbed again, look for the signs that someone is walking away with the loot. But this would only be possible with a nationalised bank, and housing safeguarded by the state.

Nationalising home lending would be as radical as having health and education provided for by the state. That was opposed in 1929, but most affluent countries now have comprehensive health insurance and free secondary education.

Markets are brilliant mechanisms for distributing trivia and trinkets. Souks are wonderful places to pick up clothes, decorations and gifts. But when it comes to putting roofs over people's heads, giving them learning and relief from the fear of illness, free markets are frighteningly inefficient.

The map below was not included in the original article but is from *Bankrupt Britain: An atlas of social change.*[2]

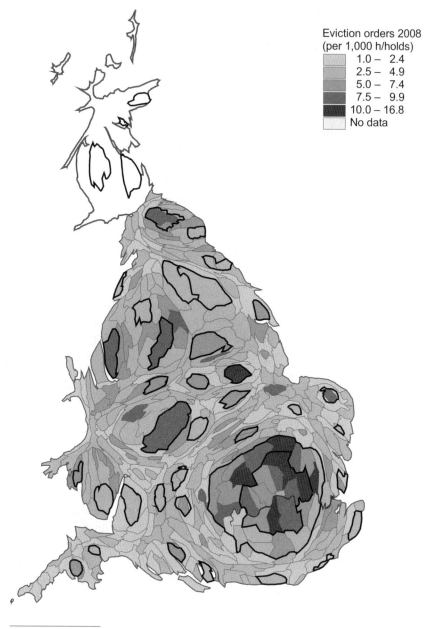

Eviction orders 2008
(per 1,000 h/holds)
1.0 – 2.4
2.5 – 4.9
5.0 – 7.4
7.5 – 9.9
10.0 – 16.8
No data

---

[2] Dorling, D and Thomas, B (2011) *Bankrupt Britain: An atlas of social change*, Bristol: The Policy Press (page 39).

# 35

# The influence of selective migration patterns[1]

*Annals of the Association of American Geographers* (2010)
vol 100, no 2, pp 393–409

**Abstract**

The research reported here uses New Zealand data on smoking behaviour that was collected in the 1981, 1996, and 2006 national censuses. Evaluation of the extent to which differential migration patterns among smokers, former smokers, and nonsmokers have contributed to geographical inequalities in health in New Zealand suggests that the effect of selective migration appears to be significant over the long term. This effect includes the arrival of large numbers of nonsmokers from abroad to the most affluent parts of New Zealand. The recording of these events and the high quality of the census in New Zealand provides evidence of one key mechanism whereby geographical inequalities in health between areas can be greatly exacerbated across a country – differential migration by health status. This assertion has important implications for studies monitoring spatial inequalities in health over time, and research investigating "place effects" on health.

**Key words:** health inequalities • migration • mobility • New Zealand • smoking

---

[1] Written with Jamie R. Pearce, now at the Institute of Geography, School of GeoSciences, University of Edinburgh. Original title ended "... among smokers and nonsmokers on geographical inequalities in health". Just a small part of the original paper is reproduced here.

Recent studies have consistently demonstrated that in most Organisation for Economic Cooperation and Development (OECD) countries over the past twenty to thirty years, there has been a polarisation in health between geographical areas (Davey Smith et al, 2002). Using various area-level measures of mortality and morbidity, researchers have tended to find that, although there have been considerable improvements in health at national levels, these gains have not been consistent in all regions. In particular, there is clear evidence that less socially deprived areas have tended to benefit disproportionately from these improvements. For example, in the United States, there are extensive health inequalities among local counties, and this divide has widened considerably in recent decades (Singh and Siahpush, 2006). Between 1980 and 2000 there was a 60 percent increase in the size of the gap in life expectancy between the poorest and richest tenths of the population (Pearce and Dorling, 2006). In New Zealand, life expectancy increased between 1981 and 2001 from 70.4 and 76.4 years to 76.3 and 81.1, for males and females, respectively, but these increases were not consistent for all regions of the country, and in some (more socially deprived) places, mortality rates actually grew (Pearce et al, 2006; Pearce, Tisch and Barnett, 2008). Regional inequalities in life expectancy in New Zealand increased by approximately 50 percent over this period (Pearce and Dorling, 2006), during a phase of rapid social and economic change in New Zealand society (Le Heron and Pawson, 1996).

There has been considerable attention given to unravelling the processes that establish and perpetuate geographical inequalities in health, and to include explanations relating to the characteristics of the people living in the areas (eg, age, sex, socioeconomic status, and ethnicity) but also features of the places themselves (eg, local resources and health services, area deprivation, and environmental disamenities such as air pollution). One potential driver of spatial inequalities in health is the process of health selective migration (Anderson, Ferris and Zickmantel, 1964; Kelsey, Mood and Acheson, 1968; Bentham, 1988). Research into health selective migration has considered whether "healthy" or "unhealthy" people have a greater or lesser propensity to move residence, as well as the implications of such movements for changing patterns in area-level health inequalities. If a sorting process occurs in which people in better health are more likely to move to (or remain in) less deprived areas, and those in poorer health are more likely to move into (or remain in) more deprived areas, then spatial inequalities in health will be exacerbated. Although the potential significance of selective migration effects for geographical studies has long been recognized (Anderson, Ferris and Zickmantel, 1964; Fox and Goldblatt, 1982), only recently have researchers attempted to quantify the effects of these processes on spatial inequalities in health. The health inequalities literature has not tended to examine selective mobility proactively as a partial account for the geographical patterning in health status and health-related behaviours. At best, health-related migration and mobility has been considered as a statistical artefact rather than a substantive area of academic enquiry (Smith and Easterlow, 2005).

Research in Great Britain has tended to demonstrate that selective migration and immobility has strengthened the relationship between area deprivation and various health outcomes including mortality (Brimblecombe, Dorling and Shaw, 1999; Norman, Boyle and Rees, 2005; Connolly, O'Reilly and Rosato, 2007), Type 2 diabetes (Cox et al, 2007), and ischemic heart disease (Strachan, Leon and Dodgeon, 1995). For example, an examination of 10,264 British residents enumerated as part of the British Household Panel Survey in 1991 found that at the local (district) scale the major geographical variations in age- and sex-standardized mortality could be attributed to selective migration (Brimblecombe, Dorling and Shaw, 1999). This effect was particularly pronounced among men. Similarly, using longitudinal data in England and Wales over a twenty-year period (1971–1991), Norman, Boyle and Rees (2005) found that the migrants who move from more to less deprived areas are significantly healthier than migrants who move from less to more deprived areas, and that the largest absolute flow was by relatively healthy migrants moving away from more deprived areas toward less deprived areas.

The results from studies of selective migration effects outside of Great Britain are more mixed. The findings of research in Australia (Larson, Bell and Young, 2004) and the United States (Landale, Gorman and Oropesa, 2006) concur with the British work and suggest that differential migration patterns between healthy and unhealthy groups are a key explanation in understanding the varying health outcomes in the providing and receiving areas. On the other hand, research in the Netherlands, Northern Ireland, and Norway demonstrates that selective migration patterns have had little, if any, effect on neighbourhood (Dalgard and Tambs, 1997; Connolly and O'Reilly, 2007; van Lenthe, Martikainen and Mackenbach, 2007), or urban–rural (Verheij et al, 1998) inequalities in health.

For example, van Lenthe, Martikainen and Mackenbach (2007) studied individuals aged twenty-five to seventy-four living in the city of Eindhoven in the Netherlands and found that after adjustment for sociodemographic characteristics at the individual level, selective migration made a negligible contribution to neighbourhood inequalities in health and health-related behaviours within the city; however, although 27,070 people were targeted to participate in this study, 30 percent of those approached refused to participate, and a further 45 percent of respondents were excluded because they did not reside within the city limits. The exclusion of this group seems surprising given that it has been established that the migration patterns between urban and rural areas tend to be selective. Further, respondents younger than twenty-five, and those who moved but whose location was unknown, were also excluded. Therefore, the study design might have minimized any measurable effects of selective migration patterns.

A study in Northern Ireland for the period 2000 to 2005 found that although there was evidence of significant variations in health between migrants and non-migrants, this differential had no impact on neighbourhood inequalities in health, partly because migrants out of deprived areas had a similar health status to the replacement in-migrants (Connolly and O'Reilly, 2007); however, the study period was a particularly unusual period of change in the recent history of Northern Ireland. Other than the former Yugoslavia and Cyprus, there are few other European examples where residential migration has been more disrupted by violence in the last three decades. Until recently, few people from affluent areas of the United Kingdom would consider moving even to prosperous areas of Northern Ireland and outmigration flows were high from many parts of Northern Ireland, not simply the poorest places (Dorling and Thomas, 2004). The unusual circumstances in Northern Ireland might have hindered the general patterns of differential migration that are evident in most OECD countries.[2]

## Migration effects

Demographic accounting was undertaken to first ascertain the net movement of smokers into each area due to internal migration within New Zealand. To determine the overall migration balance it was necessary to examine the movement of both smokers and nonsmokers into and out of each District Health Board (DHB, see Figure 1 for their boundaries). The methodology is best described by using an example (see Figure 2 for an outline of the methods). If more male smokers came to Auckland than left Auckland, then all else being equal, we would expect males living in Auckland to report worse health over time. In 1981, there were 108,711 males (aged fifteen and older) living in the Auckland DHB. Of these, 36,651 were smokers, and of this total 10,431 were living outside of Auckland five years previously (and of these migrant smokers, 3,264 had migrated into New Zealand during that period). Therefore, in 1981 just over one third of the males in the Auckland DHB were smokers; a third of male smokers had arrived in the Auckland DHB within the previous five years; and of this group of migrant male smokers, one third were new (past five years) arrivals into New Zealand. In addition, it is possible to calculate that a further 34,584 male smokers who had lived in Auckland in 1976 were living elsewhere in New Zealand by 1981. However, we cannot ascertain how many had left Auckland to live overseas, as these data are not collected. Therefore, ignoring

---

[2] Editorial note: See original article for remainder of introductory text and information on data and methods.

emigrants, there were 2,067 (36,651 – 34,584) more smokers in Auckland in 1981 than in 1976.

**Figure 1:** District health boards across New Zealand (2006)

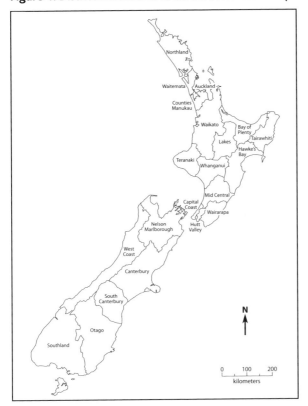

Although there were more male smokers in Auckland in 1981 than in 1976, it does not necessarily follow that a higher proportion of males in the Auckland DHB were smokers in 1981 than 1976 because the overall population of the city grew over this period (and people who do not move might alter their smoking behaviour). To determine whether the overall migration balance of smokers and nonsmokers was positive or negative we must also consider the movements of those who have never smoked.

From the 1981 census we can calculate that of the 108,711 males living in the Auckland DHB, 44,568 never smoked, and of those some 12,018 had been living outside of Auckland DHB five years previously (and of these 3,705 migrated to New Zealand during this period). Therefore, in 1981 41 percent of males in Auckland had never smoked, of whom 27 percent had moved into the city, in turn of whom 31 percent had arrived into the country. Some 41,229 men who had never smoked and lived in Auckland in 1976 now lived elsewhere. So the balance of never-smokers to Auckland by 1981 was 3,339 (44,568 − 41,229). Again we have to ignore emigrants.

**Figure 2:** Flowchart depicting the methods used to calculate the smoking migration balance in the Auckland district health board (1981)

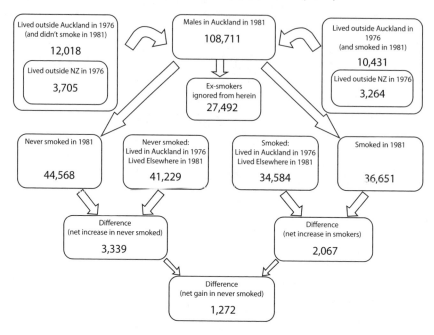

If we consider the overall change in the balance of smokers that can be attributed to selective migration patterns during the period from 1976 to 1981 in the Auckland DHB, then we find that there was a net gain of 2,067 smokers and 3,339 never-smokers, which resulted in a 1,272 net gain in never-smokers in 1981 compared to 1976. This figure represents 1.2 percent of the male population of the Auckland DHB. These calculations were completed for males and females in all DHBs across the country for each time period for which smoking data were collected (1981, 1996, and 2006). To investigate the potentially different influences of internal and international migration on the smoking balance, the analyses were repeated with immigrants excluded from the calculations[3].

---

[3] Editorial note: The remainder of this section and sections on the 'Effects on Life Expectancy', 'Overall Results', 'Trends in Smoking Rates: 1981 to 2006', the 'Smoking Migration Balance', the 'Effects of International Migration', the 'Smoking–Migration Balance and Life Expectancy' and a 'Discussion' have all been extracted to aid readability!

## Conclusion

This study has investigated the complex nature of migration streams to exemplify how geographical inequalities in health across regions of New Zealand are significantly influenced by the health (in this case smoking status) of the population entering and leaving each area. The results add to the international evidence that selective migration is an important process in explaining regional inequalities in health. It is important that future studies of spatial inequalities in health account for the potentially important effect of selective mobility that might otherwise lead to interpretations of ecological associations and area effects that are, in fact, artifactual. Accounting for the selective mobilities of people with varying health outcomes, needs, and experiences is an important domain for future research endeavour. Augmenting the understanding of health and mobility provides a considerable opportunity to enhance the appreciation of geographical processes in explaining and addressing inequalities in health.

## References

Anderson, D.O., Ferris, B.G. Jr. and Zickmantel, R. (1964) 'Levels of air pollution and respiratory disease in Berlin, New Hampshire', *American Review of Respiratory Disease*, no 90, pp 877–87.

Bentham, G. (1988) 'Migration and morbidity: implications for geographical studies of disease', *Social Science and Medicine*, vol 26, no 1, pp 49–54.

Brimblecombe, N., Dorling, D. and Shaw, M. (1999) 'Mortality and migration in Britain: first results from the British Household Panel Survey' *Social Science and Medicine*, vol 49, no 7, pp 981–88.

Connolly, S. and O'Reilly, D. (2007) 'The contribution of migration to changes in the distribution of health over time: five-year follow-up study in Northern Ireland', *Social Science and Medicine*, vol 65, no 5, pp 1004–11.

Connolly, S., O'Reilly, D. and Rosato, M. (2007) 'Increasing inequalities in health: is it an artefact caused by the selective movement of people?', *Social Science and Medicine*, vol 64, no 10, pp 2008–15.

Cox, M., Boyle, P. J., Davey, P. and Morris, A. (2007) 'Does health-selective migration following diagnosis strengthen the relationship between Type 2 diabetes and deprivation?', *Social Science and Medicine*, vol 65, no 1, pp 32–42.

Dalgard, O. S. and Tambs, K. (1997) 'Urban environment and mental health: a longitudinal study', *British Journal of Psychiatry*, no 171, pp 530–6.

Davey Smith, G., Dorling, D., Mitchell, R. and Shaw, M. (2002) 'Health inequalities in Britain: continuing increases up to the end of the 20th century', *Journal of Epidemiology and Community Health*, vol 56, no 6, pp 434–5.

Dorling, D. and Thomas, B. (2004) *People and places: A 2001 census atlas of the UK*, Bristol: The Policy Press.

Fox, A. and Goldblatt, P. (1982) *Longitudinal study: Sociodemographic mortality differentials*, London: HMSO.

Kelsey, J.L., Mood, E.W. and Acheson, R.M. (1968) 'Population mobility and epidemiology of chronic bronchitis in Connecticut', *Archives of Environmental Health*, vol 16, no 6, pp 853–61.

Landale, N. S., Gorman, B. K. and Oropesa, R. S. (2006) 'Selective migration and infant mortality among Puerto Ricans', *Maternal and Child Health Journal*, vol 10, no 4, pp 351–60.

Larson, A., Bell, M. and Young, A.F. (2004) 'Clarifying the relationships between health and residential mobility', *Social Science and Medicine*, vol 59, no 10, pp 2149–60.

Le Heron, R.B. and Pawson, E. (1996) *Changing places: New Zealand in the nineties*, Auckland, New Zealand: Longman Paul.

Moon, G. and Barnett, J.R. (2003) 'Spatial scale and the geography of tobacco smoking in New Zealand: a multilevel perspective', *New Zealand Geographer*, vol 59, no 2, pp 6–15.

Norman, P., Boyle, P. and Rees, P. (2005) 'Selective migration, health and deprivation: a longitudinal analysis', *Social Science and Medicine*, vol 60, no 12, pp 2755–71.

Pearce, J. and Dorling, D. (2006) 'Increasing geographical inequalities in health in New Zealand, 1980–2001', *International Journal of Epidemiology*, vol 35, no 3, pp 597–603.

Pearce, J., Tisch, C. and Barnett, R. (2008) 'Have geographical inequalities in cause-specific mortality in New Zealand increased during the period 1980–2001?', *New Zealand Medical Journal*, vol 121, no 1281, pp 15–27.

Pearce, J., Dorling, D., Wheeler, B., Barnett, R. and Rigby, J. (2006) 'Geographical inequalities in health in New Zealand, 1980–2001: the gap widens', *Australian and New Zealand Journal of Public Health*, vol 30, no 5, pp 461–66.

Singh, G. K. and Siahpush, M. (2006) 'Widening socioeconomic inequalities in US life expectancy, 1980–2000', *International Journal of Epidemiology*, vol 35, no 4, pp 969–79.

Smith, S.J. and Easterlow, D. (2005) 'The strange geography of health inequalities', *Transactions of the Institute of British Geographers*, vol 30, no 2, pp 173–90.

Strachan, D.P., Leon, D.A. and Dodgeon, B. (1995) 'Mortality from cardiovascular disease among interregional migrants in England and Wales' *British Medical Journal*, 310 (6977), pp 423–27.

van Lenthe, F.J., Martikainen, P. and Mackenbach, J.P. (2007) 'Neighbourhood inequalities in health and healthrelated behaviour: results of selective migration?', *Health and Place*, vol 13, no 1, pp 123–37.

Verheij, R.A., van de Mheen, H.D., de Bakker, D.H., Groenewegen, P.P. and Mackenbach, J.P. (1998) 'Urban–rural variations in health in The Netherlands: does selective migration play a part?', *Journal of Epidemiology and Community Health*, vol 52, no 8, pp 487–93.

<h1 style="text-align:center">36</h1>

# The geography of poverty, inequality and wealth in the UK and abroad[1]

*Journal of Applied Spatial Policy* (2010) vol 2, nos 2–3, pp 81–106

**Abstract**

This paper considers the temporal changes in levels of recorded poverty in Britain distinguishing between times of anecdotal reporting (1845–1901); the first national counts and geographical distribution descriptions (1895–1965); to the current era of an industry dedicated to poverty counting and cartography (1968–2008). The persistence to the geography of poverty over time is remarked upon and speculated over. In conclusion it is argued that it is important to understand the distribution of wealth to better understand poverty.

**Key words:** poverty • inequality • wealth • history • United Kingdom • income

## The origins of the statistics and cartography of poverty in England and Wales (1845–1901)

At the very centres of the twin hearts of the world economy, in London and New York, great wealth and miserable poverty are located only a stone's throw apart. We now know how unequal we are in great detail. But how did we get to know this detail so well? There are many stories that give

---

[1] Paper written jointly with John Pritchard when he was working at the University of Sheffield in the Social and Spatial Inequalities Group. The original article had the subtitle "because enough is never enough".

an answer. This particular story goes back a century and more to the four hundredth odd page of the 186th volume of the Philosophical Transactions of London. London is the most unequal part of the United Kingdom, a city of even greater social contrasts now than it was then.

At the foot of page 404 of Volume 186 of the Philosophical Transactions of the Royal Society of London, Series A (Mathematical), is a reference to an obscure diagram labelled "Plate 14, Figure 17: Statistics of Pauperism in England and Wales, distribution of 632 Unions, 1891." The diagram shows several curves and is reproduced as Figure 1 here. The curves describe the probability distribution for paupers by Poor Law Union (area), ranging from 1% up to almost 8.5% of the population of some areas of England and Wales, but with a mean about 3.5% and: "the observations are at once seen to give a markedly skew distribution" (Pearson 1895, p. 404–405). This is the first description of the national geography of poverty on these islands, but that is not what this graph is remembered for. It is remembered as the first example of a graph of chance, and as the one of the first examples of the suggestion that poverty is somehow inherited.

Squeezed between pages on the latent heat of evaporation of fluids and the specific heat of water, Series A of the *Transactions* appears now to be an odd home for one of the first scientific papers to describe the geographical

**Figure 1:** The first estimate of the geographical distribution of poverty in England and Wales

*Statistics of Pauperism in England and Wales, distribution of 632 Unions, 1891*

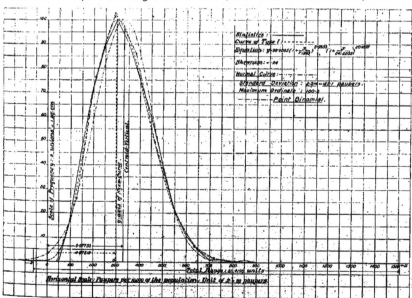

Source: Karl Pearson, Volume 186 of the Philosophical Transactions of the Royal Society of London, Series A (Mathematical).

distribution of poverty in England and Wales. The paper was written by Karl Pearson (MacKenzie, 1999) who later founded the first university statistics department in the world. His paper is mainly referred to today as containing one of the first examples of the curve of a probability distribution. However, amongst social scientists Pearson's work is now remembered as one of the early attempts to apply Charles Darwin's theory of evolution to people and to suggest that the poor have children often destined to be poor by dint of some biological mechanism (Dorling, 2010, Sections 4.2 and 4.3).

The curve Pearson drew shows how many Poor Law Union Areas contained just a few paupers and how many areas were home to far more poor people. Paupers were folk who were forced to rely on relief from the poor law and included those who lived in the workhouse in late nineteenth century England and Wales (Scotland was not included in this work). Paupers were the poorest of the poor of those times. To try to understand why there might be more poor folk in some areas than others Pearson fitted various models to the basic curve that described the data. He concluded that the point-binomial distribution fitted particularly well and that "the suggestiveness of such results for social problems needs no emphasising" (*ibid* page 405). Pearson went on to speculate that "if the statistical curve of pauperism for 1881 be compared with that of 1891 [the] curve is sliding across from right to left." (*ibid* page 406). In other words, poverty breeds poverty, and the result of that breeding is ever growing concentrations of the poor.

For Pearson and most other progressive learned folk of his time, poverty breeding poverty was a literal belief. This was the key influence of Darwin's work on those who study people. *The Origin of Species* (or *The Preservation of Favoured Races in the Struggle for Life*, to give it its poorly remembered alternative title; Darwin 1859) had been published shortly after Pearson was born, and *Hereditary Genius* just a decade later (by Galton in 1869). Galton was Darwin's half cousin and Pearson's mentor. Karl Pearson drew the curve to help establish part of his Mathematical Theory of Evolution (in "homogeneous material"). He saw pauperism as a biological outcome (the opposite of the "inherited genius") and the rise and geographic concentration of paupers as a great social problem clearly requiring eugenic solutions (although even in 1895 the language was coded as "social problems"). Pearson used the pauperism statistics to add supposed-weight to his discussion on heredity that began, if you look up the 1895 paper, on the frequency of the emergence of blossom in white clover and ended with discussions of skull shape, school-girl height, and school-boy short-sightedness.

Karl Pearson's data came from Appendix I of Charles Booths' 'Aged Poor' study (Booth, 1894). Booth was a contemporary of Pearson and drew the first detailed maps of poverty and wealth in London around this time; an example is shown in Figure 2. Thus the very first poverty statistics in England and

Wales, and the first poverty maps (of London) were closely related. A few short years later, in 1901, (Benjamin) Seebohm Rowntree, partly influenced also by Booth, drew his map of poverty and wealth in York (shown here as Figure 3). Just a couple of years after that a young man called William Beveridge wrote that there was a class that were unemployable, and that "they include those habituated to the workhouse and to the casual ward, and the many regular inmates of shelters who are paupers in all but name. For these, long periods of regular work and discipline in compulsory labour colonies are essential". (Beveridge and Maynard, 1904, quoted in Welshman 2006, page 591). Welshman argues eloquently that our current debates over the poor and their claiming of incapacity benefit for worklessness are now "shaped as much by ideological and political factors as by broader economic trends" (*ibid* page 604). By which he means as much as they were at the times of Rowntree, Beveridge and Booth. And that is just one of the reasons why this history needs to be told in contemporary analysis.

**Figure 2:** A fragment of Booth's descriptive map of London poverty

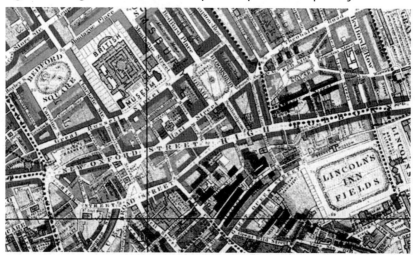

*see colour version in plate section*

*Source:* Dorling et al (2000) Figure 1. Detail: Booth's maps. Key: Yellow: Upper-middle and Upper classes. Wealthy, Red: Well-to-do. Middle-class, Pink: Fairly comfortable. Good ordinary earning, Purple: Mixed. Some comfortable, others poor, Pale Blue: Poor. 18s. to 21s. a week for moderate family, Dark blue: Very poor, casual. Chronic want, Black: Lowest class. Vicious, semi-criminal.

To bring this short story of the origins of the statistics and cartography of poverty in Britain to a close, Seebohm's father, Joseph Rowntree, had written a pamphlet on the very same subject as mentioned in Pearson's paper: "Pauperism in England and Wales", but thirty years earlier: in 1865. Joseph went on to give his name to the Foundation, Charitable Trust and Reform Trusts that have been so influential in British poverty politics during the last century and decade. However, not that much has changed in the intervening 150 years as to how we construct and then view the statistics and cartography of poverty (today). We still draw maps that label streets in particular ways – even if now through the geodemographics industry – and we still have a tendency to consider the geographical distribution of poverty as if others are people not like us – objects to be studied – paupers in all but name. To understand why it may be a good time to change some of the fundamental ways in which we look at poverty today – and in particular why it makes sense to simultaneously consider wealth – it is worth looking back at why most of these men who first studied poverty did not look in that direction.

**Figure 3:** Plan of the city of York – slum areas to servant keeping classes

see colour version in plate section

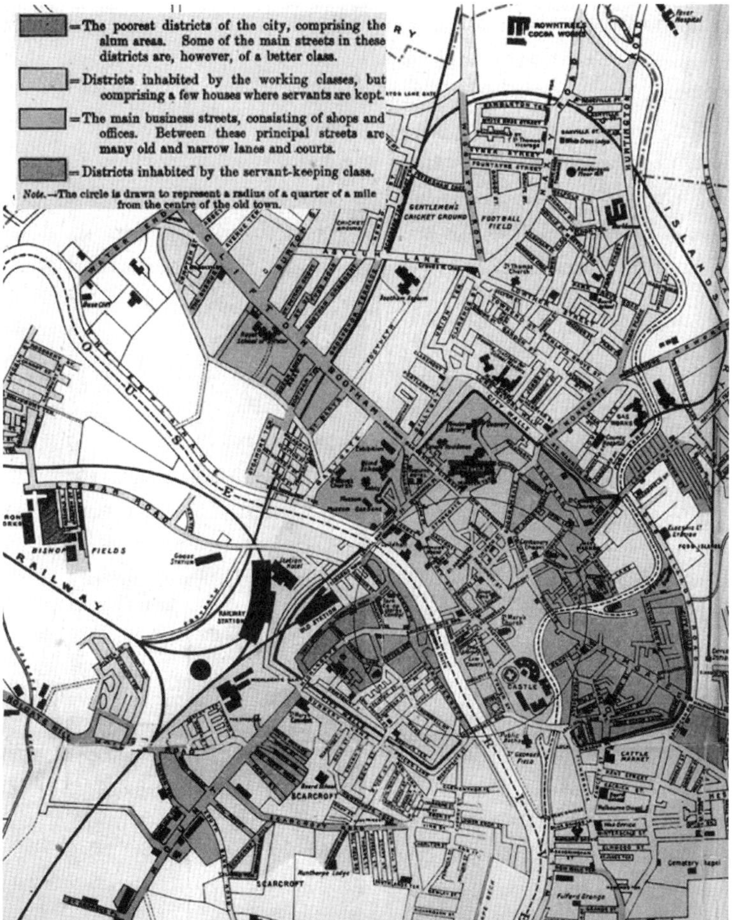

*Source:* Seebohm Rowntree, B. (2000 [1901]) *Poverty: A study of town life*, Bristol: The Policy Press.

All of these folk were connected – not just by similar social background but much more. Pearson was brought up a Quaker, his father was brought up by Quakers in York (as was Joseph Rowntree), and his mother's family were involved in shipping from Hull. Charles Booth was similarly born into a Liverpool ship-owning family. The Galtons were Quaker gun-smiths (presumably they did not use their own weapons given Quaker beliefs in non-violence). The Galtons were also bankers, from the city of Birmingham (those bankers had a lot to answer for even then!). Wealth, provincialism and Puritanism came together in the early study and mapping of poverty. This mix may also have obscured the views a little (or a lot) of those from these background. These men were not operating in a knowledge vacuum, but they had collectively decided to ignore much previously published work. Most obviously they ignored the writing of an immigrant (albeit a wealthy immigrant), who twenty years prior to Joseph Rowntree's pamphlet publication, and exactly fifty years before Pearson's graphs were drawn, had these words on poverty published:

> Society, composed wholly of atoms, does not trouble itself about them; leaves them to care for themselves and their families, yet supplies them no means of doing this in an efficient and permanent manner. Every working man, even the best, is therefore constantly exposed to loss of work and food, that is to death by starvation, and many perish in this way. The dwellings of the workers are everywhere badly planned, badly built, and kept in the worst condition, badly ventilated, damp, and unwholesome. The inhabitants are confined to the smallest possible space, and at least one family usually sleeps in each room. The interior arrangement of the dwellings is poverty-stricken in various degrees, down to the utter absence of even the most necessary furniture. The clothing of the workers, too, is generally scanty, and that of great multitudes is in rags. The food is, in general, bad; often almost unfit for use, and in many cases, at least at times, insufficient in quantity, so that, in extreme cases, death by starvation results. Thus the working class of the great cities offers a graduated scale of conditions in life, in the best cases a temporarily endurable existence for hard work and good wages, good and endurable, that is, from the worker's standpoint; in the worst cases, bitter want, reaching even homelessness and death by starvation. The average is much nearer the worst case than the best. And this series does not fall into fixed classes, so that one might say, this fraction of the working class is well off, has always been so, and remains so. (Engels, 1845, p 109)

Thus the first maps and statistics of poverty in Britain were drawn by folk who were rediscovering what had been written about in detail years earlier. But they were also ignoring one of the key discoveries of 1845, that the poor do not fall into fixed classes, but that each individual, family and community circulates between various degrees of destitution and coping over time. Poverty was rediscovered just over a century ago as still existing and affecting a huge proportion of the population (around a third according to both Rowntree and Booth), and this despite the absolute dominance and unimaginable wealth of the British Empire. Poverty in the midst of plenty and the constant rediscovering of endemic poverty are themes that arise again and again in the study of poverty in Britain.

## From the First National Counts to the First National Surveys (1895–1965)

The story of poverty into the twentieth century was a continuation of the story of a hobby. Poverty studies were something that well-meaning capitalists conducted in their spare time. And these were studies mostly for the otherwise idle but not without-conscience rich. Poverty was rife a long time before Friedrich Engels wrote on Manchester (King, 2000; Tomkins and King, 2003; Tomkins, 2006) and is rife in our times (see below). It also continues to be a concern for the paternalistic rich today. Worldwide the best example of this concern of the unbelievably rich for the plight of the extremely poor is given by the actions of Bill and Melinda Gates. They are not shy about their actions or their Foundation, so it is not hard to find out about just how charitable they have been. Back in Britain it does not take many jumps of historical figures to go from the interest in poverty amongst those who helped create the Labour Party in Britain back then, to those who helped turn it into something "new" in 1997, as the next two paragraphs show. The year 2009 marked the centenary in Britain of the key Royal Commission on the Poor Laws, which continued the story of the interest of the rich and famous into the early years of the last century, although now for the first significant time there are women involved too.

These women were Helen Bosanquet and Beatrice Webb – key figures in the majority and minority reports respectively of the 1909 Royal Commission on the Poor Laws. Helen was the daughter of a Manchester business man, and had clashed publicly with Seebohm Rowntree in 1902. Beatrice was the daughter of a Wigan railway entrepreneur. Neither Beatrice nor Helen needed to work due to the wealth of their husband and father respectively. Beatrice was influential in the early work of the Fabian Society, and fledgling Labour Party, and had worked for Charles Booth, helped establish the London School of Economics, and the weekly publication *New Statesman*. In contrast, Helen Bosanquet, arguing on the less progressive side of the debate has left little impact. But both were establishment figures and neither was responsible for there being a Royal Commission in the first place.

The Royal Commission came about due to the interest of another immigrant (to England at least): David Lloyd George (initially not wealthy) who in turn influenced greatly William Beveridge (born wealthy), who was appointed director of Labour exchanges in 1909 – the geographical heirs of Poor Law Union Areas. Following the implementation of much of what Beveridge and his colleagues suggested in a later report (now best known by his name), an aging Seebohm Rowntree, with George Russell Lavers, suggested that poverty had mostly disappeared in Britain by 1951 (Rowntree and Lavers, 1951). What happened next has been neatly summarised by Howard Glennerster, in an extract from his essay on "One hundred years of poverty and policy" selected, in theory, to help Tony Blair think better about poverty in 2000. Glennerster wrote this:

> Abel-Smith and Townsend (1965) used the national sample provided by the Family Expenditure Survey and updated Rowntree's poverty line in line with prices as a check on their own findings for 1953/54 (see below). They found 5.4% of households in poverty. When Atkinson et al. (1981) reanalysed Rowntree's data using the then National Assistance Board scales as the poverty line they found that 14.4% of working class households would have been judged poor. More recently Hatton and Bailey (2000) have reanalysed the same material to test Rowntree and Lavers' claim that poverty had fallen so dramatically because of the impact of post-war social policy. They found it did fall, but by nothing like as much as the earlier study claimed. Rowntree and Lavers claimed that the fall in poverty had been 20 percentage points. Hatton and Bailey suggest it was about 10 percentage points and much of that was the result of food subsidies: 'It is unfortunate that, in the absence of other comparable studies for the 1950s, this produced a somewhat distorted picture of poverty in the early post war period, an impression which took two decades to counteract' (Glennerster 2000, in Glennerster et al, 2004, p 537).

Peter Townsend, as a new young researcher at the Institute for Community Studies, was asked to review Rowntree and Lavers and was not convinced. It led him to a lifetime of work that has changed the way we think about poverty in most developed economies, with the exception of the United States (Glennerster, 2002).

Townsend's central point was that we cannot determine a level of adequacy simply by virtue of some expert calculation of dietary or health needs.

Social custom requires that we share cups of tea with neighbours or buy presents for our children at Christmas, even have the occasional pint. (see also Glennerster et al, 2004, pp 86–7).

Peter Townsend, who died in 2009 (and those who worked with him), changed fundamentally the way that poverty was thought of and mapped in Britain, in Europe and now in much of the world outside of the United States. His ideas of poverty have been further developed by David Gordon and colleagues as illustrated in Figure 4 (Gordon and Townsend, 2000; Gordon et al, 2000). And, ironically, just as Townsend, Atkins, and Hatton

**Figure 4:** A model of the dynamics of poverty and five categories of household

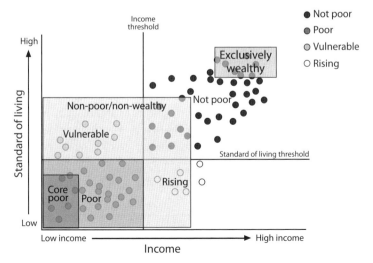

*Source:* Adapted from David Gordon's original (personal communication)

and their colleagues all referred to above found more poverty in York than Rowntree and Lavers' 1951 publication had suggested at the time, so too has contemporary re-analysis of Townsend's work of the 1960s found levels of poverty to have been higher then than was previously thought to have been the case (Dorling et al, 2007).

In Figure 4 a dynamic model of poverty is drawn to illustrate Friedrich Engels' assertion referenced above that: "The average is much nearer the worst case than the best. And this series does not fall into fixed classes, so that one might say, this fraction of the working class is well off, has always been so, and remains so". Each circle in the figure represents a hypothetical household. Poverty is defined using a relative poverty line – defined theoretically by Townsend (1979) as the resource level which is so low that people living below it are excluded from participating in the norms of society. This resource level can be determined using the Breadline Britain Index which is detailed in Gordon and Pantazis (1997). In practice those people living in households with a standard of living measured by the index to be below the crucial level, and with an income below that needed to raise this standard of living above that level are the "breadline poor", and are labelled as poor in the lower left hand box in the graph at the top of Figure 4. If and when their household incomes rise they move rightwards, and later increase their spending and are no longer poor (now being in the top right hand corner of the top diagram). For those in that corner whose income falls substantially, they move leftwards, but tend to attempt to maintain their standards of living despite falling incomes. They are thus "vulnerable". It is then only when they can no longer maintain living standards, often nowadays when debts are too high, that their standard of living falls too, the circles representing them fall downwards on the graph, and they are (in many cases again) poor.

The version of the model at the bottom of Figure 4 is the same as that at the top of Figure 4, now except that new subsets of the population have been defined from the poorest of the poor ("core poor") to the rich, and exclusively rich in the more elaborate version of this illustrative figure. These are not fixed classes. Households do move between them and lie on the borders of them, but they are a useful way of thinking about what people fall into, and how they have to climb over the backs of others to get out. These new categories have been defined as follows.

- Core poor: people who are income poor, materially deprived and subjectively poor
- Breadline poor: people living below a relative poverty line, and as such excluded from participating in the norms of society
- Non-poor, non-wealthy: the remainder of the population classified as neither poor nor wealthy

- Asset wealthy: estimated using the relationship between housing wealth and the contemporary inheritance tax threshold
- Exclusive wealthy: people with sufficient wealth to exclude themselves from the norms of society

Note that the core poor and exclusive wealthy households are subsets of the Breadline Poor and Asset Wealthy respectively. Reanalysis of Townsend's 1968 poverty survey finds that just under a quarter of households were breadline poor around then, around 1 in 7 were core poor and only 1 in 14 were exclusively rich (see Dorling et al, 2007 for more details, the text that follows, and Figure 7 for the 2001 distribution).

Thus, in moving from 1895 to a reanalysis of work first started in 1951, we no longer have folk simply labelled as 'paupers'; but those who are extremely poor; functionally poor; neither poor nor wealthy; asset wealthy; and a subset of them so wealthy that they can exclude themselves from the

**Figure 5:** Poverty in London, 1896, 1991 and mortality (1990s)

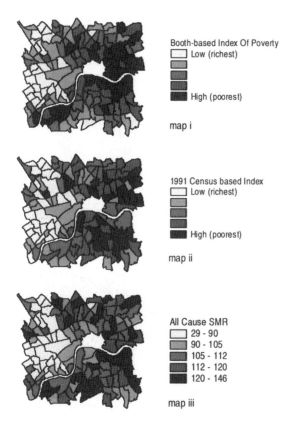

Booth-based Index Of Poverty
Low (richest)

High (poorest)

map i

1991 Census based Index
Low (richest)

High (poorest)

map ii

All Cause SMR
29 - 90
90 - 105
105 - 112
112 - 120
120 - 146

map iii

*Source:* Dorling et al (2000) Figure 3. *London poverty (1896 and 1991) and mortality (1990s).*

norms of society through their access to wealth. In this way the statistical categories begin to resemble the colour keys to the early maps of poverty (Figures 2 and 3) – where the rich had to be included because there is nowhere to hide on a map. It has taken over a century for the statistics of poverty to catch up with its cartography.

## Current era and the persistence of poverty over time (1968–2008)

The reassessment of Rowntree's work of the late 1940s and of Townsend's in the late 1960s (and that of their colleagues) suggests that the general level of poverty in Britain has had a persistence that is stronger than we thought during much of the middle of the last century. If a longer perspective is taken then, as Figure 5 illustrates, the map of poverty in London and elsewhere in Britain (Dorling et al, 2000; Dorling, 2003, 2004, 2006; Gregory et al, 2001) has not changed greatly. In fact the map of 1890 is slightly more closely linked to mortality outcomes in the 1990s than the poverty map of 1991! The persistence is so strong that two of the towns (Salford and Oldham) that Engels identified as having the highest mortality rates in England in 1845 were the two with the highest standardised rates by 1995. And conveniently – for those who do not believe that poverty (or much else that affects life

**Figure 6:** Vickers' map: York 2001

see colour version in plate section

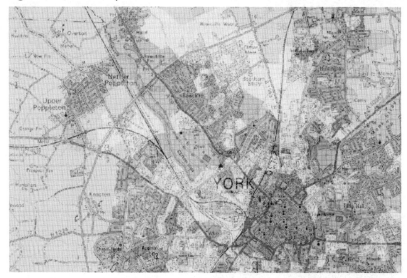

*Key:* Blue: "Idyllic Countryside"; Orange: "Comfortable Estates"; Light Green: "Typical Traits"; Brown: Inner City Multi Cultural (not found in York); Dark Green: "Blue Collar"; Red: "Melting Pot"; Purple: "Constrained by Circumstances". Source: Map supplied by Dan Vickers, when PhD student, University of Leeds. Based on analysis of the 2001 census jointly with the Office for National Statistics, unpublished at that time.

expectancy) is inherited – population turnover in these towns over those 150 years has been such that the great grandparents of many dying there today grew up in what is now Pakistan; areas inherit disadvantage and advantage much more than people do.

Poverty and wealth are fractal in their geographies. Similar to the pattern in London and in Britain more widely, there is still gross poverty within the city of York (see Figure 6), the area which was studied and became a catalyst of social change at the start of the last century and which is now often seen as a rich town (and which Helen Bosanquet labelled as rich also when Seebohm wrote on it!). In fact, there is no town or city within the United Kingdom where neither poverty nor affluence is found. The forces which operate to both maintain and transform places are in operation across the country, varying little (see Dorling, 2010, Chapter 6). The forces are also extremely resistant to intervention. Over time when a town or city fares well its poorer areas contract compared to the spreading seen elsewhere, and affluent suburbs expand in area. Thus, in comparison to most towns and cities in the North of England, there are fewer poor enclaves in York than elsewhere, but nevertheless poor enclaves remain and have spread since 1901 (Figure 7).

**Figure 7:** Distribution of households by poverty and wealth in Britain in 2000

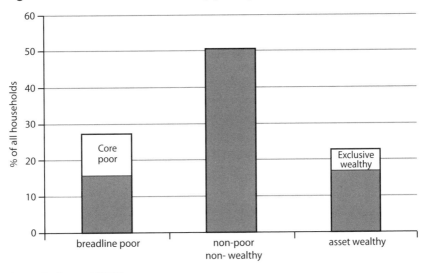

*Source:* Dorling et al (2007)

The persistence of poverty is of course not just an issue for research in Britain, it is the subject of much current debate in America too. There, the Brookings Institute (Jargowsky, 2003) suggests that despite the numbers of (extremely) poor people in the US rising from 31.7 million to 33.9 million between 1990 and 2000, the number of high-poverty neighbourhoods where over 40% of the population were poor declined by a quarter. This, if true would be a reversal of the rises in concentrated poverty seen in the United States between 1970 and 1990. The US poverty line is set notoriously low, raised only by inflation, and thus the proportion of the population who fell beneath it reduced from 13.1% to 12.4% over the 1990s (the absolute numbers only rose because the population in total rose). Nevertheless, this change in the spatial concentration of the poor is dramatic if it turns out to have happened. In the poorest parts of the US, disproportionate numbers of residents saw their incomes increase by just enough to raise them over the poverty line in the 1990s, more than for the poor elsewhere. The effect on cities such as Detroit is, at first glance, stunning (see Figure 8).

**Figure 8:** Highest poverty neighbourhoods in Detroit, 1970–2000

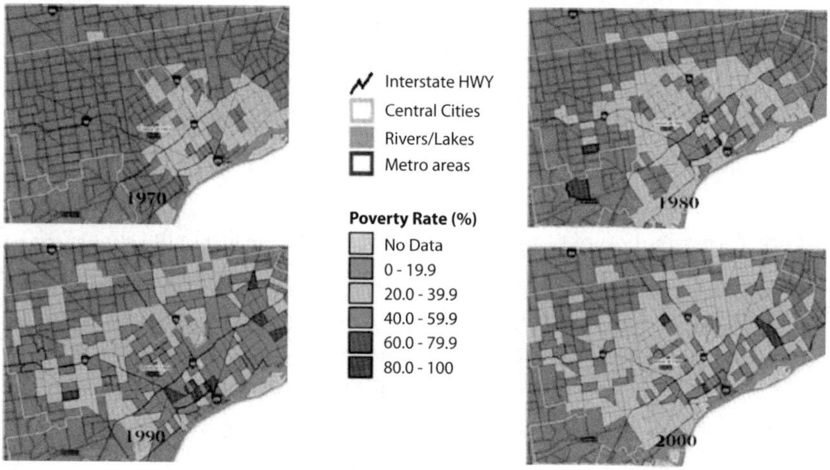

*Source:* Jargowsky (2003) Figure 5.

There are themes that re-emerge and repeat, across times and places. From the 1840s Manchester that Engels described in the first long quotation above, to twenty-first century America – extreme rates of poverty were and are tolerated – there are no immune groups, and the spectre of hunger (or malnutrition) is ever present. That hunger and desperation may be hidden away from the main streets, whereas the rich parade their wealth around the squares (see Figure 2 on page 266), but it was and is there nevertheless, and has been for some time. There is a tendency to assume progress in reducing poverty and then to be shocked when it does not materialise. Charles Booth's maps of 1880s and 1890s London were drawn as its author tried to disprove that poverty was still rife in the capital of that country half a century after Friedrich Engels had documented the excess in newly industrialised Manchester, and following decades of supposed reform between 1845 and

1895. In Figure 9 we show changing poverty rates in and around Manchester in the decades over a century later; decades which again were supposed to include huge social reforms, including the demolishing and rebuilding of entire estates within Manchester.

**Figure 9:** Breadline poor households across the Liverpool/Manchester area, 1970 to 2000

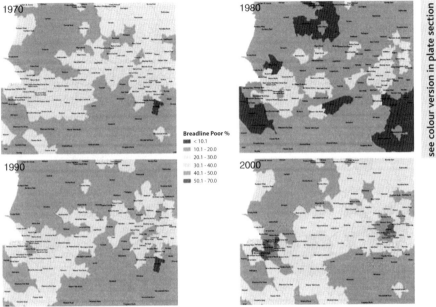

*Source:* Figure 2. Dorling et al (2007)

The labels we give areas and people change (contrast the keys to Figures 2 and 6 for instance), but the inequalities persist, as does their importance. It is hard to resist the conclusion that because so much else of our means of production, distribution, reward and threat is similar now to what was common in the 1840s, that we should not be surprised to find rates of relative poverty that are similar over time. Thus an unimaginable change in absolute levels of material wellbeing can coincide with so little change in the relative ranking of people and areas. Levels of income inequality and even murder rates with Britain have now returned to their Victorian highs despite increases in overall material wealth.

When poverty in London measured by house to house visits in the 1880s and 1890s is compared to that estimated from a survey and a census taken in 1991, it is evident that the map changes ever so slowly. Compare maps i and ii of Figure 5. There are differences – but many areas that changed – went downhill for instance since Victorian times – have since reverted back to their former socio-geographical positions: the Notting Hills of London (as opposed to its 'Notting Dales' – the first ever 'special area'). When change has happened in as packed an area as London it has not been as a result of new transportation systems being introduced (the train, tram and car), or cataclysmic events such as war and the blitz. Instead it was the arrival of a few darker skinned people from the West Indies and where they could find to call home that is most closely associated with visible differences between these maps that separate a century.

**Figure 10:** Breadline poor households across the Home Counties (including London), 1970 to 2000

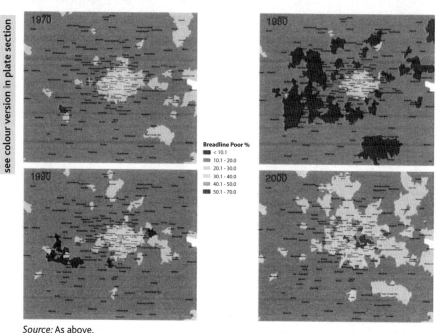

*Source:* As above.

Figures 10, 11, 12 and 13 show how there is change over time, decade by decade, that is often of an extent that matters. Currently the pendulum is swinging away from slight equality and so, for the first time in at least 60 years, by the year 2000 in many parts of inner London over half the population were poor. In similar parts of the capital in 1980 just a third of households were deemed to be poor. In contrast, Figure 11 shows how, outside of London, in the better-off parts of the Home Counties over half the population of many neighbourhoods were asset wealthy by the year 2000 and that in only three places over the same broad sweep of southern England was the same true in the 1980s. Thus in one sense as the numbers of asset wealthy rise, so too do those living nearby (but elsewhere) that have the least. (Dorling et al, 2007)

**Figure 11:** Asset wealthy households across the Home Counties (including London), 1980 to 2000

see colour version in plate section

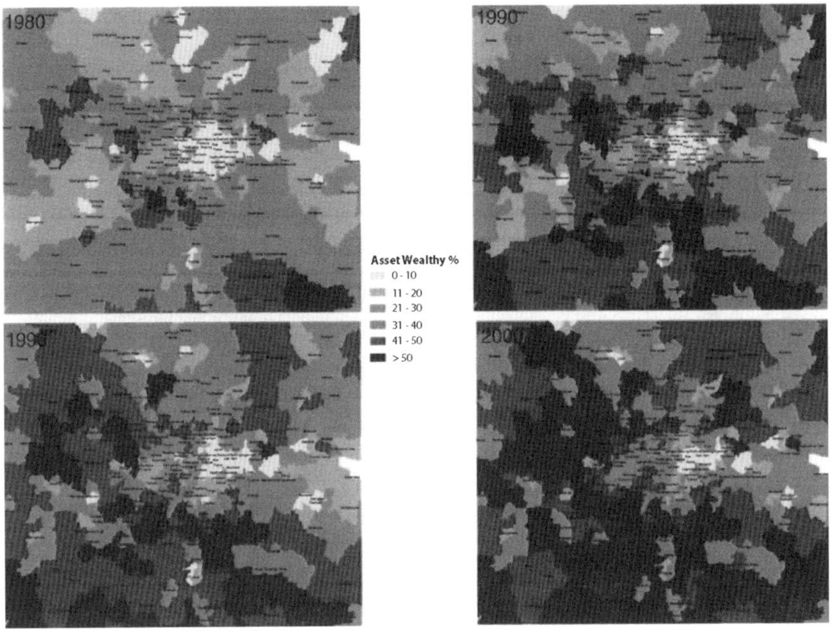


*Source:* As above.

Figure 12 first shows the spatial concentration of the poor in 2001 using local authority rather than neighbourhood geography and upon a cartogram rather than on a conventional map. Glasgow and Northern Ireland are included here and the averaging effect of using slightly larger areas, especially boroughs in London, results in no area having half its population poor. The map uses a slightly earlier definition of poverty (Dorling and Thomas 2004). The second map in Figure 12 is of the change in the proportion of households living in poverty 1991 to 2000 by these areas and shows how across almost all of Britain rates rose, even in generally wealthy areas – and how very different things were occurring in London (not commented on elsewhere here, see Dorling, 2010 for speculation).

Figure 13 highlights how the exclusive wealthy are concentrated in a far narrower group of areas, and returns to the large neighbourhood scale for mapping their proportions in contrast with the homes of the poorest of the poor – who never exceed more than about 1 in 6 of the households of any large neighbourhood. These geographies of where the extremely rich and poor live, in contrast to the rest, should be born in mind when considering the terrible position the United Kingdom has when compared internationally, as the graphs in Figures 14 and 15 demonstrate.

**Figure 12:** Distributions of the breadline poor in 2001 and the change in their numbers 1991–2001 by constituency

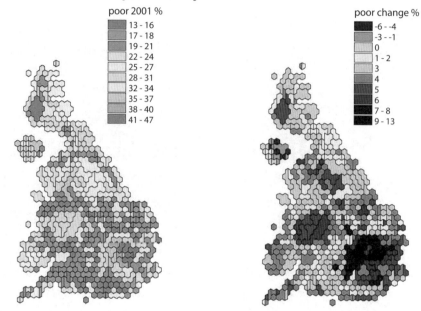

*Source:* Dorling, D and Thomas, B. (2004) *People and places: A 2001 census atlas*, Bristol: The Policy Press.

**Figure 13:** Distributions of the 6% exclusive wealthy and the 11% core poor around the year 2000

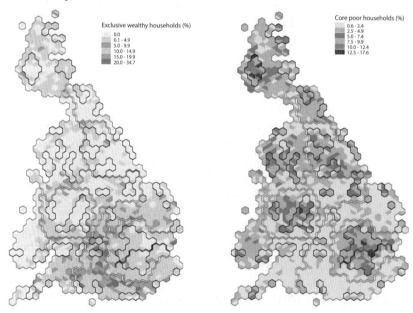

*Source:* Thomas, B. and Dorling, D. (2007) *Identity in Britain: A cradle-to-grave atlas*, Bristol: The Policy Press.

## Poverty, inequality and wealth and why enough is never enough

Income inequality is just a part of the picture of poverty and wealth, both worldwide and closer to home. Neither the very poor nor the very rich have conventional incomes: salaries, wages, or some other relatively steady inflow of monies (Scott, 1994; Clark, 2002). The very poor beg and die in poor countries and live only on welfare in rich countries. The very rich could not imagine what it is to work, let alone be poor. Nevertheless, for most people their steady income matters and it matters also for the most, on the face of it, intangible of things. Take for instance the subjective well-being of children in some of the richest nations on earth, mainly found in Europe (but also North America, and although not shown here, Japan). Figure 14 shows the propensity of children in these nations to report subjective indicators of well being with the average for the countries set to 100.

Why should the Netherlands lead the table of subjective well-being amongst young folk of the rich nations and the United Kingdom be at its tail? Elsewhere in the *Innocenti* Report (Adamson, 2007), from which this figure was drawn, the United States was shown to closely mirror the United Kingdom, with the UK only pipping the US at the post for being the worst performing rich nation in terms of the wellbeing of its children because children in the UK are a little more sanguine when asked whether they are happy in comparison with their US counterparts. Children in the US are perhaps a little more socialised, taught and brought up to sound "up-beat" even if their circumstances do not warrant it.

**Figure 14:** The rich nation league table of child well being 2007

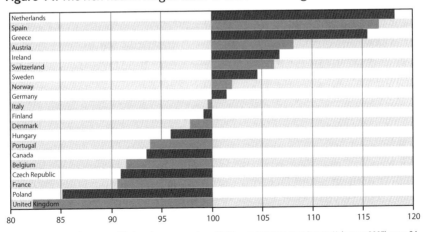

Source: Figure 6.0 Subjective well-being of young people, an OECD overview, Innocenti Report (Adamson 2007), page 34.

**Figure 15:** The European union league table of child poverty 2005

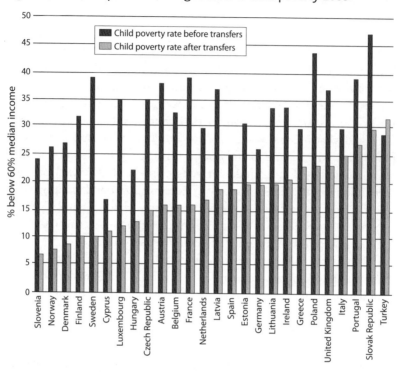

*Source:* www.hirsch.demon.co.uk/endchildpoverty.pdf. Donald Hirsh — what will it take to end child poverty? York: Joseph Rowntree Foundation 2006: Figure 5: Child Poverty rate before and after cash benefits.

As with any statistics that matter, those concerning poverty and wealth are much contested. This is especially true when considering worldwide estimates (Figure 15). Nevertheless there are some basic truths to the extents of poverty, inequality and wealth that is born out almost everywhere, repeatedly and which has been true for some considerable time (although hardly forever).

Large numbers of people are poor; a few are rich; fewer still are truly wealthy; and, for the truly wealthy – enough is never enough. For the poor it makes no sense to talk of assets, only income, spent almost as soon as it is received. For the truly wealthy it makes no sense to work for an income, nor to talk of one, their assets are self-replicating – in fact it is very hard to dispose of them, as until recently they have grown faster than they could be spent. This was part of the problem for the super rich as Bill and Melinda had discovered. The economic crash of 2008, by reducing the wealth of people like Bill and Melinda so greatly, relieved a little of their problems of what to do with their money, but it may well not as yet have reduced

**Figure 16:** Worldmapper maps of the lowest and highest incomes living on under 1$ a day:...over 200$ a day

*living on under 1$ a day:*

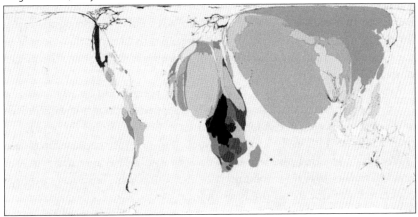

*...over 200$ a day*

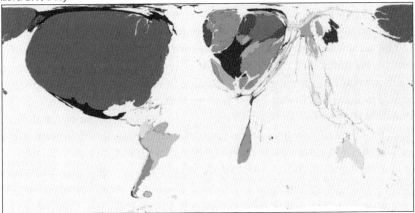

*Note:* All in Purchasing Power Parity (PPP) $'s.
The area of each country is proportional in size to the subject being mapped.
*Source:* www.worldmapper.org

see colour version in plate section

overall global inequalities.[2] At exactly the same time that the Gate's were losing billions of dollars, billions of the poorest people on earth saw their meagre relative incomes also fall as the price of food rose. Almost everyone became poorer, it is just that for the very rich that meant they suffered by being able to give a little less to charity than before, and that too hurt the very poorest, but perhaps not for the long term.

---

[2] Editorial note: Of course, a year after this was written we discovered that the wealthy had quickly recouped their losses. See table at the end of Chapter 27 (p 212) in this volume showing just how dramatic the change was.

The poor in countries like Britain used to have to rely on charity hospitals and charity for clothes and food and for schools for their children. There are better ways to live than relying on charity. In Britain the rich were helped to part with their money through taxes rather than as gifts to pay for things like hospitals for all. The British now live longer than people in the United States. In the US they are still arguing in 2009 about the merits of state funded health care!

Around the year 2002, over a billion people were living on an income of less than one dollar a day. The world when shaped by their bodies is shown at the top of Figure 16. By definition their collective annual income is less than $365 US billion. It is in fact much less, not just because many are surviving on less than the wretched dollar a day, but because these are not real US dollars that their income is being counted in, but local currency converted into dollars on the basis of local prices. A real US dollar would buy far more rice in all of the places drawn large at the top of Figure 16 than would that fictional "PPP" dollar used to calibrate the incomes of the poor. A further one and a half billion survive on between 1 and 2 of these adjusted dollars a day, and another billion on more than two but less than ten.

The wealth of the richest people on earth is similarly hard to nail down precisely. Estimates of the wealth of Mr Gates vary. Even in early 2009 after the big write-downs of the crash, according to Forbes his value was estimated at $40 billion (Kroll et al, 2009). But again these are not the same kinds of dollars as the incomes of the poor are measured in, or even American dollars. This money is mostly held in the form of investments, stock options, trusts or charities – it grows by itself, it avoids taxation, and if even a fraction of it had been enough he'd have stopped amassing it by now. It is wealth that falls at times, precariously in 1929 and 2008, but in most years it is wealth that grows quickly. The wealth of this one man would save the labours of the poorest billion for a year, if converted into the same kind of money and goods the poorest billion receive. But it is not the same kind of money – it is not convertible, because it is never enough.

Money is not liquid, it is not like water. The money in your pocket is not the same kind of stuff as the money in your bank account. You almost certainly have both kinds if you are reading this. It is not the same as a salary you can expect to continue to receive, or the less certain wages of others who work where you work. It is not the same kind of money as the assets of your extended family, as the reserves or debts held by the company or university you might work for. It is not the same kind of money that is awarded in research grants; matched by development grants; doubled by some other scheme; reported in company and then national accounts; sent spinning around the world by wire; or represented by a few copper coins in the pocket of a child working in a mine excavating copper worth less itself than were those coins to be melted down. This is not the same kind of money as £175 billion that the government in Britain had 'borrowed' to bail out banks by autumn 2009, the billions more it was "quantitatively easing" out of the Bank of England as recovery stalled, or the trillions of dollars the United States had 'made' appear when needed. Money is not money is not money. This makes calculations of inequalities difficult.

Money might be slippery but location is more solid. What is obvious is that the highest earners worldwide no longer live anywhere near the poorest, other than in the hearts of our financial capitals (London and New York). The map in the bottom half of Figure 16 is of the world shaped to show with equal importance the homes of the best rewarded one percent of people. International estimates are only made for the very poor, not for the rich and so this map is based on an income model described in the note to Table 1 (below). The lower map in Figure 16 is the antithesis of the map above it.

**Table 1:** World income distribution

| Estimates of Household Annual GDP/capita ($PPP) | Central Africa | Southeastern Africa | Northern Africa | Southern Asia | Asia Pacific | Middle East | Eastern Asia | South America | Eastern Europe | North America | Western Europe | Japan | Total |
|---|---|---|---|---|---|---|---|---|---|---|---|---|---|
| 32 | 0 | 0 | 1 | 0 | 0 | 0 | 0 | 0 | 0 | 0 | 0 | 0 | 1 |
| 64 | 1 | 1 | 3 | 0 | 0 | 0 | 0 | 0 | 0 | 0 | 0 | 0 | 5 |
| 128 | 4 | 6 | 10 | 0 | 1 | 0 | 0 | 1 | 0 | 0 | 0 | 0 | 22 |
| 256 | 13 | 23 | 27 | 1 | 4 | 2 | 4 | 6 | 0 | 0 | 0 | 0 | 80 |
| 512 | 23 | 59 | 54 | 23 | 19 | 9 | 27 | 18 | 1 | 2 | 0 | 0 | 235 |
| 1,024 | 27 | 80 | 81 | 174 | 62 | 29 | 113 | 43 | 3 | 6 | 0 | 0 | 618 |
| 2,048 | 19 | 52 | 98 | 496 | 139 | 62 | 275 | 74 | 17 | 14 | 0 | 0 | 1,246 |
| 4,096 | 8 | 25 | 92 | 503 | 168 | 86 | 386 | 94 | 58 | 26 | 3 | 0 | 1,449 |
| 8,192 | 3 | 15 | 53 | 172 | 102 | 90 | 317 | 88 | 87 | 47 | 25 | 0 | 1,001 |
| 16,384 | 1 | 10 | 17 | 19 | 43 | 62 | 164 | 59 | 62 | 87 | 99 | 19 | 641 |
| 32,768 | 0 | 6 | 3 | 1 | 19 | 27 | 55 | 29 | 21 | 115 | 161 | 77 | 514 |
| 65,536 | 0 | 2 | 0 | 0 | 8 | 7 | 11 | 11 | 2 | 86 | 86 | 31 | 244 |
| 131,072 | 0 | 1 | 0 | 0 | 2 | 1 | 1 | 3 | 0 | 34 | 15 | 1 | 58 |
| 262,144 | 0 | 0 | 0 | 0 | 0 | 0 | 0 | 1 | 0 | 7 | 1 | 0 | 9 |
| 524,288 | 0 | 0 | 0 | 0 | 0 | 0 | 0 | 0 | 0 | 1 | 0 | 0 | 1 |
| 1,048,576 | 0 | 0 | 0 | 0 | 0 | 0 | 0 | 0 | 0 | 0 | 0 | 0 | 0 |
| Total | 99 | 280 | 439 | 1,389 | 566 | 374 | 1,353 | 428 | 251 | 425 | 391 | 128 | 6,123 |

*Source:* http://www.worldmapper.org/data.html, data file 3, Table 14

Most studies of global income inequalities argue over the precise magnitude of those inequalities, the extent to which they are manifest between nation states as well as within them and what the trends in all those aspects of these inequalities are. Recently estimates have also been made of global wealth inequalities (Davies et al, 2006). More important than all of this, though, is the staggering extent of those inequalities. There is no easy way to even draw a graph of the 221 numbers in Table 1 (192 of which are not totals). All these numbers show are estimates of how many million people in each World region, fall into each of 16 household income bands and into each of the 12 regions used as the primary shades in Figure 16. Each income band is twice as wide as that above it in the table and half as wide as that beneath it.

**Figure 17:** Visualisations of world income, a and b

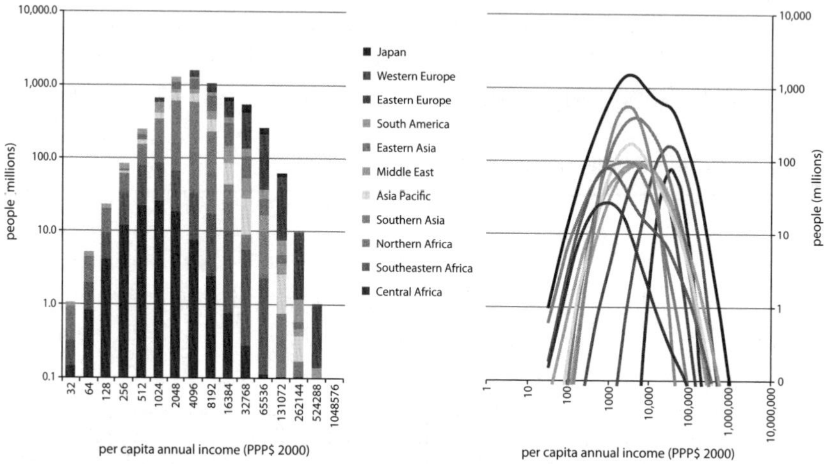

Source: Table 1

Figure 17 shows two visualisations of Table 1. The income distribution of the world is divided into twelve regions, and the world total is shown as a black line. The variation in income means that it is necessary to use log scales on both axes of Figure 17a. Figure 17b shows the numbers of people in each of the sixteen annual income bands and how many within each band live in each of the twelve regions. Again, it is necessary to use log scales in order to be able to see the whole picture. The distributions within Africa can be seen but it is far from simple to compare them with other regions. In short, while many different facets of inequality can be visualised, the whole is never visible, even when summarised in less than a couple of hundred well ordered numbers.

Figure 15 shows children affected by poverty in Europe. Wider international comparisons often have the United States missing, as US civil servants do not collect the information needed, do not feel the information needs to be collected, or – most fundamentally – cannot collect the information because the population has been conditioned to answer surveys in particular ways.

Americans tend to report that they are happy almost instinctively when asked in a nation brought up to "have a good day".

If the US were included, it would be to the extreme right of the chart. Note again how far over the United Kingdom is in that direction. Almost a quarter of children in the UK live below the family income poverty level now set across Europe at 60% of median national household income. This is a relative limit, unlike the absolute measures used in the United States which have hardly altered since their 1960s inceptions. Poverty and inequality are inexorably intertwined – one and the same thing. And it is where there is income inequality, and hence high poverty, even in the richest of nations that many more children grow up feeling worthless – that they cannot trust their friends – those that are not poor as well as those that are rich. Thus even children growing up in the highest income areas of Britain are not very mentally healthy in many ways we would consider important. Table 2 shows precisely where the homes of the highest income earners in Britain tend now to be located.

**Table 2:** Areas of Britain where the highest income earners most commonly live in recent years.

| Constituency | Proportion | Number |
|---|---|---|
| Kensington and Chelsea | 8% | 4,884 |
| Cities of London and Westminster | 6% | 4,048 |
| Hampstead and Highgate | 5% | 3,543 |
| Richmond Park | 5% | 3,677 |
| Esher and Walton | 5% | 3,697 |
| Beaconsfield | 5% | 3,190 |
| South West Surrey | 4% | 3,086 |
| Maidenhead | 4% | 2,756 |
| Mole Valley | 4% | 2,869 |
| Hammersmith and Fulham | 4% | 2,934 |
| Finchley and Golders Green | 4% | 2,729 |
| Tonbridge and Malling | 4% | 2,435 |
| Sevenoaks | 4% | 2,380 |

*Source:* Some of the wealthiest areas in the world are in the UK Adults with an income over £100,000 per annum in 2004 (Source Barclays Bank): most concentrated 10% in all parliamentary constituencies of England and Wales

## Conclusion

One reaction to our current state of affairs, a state of affairs that has changed far less in 150 years than we might think, is that we continue to blame the poor for the state we collectively find ourselves in. The continued re-labelling of the poor as ill, lazy, illegal, and stupid and in a multitude of other ways potentially undeserving is all around us. The paupers are still here. However, given how hugely expensive it is to maintain an exclusively rich elite, even one that only about 5% of people can be in, it is necessary that large numbers of people live in poverty in a country like Britain. The same is far less the case in many other European nations and in Japan. It is thus vital to understand the distribution of wealth to better understand that of poverty. The huge cost of maintaining the lives of a tiny proportion of people in luxury has to be born by the rest. A few of the rest can be asset wealthy – hold some noticeable wealth even if not enough to exclude themselves. More can be normal – neither rich nor poor – but they are now only half of all households in Britain. Nationally, a quarter of households in Britain are now poor and today, in large parts of the country, over half of all households are breadline poor, and up to a sixth are extremely poor in the supposedly united United Kingdom.

Money does not come out of the ether. As the exclusive rich become richer and richer their rights to others' time, labour and subservience grows. Even if their wealth falls, if the incomes of others also falls then they will even more desperately work for the rich; labour in factories in China, grow cash crops in Bangladesh, work in service in the new grand houses in London. This truism holds at a wide range of geographical scales, from within cities in England, to globally. If you are rich, enough is never enough, and for the rich, social position is relative too. Losing even a small proportion of your wealth could be very hard to take. No matter how much you have to begin with.

## References

Abel-Smith, B. and Townsend, P. (1965) *The poor and the poorest*, Occasional Papers in Social Administration, 17, London: Bell.

Adamson, P. (2007) *Child poverty in perspective: An overview of child well-being in rich countries*, Innocenti Report Card 7, Florence: UNICEF Innocenti Research Centre

Atkinson, A.B., Corlyon, J., Maynard, A.K., Sutherland, H. and Trinder, C.G. (1981) 'Poverty in York: a reanalysis of Rowntree's 1950 survey', *Bulletin of Economic Research*, no 33, pp 59–71.

Booth, C. (1894) *The aged poor in England and Wales*, London: Macmillan and Co.

Clark, C. (2002) 'Wealth and poverty: on the social creation of scarcity', *Journal of Economic Issues*, vol 36, no 2, pp: 415–21.

Darwin, C. (1859) *On the origin of species by means of natural selection, or the preservation of favoured races in the struggle for life*, London: John Murray.

Davies, J.B., Sandstrom, S., Shorrocks, A. and Wolff, E.N. (2006) *The world distribution of household wealth*, UNU-WIDER, Katajanokanlaituri 6 B 00160 Helsinki, Finland.

Dorling, D. (2003) 'A century of progress? Inequalities in British society, 1901–2000', in D. Gilbert, D. Matless and B. Short (eds) *Geographies of British modernity: Space and society in the twentieth century*, Part 1, Chapter 2, Oxford: Blackwells, pp 31–53.

Dorling, D. (2004) 'Distressed times and areas: poverty, polarisation and politics in England 1918- circa 1971', in A.R.H. Baker and M. Billinge (eds) *Geographies of England: The North–South divide, material and imagined*, Cambridge: Cambridge University Press.

Dorling, D. (2006) 'Infant mortality and social progress in Britain, 1905–2005', Chapter 11, in E. Garrett, C. Galley, N. Shelton and R. Woods (eds) *Infant mortality*, Aldershot: Ashgate.

Dorling, D. (2010) *Inequality: Why social inequality persists*, Bristol: The Policy Press.

Dorling, D. and Thomas, B. (2004) *People and places: A 2001 census atlas*, Bristol: The Policy Press.

Dorling, D., Mitchell, R., Shaw, M., Orford, S. and Davey Smith, G. (2000) 'The ghost of Christmas past: health effects of poverty in London in 1896 and 1991', *BMJ*, 7276(23–30), pp 1547–51.

Dorling, D., Rigby, R., Wheeler, B., Ballas, D., Thomas, B., Fahmy, E. et al (2007) *Poverty, wealth and place in Britain, 1968 to 2005*, Bristol: The Policy Press.

Engels, F. (1845, 1987) *The condition of the working class in England*, Harmondsworth: Penguin Books.

Galton, F. (1869, 1892) *Hereditary genius: An inquiry into its laws and consequences*, London: Macmillan and Co.

Glennerster, H. (2002) 'United States poverty studies and poverty measurement: the past twenty-five years', *Social Service Review*, no 76, 83–107.

Glennerster, H., Hills, J., Piachaud, D. and Webb, J. (2004) *One hundred years of poverty and policy*, York: Joseph Rowntree Foundation, www.jrf.org.uk/bookshop/eBooks/1859352227.pdf.

Gordon, D. and Pantazis, C. (eds) (1997) *Breadline Britain in the 1990s*, Aldershot: Ashgate.

Gordon, D. & Townsend, P. (eds) (2000) *Breadline Europe: The measurement of poverty*, Bristol: The Policy Press.

Gordon, D., Adelman, L., Ashworth, K., Bradshaw, J., Levitas, R., Middleton, S. et al (2000) *Poverty and social exclusion in Britain*, York: Joseph Rowntree Foundation.

Gregory, I., Dorling, D. and Southall, H. (2001) 'A century of inequality in England and Wales using standardised geographical units', *Area*, vol 33, no 3, pp 297–311.

Hatton, T.J. and Bailey, R.E. (2000) 'Seebohm Rowntree and the post-war poverty puzzle', *Economic History Review*, vol 53, no 3, pp 517–43.

Jargowsky, P.A. (2003) 'Concentration of poverty declines in the 1990s', *Poverty and Race Research Action Council*, vol 12, no 4, pp 1–2.

King, S. (2000) *Poverty and welfare in England 1700–1850*, Manchester: Manchester University Press.

Kroll, L., Miller, M. and Serafin, T. (2009) *The world's billionaires*, [online] www.forbes.com/2009/03/11/worlds-richest-people-billionaires-2009-billionaires_land.html. Last accessed 19.04.09.

MacKenzie, D. (1999) 'Eugenics and the rise of mathematical statistics', in D. Dorling and S. Simpson (eds) *Statistics in society: The arithmetic of politics*, London: Arnold.

Pearson, K. (1895) 'Contributions to the mathematical theory of evolution. -II. Skew variation in homogeneous material', *Philosophical Transactions of the Royal Society of London, Series A, Mathematical*, no 186, pp 343–414

Rowntree, B.S. (1901, [2000]) *Poverty: A study of town life*, Bristol: The Policy Press.

Rowntree, B.S. and Lavers, G.R. (1951) *Poverty and the welfare state: A third social survey of York dealing only with economic questions*, London: Longmans.

Scott, J. (1994) *Poverty and wealth: Citizenship, deprivation and privilege*, London: Longman.

Thomas, B. and Dorling, D. (2007) *Identity in Britain: A cradle-to-grave atlas*, Bristol: The Policy Press.

Tomkins, A. (2006) *The experience of urban poverty 1723–82: Parish, charity and credit*, Manchester: Manchester University Press.

Tomkins, A. and King, S. (eds) (2003) *The poor in England 1700–1900: An economy of makeshifts*, Manchester: Manchester University Press.

Townsend, P. (1979) *Poverty in the United Kingdom: A survey of household resources and standards of living*, London: Penguin Books and Allen Lane.

Welshman, J. (2006) 'The concept of the unemployable', *Economic History Review*, vol 59, no 3, pp 578–606.

# 37

# All connected? Geographies of race, death, wealth, votes and births

*Geographical Journal* (2010) vol 176, no 3, pp 186–98

## Knowing less and less of each other's lives

Figure 1 charts the share in annual incomes received by the richest single percentile of Britons as recorded between 1918 and 2005, both pre- and post-tax. The richest percentile of people in Britain receive some of their income from earnings, but a greater proportion from interest on wealth, dividends and shares, and the returns on investments made in stocks and rent on their land. At the end of World War I, one in every 100 people lived on about a sixth of the national income, 17 or 18 times more than the average family, 100 times more money than the poorest 10th saw in a year.

From 1918 through the 1920s, 1930s, 1940s, 1950s and 1960s the share of national income the affluent received fell. As many of the heirs to great estates had died in the Great War, the government taxed the aristocratic families, but just as crucially, the 'great' families became just a little more lax over who they slept with and subsequently married. The arithmetic of homogamy (assortative mating) is simple. Should you be a member of a family in the top percentile of income earners in 1918 you might expect to receive around £150,000 a year in today's money, or 18 times average individual incomes. If you are careful and ignore 99 potential life partners in every 100, you might in theory meet and only choose from the one percentile like you. Because social networks were so limited it was not hard to avoid at least 90 of the other 99, or meet and mistreat them only as servants, but the other nine you had to tell yourself were beneath you when you did meet them. Then as a couple, and later possibly a family, you will remain in that top 1% of earners.

**Figure 1:** Share of all income received by the richest 1% in Britain, 1918–2005

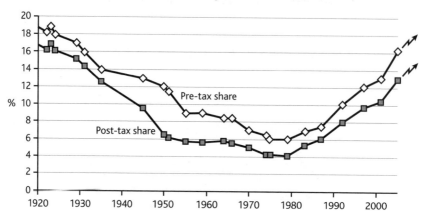

*Note:* Lower line is post-tax share. *Editorial note:* Arrows added to show most recent trend.

*Source:* Atkinson (2003, figures 2 and 3); from 1922 to 1935 the 0.1% rate was used to estimate the 1% when the 1% rate was missing, and for 2005 the data source was Brewer et al (2008, 11); the final post-tax rate of 12.9% is derived from 8.6%+4.3%, the pre-tax rate scaled from 2001.

If you are very rich you are told 'be careful', should your eye stray and you find a young man or woman from the bottom of the top decile more attractive, or caring, or just more understanding or interesting, and you had successfully ignored 90 out of 100 other possible suitors, but not the 91st, and you pair up, then you *as a pair* will drop out of the top percentile. Another couple or individual will enter it, but they will not have been as well-off as you (or else they would have been in that group already) and so the average income of the best-off falls. Figure 1 shows a combination of many things, but it also includes the effect of that equalising process at work, increased freedom to choose who you love, gaining in strength right through to the 1970s. Note that this is especially true for the very rich as a large proportion of the income of the richest 1% is interest earnings from holding wealth, and high wealth is thus largely maintained over generations by marrying 'correctly'.

In England debutantes (young aristocratic or upper class girls) were presented at court at the start of each social season right up until 1958. They were presented to make it clear that they were available for marriage, only marriage into the 'correct' families, of course. It became progressively harder after 1958 to know exactly who was most 'respectable'. The process carries on today, especially in the USA at various huge 'charity' balls, but is less overtly state-sponsored than when the most suitable of young ladies were regularly presented to the Queen of England at court, just half a century ago. The very same Queen that we British remain subjects of today.

A combination of high mortality among even the upper classes in World War I, increased death duties, loss of wealth during the depression and later redistribution by increases in income and inheritance taxation all helped to bring down inequalities in income and wealth from 1918 to the end of the 1970s. However, it is also not hard to see, as collars became less starched, as Victorian norms became only a memory, and as the sexual revolution slowly developed, that as wealth became a little more equally spread, there were ways in which people could choose a little more often to be with someone they might actually love, and a little less often tolerated those they were expected to choose just to maintain the family silver.

Figure 2 shows how the average age of mums fell and rose too. It was not just better knowledge of contraceptives or better chances for women to have careers that drove this trend up after it first went down. The timing also follows the trends described above. Figure 2 also shows why it is worth being wary of thinking that casual mechanisms are obvious when you first see two trends that are so similar. Average ages of mothers giving birth initially fell as it became possible to marry earlier and earlier, no longer having to wait until savings were sufficient for a new home to be afforded for the new couple. Greater financial and social equality, and the huge house building program that resulted from the growing belief that everyone deserved a home, made marrying earlier and then having children earlier much more conceivable.

Lower ages of motherhood was not the result of greater promiscuity but of having far fewer 'great' houses staffed by armies of mainly childless servants, and far more small houses built for new working class families. The middle classes saw their sexual freedom grow too as a result, and there was much more marrying between classes. Then, as social and economic inequalities rose, fewer new homes were built and the houses we had were more and more inefficiently shared out as market forces grew stronger in housing. Middle class people put off having children to very late ages and working class people did the same, if not so quickly. Age of parenthood both rose and socially polarised at the same time, so that the average age of 29 by 2004 was far less representative than the much lower average just 29 years earlier. Improved access to contraceptives helped people delay parenthood more effectively but were not the reasons why so many did, nor was it increased hedonism, although advertising that told you to 'live for today' because 'you're worth it' became far more ubiquitous. More young adults talked about not being able to 'afford' to become a parent in the 1990s than

**Figure 2:** Average age of mothers giving birth in England and Wales, 1938–2004

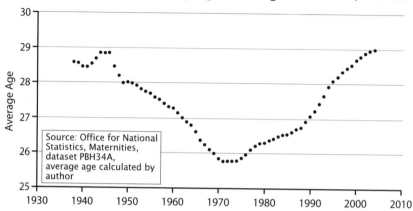

did so in the 1970s. Why should that happen in a country that was overall so much richer?

Why too, from the late 1970s onwards, should we see individual earnings again concentrating within the best-off percentile (see Figure 1)? It was not just the progressive tax structure being dismantled after 1979. Earnings before tax (shown in the same figure) follow almost exactly the same trend. The rise is so quick that by 2005 the trend line suggests that we had returned to early 1930s levels of income inequality at the very top end. Add falling actual national wages during 2009, but bankers' bonuses continuing, and we are back to 1918 levels of income inequality in 2010. Wealth inequalities in 2010 have skyrocketed. The *Sunday Times* 'rich list' of April 2010 reported that the wealth of the 1000 richest people in the UK had risen by 29.9% in just 1 year to stand at £335.5 billion.[1] The annual rise itself was enough to more than wipe out the UK's newly grown structural deficient to £70 billion! But step back in time a little to see how we got to such excesses again.

The Pearson product-moment correlation coefficients between the pre-tax income share of the richest percentile and the excess mortality of the poorest 30%, the health advantage of the best-off 10th, and the geographical concentration of Conservative votes over the 1918–2005 period are: 0.57, 0.82 and 0.51 respectively (see Table 1 in the original article this is an extract of). Again, this is no evidence of a causal link – clearly the health advantages of the rich are most closely connected to their share of wealth. But these are also both in some way related to trends in inequalities in voting and to the fluctuations in the rates of premature mortality suffered by the poor. There is only a one in 100 chance that even the lowest of these correlations

---

[1] Editorial note: This rise in the wealth of the super-rich of the UK has been referred to at many points in this book, but it really cannot be referred to enough, given how much money is now held by them, and those just below them, and how from 2010 to 2011 their wealth rose again by a further 25%.

occurred by chance. The correlations with the post–tax income trend shown above are even stronger: 0.60, 0.86 and 0.58 respectively, and they are both higher and even more statistically robust. When the rich take even more of the national income of a country (and almost all of its wealth), the health of the poor suffers and voting in general elections becomes more spatially polarised. Similar trends have been suggested in the USA (Krugman, 2007): a kind of growing racism against the poor emerges. The poor are not seen like the rest of society, as people deserving to be treated as you would wish to be treated. How else can you defend holding individual wealth in its billions? To justify being so very rich you have to believe you would look after that wealth better than the poor would.

### References

Atkinson, A.B. (2003) *Top incomes in the United Kingdom over the twentieth century*, Nuffield College Working Papers, Oxford (http://ideas.repec.org/p/nuf/esohwp/_043.html) accessed 12 May 2010.

Brewer, M., Sibieta, L. and Wren-Lewis, L. (2008) *Racing away? Income inequality and the evolution of high incomes*, London: Institute for Fiscal Studies.

Krugman, P. (2007) *The conscience of a liberal*, New York: W.W. Norton.

# SECTION VIII
# Well-being and misery

This section begins with a paper I was invited to write for the journal *Social Science and Medicine* in response to the publication of the Marmot review of February 2010.[1] I asked Kate Pickett to help me and she led the writing and so is first author of that piece (but you have to read the footnotes to find that out!). The Marmot review was published in the dying days of the Labour administration, which was in power from 1997 to 2010, and may have been drafted with an eye towards placating the likely prejudices of an incoming Tory regime and – in good medical tradition – trying to help it to cause the least harm. In the event the review was both unsatisfactory for the reasons we detail below and also largely ignored by the incoming coalition government, which had its own agenda.

The second chapter of the section returns to the theme of murder as a social disease, with which this book began, and discusses what such callousness can lead to. This chapter originally appeared as an article in the magazine *Red Pepper* in 2006, but it is possibly more relevant today than it was then. The third chapter moves the perspective on, from local to regional and then to worldwide inequalities, reproducing a series of graphs and maps that were first put together in a lecture designed to show epidemiologists how information on inequalities in health and the subsequent well-being and misery caused by such inequalities could be visualised. The lecture has not been previously published in print. It is followed by Chapter 41, a book review that first appeared on an obscure academic website for people studying the humanities and social sciences and which is reproduced here to illustrate the extent to which many academic cartographers are concerned with the subliminal as well the more liminal physiological and psychological responses to images; in this case of the distribution of suffering and the apparent organisation of misery.

---

[1] Marmot, M. *et al* (2010) *Fair society, healthy lives*, London: The Marmot Review.

The fifth chapter of this section is a response to a paper published in the *International Journal of Epidemiology* concerning growing inequalities in health in the US, where, among rich nations of the world, we first saw life expectancy begin to fall in the poorest parts of the USA as social and economic inequalities reached new heights during the 1980s and into the 1990s and beyond. Only very recently have the full repercussions of this become evident in terms of the current generation of the poor now living shorter lives than the majority of their parents in some of the worst-off areas of what is labelled 'the land of the free'. The section ends with a commentary on inequalities in the next most unequal of large affluent countries, the United Kingdom, written to introduce a set of papers in the social science journal *Environment and Planning A*. That commentary tells you a little more of where I am coming from and why I think things fit together as they do.

# 38

# Against the organization of misery? The Marmot Review of Health Inequalities[1]

*Social Science and Medicine* (2010) no 71, pp 1231–3

In February 2010, the UK Government published *Fair Society, Healthy Lives: Strategic Review of Health Inequalities in England Post- 2010*, better known as "The Marmot Review" after its lead author Professor Sir Michael Marmot. The very first words of the report are a variation on a quotation from Pablo Neruda:

> "Rise up with me against the organisation of misery"
> Marmot et al, 2010, p 2

Pablo Neruda was a Chilean writer, a left-wing politician, and a confidant of president Salvador Allende; he died within days of August Pinochet's coup. An official British document that begins with a quotation from a revolutionary communist would seem to promise unusually radical content.

The Marmot Review (2010) received extensive coverage and acclaim from London's *Guardian* newspaper and was covered, albeit more briefly, in the *Times* and the *Daily Telegraph*, but few of the initial commentators seemed to believe that any of its main recommendations would actually be

---

[1] Written with Kate Pickett and with Kate as first author (She is based at the Department of Health Sciences, University of York).

implemented. These included improving prenatal and early years provision, better drug addiction treatment, and raising social security payments. Rather than anticipating real progress in tackling health inequalities in the wake of the financial crash, one journalist suggested that:

> "This grim situation makes those few Marmot recommendations that need not involve great public expense, such as better workplace procedures to deal with stress at work, all the more important, and everyone should now get behind these." (*Guardian*, 2010, March 15, p 30)

If all that can be done to reduce Britain's grievous and persistent inequalities in health is to try to abate stress in the workplace, what does that say about the commitment of the British (government, academics, public health professionals, and public alike) to truly creating a fairer and healthier society?

The Marmot Review (2010) followed an earlier report also led by Sir Michael. Published just over a year earlier, again with a large cast of distinguished colleagues, he authored the acclaimed WHO Commission on Social Determinants of Health treatise: *Closing the Gap in a Generation: Health Equity Through Action on the Social Determinants of Health* (CSDH, 2008). Many reviews of this report have now been published, in both high-impact (Davey Smith and Krieger, 2010) and less well-known journals (Pearce and Dorling, 2009). Most of the responses to this earlier global report were positive, welcoming its well-argued call for a shift in focus for WHO, from disease control to improving the social determinants of health.

> "The conclusions of the WHO report are a salient reminder to the governments of member states that reducing health inequalities should be a political priority. (Davey Smith and Krieger, 2010, p 530).

Like most other commentators, we welcomed the publication of the UK Marmot Review, but think it is now apposite to suggest that, in comparison to the earlier WHO report, and in contrast to its early precursor in Britain, the *Black Report* (Black et al, 1980, 1992), it has not succeeded in putting health inequalities back onto the political agenda, even as we write this review (in the days approaching a UK general election).

We suggest that a major (but significant) problem with the UK Marmot Review is that it fails to deal with the need to reduce inequality by failing to focus on the top end of the social hierarchy, as well as the bottom. Although the Review calls for the establishment of a 'minimum income for healthy living', there is no suggestion that a maximum income or a constraint on the ratio of top-to-bottom incomes in institutions would also help reduce inequalities, and so improve the health and well-being of the population as a whole.

In a time of severe financial restraint it is far easier to reduce spending by curtailing top incomes than it is to raise incomes at the bottom. However, taxation is only discussed in the Marmot Review with respect to improving low incomes. This is odd because the Review demonstrates in great detail that inequalities in health exhibit a social gradient; these are not simply problems of the poor, so why direct all policy solutions towards the bottom? It makes sense to target services to those who need them most, but even more sense to reduce the social inequalities that actually produce social disparities in health in the first place. We suspect that more radical policy measures were not proposed because the political climate in Britain across the mainstream party spectrum, whilst accepting the rhetoric of 'fairness', is actually diffident in its support for the policies needed to create more equality.

If the Marmot Review had suggested curtailing the excesses of the rich it might have been more difficult for those who ideologically oppose it to criticise it on the grounds that its recommendations would support and sustain those who are stereotyped as the feckless poor. Those who actually favour inequality and elitism would have to defend the harmful impact of the extremely affluent on society, rather than turn their attention to the supposed failings of the people who cost society least: the poor.

The vast majority of people benefit when incomes are curtailed at the top. If we curtail top incomes, it is easy to model the benefits – there is far more to go round. The taxation of excessive wealth (perhaps through a land-value tax), regulatory restraint of the bonus culture, and other measures aimed at reducing economic inequalities would help the vast majority of us (in the UK and other rich market democracies) enjoy an improved quality of life, even if such policies did not improve things much for the tiny minority of the super-rich (Wilkinson and Pickett, 2010).

Evidence of hostility towards the poor abounds on the Internet. When poor people joined what little public debate took place on the Marmot Review they were immediately abused. One of the *Daily Mail*'s online readers, responding to a criticism of his extreme views, said:

> *"Why are the poor replying to my thread?*
> *GET A JOB and stop scrounging.*
> *Who is paying for your Internet?*
> *I'd sterilise the lot of you!"*
> *– Anthony, Esher, Surrey, 11/2/2010 12:56*

Another wrote:

> *"I would put you up against a wall and put a bullet in your*
> *pathetic brain.*
> *I doubt this will be published but oh boy do I feel better now.*
> *– Alan, Gloucester UK, 13/2/2010 15:57"*

Obviously the *Daily Mail* did publish these views; otherwise we would not
be able to report them here. The paper published many similarly extreme
comments in its online edition. Typical reactions included:

> *"Perhaps Prof. Sir Michael might revise his recommendations*
> *from hard working taxpayers being bled even more*
> *to pay for feckless wastrels, to relocating 'poor' people to*
> *remote mountainous regions and subsistence occupations?*
> *– Penny, London, 14/2/2010 19:34"*

These angry reactions towards the poor in Britain, and to academics who
research their suffering and support their rights, have become much more
common than they were thirty years ago (Dorling 2010, p 28). They reflect
a general trend in many affluent countries, but especially in those that have
become increasingly unequal. Poor people are increasingly seen as an 'out'
group. The laziness and innate incapability of the poor, sponging off the rest
of us, cost society dear; at the extreme, in the USA, Americans are told more
and more often that it is the poor who make you poor (Tropman, 1998).

Britain is not yet as bad as the United States when it comes to public
expressions of hatred for those with less money, but it is not that much better,
and is certainly a society with less social solidarity than almost anywhere else
in Europe. In such an environment of hate, with huge public sector cuts in
the offing, with an unregulated media allowing the online promulgation of
views that border on fascism and hate crimes, whichever political party forms
the next government, it is worth asking whether, in hindsight, the Marmot
Review could have painted a more positive picture for societal change.

We believe it could have. We believe there is still time to change attitudes
rather than plead for a little more charity for those with less. Much of
the strong evidence lies within the hundreds of tables and appendices of
the Marmot report. The full Review includes abundant evidence on the
importance of the social determinants of health. What is missing is the
political courage to deal with the root causes of those social determinants.
Why people smoke, rather than trying to get them to stop… why people
eat too much, commit violence, trust each other less, invest more money
in their children's education, rather than trying to understand the social
inequalities that stand in their way.

We have to look back more than 30 years to see when academics last showed true political commitment to health inequalities. Thirty years ago *Inequalities in Health: Report of a Research Working Group* chaired by Sir Douglas Black was published (Black et al, 1980, 1992). Among many other recommendations, that Report suggested the following six main aims and measures:

- "To give children a better start in life" (Black et al., 1980, 1992, p. 336).
- "…child benefit should be increased to 5½ per cent of male earnings" (Black et al, 1980, 1992, p 342).
- "…minimally acceptable and desirable conditions of work" (Black et al, 1980, 1992, p 343).
- "…abolition of child-poverty should be adopted as a national goal…" (Black et al, 1980, 1992, p 342).
- for communities: "Additional funding for ten special areas" (Black et al, 1980, 1992, p 341).
- strengthen "…preventive and educational action" (Black et al, 1980, 1992, p 337).

Although the Marmot Review opens with a revolutionary quotation, the six main recommendations of the Marmot Review are unlikely to scare the horses, indeed they are remarkably similar (if in places a little less ambitious) to those of the Black Report. The main recommendations of the Marmot Review, for comparison with the above, are:

- Give every child the best start in life.
- Enable all children … to maximise their capabilities and have control over their lives.
- Create fair employment and good work for all.
- Ensure a healthy standard of living for all.
- Create and develop healthy and sustainable places and communities.
- Strengthen the role and impact of ill health prevention.

Is the Marmot Review really saying – by repeating so much of it – that it is about time we looked back again at the Black Report and realise how little progress we have made? The UK has led the world in research and policies designed to reduce health inequalities. Not only did it commission a series of important reviews, when the UK held the Presidency of the European Union (EU) in the second half of 2005, but one of the issues it chose to highlight during its Presidency was inequalities in health. As part of this effort, it commissioned two reports, one on the extent of health inequalities in EU countries (Mackenbach, 2005), the other summarising policy initiatives adopted to tackle them (Judge et al, 2006). What was clear from these reports was that Britain was ahead of other countries in implementing health policies to reduce health inequalities, but also that health inequalities in the UK have shown no tendency to decline. The growth in inequalities in health between geographically defined communities in Britain is currently accelerating (Thomas, Dorling, and Davey Smith, 2010).

No reviews or policies 'boldly go' where all public health researchers know they need to go. And yet our evidence base for the social determinants of health proceeds apace; we learn more and more about the futility of trying to change individual behaviour, and more and more about the importance of influences in the womb and early years of childhood. Indeed, the Marmot Review could have gone much further, if it had only placed greater reliance on Sir Michael Marmot's own research and that of his colleagues studying life-course effects on health in the British birth cohorts. In contrast to 1980 when the Black Report was published, we now, thanks especially to his work, know much more about the importance of psychosocial influences on population health. We also know much more about the biology of chronic stress (Sapolsky, 2005), about how rank and status harm health (Marmot, 2004). We know that children get the best start in life by being brought up in more equitable societies, rather than in rich ones (Pickett and Wilkinson, 2007). Why did the Marmot Review not make hard hitting recommendations to reduce the harm created by great differences in rank and status? Crucial parts of the contemporary tale are missing in this latest review of health inequalities.

Instead, there is a focus on maximising the 'capabilities' of children and young adults. This is the language of economics, not social epidemiology or progressive public health. It is a language that has seeped into our everyday vocabulary and thinking, and it permeates the Marmot Review.

The Marmot Review is indeed welcome, but it tells only part of the story, and provides far less than its authors and most readers already know about what needs to be done.

Were Pablo Neruda around today he might feel that what the Marmot Review recommends is not to actually "rise up with me against the organisation of misery". There are ways of rising up against the organisation of misery, but they all require far more than attempting the slight abatement of suffering.

At the start of the Marmot Review, when Neruda's words are quoted, five lines of text have been left out from the relevant stanza (Davey Smith, 2010). Here is the full text including the missing lines:

*But stand up,*
*you, stand up,*
*but stand up with me*
*and let us go off together*
*to fight face to face*
*against the devil's webs,*
*against the system that distributes hunger,*
*against organized misery*
**(Neruda, 1972, p 99)**[2]

## References

Black, D., Morris, J.N., Smith, C. and Townsend, P. (1980) 'Key conclusions' published as Chapter 27, in G. Davey Smith, D. Dorling, and M. Shaw (2001) (eds) *Poverty, inequality and health in Britain: 1800–2000: A reader*, Bristol: The Policy Press.

Black, D., Morris, J.N., Smith, C., and Townsend, P. (1992) 'Inequalities in health: The Black Report', in M. Whitehead, P. Townsend and N. Davidson (eds) *Inequalities in health*, London: Penguin.

Commission on the Social Determinants of Health (CSDH) (2008) *Closing the gap in a generation: Health equity through action on the social determinants of health*, Geneva: World Health Organization.

Davey Smith, G. (2010) (Per. comm. Recital of '*The Flag*' by Pablo Neruda).

Davey Smith, G. and Krieger, N. (2010) 'Tackling health inequities', *BMJ*, 337: a1526.

Dorling, D. (2010) *Injustice: Why social inequality persists*, Bristol: The Policy Press.

*Guardian* (2010) The editorial: for richer, for poorer, Britons overall are getting steadily healthier, but being poor still carries a vast penalty, www.guardian.co.uk/commentisfree/2010/mar/15/health-divide-betweenrich-poor, 15 March.

Judge, K., Platt, S., Costongs, C. and Jurczak, K. (2006) *Health inequalities: A challenge for Europe*, London: Presidency of the EU, www.dh.gov.uk/assetRoot/04/12/15/83/04121583.pdf, accessed 3 March 2006.

Mackenbach, J.P. (2005) *Health inequalities: Europe in profile*, London: Presidency of the EU.

Marmot, M. (2004) *The status syndrome: How social standing affects our health and longevity*, London: Bloomsbury.

---

[2] Editorial note: On 21 July 2011 the Associated Press revealed that a judge in Chile had ordered an investigation into whether Pablo Neruda had been mudered in 1973.

Marmot, M. (2010) *Fair society, healthy lives. The Marmot review Executive Summary*, London: The Marmot Review, www.ucl.ac.uk/gheg/marmotreview/FairSocietyHealthyLivesExecSummary.

Neruda, P. (1972) *The captain's verses* (D.D. Walsh, Trans.) New York: New Directions Books.

Pearce, J. and Dorling, D. (2009) 'Tackling global health inequalities: closing the health gap in a generation', *Environment and Planning A*, 41, 1e6, Commentary.

Pickett, K.E. and Wilkinson, R.G. (2007) 'Child wellbeing and income inequality in rich societies: ecological cross sectional study', *BMJ*, 335(7629), pp 1080–7.

Sapolsky, R. (2005) 'Sick of poverty', *Scientific American*, vol 293, no 6, pp 92–99.

Thomas, B., Dorling, D., and Davey Smith, G. (2010) 'An observational study of health inequalities in Britain: geographical divides returning to 1930s maxima by 2007', *BMJ*, 341:c3639, doi:10.1136/bmj.c3639.

Tropman, J.E. (1998) *Does America hate the poor?: The other American dilemma – lessons for the 21st century from the 1960s and the 1970s*, Santa Barbara: Greenwood Press.

Wilkinson, R. and Pickett, K. (2010) *The spirit level* (2nd edn) London: Allen Lane.

# 39

# Inequality kills

*Red Pepper Magazine* (2006)

The murder rate tells us far more about society and how it is changing than any particular murder tells us about the individuals involved.

For most people the chances of being murdered are the same or lower than they were 20 years ago. For young men in the poorest parts of the country, they are considerably higher. Murder is like a disease – it affects different groups disproportionately, and its cause is an unequal society.

Inequality kills. It kills indirectly, of course, by robbing people of protection from physical and mental illness. But it also kills directly by increasing the rates at which people are murdered.

Between January 1981 and December 2000, over 13,000 people were murdered in Britain – a rate of just under two murders per day. But the chances of being a victim vary greatly according to gender and geography. The general rise in murder rates in the UK, with more murders committed in the past 15 years than in the preceding 20-year period, is almost exclusively concentrated amongst men of working age living in the poorest parts of the country. A more detailed look at these figures shows a close relationship between this fact and the rising levels of inequality in Britain since the early 1980s.

Before exploring this relationship further, it is important to understand the role of murder in our growing awareness of broader health inequalities. This connection may seem surprising, but murder is a form of death, just as all health inequalities eventually are, and, increasingly, research is showing that inequalities in health tend to both reflect and be caused by other inequities in society.

For instance, Richard Wilkinson, writing in the recent UK Health Watch 2005 report, reviews research findings showing that levels of poor health and extreme violence are consistently worse in more unequal societies. High levels of inequality play a crucial part in corroding social relations reducing trust, increasing levels of shame and embarrassment, and reducing the positive feedback of friendship. In general, he concludes that inequality affects people's sense of their own 'worth':

> "In more unequal societies it is as if some people count for everything and others for nothing, making us all more concerned with how we are seen. More hierarchical societies are marked by greater social divisions and more downward discrimination and prejudice against those lower on the social ladder."

Income differences are closely correlated to social mobility, with countries like Britain and the USA (the 'land of opportunity') enjoying significantly less social mobility than, for example, Norway and Sweden. These divisions also play out geographically, with inequality increasing 'the segregation of the population into rich and poor neighbourhoods', according to Wilkinson, who concludes that: 'it is unrealistic to pursue greater equality of opportunity without at the same time moving towards greater equality of outcome.' In Britain, income differentials have widened over the past two or three decades – which explains, Wilkinson says, why social mobility has actually decreased in the period since Margaret Thatcher became prime minister.

Understood in this context, patterns of murder in Britain can be seen in a new light, starting from an understanding that greater inequality causes worse health and poorer social relations. Looking at the changing rate of homicide in Britain (defined as murders and manslaughters combined) from the viewpoint of who is most likely to be killed reveals some crucial patterns.

Think of murder as a disease that has been spreading. Tackling this disease is not simply a question of finding the immediate causes of individual cases – the person who wields the knife or pulls the trigger – but is a search for the underlying pattern of infection and the signs of susceptibility to that infection. In particular, we should be concerned with why the disease takes holds in certain areas and in particular circumstances most while other areas seem to be almost immune, and why some people are increasingly susceptible to it.

Analysing murder according to the age and gender of the victims, and how and where they were murdered, reveals an increasingly unequal picture. Despite regular panics in the mainstream media, the evidence shows that for the majority of the population the chances of being murdered have fallen, in some cases considerably. For males aged over 60 and under five, and for females of all ages, the chances of being murdered have either fallen or remained constant over the past 20 years.

The large majority of murders are committed by men and the large (and growing) majority of victims are men, especially young men. Women are now far less likely to be murder victims because they are in a better position than they were two decades ago to escape violent relationships before those relationships become deadly. By contrast, the chances of being murdered have increased significantly for most men – with those between 20 and 24 facing twice the risk now compared with 20 years ago. Today, men aged between 17 and 32 make up 7 per cent of the population but 25 per cent of all murder victims.

A more detailed look shows that most murders of men by men occur within relationships of friendship turned bad – situations in which the murderers and victims know each other well. For some reason, quarrels between men in western societies (and Britain in particular) are turning more violent. For a clue as to why, we need to look at where, for whom and when this changed.

Gender differences are reinforced by profound residential inequalities. In all countries, where you live matters more than who you are. In Britain, growing inequality between neighbourhoods has occurred alongside more unequal patterns of murder. Between 1981 and 1985, people living in the poorest 10 per cent of areas were 4.5 times more likely to be murdered than those living in the richest ten per cent. By 2000, the poorest 10 percent were six times more likely to be murdered.

Some simple projections using figures for the 1980s and 1990s help illustrate these trends. In the richest neighbourhoods, for every 100 murders that we might 'expect' to take place if the national average were applied equally, only 50 occurred. In the poorest 10 per cent of council wards, using the same measure, there were around 300 murders compared to the 100 expected.

In fact, the rise in murders in Britain has been concentrated almost exclusively amongst men of working age living in the poorest parts of the country. Living in the areas most affected by the recession and high unemployment of the early 1980s, many of these men left school at 15 or 16 and were unable to find work. In each case, there is no simple causal relationship at play. Murders typically result from a complex interplay of factors – including social exclusion, esteem and status – as well as a considerable degree of bad luck. For every murder victim, dozens of others have been 'almost murdered'.

There is a common myth that gun crime is behind high murder rates in poor areas. In fact, a higher proportion of rich people are killed by guns than poor people. The most common way of being murdered in poor areas is through being cut with a knife or broken glass. Most murders are shockingly banal – such as a fight after a night out drinking in which a threat was made and someone died. Such murders do not make the headlines. Most are extensions of fighting, not carefully planned and executed events. Real life is not like Morse or Taggart, and cases very rarely take great detective work or remain unsolved for a generation. Murder, although extreme, is a fact of life – but it need not be a growing part of our lives.[1]

Murder rates are still very low compared to the US, but murder is a stark and powerful social indicator and there can be no cause for complacency. The murder rate tells us far more about society and how it is changing than any particular murder tells us about the individuals involved. The changing pattern of the victims is consistent with new evidence that inequality kills. While the majority of people are less likely to become a victim, the poorest people in the most deprived communities are becoming more and more likely.

I argued earlier that it helps to think of murder as a disease. As with many diseases, we do not have a cure for murder. There is no childhood inoculation. We can, however, increase our efforts to stop its spread and better protect those most likely to fall victim. There is nothing inevitable about murder and the falling rates for most of the population show that there is no need for the rest of us to experience the level of violence and inequality of which murder is such a powerful indicator.

### Further reading

*Prime suspect: Murder in Britain* by Danny Dorling, www.crimeandsociety. org.uk/ pdfs/monograph1_17Oct05.pdf

UK Health Watch (2005) *The experience of health in an unequal society* (Politics of Health Group). The full report is available at www.pohg.org.uk/ support/downloads/ukhealthwatch-2005.pdf

Davey Smith, G. (2003) *Health inequalities: Lifecourse approaches*, Bristol: The Policy Press.

---

[1] Editorial note: In 2011 a group within the very small gun-lobby that exists in Britain questioned whether a claim I had made about people being more likely to be shot in the countryside was valid. They pointed out that officially recorded gun crime was high in some urban areas. What they failed to point out was that in the large majority of these cases no gun was fired. The crime being that someone found carrying a gun. In contrast, it appears very likely that the majority of gun crime recorded in rural areas involves the actual discharging of a fire-arm.

# 40

# The geography of social inequality and health[1]

Swiss Public Health Lecture (2005)

## Some statistical pictures of the rich world, the local, and the global

This chapter documents a lecture that presented some 30 pictures: maps, graphs and 'map-graphs' that were intended to show a group of public health physicians what a geographical perspective can bring to the understanding of social inequality and inequalities in health. Here those images have been grouped into eight figures to provide some food for thought. The mapping of disease is rumoured to have been initiated by a medical doctor in charge of a lunatic asylum who gave his patients crayons to colour in maps by disease rate. Maps and map-like graphs can have a wide appeal and can draw people into issues that might otherwise not interest them. I begin with changing gender inequalities in the rich countries of the world, move on to local health inequalities in one country (the UK) and then to new emerging global patterns in social inequality and health inequalities as depicted geographically and graphically. The images were originally drawn in colour but have to be reproduced in black, white and grey here. However, the original versions of most can be found in the plate section of this book.

---

[1] This chapter is made up of the text and images used in a lecture given to the Swiss Public Health Society which took place in Berne, 24 June 2005. I am grateful to Matthias Egger, Professor of Epidemiology and Public Health at the Department of Social and Preventive Medicine (ISPM), Finkenhubelweg, Berne, for the invitation to speak there.

## Graphs that look like maps: mortality by age, year and sex

**Figure 1a:** Rich world female mortality rates 1850–2000 (per year per 1,000)

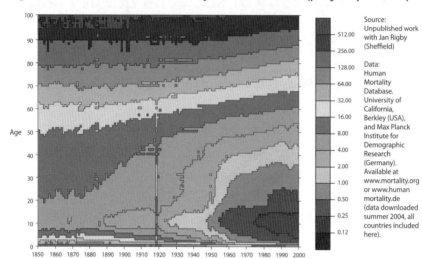

**Figure 1b:** Rich world male/female mortality rates 1850–2000 (per year per cohort)

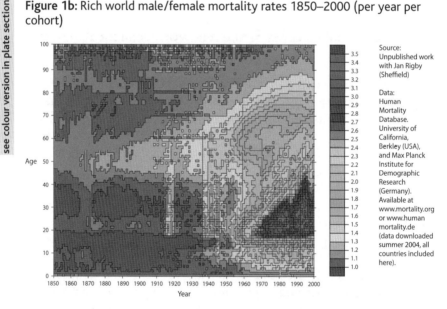

**Figure 1a:** Rich world female mortality rates (top half of diagram)

This first image is a graph which looks like a contour map. Along the bottom axis are marked 150 years in time and along the side axis 100 years of age. The colours of the cells in the graph depict 15,000 mortality rates. The bottom left-hand corner of the graph is the mortality rate of infant girls who were born in 1850 into what are now the rich countries of the world. Between an eighth and a quarter died before their first birthday. The top right-hand corner of the graph shows that by the year 2000 between a quarter and a half of the women aged 100 in the rich world died before their 101st birthday. The contours in the graph show that it is for the young that progress has been most rapid and that only one event, the influenza epidemic of 1918, interrupts the trends shown in data involving more than half a billion people. Data sources are given in the figure, and this work was carried out in collaboration with Dr Jan Rigby.

The technique of mapping deaths by birth year and age is called drawing a lexis diagram and a useful primer is to found at www.demog.berkeley. edu/~bmd/lexis.html where it is explained how all human lives flow at 45 degrees from the base of the graph upwards.

When the graph showing male mortality rates is divided by the graph just shown (Figure 1) for women then a clear pattern emerges for the richest countries of the world. Note that at different times different countries enter the world mortality database but this does not have a great effect on the patterns shown and, if anything, ensures that countries are included only when they are sufficiently wealthy to be able to record mortality rates accurately. Figure 1b shows that before 1914 mortality rates for men and women were very similar at all ages. The First and Second World Wars are evident in the graph above as is the 'smoking plume' (the 'cloud-like' structure) centred around age 60 in 1975 (of the men born in 1915). The striking inequality in Figure 1b is the triangle to the right with an apex around age 20 in 1960 (the men born in 1940). Men of my age (when I

**Figure 2a:** USA male/female mortality ratios 1900–2071 (per year per cohort)

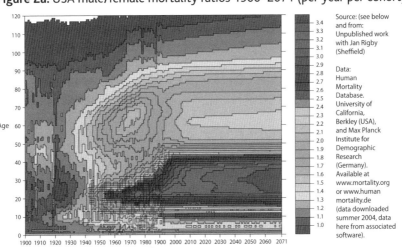

Source: (see below and from: Unpublished work with Jan Rigby (Sheffield)

Data: Human Mortality Database. University of California, Berkley (USA), and Max Planck Institute for Demographic Research (Germany). Available at www.mortality.org or www.human mortality.de (data downloaded summer 2004, data here from associated software).

see colour version in plate section

Source: Life Tables for the United States Social Security Area 1900-2080 by Felicitie C. Bell et al.

gave this talk) across the rich world are now three times more likely to die, this year, than are women of my age.

**Figure 2a:** US male/female mortality ratios, 1900–2071 (diagram on page 313)

Data for individual countries show local variation. The First World War had little effect on mortality rates of the citizens of the US; their smoking plume is centred on those slightly older men who could afford large numbers of machine-rolled cigarettes a little earlier, and were kept alive a little longer perhaps, but in essence the pattern is the same. The horizontal bands in the figure for future years show that US actuaries predict a remarkably uneventful future as current trends become embedded. I don't think we should be so hopeful. We are likely to live in more interesting times than these.

**Figure 2b:** England–Wales male/female mortality ratios 1840–2050 (year/cohort)

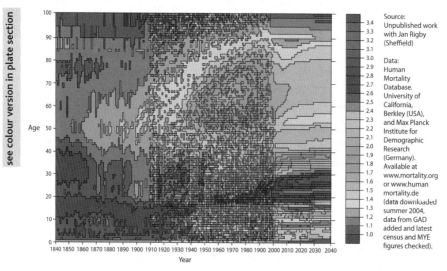

**Figure 2b:** England and Wales male/female mortality ratios, 1840–2050 (diagram at the top of this page)

For the UK, with only one-twentieth of the billion total population from the world mortality dataset, the patterns are less clear but still similar to those of the US. The First World War is more significant; the inequalities attributable to differential rates of smoking between men and women in the past peak a little later, but by only a few years, and the variability in the figure suggests that UK actuaries are perhaps slightly more imaginative than their US colleagues, but they are still naturally conservative in their predictions. Growing inequalities in mortality at young ages are, of course, based on low numbers of deaths, but for many age groups of younger men their deaths rates remain at levels reached shortly after the Second World War. Diseases of despair such as cirrhosis of the liver and deaths from overdoses are on the rise for younger men in the rich world and especially in more unequal rich nations such as the UK and the US.

**Figure 3a:** Sickness and disability in the UK in 2001 and change from 1991

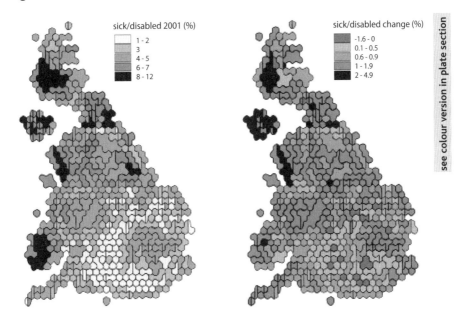

**Figure 3b:** Limiting long-term illness in the UK in 2001 and change from 1991

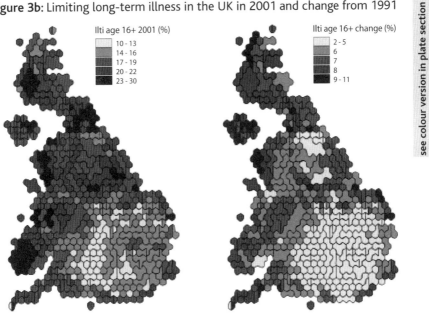

## Inequality in morbidity across the districts of the UK

**Figure 3:** Sick/disabled and limiting long-term illness

Turning to the local and returning to both sexes, what might these diseases of despair be? Above are two maps of the UK each showing over 400 areas, with each area in each map drawn roughly in proportion to its population. The first map shows the proportion of people who could not work because they were sick and disabled in the year 2001; the second shows the percentage point change in that rate since 1991. None of these rates are age- or sex-standardised because, in these areas where population demography is similar, that confuses unnecessarily. Note that the rate reaches 12 per cent of the population in some areas in the North, and has risen almost everywhere over time. Physically the population now have better health than a decade ago, but everywhere higher rates of overall sickness are reported as mental health worsens. Geographically the worst reported health is where people are poorest and have become poorer.

Limiting long-term illness rates are at their maximum in northern and Welsh areas, where up to almost a third of the population in particular places report that they suffer from an illness which limits their daily activities. These rates of illness have risen everywhere in the UK since 1991, but have increased the most furthest away from a population circle centred on London.

## Inequality in education and affluence, mortality, income and health over time in the UK

**Figure 4a:** Key to the human geography of the UK (top third of figure and right-hand list)

The population circle of constant health, centred on London, also coincides with the area from which children are most likely to attend university in the UK: a 'T'-shaped 'valley' (as shown on this map) where height of areas is drawn in proportion to children not attending university. The 'T' is made up of areas of low height indicating that the highest proportions of all young people living in the UK attending university are found here.[2]

**Figure 4b:** The geography becomes simpler over time (middle third of figure)

Here are shown simple cartograms of all-cause and lung cancer age- and sex-standardised mortality ratios (SMRs) to illustrate just how simple many

---

[2] Dorling, D. and Thomas, B. (2004) *People and places: A census atlas of the UK*, Bristol: The Policy Press. Shows this map in relation to other influences.

**Figure 4a:** Key to the human geography of the UK

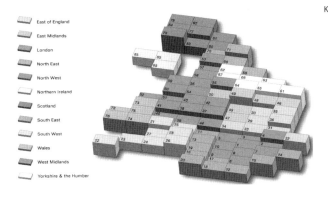

Key to the Human Geography
of the UK

| | |
|---|---|
| 1 | London Central |
| 2 | London East |
| 3 | London North |
| 4 | London North East |
| 5 | London North West |
| 6 | London South & Surrey East |
| 7 | London South East |
| 8 | London South Inner |
| 9 | London South West |
| 10 | London West |
| 11 | Buckinghamshire & Oxfordshire East |
| 12 | East Sussex & Kent South |
| 13 | Hampshire North & Oxford |
| 14 | Kent East |
| 15 | Kent West |
| 16 | South Downs West |
| 17 | Surrey |
| 18 | Sussex West |
| 19 | Thames Valley |
| 20 | Wight & Hampshire South |
| 21 | Bristol |
| 22 | Cornwall & West Plymouth |
| 23 | Devon & East Plymouth |
| 24 | Dorset & East Devon |
| 25 | Gloucestershire |
| 26 | Itchen, Test & Avon |
| 27 | Somerset & North Devon |
| 28 | Wiltshire North & Bath |
| 29 | Bedfordshire & Milton Keynes |
| 30 | Cambridgeshire |
| 31 | Essex North & Suffolk South |
| 32 | Essex South |
| 33 | Essex West & Hertfordshire East |
| 34 | Hertfordshire |
| 35 | Norfolk |
| 36 | Suffolk & South West Norfolk |
| 37 | Birmingham East |
| 38 | Birmingham West |
| 39 | Coventry & North Warwickshire |
| 40 | Herefordshire & Shropshire |
| 41 | Midlands West |
| 42 | Staffordshire East & Derby |
| 43 | Staffordshire West & Congleton |
| 44 | Worcestershire & South Warwickshire |
| 45 | Leicester |
| 46 | Lincolnshire |
| 47 | Northamptonshire & Blaby |
| 48 | Nottinghamshire & Leicestershire North West |
| 49 | Nottinghamshire North & Chesterfield |
| 50 | Peak District |
| 51 | Cheshire East |
| 52 | Cheshire West & Wirral |
| 53 | Cumbria & Lancashire North |
| 54 | Greater Manchester Central |
| 55 | Greater Manchester South |
| 56 | Greater Manchester West |
| 57 | Lancashire Central |
| 58 | Lancashire South |
| 59 | Merseyside East & Wigan |
| 60 | Merseyside West |
| 61 | East Yorkshire & North Lincolnshire |
| 62 | Leeds |
| 63 | North Yorkshire |
| 64 | Sheffield |
| 65 | Yorkshire South |
| 66 | Yorkshire South West |
| 67 | Yorkshire West |
| 68 | Cleveland & Richmond |
| 69 | Durham |
| 70 | Northumbria |
| 71 | Tyne & Wear |
| 72 | Mid & West Wales |
| 73 | North Wales |
| 74 | South Wales Central |
| 75 | South Wales East |
| 76 | South Wales West |
| 77 | Central Scotland |
| 78 | Glasgow |
| 79 | Highlands & Islands |
| 80 | Lothian |
| 81 | Mid Scotland & Fife |
| 82 | North East Scotland |
| 83 | South of Scotland |
| 84 | West of Scotland |
| 85 | Northen Ireland: (3 seats) |

Legend:
East of England
East Midlands
London
North East
North West
Northern Ireland
Scotland
South East
South West
Wales
West Midlands
Yorkshire & the Humber

*see colour version in plate section*

**Figure 4b:** The geography becomes simpler over time

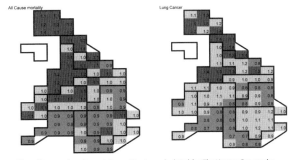

All Cause mortality — Lung Cancer

*Source:* Mortality records and population estimates, calculated for *The Human Geography of the UK* book

*see colour version in plate section*

**Figure 4c:** Trends in UK inequalities – life expectancy and income

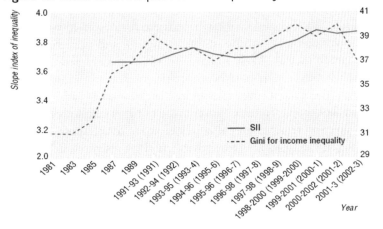

*see colour version in plate section*

local geographical patterns are. Rates of 40% and even of 120% above national mean levels can be seen in Glasgow – some of the highest rates in Western Europe.[3]

**Figure 4c:** Trends in UK inequalities – life expectancy and income (bottom third of figure)

In the UK inequalities in income, both socially and geographically, rose quickly in the 1980s and this was mirrored by rising and then stable but still high inequalities in life expectancy between areas. Only for the most recent year of data have inequalities in income been seen to fall – seven years after the current Labour government came to power.[4]

## The geography of supply and demand of physicians in England and Wales

**Figure 5a:** Demand for the health industry (top half)

If even simpler geographical boundaries are used in one country then patterns often become clearer as this figure demonstrates by plotting rates for large counties. Here are the proportion of people who suffer both poor health and a limiting long-term illness (combined) in England and Wales. Note that rates are lowest to the north and west of London. The rate at which the population expresses a demand for health care varies by more than fourfold between these large areas. If these rates were age- and sex-standardised the gap would actually widen slightly.

**Figure 5b:** Supply for the health industry (lower half)

Health professionals, in this case qualified and working medical practitioners, generally prefer to live and work where there are fewer ill people, in university towns and cities of the south of England and in places similar to those in which they are likely to have grown up and entered university from. Thus they remain distributed geographically away from the majority of their prospective patients, even after more than 50 years of national health planning and allocation formulae. Nurses in the north of England reduce the size of the gap considerably, being the only group of health professionals in the UK who tend to be located towards where there are more sick people. The inverse care law in the UK is as strong as ever.

---

[3] Dorling, D. (2005) *Human geography of the UK*, London: Sage.

[4] Editorial note: As Chapter Seven of this volume makes clear, that gain was short-lived. See also Shaw, M., Davey Smith, G. and Dorling, D. (2005) 'Health inequalities and New Labour: how the promises compare with real progress', *BMJ*, vol 330, pp 1016–21.

**Figure 5a:** Demand for the health industry

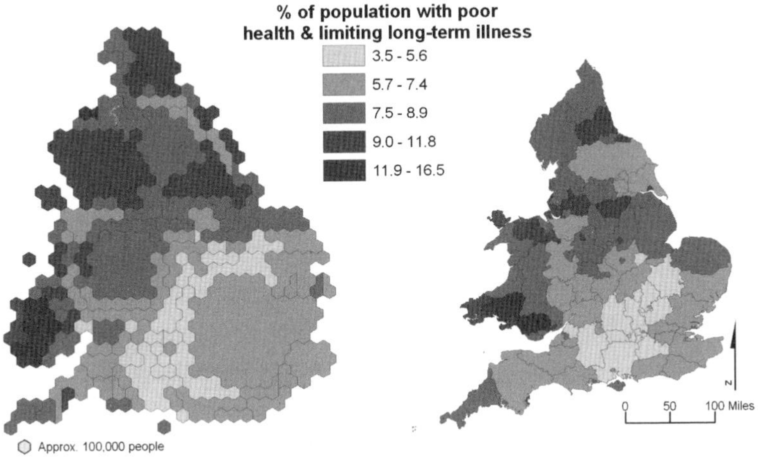

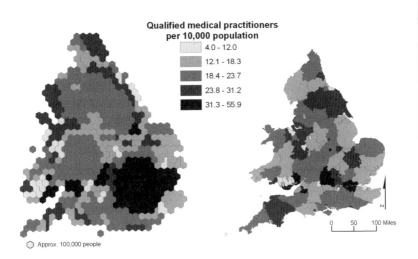

**Figure 5b:** Supply for the health industry

## Turning from inequality within a rich country to inequality across a poor world

**Figure 6:** A global context: the world's children

Two billion of the six billion[5] people on earth are children and half of them are growing up in countries within Africa, or in India or China. Moving from local inequalities in the UK (which contains only 0.5% of the world's

---

[5] Note the data here refer to the year 2000 – over ten years ago. The figure is now nearer 6.8 billion, by the end of of 2011 it is forecast to pass 7 billion.

children) to global inequalities in health involves reporting illness and mortality rates which were last experienced in the UK in the 1850s [the point in time this lecture began with; see Figure 1]. Figure 6 shows one possible map of the world's children, which can be coloured according to the rates at which they are deprived of shelter, clean water, education, health care, information, food, and so on – but, in essence, global inequalities in health can be summarised more clearly by concentrating on a dozen regions of the world rather than all 200 (or so) countries. All the data that follow were derived from the UNDP World Development Report 2004.[6]

**Figure 6:** A global context – the world's children

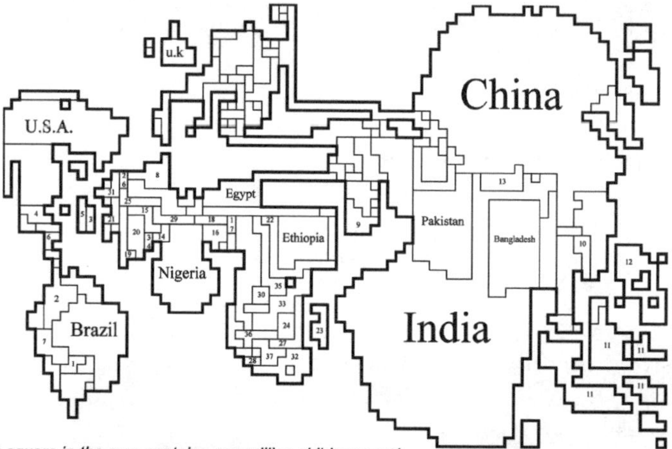

*Each square in the map contains one million children aged under 18 as recorded as living by the United Nations in 2000. National borders are shown. Other than the UK and USA countries named or numbered were surveyed and so are shaded below.*

Source: Human Geography of the UK, London: Sage, February 2005

---

[6] Editorial note: Were the figures to be redrawn using data from more up-to-date reports the changes would be so small in most cases as to be imperceptible.

**Figures 7a-7e:** Population, life expectancy, health spending

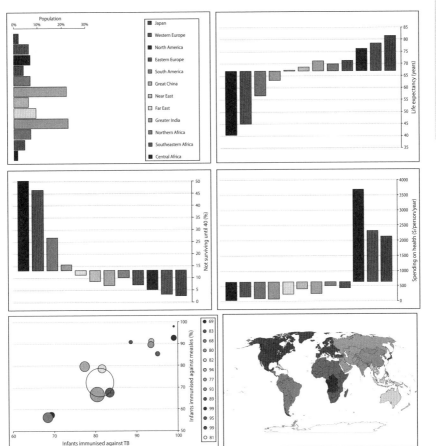

Note: In the three horizontal bar charts above the bars rise up if above the world average rate and descend if they represent below average rates.

**Figure 7a:** Population (top left panel)

Here are shown the 12 regions used in the Worldmapper project and their respective shares of the world's population. These regions are used in the rest of the panels in Figure 7. The two smallest regions are the islands of Japan and the countries of the Congo basin (Central Africa) – each containing over 100 million people. These regions are defined by continental location, income and by the locations of the world's two largest states (India and China), which contain over a billion people each; globally these 12 regions of the earth order the population by space into social groups which suggest that there is a continuum to global social and health inequalities.

**Figure 7b:** Life expectancy in years (top right panel)

By 2002 the best-off 100 million people on earth (by large area) lived twice as long as the worst-off 100 million. The main irregularity in the continuum is that the people of China now live a little longer, on average, than do those of South America. Within Africa there are regional inequalities that are mirrored, at the opposite end of the global scale, by inequalities between geographically contiguous groups of OECD nations.

**Figure 7c:** Population not surviving up to age 40 (%) (middle left panel)

By 2002 a majority of people living in central Africa did not survive up to age 40. In both China and the Near East a higher proportion do survive to age 40 than in South America, but again the regional continuum is clear.

**Figure 7d:** Spending on health in $ per person per year (middle right panel)

When compared by equal purchasing power parity dollars, the spending on health care per person is higher in North America than in Western Europe and higher there again than in Japan. This is total public and private spending. Thus the country with the longest life expectancy is not that which spends most on health care. Nevertheless the global inverse health care law is still stark. The spending per person in Central Africa is near zero. The reverse continuum is clearer on a log scale (not shown here).

**Figure 7e:** Proportion of infants immunised against TB and measles (bottom panel)

Globally around four in every five infants are immunised against TB and three in every four against measles, annually. More are immunised where the diseases are least common. Regions are drawn in proportion to the number of infants in each region (135 million infants a year now worldwide).

**Figures 8a-8f:** HIV, GDP, infant mortality, life expectancy, income

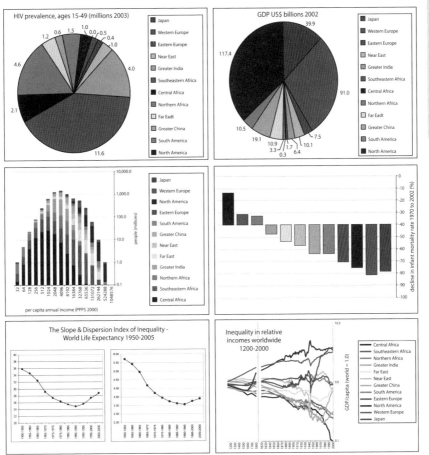

Note: In the horizontal bar chart above the bars rise up if above the world average, similarly with the multiple-line graph.

**Figure 8a:** HIV prevalence, ages 15-49, in millions in 2003 (top left panel)

Three quarters of all people dying with HIV live in Africa and India and, to all intents and purposes, almost none in Japan.[7]

---

[7] Editorial note: Although unknown to me while I was giving this lecture, my colleague Tomoki Nakaya and his colleagues were mapping the spread of AIDS in Japan even using very small numbers: T. Nakaya, K. Nakase and K.Osaka (2005) 'Spatio-temporal modelling of the HIV epidemic in Japan based on the national HIV/AIDS surveillance', *Journal of Geographical Systems*, vol 7, pp 313–36. Later the results were shown here: (www.envplan. com/epa/editorials/a4320.pdf

**Figure 8b:** GDP in US$ billions, 2002 (top right panel)

Three quarters of the world's income is enjoyed in North America, Western Europe and Japan. To all intents and purposes, as near to none is enjoyed in Central Africa as can be shown without employing a log scale.

**Figure 8c:** Per capita annual income in PPP$, 2000 (middle left panel)

The world income distribution appears to be essentially log normal, formed by the addition of these 12 log normal distributions. It is continuous, not bimodal – although this graph relies on estimates made for individual countries. Almost no one earns (rather than receives) more than 1 million US$ a year. One million people, almost all in Africa, live on less than $64 a year. Of course, with the limited real data we have, rather than the estimates shown here, we know that the richest people in the world have incomes very much higher than the combined incomes and assets of groups of ten thousand of the poorest of peoples. In this figure inequalities are underestimated.

**Figure 8d:** Decline in infant mortality rate 1970–2002 (%) (middle right panel)

Infant mortality rates have declined most since 1970 where they were lowest to begin with. Globally inequality in infant mortality has been growing since the 1970s.

**Figure 8e:** Slope and dispersion index of inequality – world life expectancy, 1950–2005 (bottom left panel)

Continental variations in life expectancy have been rising since the mid-1980s using the SII measure and since the early 1990s using the DII measure.[8] Irrespective of how global inequalities in mortality are measured, they are continue to rise as much because of events in Eastern Europe and the Near East as because of what is occurring in Africa, and because health improvements are still rapid in the richest regions of the world.

**Figure 8f:** Inequalities in relative incomes worldwide, 1200–2000 (bottom right panel)

When OECD estimates by Angus Maddison for GDP and population are amalgamated for the 12 regions used here it becomes evident that average incomes in Central Africa have now fallen to a tenth of the world average (which is itself low). India and the remainder of Africa live half an order of magnitude away. China, Japan and the Far East each, at different points in the last 60 years, broke away from the group of regions they were travelling downhill with, in relative terms. However, globally income inequalities are

---

[8] SII is the Slope Index of Inequality and DII an alternative measure – the 'Dispersal Index of Inequality'.

now widening at an exponential rate, with the acceleration beginning just as inequalities in mortality began to rise for the first recorded time. The world is dividing rapidly by health and by wealth.

## Conclusion

This talk has drawn on new data made available in recent years locally and globally. Most results are unpublished, but some are included in an atlas titled *People and places* (The Policy Press, 2004), and more analysis of the changing social make-up of one country is now published in *The human geography of the UK* (Sage, 2005); see www.shef.ac.uk/sasi for more information. Locally, in the UK, rates of poverty have risen as increased affluence has been accompanied by increased inequality. Worldwide, inequalities in income and health are widening. In rich nations the future looks most bleak for younger men who do not succeed – however success is measured. In poorer nations the future is most bleak for children.

# 41

# The cartographer's mad project[1]

Review of: Christian Jacob (2006) *The sovereign Map: Theoretical approaches in cartography through history*, Translated by Tom Conley, Edited by Edward H. Dahl, Chicago: University of Chicago Press, 464 pp

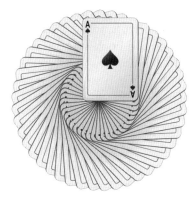

"Something has disappeared: the sovereign difference between them that was the abstraction's charm. For it is the difference which forms the poetry of the map and the charm of the territory, the magic of the concept and the charm of the real. This representational imaginary, which both culminates in and is engulfed by the cartographer's mad project of an ideal coextensivity between the map and the territory, disappears with simulation, whose operation is nuclear and genetic, and no longer specular and discursive. With it goes all of metaphysics. No more mirror of being and appearances, of the real and its concept."[2]

In the twenty-six years since Jean Baudrillard described the cartographer's mad project in this manner, the worlds of both geography and cartography have had their gaze utterly inverted from looking out on the world to looking

---

[1] Editorial note: This book review first appeared on-line in the series H-HistGeog, H-Net Reviews. It is included here because I really like the title that the review editor chose for it, and because it shows what kind of obscure things people like me worry about when we write about why we draw maps. H-Net is short hand for "the Humanities and Social Sciences". See: www.h-net.msu.edu/reviews/showrev.cgi?path=92111211471469

[2] This extract, translated from the French, appears in Poster, M. (1988) (ed) *Jean Baudrillard, Selected writings*, Stanford: Stanford University Press, p 166.

in on themselves. Christian Jacob did not write *L'empire des Cartes*, published in 1992, to reinforce the achievement of this. But reviewing in hindsight we can say that it was a significant force in what drove that shift of view.

To fit this book into a lineage: Christian Jacob cites the late Brian Harley as particularly influential, who in turn was influenced by the writing of many French academics.[3] But the influences are not all contemporary. For instance on how cartography verges with madness (a word he never uses), he draws from *The Hunting of the Snark* (1876) by Lewis Carroll (definitely English, with a little Irish) (p 103), not Jean Baudrillard. Thus the formative thinking that leads to our now-introverted contemplation has bounced around the globe, slowed only by time for publication and the number of people writing, and time for translation.

In the fifteen years since this book was first written, many of its ideas have come to be accepted as the new truth (for all that Jean Baudrillard said about simulacra). Those ideas have been propounded by many others independently of Christian Jacob – although I doubt by any others in such encyclopaedic detail and based on so many concrete examples, nor so well written and translated (by Tom Conley).

Ed Dahl edited this edition and, given the book's iconic status, a good job was done in preserving the detail. The downside is that, at times, the slow reader can begin to wonder if they will ever finish the text; but read in fits and starts it is constantly rewarding. It ranges in content from consideration of near contemporary puzzle maps, such as the world on a Rubik's cube (p 86), to Pierre Duval's cartographic snakes and ladders type map game of 1654 (opposite p 269).

The sovereign map is a very substantial work, its scope includes the entire temporal history of cartography, although, as its author readily admits, with a spatial bias for maps drawn north of the Mediterranean. Despite this temporal scope, reading a book for the first time that was written fifteen years ago, and which was at the cutting edge then, is an odd experience. The reader can find themselves thinking "so what" or "of course" or "why go on" to ideas that required more careful explanation when first introduced to a potentially more sceptical audience. Indeed, in the preface to the current edition, the author confesses that he would not choose to write the same book now. So why read it now?

The obvious answer is because, like me, you could not read it prior to translation. A better answer is that, despite this being a long and at times tortuous read (with some passages being difficult to absorb in anything but small chunks), the book rewards the reader not just with grand ideas (albeit most now well known) but with a myriad of nuggets of priceless information

---

[3] He is described as an American in the text (p xxii); as he worked there towards the end of his life, it is an easy error to make.

to those fascinated with mapping. As an example of this, the book proper begins with a discussion of the proper definition of a map and does not actually venture one until it reaches page 98. That is still very early on in its argument. For those too mean to buy the book, the definition of a map is:

> "It is an object likely to be materialized in many ways; an anonymous object in that it bears so many different names that do not name it" (p 98).

This definition carries on in a similar vein for one hundred more lines and there is no obvious ending to the definition.

Pretentious (*moi*)? Anyone who ploughs through 98 pages is not going to mind reaching a 100 line definition when they do. They might well feel cheated had they not! This is a book about changing underlying beliefs and can now be read with great current interest as a study in how that was done. As Paul Carter is quoted as saying on the back-flap blurb, the book "not only charts the sovereign and ubiquitous reach of maps: it supplies the wise ways of reading between the signs, so that we might bend back the bars of latitude and longitude, escape the prison house of our imperial projections, and to begin to write the earth less schematically, more inclusively."

I could not agree more on the need to escape the imperial prison of our current projections, bend back the bars of graticule and write the earth inclusively; but what of reading between the signs? At an early point in the book, the Bronze age petroglyph map of Bedolina is deconstructed for its meaning over the course of two pages, only to end: "To go any further in interpretation would be mere extrapolation" (p 26). However, neither there, nor often elsewhere in the book, was it clear to me why ending precisely there was any better than ending the speculation a little early, or just letting rip with your imagination.

For me it is the comprehensive nature of the research involved that is most valuable about this work. Not its contribution to our current fad of navel gazing and reading between the lines in recursive obsession. For those that have time to spare (but not so much time that they can wade through the now multiple-volume History of Cartography project) this book provides a particular history of cartography as well as an excellent reinterpretation. The links that can be made to some current mental maps from some classical ones are also staggering.

Take, for instance, a 2,500 year old Chinese map in which the center of the world is the Imperial Palace, surrounded respectively by "imperial domains, the nations of the nobility that pay tribute, the zones of pacification (on the borders, where the people adapt to Chinese customs), the nations of friendly barbarians, and, finally, the nations of those who do not fall under the purview of civilization" (p 134; see Figure 1, reproduced here on page

331). Compare today the Imperial Palace to the White House, surrounded by its domains (the United States), nations like the United Kingdom, France, Pakistan, and Afghanistan respectively. It is only this year that the United Kingdom stopped paying tribute to the United States (in the form of lend-lease repayments). Imperial projections and similar schematic images are no modern creation.

The book (when not too engrossed in lists) can also give a sense of pace to developments that a larger project cannot. One description that is particularly effective concerns the motives for the development of the first printed map in 1472, to Mercator's 1578 Ptolemaic publications, to the first atlas of one-hundred maps in 1654, ending with the first 3000 leaves printed in 1662 (pp 61-73). Now there's a challenge for today's cartographers!

This is a wonderful book. I think it shows through a careful historical reading how cartography has not been a mad project to achieve the unachievable; rather it has always been both the product and the driver of the thinking in particular places and times where each map was made. The map remains sovereign regardless of how well we may think we understand it. Today's maps matter just as did those of the entire world stretched about the Imperial Palace, or the small valley around Bedolina – which was slowly drawn and redrawn in rock above the Oglio River plain over the course of a millennia (1500–500 BC) (p 26).

The map has always been the symbol of how we think of our world. The better we understand that, the easier it is to map in new ways. Christian Jacob has helped many along this road. Most could not know it until this careful translation was made.

**Figure 1:** From the Chhin-Ting Shu Ching T'u Shuo

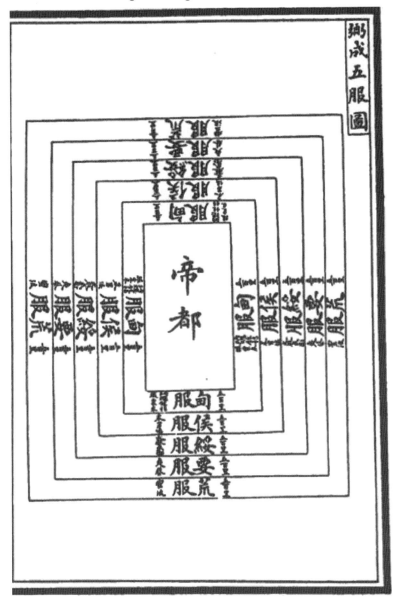

"Translation: outward from the metropolitan area (center), there is, in concentric rectangles: (a) the royal domains; (b) the lands of the tributary feudal princes and lords; (c) the 'zone of pacification', i.e., the marches, where Chinese civilization was in course of adoption; (d) the zone of allied barbarians; and (e) the zone of cultureless savagery".

*Source:* http://cartographic-images.net/Cartographic_Images/209_Chhin-Ting_Shu_Tu_Shuo.html

# 42

# The fading of the dream: widening inequalities in life expectancy in America

*International Journal of Epidemiology* (2006) vol 35, no 4, pp 979–80

'Oh give me a home, where the buffalo roam and the deer and the antelope play Where seldom is heard a discouraging word And the skies are not cloudy all day.' [Popular Cowboy Song, undated, verse]

Studies of health inequalities in the United States are relatively rare, especially considering the extent of those inequalities in comparison with other countries;[1] the population size of the United States in comparison with far smaller but more studied peoples;[2] the concentration of resources available to

---

[1] Wilkinson, R. (2005) *The impact of inequality: How to make sick societies healthier*, New York: The New Press.

[2] Fawcett, J., Blakely, T. and Kunst, A. (2005) 'Are mortality differences and trends by education any better or worse in New Zealand? A comparison study with Norway, Denmark and Finland, 1980–1990s', *European Journal of Epidemiology*, no 20, pp 683–91.

academics in that country;[3] and the hegemonic status of the world's 'leader'[4] making it odd that it does not lead in this field. Health and wealth are old acquaintances, but best related where riches are best shared.[5] If riches were to trickle down naturally anywhere, they should have done so in the land where they have been most abundant. That they have not done so can be counted in years of lives lost as well as in dollars. That is not in dispute, even if the precise mechanism is keenly debated.[6] Thus Singh and Siahpush[7] have demonstrated what many long suspected: that health inequalities within the United States have widened considerably in recent decades. At the county level of geographic discrimination there has been a 60% [(4.5–2.8)/2.8] increase in the size of the gap in life expectancy between the poorest and richest tenths of the population from 1980 to 2000. The poorest tenth of the population, by area, can now only expect to live to just under 75 years of age while the people living in the best-off counties live on average to almost 80. Some counties are as populous as Los Angeles city. This is not a fine-grained analysis. That is not possible as much detailed demographic data is concealed in many States of the Union. Thus the 4.5 year life expectancy difference is a very wide gap considering the degree of averaging involved.

One reason for not being surprised to find widening inequalities in mortality in the United States is that inequalities have been widening in many Western European countries over the same period – albeit assessed more often as measured between socioeconomic groups within countries[8] rather than between areas. However, when geographical comparisons have been made, similar results of increasing inequalities have been found, but usually not as rapid increases (as have occured recently in America).[9] Inequalities within the United States also appear to be much larger than within most countries in Western Europe and to have grown more rapidly.

---

[3] Carvalho, R. and Batty, M. (2006) 'The geography of scientific productivity: scaling in US computer science', *Physics Abstracts*: arXiv:physics/0603242v1, available at: http://arxiv.org/abs/physics/0603242, accessed 28 March.

[4] Wallerstein, I. (2003) *Decline of American power: The US in a chaotic world*, New York: The New Press.

[5] Ross, N., Dorling, D., Dunn, J.R., Henriksson, G., Glover, J., Lynch, J. and Weitoft, G.R. (2005) 'Metropolitan income inequality and working-age mortality: a cross-sectional analysis using comparable data from five countries', *Journal of Urban Health*, no 82, pp 101–10.

[6] Lynch, J.W., Smith, G.D., Kaplan, G.A. and House, J.S. (2000) 'Income inequality and mortality: importance to health of individual income, psychosocial environment, or material conditions', *BMJ*, no 320, pp 1200–04.

[7] Singh, G.K. and Siahpush, M. (2006) 'Widening socioeconomic inequalities in US life expectancy, 1980 2000', *Int J Epidemiol*, doi:10.1093/ije/dyl083.

[8] Mackenback, J.P. (2006) *Health inequalities: Europe in profile*, Independent report commissioned by the UK Presidency of the EU, available at: www.fco.gov.uk/Files/kfile/HI_EU_Profile,0.pdf.

[9] Shaw, M., Orford, S., Brimblecombe, N. and Dorling, D. (2000) 'Widening inequality in mortality between 160 regions of 15 countries of the European Union', *Social Science and Medicine*, no 30, pp 1047–58.

When compared internationally, Western European inequalities are found to be larger again than those prevailing in Japan[10] and are comparable or can be exceeded by those found elsewhere in the rich world.[11] And, if poorer countries are included also, it becomes increasingly clear that where there is higher inequality, especially income inequality, there is higher inequality in health[12] and that occurs as much between groups of people arranged by occupational social class as it does amongst groups arranged by class as indicated by place of residence.[13] It is worth highlighting that no other rich country with such a large population has such wide inequalities as the United States, a country that can be considered a natural experiment for studying the effects of exposing millions of human beings to relatively high levels of the various insults of inequality.

The details that Singh and Siahpush give on how the changing trends have differed for men and women, how they have had effects at different points in the life-course, and which areas are doing worse, are all worth referring to in their original paper for clues as to the processes that may well be occurring outside the United States as well as within. To reiterate, no other rich country has so large a population that such patterns could be as clear when disaggregated by area, age, sex, and time. To take one example, Singh and Siahpush find that in 1980 the best-off in the United States by county had a life expectancy of on average only 75.8 years (men and women combined). However, this was a year more than those from the poorest areas could expect to live almost a generation later. In general the poor, whether defined by occupational class, income, or residential area, tend not to experience the living standards of the rich until a generation has passed – but standards for both the rich and poor tend to rise in parallel and so too does life expectancy. It is when those parallel improvements diverge that inequality is most keenly felt: when you cannot even expect your children to have what you do not have (and there is a fear that their children might not too). And it is when those parallel rates of improvements converge slightly that great social progress is said to have occurred. Currently the trends worldwide are more often than not diverging, both within countries and between them.[14] Given current trends within the United States we should expect the gap in living standards between future generations

---

[10] Nakaya, T. and Dorling, D. (2005) 'Geographical inequalities of mortality by income in two developed island countries: a cross-national comparison of Britain and Japan', *Social Science and Medicine*, no 60, pp 2865–75.

[11] Pearce, J. and Dorling, D. (2006) 'Increasing geographical inequalities in health in New Zealand, 1980–2001', *International Journal of Epidemiology*, no 35, pp 567–603.

[12] Ram, R. (2005) 'Further examination of the cross-country association between income inequality and population health', *Social Science and Medicine*, no 62, pp 779–91.

[13] Dorling, D. (2006) 'Class alignment renewal', *Journal of Labour Politics*, no 14, pp 8–19.

[14] Dorling, D., Shaw, M. and Davey Smith, G. (2006) 'HIV and global health: global inequality of life expectancy due to AIDS', *BMJ*, no 332, pp 662–4.

there to widen considerably – unless there are some radical changes to the structure of US society.

Perhaps the most stunning observation in the study by Singh and Siahpush is not the results – the direction of which was expected, if not the magnitude, but this observation:

> 'To our knowledge, no attempt has yet been made to conduct a systematic analysis of how socioeconomic inequalities in US life expectancy have changed in recent decades.'

My view will be conditioned by my experiences of the United States, but I still find it amazing how inequality there can be ignored by so many. A dozen years ago I walked into a vast lecture theatre at a convention centre in San Francisco to join the audience to hear a series of plenary talks on 'poverty in America'. These talks were being given at the annual Association of American Geographers' conference, which had just topped the 5000 delegates mark – I think then for the first time. I had only been to the States once before and was overawed with the vastness of the stage in front of me; by the then novel PowerPoint display playing (three times taller than the speaker standing in front of it); and the detail and pain of the geographies of destitution and despair being shown on it. The talks were illuminating. I learnt a lot about where those with least lived and why, as I guess did the other four members of the audience in the theatre that would seat many hundreds. At least two of the other four were from Britain. I don't know whether a single American saw a slide that day or heard a word about their country. That empty lecture theatre and the difficulty of walking through scores of beggars who were then allowed on the streets of San Francisco were the images I took away with me from one of my first visits to the US.

The country I come from is hardly a paragon of social virtue, progressive policy, or a world leader in reducing inequalities, far from it. However, the most important inequality of all (as it has been termed by British government ministers) is both more vast and more quickly widening between the places that people call home in the United States of America than has been recorded almost anywhere else in the rich world. So much of that increase has happened since 1980, the year in which Ronald Reagan was first elected as president, that these levels of inequality should not be seen as having been inevitable. They need not have risen, they need not be sustained, and they could be reduced. But unless inequalities in America are more studied and comparisons with other rich countries made and made frequently – why should we expect people in America to know that they have a problem costing them hundreds of millions of years of life each year – of their lives?

Without the evidence why not simply believe the old songs:

'How often at night when the heavens are bright
With the light from the glittering stars
Have I stood there amazed and asked as I gazed
If their glory exceeds that of ours.'

[Popular Cowboy Song, undated – verse 2][15]

---

[15] Lyrics from hwww.kididdles.com/mouseum/h020.html (available for purchase on cassette on the album 'Wee Sing in the Car' from the KIDiddles Online Store).

# 43

# The importance of circumstance[1]

*Environment and Planning A* (2001) vol 33, no 8, pp 1335–40

'Everything is real estate. You're a product of your geography.' [2]

From the ages of six to eighteen I got to school on foot or bike through a subway. The subway ran under a large roundabout connecting what was then one of the main roads from London to Wales and the Midlands, to the Oxford ring road.[3] It connected the four estates divided by these dual carriageways. It was entered by steep sloping ramps, was damp, long, and usually very dark as the lighting was smashed. The walls were graffiti covered. Among the names of children I knew, or thought I knew, were nastier slogans. The National Front were strong at the time and appended a swastika to their two joined-up initials. Swastikas are easy to spray-paint. Most importantly, however, to me, the subway was curved. You couldn't see who was inside when you were going down into it. Once inside you could not see who was round the corner. Only when coming up again to the surface could you see light. And it mattered who you bumped into, depending on where you were entering and exiting from, how old you were, how small you were, whether you were a boy or a girl, black or white.

---

[1] Editorial note: This is a section entitled in the original paper, "The importance of circumstance", taken from a longer piece entitled: "Anecdote is the singular of data".

[2] Thanks to Nick Phelps for this. Source: Lenny Bruce, comedian character, in Don DeLillo's *Underworld*, (1998, p 544). 'Anecdote is the singular of data' came from an e-mail forwarded to me by Charles Pattie.

[3] Directions have also been anonymised somewhat.

The roads divided a large council estate to the north, from the 1930s semidetached housing of my estate to the east, from the picturesque 'urban village' to the south, and the mixed development of the west. The subway connected these four corners and was where children in the 1970s and 1980s met between these different worlds. Adults often preferred to risk crossing the dual carriageways. Each morning and evening what appeared to be thousands of men cycled four abreast from the council estate round the roundabout to work in a large car factory half a mile south. Mums with prams would walk their smallest children to schools in each direction from each direction, over the surface, crossing the roads. Older children and teenagers (and a few pensioners, too slow for the roads) would go underground. There were half a dozen primary/junior schools and two middle schools. Which you went to said something about where your parents thought you were coming from and going to. Everyone I met in the subway ended up at the same secondary school at age thirteen.[4] But by then where they were going to next (how they would add to the sediment of society) was often largely decided.

No child I knew from the large northern estate left the city after school and only a couple from the estates east and west left Oxford. The boys were some of the last to be employed by the factory in large numbers; the girls could have children or take a secretarial course (but not both). Both sexes went into 'service' in the university, three miles into town waiting on academics and keeping tourists out of colleges, cleaning the buildings and rooms. Painting, decorating, building, and labouring appeared the only other main alternatives. The small number of children who stayed on at school after fifteen/sixteen mostly came from the southern and eastern estates. They took and largely failed A-levels, it seemed to me later, so that other people's children could be told how well they had done when they passed. The most common grades were Us and Fs followed by a few Es and Ds. Only a few of my contemporaries got a higher grade than this without help from a parent (in almost all cases a parent who was a teacher). But these children who failed A-levels or did poorly at age seventeen/eighteen largely avoided manual, servile, or casual work and went into town to work in estate agents, other shops, banks, and building societies. These children were at least immune from unemployment for a while, as the car factory began to close, the university started to save money by sacking its servants and cleaners, and the housing market collapse ended painting, decorating, and casual building for a while. However, the current rationalisation of the financial and retail sectors is beginning to bite. Other jobs have come, new

---

[4] Children going to private school did not use the subway – I think they must have travelled by car.

housing has been built, and a science park has been established over part of the factory site.

Why did I begin to learn that place mattered at age twelve? Because it was then that I began to notice who came into the subway from where and by which exit they left (in effect, where they lived and where they went to school). What happened to my neighbours six years later appeared, to me, to depend acutely on children's comings and goings in the subway earlier. You did not need to read for a geography degree to learn that children's options in life are largely controlled and constrained by the places in which they grow up, the local expectations, resources, schools, job opportunities, child-care expectations, and housing opportunities. If you saw how the political posters coloured each quarter red, yellow, or blue with sometimes near uniformity in a street – you did not need to know there was a neighbourhood effect to voting and campaigning – neater even than the social geography. If you worked in education, the police, in health, or most obviously as an estate agent – you knew that place mattered. If you got a kicking at age twelve because you came in from the wrong entrance of a subway, you learnt quickly that place matters. There were exceptions to the monotonous predictability of children's lives from their subway journeys – but the very fact that these were pointed out illustrated their rarity: "didn't he do well," "she let them down,'" and so on.

Why, then, if it is all so obvious, do we endlessly debate 'area effects'? Perhaps we were not all lucky enough to have such neatly laid out subways in our childhoods? More likely, I suspect, we have forgotten them, consciously or unconsciously. One thing academics have in common is that they tend to be good at passing exams. The temptation to put your success in exams down to personal ability or 'being clever' is high. For men like me it might, for instance, make up for not being so good at football or fighting as a boy. Increasingly concentrate your solution of 'higher achievers' as you move through academic careers, and the pages of a journal such as this become full of the self-supporting writing of the children who 'did well' in this one area of life. We give marks to children or young adults ourselves – supposedly to reward individual talent. We can begin to believe what we once knew was a myth – that achievement is due to individual effort, not largely a product of environment.

You are very likely to know the places where I grew up through having read at least one other person's very different description of them. Alongside cars from the factory and papers from the university, a third Oxford export has been its children's books. At least two of the most famous of children's authors lived long parts of their lives within a short distance of the roundabout which I later passed under twice a day for twelve years. To my mind all of these books are partly writing about how place mattered in one way or another. None of these writings was complimentary about the particular parts of the city their authors lived in and particularly about the area I walked through and came from. I will list a few below, but before you read the list, think what messages about the importance of space you were told. Did you read, or were read to you in childhood? Can you recognise them, from people writing about, or at least writing in, this one city and neighbourhood?

When Charles Lutwidge Dodgson (alias Lewis Carroll), of Christ Church, Oxford, wrote *Alice's Adventures in Wonderland* (in 1865) there was obviously no roundabout, there was only farmland and a quarry where the estates are now. The Oxford meadows and farmlands were portrayed in some ways as a safe place to play (although there were many other dangers to children in Alice's Victorian world). Less than half a century later the second most famous children's book to be inspired by a Thames boat trip was published. Kenneth Grahame, wrote *Wind in the Willows* in 1908. The map in the book is based closely on Oxford itself and shows the stoats and weasels living towards where the roundabout now lies. Forty years on John Ronald Reuel Tolkien wrote *The Lord of the Rings* in 1948 while living in Oxford. He lived in one of the four quarters described above from 1953 to 1968. In this children's tale the 'world' map clearly reflects European wartime geography, but the description of the 'shire' becoming corrupted reflects one view of the postwar estate building in this area (it appears in the third of the trilogy published in 1955). Finally, Clive Staples Lewis, another Oxford academic (although he commuted between weekends to Cambridge from 1955) wrote *The Lion, the Witch, and the Wardrobe* in 1950. He lived in a house made famous through the film *Shadowlands* at the edge of another of the four quarters, a few hundred yards from the roundabout. His garden of small lakes, many trees, and the odd lamppost is now a nature reserve, although hidden from children growing up in the area. The children he described ruling over lesser species did not live in the houses his home overlooked. The parochial description I have given you above is of a place you have probably already been to in your imagination, it just looks a little different on the ground.

So where are we now? For me, given my past and my places, I am unlikely ever to be impressed by an A-level grade on its own (or even a string of As) – to believe it is much more than a signpost to your street, school, and socialisation. I am unlikely to think that if you do not have a job it is because of your personal failing rather than the choices of the employers in your area, and what in turn affects them and your luck and status when you enter that market. I am unlikely to be convinced that people in Britain do not know these things themselves – that when they choose and are forced where to live they are not expressing their intimate knowledge that place matters. I am unlikely to read a book by someone who has lived in Oxford (many famous geographers included) and not to have read something into where precisely they lived in that city. I made my mind up a long time ago about geography. However, proving that place matters to the satisfaction of others is much more difficult.

Finally, you might like to know what has happened to the subway. Around the time that the new M40 motorway was finished – through an area of outstanding natural beauty (but thankfully taking the London traffic to Birmingham away from many of the children of east Oxford) – the roundabout was reengineered. The subway was dug up and a new one built in which from every entrance you can see through to an exit. A lot of the graffiti has now gone. Thankfully the National Front have too; although there are few new jobs in the car factory for the white men to 'defend' (but it is producing the new Mini car). To keep some pretence of olden days going, the university still hires a few younger, cheaper servants from the estates in preference to their more expensive parents (lower minimum wage regulations make under twenty-fives more attractive servants). Traffic lights and pedestrian crossings have been placed over the dual carriageways which so neatly divided the estates before. Some council houses have been bought, including even some of wartime pre-fabs (that I suspect Tolkien and C S Lewis despised). Despite many protests, a small council estate has been built in another of the quarters (very near to C S Lewis's old house). Many children are now taken to school by car. Almost no men cycle to work by the road any more. And so – all in all – the lines of demarcation are more blurred and the connection between where you are and where you are going is now less clear to me at least. But perhaps not to a twelve-year-old child growing up there today? On one of the walls of the subway in May 2001 some child has written (geographically correctly):

← good puppies this way            lost puppies this way →

Perhaps I grew up in a strange place – but if that is true, place obviously matters in terms of what might inspire (or condition) you. Circumstances matter . . . there is a human as well as quantitative answer to the extent to which geography matters.

### Acknowledgements

Thanks to Nick Phelps and Mary Shaw for comments on a draft of this, also to the authors of the responses for writing them so quickly, to Andrew McCulloch for the original paper, for agreeing to this debate, and for his response, and to Ron Johnston for refereeing the articles submitted for the special section this paper introduced.

## References

Caroll, L. (1865) *Alice's adventures in wonderland*, London: Macmillan.

DeLillo, D. (1998) *Underworld*, London: Picador.

Grahame, K. (1908) *Wind in the willows*, London: Methuen.

Lewis, C.S. (1950) *The lion, the witch, and the wardrobe*, London: Geoffrey Bles.

McCulloch, A. (2001) 'Ward-level deprivation and individual social and economic outcomes in the British Household Panel Study', *Environment and Planning A*, no 33, pp 667–84.

Plummer, P. and Taylor, M. (2001) 'Theories of local economic growth (part 2): model specification and empirical validation', *Environment and Planning A*, no 33, pp 385–98.

Putnam, R.D. (2001) *Bowling alone: The collapse and revival of American community*, New York: Simon and Schuster.

Tolkien, J.R.R. (1948) *The lord of the rings*, London: George Allen and Unwin.

Tolkein, J.R.R. (1955) *Return of the king*, London: George Allen and Unwin.

# SECTION IX
## Advocacy and action

The final section in this volume is the largest and concerns what can be argued for and what can be done, but also why it is often so hard to achieve very much at all. The section begins with a paper published in the *New Internationalist* magazine which suggests that, in very unequal affluent countries, people's individual and collective abilities to argue cogently for change have been greatly curtailed. We are made a little more stupid and selfish the longer we live in a stupid and selfish society.

Next, an example is given from a short piece reproduced from the journal *Criminal Justice Matters* concerning how, in criminology, people stop thinking straight when they start thinking of 'us' and 'them'. This is followed by an extract from the newsletter of the Regional Studies Association, *Regions*, giving an example of when government ministers commissioned research and then ignored the results because they did not fit their way of thinking. The result, as the fourth article of this section, written initially for *Public Servant Magazine*, argues, is that inequalities rose in many areas under a New Labour administration supposedly committed to reduce them.

The worst, and growing, inequalities are inequalities in health, and so the fifth short article for this section gives an example of advocacy in that area through the simple listing of what kills most people at each age in Britain. The result was used in evidence by the House of Commons Select Committee on Transport in their 2010 report on the scandal of road deaths in Britain (see page 366). This is followed by a piece from *The Yorkshire Post* newspaper which illustrates that, in general, as social inequalities rise, we tend to confuse becoming more unequal with becoming more free. Chapter 49, an article from *Poverty* (the journal of the Child Poverty Action Group) then lists how children did not necessarily benefit from a government committed to the eradication of child poverty. Commitment is necessary but not sufficient.

Next a very different chapter is included from an article on new ways of mapping the world written with three colleagues for *ArcUser*, a magazine that is almost exclusively read by people who use expensive mapping software. Almost no one who reads *Poverty* will read *ArcUser* and vice versa, but the new ways of visualisation are about mapping using projections that are more equitable.

To my mind, advocacy is about very different little bits of action in very many very different places. What works in one place does not often work in other places, but if you have a rough idea of where you are trying to get to, and you try most of the time to make steps towards that, you won't go too far wrong. The section ends with a chapter taken from a very short article first printed in *The Big Issue* (a magazine mostly sold by homeless people, often to students) on imagining if you could be king, just for one day, what roles, as a king, queen or emperor, you would play, should you get the chance.

# 44

# Mean machine: how structural inequality makes social inequality seem natural[1]

*New Internationalist* (2010) June

Don't be so hard on rich people who appear stupid. All of us are made less able, less imaginative and less mentally effective in more unequal, affluent societies. And it is only in very unequal affluent societies that the rich can be very rich. George Bush attended both Yale and Harvard Universities. Former Prime Minister Tony Blair, British Tory leader David Cameron and a small army of former prime ministers (and even more wanna-be-prime-ministers) studied in just a few elite Oxford colleges.

All these men were made what they became largely by their circumstances, by growing up with structural inequalities so great that they could not easily understand the lives, motivations and unlimited potential of others because their own lives were so different, literally cloistered from late teenage years onwards.

George Irvin in his 2008 book, *Super rich: The rise of inequality in Britain and the United States*, suggests: 'Perhaps the most serious problem created by growing inequality is that it facilitates the reproduction of the politics and ideology of inequality.' Jane Kelsey in her 1997 study: *The New Zealand experiment* showed how an entire nation could be made to think more callously through the introduction of greater inequality.

The level, content and clarity of public debate in more unequal, affluent nations falls far below that which most citizens of OECD countries enjoy. The outpouring of anger in the US over President Obama's watered down 'socialised medicine' proposals are testament to that. Almost anyone who lives outside of the US understands this and yet in that country 'Tea Party

---

[1] First published in Issue 433 of *New Internationalist*, pages 20-21.

politics' passes for rational debate. Ask Canadians about why they would not live in the United States, but make sure you have plenty of time to listen.

In more unequal European countries, such as Britain and Portugal, claims are made about people that would simply not be countenanced elsewhere in Europe. Elsewhere most people are far more trusting of their neighbours and do not look down on others so often as feckless and worthless. Nor do they consider that a few are worth their multi-million euro/dollar/pound salaries because they are somehow wonderfully gifted and need to be encouraged to get out of bed by such vast sums – because no-one else could substitute.

Living in a country where huge income and wealth inequalities are accepted as normal dulls everyone's capacities, from top to bottom. The well-known social critic, Noam Chomsky, was once asked how he responded at talks given to American audiences when he was asked, 'What should I do?' He replied he was only asked this by American audiences: 'I'm never asked this in the Third World… they don't ask you, "What should I do?" They tell you what they're doing… enormous privilege and freedom carries with it a sense of impotence, which is a strange but striking phenomenon…'

Evidence is slowly amassing that the impotence of US citizens is not a result of their apparent privileges or freedoms, but of the huge inequalities they live with. Equally affluent but far more equitable Norway, with a population at least 66 times smaller than the United States, shows what a people can do when not so encumbered by inequality. Norwegians each generate 5.55 times more international assistance than US citizens and they spend it far more effectively.

In Japan, through a translator, I can have conversations with young people from the poorest fifth of society about income distribution and inequality that would simply not be possible in England. In England I would have to try not to use the word 'distribution' and I would have to cope in my conversation with the near certainty that the people I was talking to would have no accurate idea what average wages were or what the best-off fifth of households received in income a year, what their wealth was, or even what a 'fifth' was – or even with what a fraction means as a concept.

Sadly it is because the poorest young people in unequal rich countries are so badly schooled – that the richest don't even realize that their education was not great. They assume that they, the richest fifth, have received a 'good' education and often say they are 'privileged'. The richest fifth in Britain and the US also have almost no idea of how unequal income and wealth distributions have become, but they are often taught to bluff an understanding of the word 'distribution', or the mathematics of fractions.

So how does a nation made stupid by rising inequality get out of its hole? People have to think their way out. They did this before when inequalities fell in the United States and United Kingdom, consistently from 1918 to 1978. They can do this again with the help of lessons from abroad. And they can do it by waking up one day and thinking: "I'm never going to be rich, but there is no need for me to be ignorant. I can start to teach myself about what's going on."

**Table 1:** Highest rates of income inequality – among the world's richest countries with a population of 1 million or more

| Ratio of incomes/consumption of the best-off 10% as compared to the worst-off 10% | | |
|---|---|---|
| 17.7 | Singapore | 🚶🚶🚶🚶🚶🚶🚶🚶🚶🚶🚶🚶🚶🚶🚶🚶🚶🚶 |
| 15.9 | United States | 🚶🚶🚶🚶🚶🚶🚶🚶🚶🚶🚶🚶🚶🚶🚶🚶 |
| 15.0 | Portugal | 🚶🚶🚶🚶🚶🚶🚶🚶🚶🚶🚶🚶🚶🚶🚶 |
| 13.8 | United Kingdom | 🚶🚶🚶🚶🚶🚶🚶🚶🚶🚶🚶🚶🚶🚶 |
| 13.4 | Israel | 🚶🚶🚶🚶🚶🚶🚶🚶🚶🚶🚶🚶🚶 |
| 12.5 | Australia | 🚶🚶🚶🚶🚶🚶🚶🚶🚶🚶🚶🚶 |
| 12.5 | New Zealand | 🚶🚶🚶🚶🚶🚶🚶🚶🚶🚶🚶🚶 |
| 11.6 | Italy | 🚶🚶🚶🚶🚶🚶🚶🚶🚶🚶🚶🚶 |
| 10.3 | Spain | 🚶🚶🚶🚶🚶🚶🚶🚶🚶🚶 |
| 10.2 | Greece | 🚶🚶🚶🚶🚶🚶🚶🚶🚶🚶 |
| 9.4 | Canada | 🚶🚶🚶🚶🚶🚶🚶🚶🚶 |
| 9.4 | Ireland | 🚶🚶🚶🚶🚶🚶🚶🚶🚶 |
| 9.2 | Netherlands | 🚶🚶🚶🚶🚶🚶🚶🚶🚶 |
| 9.1 | France | 🚶🚶🚶🚶🚶🚶🚶🚶🚶 |
| 9.0 | Switzerland | 🚶🚶🚶🚶🚶🚶🚶🚶🚶 |
| 8.2 | Belgium | 🚶🚶🚶🚶🚶🚶🚶🚶 |
| 8.1 | Denmark | 🚶🚶🚶🚶🚶🚶🚶🚶 |
| 7.8 | S Korea | 🚶🚶🚶🚶🚶🚶🚶🚶 |
| 7.3 | Slovenia | 🚶🚶🚶🚶🚶🚶🚶 |
| 6.9 | Austria | 🚶🚶🚶🚶🚶🚶🚶 |
| 6.9 | Germany | 🚶🚶🚶🚶🚶🚶🚶 |
| 6.2 | Sweden | 🚶🚶🚶🚶🚶🚶 |
| 6.1 | Norway | 🚶🚶🚶🚶🚶🚶 |
| 5.6 | Finland | 🚶🚶🚶🚶🚶🚶 |
| 4.5 | Japan | 🚶🚶🚶🚶 |

Note: of all the 25 richest countries in the world (excluding very small states), Singapore, the United States, Portugal, the United Kingdom and Israel are the top five most unequal when the annual income of the best-off tenth of the population is compared with the poorest tenth. For example, the top 10% in the US makes 15.9 times more than the bottom 10%.

Source: See footnote 37, p 323 of Dorling, D., 2010, *Injustice: why social inequalities persist*, Bristol: The Policy Press. [Editorial Note: These figures are derived from tables that appeared in the United Nations Development Programme World Human Development Report of 2009. That table was not repeated in the 2010 report so these remain the most up-to-date figures at the time of reprinting this short article as a book chapter, September 2011].

# 45

# Policing the borders of crime: who decides research?

*Criminal Justice Matters* (2005/06) no 62, pp 28–9

## The relationship between poverty and mortality

Who decides which actions and events constitute a crime and which underlying aspects of crime are worthy of research funding and investigation? The short answer to the funding part of that question is that those who hold the research purse strings decide – but that is a far from satisfactory answer, as those string holders in turn react to academic debate, public opinion and political imperative. Academic debate takes place as much in newsletters and newspapers as in journals. That debate influences and is influenced by more general opinion. It drives and is driven by political imperatives. Over time, often very short spans of time, the words, meanings and truth within the discussion change.

Seventy-five years ago the Institute for the Scientific Study and Treatment of Delinquency was founded in London. At that time criminology was not a subject of academic enquiry in British universities but within those three-score and fifteen years (roughly the average length of a current British lifetime), our collective understanding of delinquency, criminology and crime itself has transformed beyond recognition. The Institute changed its name to the Centre for Crime and Justice Studies in 1993 and has published this magazine ever since then. This is of relevance because recently delinquency has become of interest again. Not the delinquency of the 1920s and 30s working class in economic recession, but systemic delinquency – a tendency to be negligent and uncaring – something that appears to underlie much current social harm.

Last year Paddy Hillyard and his colleagues Christina Pantazis, Steve Tombs and David Gordon argued that criminology needs to change to consider a wider definition of social harm and currently remains "infected with individually-based analysis, explanation and 'remedy' ... despite decades of resistance to these notions from within the discipline of criminology itself."

They illustrated the futility of much current conceptualising and counting of crime with an international example: "By contrast, given that one of the most prevalent 'crimes' in the UK is 'failure to pay the TV licence' while the most common crime in Turkey is 'being rude to a public official', there is not even a theoretical prospect of being able to make meaningful international comparisons of the extent of crime, except in relation to a relatively small sub-set of 'crimes'" (Hillyard et al, 2005).

However, in their conclusion Hillyard et al were pessimistic as to the future of the academic study of crime. "Holding out hope that this situation might change through ever greater pressure from within criminology is at best optimistic, at worst illusory." (*ibid*, p 66). However, from where I work – outside of criminology – the approach that Hillyard and his colleagues argue for makes sense and it can take social research in a very interesting, possibly useful and certainly wide variety of directions. Their definition of harm extends from the physical (itself ranging from violence to starvation) to financial harm, economic, emotional, psychological to sexual and cultural harms (*ibid*, p 14) – and they use the general term 'social harm' to encompass all objects in the study of harm.

## Murder

In several publications I argued that a social harm approach could be taken to study what is often seen as a most individual crime: murder (Dorling 2005, 2006; Shaw et al, 2005). Over the course of the last twenty five years, the chances of being murdered have fallen for most groups of people in Britain. However, the chances of young men being murder victims have risen so much that the overall murder rate for all people doubled. Young men in the most affluent parts of the country saw their chances fall too, so this increase is mostly due to rapid increases in fatal violence in the poorest neighbourhoods of the country. Furthermore, it is the cohort born after 1965 amongst whom the rise is most evident with – crucially – their chances of being a victim not falling so far as they age.[1] There is even tenuous evidence that the first generation of their male children are experiencing even worse chances in the worst-off areas of the country.

---

[1] Editorial note: See the final Table in Chapter 1 of this book, on page 23.

Viewed from the location of the victims, from where the harm impacts, the patterns of murder follow geographical and demographic trends in the recent economic and social history of Britain, characterised by a politics that had a tendency to be negligent and uncaring – I would argue a delinquent politics – which coincided with the circumstances that allowed violent harm to rise in Britain and for that rise to be concentrated only on particular groups of people while almost all others saw their circumstances improve. This evidence may appear circumstantial but such patterns are becoming ever clearer as shown in recent research in health and are well summarised by the following statement:

"Greater inequality almost certainly affects how important status is and how much people feel their social standing is taken as an indication of their 'worth'. Bigger material differences lead to bigger social distances up and down the hierarchy. In more unequal societies it is as if some people count for everything and others for nothing, making us all more concerned with how we are seen. More hierarchical societies are marked by greater social divisions and more downward discrimination and prejudice against those lower on the social ladder. The divisiveness of widening income differences during the last two or three decades explains why social mobility has actually decreased in Britain and why there is less social mobility in Britain than in many other rich societies. Among the eight countries for which there are broadly comparable measures of social mobility (Blanden et al, 2005), there is a close (and statistically significant) correlation showing that social mobility tends to be lower where income differences are greater. In this comparison, the most unequal countries with the lowest social mobility were the USA (the 'land of opportunity') followed closely by Britain. At the opposite end, with the lowest income differences and highest social mobility, were countries like Norway and Sweden. The same tendency for income inequality to lead to wider and more rigid social divisions can also be seen geographically: as inequality increases so too does the segregation of the population into rich and poor neighbourhoods. The power and divisiveness of greater income inequality suggests that it is unrealistic to pursue greater equality of opportunity without at the same time moving towards greater equality of outcome. Indeed, greater equality of outcome is likely to be the best way of achieving greater equality of opportunity." (Wilkinson, 2005).

## Social harm

Where would a research agenda that concentrated on the crime of social harm take us? Suppose that we concentrate to begin with only on those crimes that kill. Only a tiny proportion of deaths that result from social harm are legally labelled as murder. For every murder in Britain, a further ten people are killed by themselves – often, but not always, labelled suicide. Suicides are just as socially patterned as is murder, although correlates of loneliness are a key aspect of the related neglect (Dorling and Gunnell, 2003). Suicide rates too have risen most for young men, as have deaths from accidents when generally defined. However, a slow and early non-violent death from poverty is no less painful and no less harmful than murder, suicide and accident. The legacy of mass early unemployment, mass tobacco poisoning and mass neglect for over a generation are amongst the key explanations for why life expectancies stubbornly stagnate in the poorest parts of the UK, whilst they soar ahead in the richest places. Life expectancy for men in Glasgow by 2002–2004 remained below 70 years while it rose in the Royal Borough of Kensington and Chelsea by a year for both men and women in the most recent twelve months, to now stand at 80.8 and 85.8 years respectively.

In the past seventy-five years millions of short lives were begun and ended in this country. Almost none of those deaths were the result of a crime as conventionally understood, but many, if not most, were preventable and were largely the product of social harm. The correlation between poverty and mortality rates by area is amongst the highest found between any pair of social indicators in the UK. But social harm, the product of a neglectful and uncaring society, does much more than kill people young. The abuse means that people's dignity, their rights to opportunity, and their rights to respect are continuously damaged while poverty remains endemic and inequality is sustained.

The effects of social harm are evident (and again a hierarchy can be established) from relatively small numbers of obvious 'crimes' to the more widespread and general damage done to others from our collective choices and actions. The mass killing of people (most emotively civilians and especially children) by bombing overseas is one of the most visually obvious forms of social harm committed by people in London on people abroad. Whether the attorney general thought this 'illegal' is immaterial from a social harm perspective.

What, though, of the deaths spread through our commerce and industry? Two-thirds of men in China now smoke – a future Glasgow on an epic scale. How is the making of profit in London's square mile from the spread of tobacco worldwide legal? Spread the net more widely and you see a pharmaceutical industry that prices drugs beyond the reach of the world's poor, profits massively from most of the rest and concentrates subsequent wealth amongst the few (again disproportionately through London!). It is not just bad drugs that do harm. I could go on – but it is perhaps the top of the international ice-berg of harm and the potential causes of future harm that should concern us most, first.

Type "QinetiQ nanotechnology" into Google… It is not yet a crime to develop microscopic devices designed to potentially kill millions – why not?

Who decides what is researched, who polices the borders of crime? Ultimately you do.

### References

Dorling, D. (2005) 'Prime suspect: murder in Britain', in P. Hillyard et al *Why harm matters more than crime*, London: Crime and Society Foundation [Chapter 1 of this volume].

Dorling, D. (2006) *Inequality kills*, *Red Pepper Magazine*, January 2006. [Chapter 39 of this volume].

Dorling, D. and Gunnell, D. (2003) 'Suicide: the spatial and social components of despair in Britain 1980–2000', *Transactions of the Institute of British Geographers*, vol 28, no 4, pp 442–60, www.sasi.group.shef.ac.uk/publications/2003/dorling_and_gunnell_suicide.pdf

Dorling, D., Mitchell, R., Orford, S., Shaw, M. and Davey-Smith, G. (2005) 'Inequalities and Christmas yet to come', *BMJ*, 331(7529) p 1409.

Hillyard, P. et al (2005) *Social harm and its limits, in criminal obsessions: Why harm matters more than crime*, London: Crime and Society Foundation, www.crimeandsociety.org.uk

Shaw, M., Tunstall, H. and Dorling, D. (2005) 'Increasing inequalities in risk of murder in Britain: trends in the demographic and spatial distribution of murder, 1981–2000', *Health and Place*, no 11, 45–54, www.sasi.group.shef.ac.uk/publications/2005/shaw_tunstall_dorling_murder.pdf

Wilkinson, R. (2005) 'Inequality: what it does and how to reduce it', p 12 of *UK health watch 2005: The experience of health in an unequal society*, the full report is available at www.pohg.org.uk/support/downloads/ukhealthwatch-2005.pdf

# 46

# Learning the hard way

*Regions* (2007) no 266, pp 2–4

*Policy-makers should learn from all their commissioned studies,*
*not just cherry pick the convenient parts of the convenient ones*

Government in Britain is still setting a bad example to the rest of the world
in terms of the selectivity of its reporting and its summarising of its own
commissioned research. This particularly affects the debate over regional
inequalities and trends in them.

Writing in April 2007, I quote below the words of three government
ministers. Currently their roles are: Secretary of State for the Environment
(David Miliband); Minister of State for Housing and Planning (Yvette
Cooper); and the Minister for Work (Jim Murphy). I pick on these three
because they are not easy targets; indeed, they are who we should be looking
to, to be making a difference to our cities and regions in the future.

My worry is that ministers have a general concern, which is to paint a rosy
story, coupled with a spin they themselves receive from their key advisors,
that results in a general air of unreality and unsustainable comment being
made continuously. How are these people with great personal integrity
being failed by the government policy machinery?

At the very top of government, leaders are cocooned from the world to
such an extent that they find it very hard to understand why they may be
unpopular. But why, lower down in the government apparatus are junior
ministers also selectively quoting our research and statistics in an easily
misunderstood way? Here is the first of my three examples:

"*The State of the Cities* report was published just two or three weeks
ago and it looked at the fifty-six primary urban areas of England, not
just the eight biggest cities outside London, but the next forty-eight
towns and cities, and it came to a stunning conclusion.

Twenty years ago, if we'd been having a conference about cities people would have talked about decline: about declining population; declining economies; declining public services. *The State of the Cities* report – the most comprehensive analysis of urban britain for forty or fifty years – said that not only were our towns and cities getting better, not only were they getting better economically and socially faster than the national average, but that we had the best opportunity for a hundred years to make our towns and cities our leading towns and cities, not just good by British standards, but excellent in European terms."
David Miliband[1]

What the data in the report showed was that some cities were becoming better-off and some not so better-off – and a gap was growing between them. They were certainly not all getting "better economically and socially" than the national average, as the quote above implies. Nor were they amounting to be excellent in European terms. I know because I worked with a group of researchers to pull together some of the data for the report.[2]

Here's another example of a more local issue coming from a statement made by another minister almost a year later. How do you square this quote from their press release with reality or ever with the research report?

"The transformation of many of our coalfield areas has been dramatic. When the pits were closed many coalfield communities saw soaring unemployment and their communities were devastated. Now, thanks to coalfield regeneration, the jobs are coming back.

Many former miners have had training to get new jobs and whole communities are being revived. On some of the pit sites we are even seeing more jobs above ground then there were below when the pits were open. …"
Yvette Cooper[3]

Try to square that with this:

"The growth in replacement jobs in the coalfields that was evident before 1998 continued over the next five years but at a slower pace than in non-coalfield areas. Moreover,

---

[1] Speaking on 3rd of April 2006 as then Minister of Communities and Local Government, Presentation for "The Work Foundation": www.theworkfoundation.com/Assets/pdfs/Ideopolis_DavidMilibandspeech.pdf
[2] For more details and a summary table showing how each of the 56 cities actually fared see: http:/sasi.group.shef.ac.uk/publications/2006/dorling_inequalityinBritain1997_corrected.pdf or Chapters 2 or 30 of this book, pages 33 and 228.
[3] From press release DCLG 22/3/2007 "Coalfields discover they have a second life", quote: Housing Minister, Yvette Cooper, 22 March, 2007: www.communities.gov.uk/index.asp?id=1002882&PressNoticeID=2382

despite some relative improvements, the deprivation, health, educational qualifications and enterprise 'deficits' in the coalfields persisted as a long-term legacy from the loss of mining employment (see paragraphs 31–33). These deficits hampered and will continue to hamper the capacity of residents to benefit from any increased job opportunities that come their way.
*Source*: Para 24 of "Regenerating the English Coalfields"[4]

Finally (and perhaps a salutatory warning of what can happen if you are too honest over your hopes and fears as a minister) during his lunch break on Friday March 9th the Minister for Work, Jim Murphy, posted a message to his 'blog'. He may have been in a hurry to get to his next meeting, but at least it was not all carefully crafted spin. This is what he said:

"*Into the valleys*: I was visiting the Welsh valleys today to discuss how we can get more people into work. My colleagues, John Hutton, Anne McGuire, James Plaskitt and Lord McKenzie of Luton have also covered a fair few miles between them from Cardiff and Swansea to North Wales and Usk. Wales is a classic example of the success we've had in getting more people into work – there are over 130,000 more people in work and whilst cities like Cardiff have been transformed, there are still parts of the country where a life on benefits is still the norm.

This leads us to a number of questions: Why do less people find work in the valleys than in the rest of Wales? Why are you more likely to get a job in the Cynon Valley, for example, than in Merthyr Tydfil? How can we help 20 thousand more people off Incapacity Benefit and into work? Chatting to local MPs, employers and other people on the ground has given me a much better appreciation of the issues.

So what's the answer? This is probably going to sound like a typical politician's response but I believe there isn't one, single answer. There are many. What's important is making sure local areas combine the support of different organisations, private and voluntary, to best effect. We'll be on the right path when a lone parent in the valleys doesn't have to worry about who's looking after the kids or if they have the

---

[4] Extract taken from executive summary of the report the minister was referring to "Regenerating the English Coalfields" – interim evaluation of the coalfield regeneration programmes, published by DCLG: www.communities.gov.uk/pub/894/InterimEvaluationofthecoalfieldsregenerationprogrammes_id1508894.pdf

right skills for a job because they know all the back-up they need has already been sorted out in the first place.
This entry was posted on Friday, 9 March 2007 at 1:59 PM by Jim Murphy."[5]

So what thanks did Jim get for admitting that there are still parts of the country where life on benefits are the norm. That there is no easy answer. And that there are still great inequalities?

The comments to his blog are vetted by civil servants at the Department of Work and Pensions; despite that, they let this comment through:

"Robert wrote: And then you woke up at home with your family and said love I had a nice dream I made Wales a nice place to live with lots of jobs and the sick and disabled rose up and walked. Posted on 13-Mar-07 at 8:46 am."

Damned if they dream, damned if they spin, damned if they are honest, damned when they lie. It is hardly surprising that ministers and many others at the top of numerous policy ladders begin to be unsure of the plot.

The actual story of economic inequalities is revealed in statistics which receive very little coverage in government reports, or in ministerial pronouncements. Buried in the press release (15 December 2006) for the latest estimates of regional Gross Value Added[6] you find that:

"Shares of GVA: London (17.0 per cent) and the South East (15.6 per cent) had the largest share of total UK GVA in 2005. London's and the South East's share of UK GVA has increased since 1995 when it accounted for 15.2 per cent and 14.9 per cent respectively. Northern Ireland (2.3 per cent) and the North East (3.4 per cent) had the smallest share of UK GVA in 2005."[7]

A week after this statement was made another part of government, the Department of Health, released "Tackling health inequalities: 2003-05" its data update for the national 2010 PSA target on health (21 December 2006). That report showed geographically inequalities in mortality between regions continue to widened.

And it is now universally acknowledged that geographical trends in health follow those in wealth. True, there are great problems with government's

---

[5] Source: Jim Murphy's blog, www.dwp.gov.uk/welfarereform/blog/index.php/page/2/
[6] Editorial note: A measure of how much an area contributes to increasing GDP and GNP.
[7] Available on-line at www.statistics.gov.uk/pdfdir/gva1206.pdf

regional accounts, but that is not reason to ignore them. Although for an entertaining summary, read the words of the then national statistician Len Cook, in 2002, on his receipt of personal abuse and the complete mess that regional statistics are in, in general.[8]

Our cities are becoming more unequal both within and between them. Outside our cities our coalfields are not catching up with the average, let alone the affluent areas which they moved even further away from so rapidly all those years ago in 1984/85. Our regions are slowly pulling apart; and our countries are less and less united in common experience.

So here is my advice for these ministers. Before you try to find the answer, or suggest that there are a plethora of answers, you need a better picture of what the question is. The central question for you all is why we are still becoming more unequal: individually, by community, by city and by region?

Read the reports not just the press releases, and not just the two page summaries that your officials hand you as your limousine speeds off for that next visit to "the regions"!

---

[8] Available online at www.publications.parliament.uk/pa/cm200102/cmselect/cmtreasy/1289/2103009.htm

# 47

# When the social divide deepens

*Public Servant Magazine* (2008) May, p 3

It has been a hard lesson to learn that a succession of Labour victories in economic good times is no guarantee of greater social equality.

Who would have thought 10 years ago that the greatest improvements in living standards would have been realised in the areas that voted for a Conservative MP in 1997? That the largest increases in life expectancy have been in the areas which returned the shadow cabinet, while life expectancies have increased most slowly in cabinet ministers' constituencies? All since that landslide election for a progressive party that promised greater equality.

Who would have thought that the chances of children getting to participate in higher education would have increased most under Labour for those whose parents voted Conservative? Areas most loyal to Labour have felt the brunt of social polarisation. The rich are harmed too but, for them, the effects are less obvious. They live shorter lives compared with the affluent in other (more equal) OECD nations; they live in fear of others so have less freedom to choose where to live. They increasingly feel they need to opt out of state education and health provision and they don't feel rich.

Who would have thought 10 years ago that the very richest of the world would flock to live in London; and that wider London and its financial heart should attract the greatest sustained net inflow of migrants since the 1840s famine in Ireland? Do you remember the poster that asked for the last person to leave Britain to turn out the light, should Labour win? That was a very different Labour Party from the one that has presided over such a huge transfer of wealth to the already rich.

"Isn't it ironic" is an old refrain in politics, of the kind: Wasn't it funny that Margaret Thatcher created more comprehensives compared to any other Education Secretary despite her believing in them the least? This might be the only thing she did that I personally benefited from. So it's not that ironic. Neither is it ironic that one of the first governments to attempt to transfer wealth to the poor directly – through child trust funds – will see those attempts wiped into insignificance by the acceleration of market trends in the opposite direction.[1]

And what are they thinking of all this inside the Labour movement? A large part of the point of not being that radical was to be electable. The failure over inequality at home has been overshadowed (in the failure stakes) by that huge misery of a war abroad.

What should the party have done and what should it do now if it really wants to benefit the poor like previous Labour and Liberal administrations, all of which presided over narrowing social gaps? It is perhaps time to say that we now have the evidence that the "first past the post" Westminster voting system has not made the country a better place. Proportional representation would make so many more people's votes matter, especially those who Labour can currently take for granted in safe seats.

Short term, there could be another cabinet reshuffle. As for another leader, it's hardly an ideal time. There is no Barack Obama in the waiting room of British politics about to offer us at least a dream of a different world. It has been a hard lesson to learn that a succession of Labour victories in economic good times is no guarantee of greater social equality, not in the way that just one Labour victory in the worst of times was in the past. The fastest route to greater equality is not a comfortable one. It is a banking crisis, slow financial collapse and prolonged recession, which tends to bring those at the top of the social scale slightly closer to those at the bottom.[2] Funnily enough it happened once before, some 80 years ago when a bunch of old Etonians was in power.

---

[1] Editorial note: And then just to ensure no effect, by the abolition of future payments to those funds by the incoming 2010 Coalition.
[2] Editorial note: This is usually the fastest route. Three and a half years after this commentary was written it was looking as if history would not be repeating itself in quite the same way.

# 48

# Ending the scandal of complacency[1]

Supplementary memorandum from Professor Danny Dorling, The University of Sheffield (RS 70)

In my testimony I offered to provide further information on the most common cause of death of people in Britain in case of inaccuracy in my recall. With several colleagues in work in preparation for a new atlas of mortality by cause in Britain we have been studying the major causes of death across this island over the period 1981 to 2004 (inclusive). About one hundred causes of death are being mapped, including groupings of causes that are hard to classify as one group. The source data for our analysis has been provided by the General Register Office for Scotland and from the Office for National Statistics (for those deaths occurring in England and Wales). The data we are analysing does not include Northern Ireland. We analyse by 20 age groups and find:

---

[1] This Supplementary memorandum from Professor Danny Dorling, pages Ev 323– 324, 2008, *House of Commons Transport Committee: Ending the scandal of complacency: Road safety beyond 2010.*

## Most common cause of death of people dying in Britain by age 1981 to 2004

| Age | Most death due to: |
|---|---|
| 0 | Other conditions in the perinatal period |
| 1–4 | Congenital malformations of heart |
| 5–9 | Pedestrian and motor vehicle accidents |
| 10–14 | Pedestrian and motor vehicle accidents |
| 15–19 | Other motor vehicle accidents |
| 20–24 | Other motor vehicle accidents |
| 25–29 | Other motor vehicle accidents |
| 30–34 | Other motor vehicle accidents |
| 35–39 | Heart attack and chronic heart disease |
| 40–44 | Heart attack and chronic heart disease |
| 45–49 | Heart attack and chronic heart disease |
| 50–54 | Heart attack and chronic heart disease |
| 55–59 | Heart attack and chronic heart disease |
| 60–64 | Heart attack and chronic heart disease |
| 65–69 | Heart attack and chronic heart disease |
| 70–74 | Heart attack and chronic heart disease |
| 75–79 | Heart attack and chronic heart disease |
| 80–84 | Heart attack and chronic heart disease |
| 85–89 | Heart attack and chronic heart disease |
| 90+ | Heart attack and chronic heart disease |

*Note:* Motor vehicles (mostly cars) are the major killer between ages 5 and 34 in this country. This is of child pedestrians being killed in a collision with a motor vehicle between ages 5 and 14, and then through involvement in other motor vehicle accidents, most often as drivers and passengers between the ages of 15 and 34. It is possible that motor vehicles are a major factor before age 5 given that most deaths due to congenital malformations occur in the earlier years for those aged 1–4.

*Source:* Analysis by the author and colleagues of mortality records as work in preparation for a national atlas of mortality according to roughly one hundred key causes to be published by the Policy Press in autumn 2008. (see Figure 1)

Definitions: "Other conditions in the perinatal period"—over half of deaths in this category are due to trauma around the time of birth or shortly after, such as asphyxia and other respiratory distress. The deaths come under cause-codings: ICD-9 codes: 760-779; ICD-10 codes: G70.2, P00-P05, P07, P10-P11, P15, P20-P28, P29.0-P29.1, P29.8, P35-P37, P39, P50, P52, P54, P59-P61, P70, P74, P76-P78, P83, P90-P92, P94, P96, Q86.0.

"Congenital Malformations of the heart" include deaths due to medical condition present at birth ICD-9 codes: 745-747; ICD-10 codes: P29.3, Q20-Q28.

"Pedestrian and motor vehicle accidents" includes deaths to pedestrians due to collision with a vehicle of some kind ICD-9 codes: E812.7, E813.7, E814.7, E815.7, E816.7, E817.7, E818.7, E819.7, E821.7, E822.7, E823.7, E824.7, E825.7, E826.0; ICD-10 codes: V01-V04, V06, V09.0-V09.3.

"Other motor vehicle accident death are those deaths where the passenger or driver of the vehicle dies. Pedestrian deaths and the deaths of cyclists are not included here: ICD9: 810-812, 815-825 (excluding -.7's).

Heart attack and chronic heart disease: ICD9: 410-414 and 429.

**Figure 1:** All deaths in Britain during 2006 and 2007 to people aged 11 to 24 by cause of death

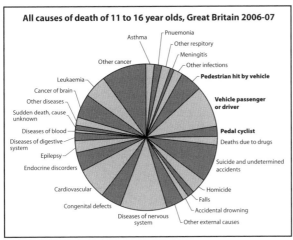

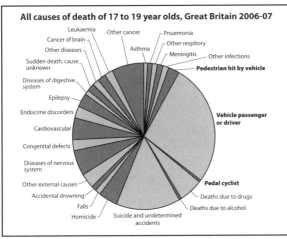

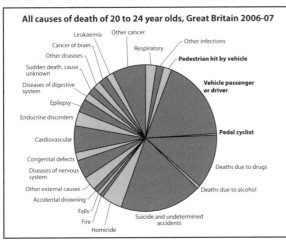

*Source:* Dorling, D. and Thomas, B. (2011) *Bankrupt Britain: An atlas of social change*, Bristol: The Policy Press – Chapter on Environmental Bankruptcy, data in turn supplied by ONS and GRO(S).

367

# 49

## Our grandchildren will wonder why we were addicted to social inequality[1]

*Yorkshire Post* (2010) 26 April

What would be your list of the most damaging social evils in Britain today and how would you explain their survival?

Many writers and commentators have tried to answer this question over the decades since an answer was first offered by William Beveridge in 1942. In recent years, the general public has also been asked what they think, many more times than they have ever been asked before. The result is that you end up with many long lists of evils.

I thought these lists might be a good place to start when writing a book I have called *Injustice: Why social inequality persists*, which attempts to explain why inequalities are allowed to rise, even having reached in some cases their highest recorded levels for almost 80 years, notably in terms of our income, health, wealth and also voting inequalities.

What I found was that almost all the entries in almost all the lists could be put into various boxes.

By comparing how the lists changed over time, I have been able to see how the nature of each social evil has changed. What began to emerge,

---

[1] When published in *The Yorkshire Post*, the title was in the present tense. I have changed 'are' to 'were' here.

for me at least, was a picture of how each old social evil has transformed into something often very different but equally as damaging in terms of maintaining inequality and hence injustice.

So, as the social evils identified by Beveridge at the dawn of the British welfare state (ignorance, want, idleness, squalor and disease) are gradually being eradicated, social injustices are now being recreated, renewed and supported by new sets of unjust beliefs.

Most troubling is the realisation that people, especially powerful people in the most unequal of large countries in the rich world – top of this list is the United States and the United Kingdom – don't appear to see their great levels of inequality as particularly problematic, despite the evidence.

Indeed, have some of us also become weaned onto the idea that inequalities are good, inequality as evidence of successful competition, as the unavoidable result of a survival of the fittest?

Are the mental habits that perpetuate inequality much harder to kick in some places and times than others?

Does living in a nation that has become adjusted to high levels of unfairness make inequalities appear more acceptable; inequalities which would not be accepted now elsewhere?

What is also interesting is why the most unequal countries of the rich world don't express any sustained wish to have their levels of social inequality reduced, say to the average levels enjoyed by the rest of the world's richest 25 countries.

In the rest of the rich world, people live longer, consume and pollute less, appear happier when surveyed, experience less crime, trust each other more, stay together more often in families, live longer and healthier lives, invent more things, recycle more, eat less meat, have more stable economies, take fewer drugs and drink less and so on and so on. Even the trains run on time more often!

People in the most unequal of affluent countries are not especially stupid, although we do worse at school on average than children of most of the other 21 rich nations. So, why don't we notice? Why don't we accept that greater equality brought about by curtailing the excesses at the top would help us all?

A good place to start in trying to answer this question, and where I started in writing, is with the answers people living in these most unequal countries themselves give when they are asked what is most wrong.

All of the new social evils are arguments for maintaining and increasing inequality. They are, I claim, what keep us addicted to inequality.

Some people used to say that smoking was good for the constitution. It helped you develop a "productive cough", cleared out the lungs. There are still people today who say that inequality is good, it rewards merit, encourages competition and fosters growth and consumption – these are in effect the "productive coughs" of 21st century society.

And, just as there were lobbyists paid to argue for tobacco long after most people came to agree it was harmful, so too are there lobbyists today who are paid to argue for injustice and call it "freedom", people paid by those who can see a short-term gain in bolstering inequality.

Had you told someone in 1942 that there would come a day when smoking was banned in all public buildings, they might well not have believed you. If you are told today that within your lifetime you could see social inequalities greatly reduced and the health and well-being of the population greatly increase as a result, would you believe it?

Will our grandchildren ever understand why some people equate inequality with freedom?

# 50

# Mind the gap: New Labour's legacy on child poverty

*Poverty* (2010) no 136, pp 11–13

'What have the Romans ever done for us?' asked the People's Front of Judea in *The Life of Brian*'s fictional recording of ungrateful subjects ignoring their rulers' largesse. But what does the People's Front of Judea have to do with modern-day critics of the 1997–2010 New Labour government?

I was first told that the views I held equated to those of the Peoples' Front when writing a book, *The widening gap*, with colleagues in 1999, which considered how, under both the Tories and the start of New Labour, the gap between rich and poor continued to grow. We highlighted that New Labour explicitly continued Conservative spending policies for those two years and, once in office, did not enact the key policies to reduce inequalities that it had supported throughout opposition. That gap became a great deal wider in the years that followed.

Perhaps people like me should have shouted a great deal louder rather than wait for the seeds New Labour had sown to bear fruit. A few of those seeds did grow into tall poppies. Success was greatest in reducing some education divides,[1] but inroads into reducing poverty were diminished because incomes were allowed to grow exponentially above those of the poor. And, more critically, Labour introduced and continued to extol a populist and punitive

---

[1] Dorling, D. (2010) 'Expert view: one of Labour's great successes', *The Guardian*, 28 January, p 10 [Reproduced as Chapter 18 of this book, page 147].

approach, labelling benefit claimants as potentially feckless. Permitting rising inequality and stoking prejudices against the poor sets a precedent for the next government which heavily outweighs the many gains made.

The most recent suggestion that those who hold views such as mine are misguided was announced in a recent *Guardian* editorial, when it transferred its allegiance to the Liberal Democrats:

> "Invited to embrace five more years of a Labour government, and of Gordon Brown as Prime Minister, it is hard to feel enthusiasm. Labour's kneejerk critics can sometimes sound like the People's Front of Judea asking what the Romans have ever done for us. The salvation of the health service, major renovation of schools, the minimum wage, civil partnerships and the extension of protection for minority groups are heroic, not small, achievements."[2]

But, in an affluent country like Britain, should the renovation of state schools be seen as an achievement rather than as business as usual? Similarly, what the *Guardian* calls a 'salvation' – managing to fund a health service still many euros per person cheaper than the European norm – is hardly a staggering feat. And putting in place a minimum wage? Even the USA has had this for many decades. Civil partnerships and removing a little of the bigotry faced by minority groups are important, but obvious, policies. Rather, it would have been heroic to have reduced income and wealth inequalities (and, by doing so, rates of real poverty). It would have been heroic to have refused to take part in America's wars. It would have been heroic to have reined in the bankers before the crash.

In comparison with other contemporary governments in the present, with progressive politics in Britain's past, and with the 1997 dream that 'things can only get better', New Labour fell far short. Here is what Julian Baggini had to say on Labour's record in office in that same issue of the paper:

> I think this has been an under-appreciated government. The last 13 years have been immeasurably better than the previous 18, and the return to Conservatism, in its current shape at least, appals me. But the game is up, both for a system which protects two parties which most people do not support, and a government that just cannot now hope to be re-elected with a majority.[3]

---

[2] www.guardian.co.uk/commentisfree/2010/apr/30/the-liberalmoment- has-come
[3] Quoted in part in *The Guardian*, 1 May 2010, p 37 and in full at www.guardian.co.uk/commentisfree/2010/apr/30/lib-dems-torieselection

What do we find when, instead of announcing 'immeasurably better', we measure? Here are my attempts (with the help of many others) to measure this apparently immeasurable betterment.[4]

Among British adults during the 1997–2005 Blair years, the proportion unable to make regular savings rose from 25 per cent to 27 per cent; the number unable to afford an annual holiday away from home rose from 18 per cent to 24 per cent; and the national proportion who could not afford to insure the contents of their home climbed a percentage point, from 8 per cent to 9 per cent. However, these national proportions conceal the way in which the rising exclusion has hit particular groups especially hard, not least a group that the Blair government had said it would help above all others: children living in poverty. Brown was in office too short a time and too recently to yet make a clear assessment yet of his years. Given that his term ended in recession, the record will not look good. But what of Blair's term that ended at the height of an economic boom?

The comparison of poverty surveys taken towards the start and end of Tony Blair's time in office found that, of all children, the proportion living in a family that could not afford to take a holiday away from home (or just to visit relatives) rose between 1999 and 2005, from 25 per cent to 32 per cent. This occurred even as the real incomes of most of the poorest rose; they just rose more for the affluent, making holidays more expensive for all and subtly changing what it meant to go on holiday. Similarly, as the rich became richer and housing became more expensive and more unequally distributed, the number of school-age children who had to share their bedroom with an adult or sibling over the age of 10 *and* of the opposite sex rose from 8 per cent to 15 per cent nationally. Encouraging buy-to-let landlords in a new wave of privatisation did not help reduce overcrowding. It was in London that such overcrowding became most acute and where sharing rooms rose most quickly. Keeping up appearances for the poor in London was much harder than in Britain as a whole, not simply because London had less space, but because within London other children were so often very wealthy.

Even among children at the same school, the incomes of their parents had diverged and, consequently, standards of living and expectations of the norm did too. Nationally, the proportion of children who said their parent(s) could not afford to let them have friends round for tea doubled, from 4 per cent to 8 per cent. The proportion who could not afford to pursue a hobby or other leisure activity also rose, from 5 per cent to 7 per cent, and the proportion who could not afford to go on a school trip at least once a term doubled, from 3 per cent to 6 per cent. For children aged below five,

---

[4] The sources for all these facts are in Dorling, D. (2010) *Injustice: Why social inequality persists*, Bristol: The Policy Press, pp 117–43

the proportion whose parents could not afford to take them to playgroup each week also doubled under the Blair government, from 3 per cent to 6 per cent.

Concealing poverty becomes ever more difficult in an age of consumption and it becomes easier for us to imagine why someone might be tempted to go further into debt in order to pay for a playgroup rather than spend another day at home with a toddler. If at all possible a child will beg their parent(s) to pay for a school trip rather than them have to pretend to be ill that day. One Farepak[5] victim made it clear what growing inequality meant:

> I have got four children, all at various ages. Like I say, you can't tell the little two, Father Christmas can call next door, but he can't call here you know. And with my husband being on sick as well, having to pay the mortgage and feed four kids and whatever, and £37 a week is not a lot.[5]

The second most expensive of all consumption items are housing costs – rents or mortgages – and these have also diverged as income inequalities have increased. Having to move to a poorer area, or being unable to move out of one, is the geographical reality of social exclusion. People get into further debt trying to avoid this.

The most expensive consumer item is a car. The combination of the expense and necessity of car ownership is the reason why not having a car is, for many, a contemporary mark of social failure. It is also closely connected to why so many car firms were badly hit so early on in the crash of 2008, as they were selling debt as much as selling cars.

By 2008/09, two out of three children in Britain living in a household without a car were living with only one parent. The chattels and behaviour that signal what it means to be poor change over time and in accordance with what most others have. By 2009, not having a car, like not being able to go on the cheapest of summer holidays, spelt stigma.

This was the outcome of having a government that was seriously relaxed about the rich becoming richer – 'as long as they paid their taxes'. (But Labour cut Her Majesty's Revenue, thereby reducing tax inspectors' abilities to chase the rich for their payments.) The gaps between all families grew: celebrity, entrepreneur, affluent, hard-working, a bit slovenly, and down-in-

---

[5] Spalek, B. and King, S. (2007) *Farepak victims speak out: An exploration of the harms caused by the collapse of Farepak*. See www.crimeandjustice.org.uk/opus419/Farepak_Web_Final.pdf. For the full report, see www.crimeandjustice.org.uk/farepakvictims.html. In April 2010, 'Customers who paid for hampers from Farepak are expected to receive less than £50 each, even as accountants and lawyers handling the liquidation rack up millions in fees.' *The Times*, 27 April 2010 and http://business.timesonline.co.uk/tol/business/industry_sectors consumer_goods/article7108918.ece

the-mouth. Council housing became social housing (with the word '*social's*' implications of charity rather than rights). Taxation became viewed by New Labour as a form of charity; something one did for the poor. Jobseeker's Allowance of £9 a day was fine (as long as one never imagined having to live off it oneself). But charity, or child tax credits or Sure Start centres are simply not enough if the income gaps between people are allowed to turn into chasms. Whether our gaps can be considered cracks or chasms can be established by looking at other similarly affluent societies.

International comparisons of the quintile range of income inequality are some of the most telling comparisons that can be made between countries. The best current estimate of UK income inequality on this measure is that, by 2005, the richest fifth received 7.2 times more income on average than the poorest fifth each year – up from 6.9 times in 1997. According to the United Nations Development Programme's Annual Report (the most widely used source), this ratio has most recently been 6.1 to 1 in Ireland; 5.6 to 1 in France; 4.0 to 1 in Sweden; and 3.4 to 1 in Japan. By contrast, in the United States that same ratio of inequality is 8.5 to 1. Between 1997 and 2005 the UK moved 0.3 points towards US levels of inequality, or almost one-quarter of the way along the path to becoming as socially unequal as people are in the United States.[6]

The gulfs between our worlds are so wide that comparisons are rarely made between the lives of the richest and poorest on the planet. Worldwide, the poorest tenth will die having hardly left a scratch on the earth. The richest tenth will each individually consume more oil through travel and minerals through gadgets than dozens of previous generations of their own families ever did, at least six times more each than their already affluent parents. In doing so, they consume the vast majority of all the resources that are consumed worldwide. It is precisely because it has become normal in affluent countries to consume, to want so much more than our parents had, especially if our parents were rich, that escapism has taken hold.

Have we all become too apathetic and individualistic? What do we do when we have all our televisions, cars and holidays, when our home is full of possessions that cost such huge amounts? The answer is: we begin to live in fear. We move to what we perceive are safer and safer environments. Eventually, we end up with a home in a gated estate, a gilded cage for the new gilded age. Our visitors must check in with guards before they can get to our door. Our children are too afraid to go outside the gates to play. They watch television.

---

[6] The change in the post-tax income ratios can be calculated from figures given in Stratton, A. (2010) 'Lib Dems to accuse Labour of failing to deliver fair taxes', *The Guardian*, 11 April 2010 and at http:www.guardian.co.uk/politics/2010/apr/11/liberal-democratslabour-unfair-taxes

People in Britain care; rich business people often care; the great and the good of New Labour mostly cared. But caring is not enough if our thinking has been rewired by too many years of living under growing inequality and growing poverty. That time is coming to an end. The people who make up what is left of the party that governed until 6 May 2010 mostly know that it made huge mistakes, that what it did was not enough compared with what most other politicians in most other affluent countries in the world achieve today; not enough compared with what the 1906 or 1910 or 1945 or 1964, or even the 1974 governments achieved, all with less time and much less money. And most importantly of all, what New Labour did was not enough… for what they dreamed of.[7]

---

[7] 'For what you dream of' is the title and chorus of the song that begins 'When the taking and the giving starts to get too much', which appeared in the sound track of the film *Trainspotting*, released a year before New Labour came to power.

# 51

# Remapping the world's population: visualizing data using cartograms[1]

*ArcUser* (2010) no 1, pp 66–69

The Worldmapper project has successfully produced a series of maps to visualize data concerning a range of issues facing the modern world based on the idea of density-equalizing maps. With this approach, ArcGIS 9.3 plays a crucial role as an interface to convert suitable raster datasets and produce updated cartograms. The data is converted using ArcMap's ArcToolbox, while the cartograms were calculated using a geoprocessing tool available from ESRI's ArcScripts site. The final visualization was performed in ArcMap. This article introduces and evaluates further new mapping approaches that move depictions beyond their simple descriptive form. It gives an insight into these new developments, focusing on subnational-level data that have, until now, been neglected.

## Worldmapper and its world population cartogram

The world population cartogram demonstrates the first attempt to include subnational density data. In the first stage of the Worldmapper project, a wide range of maps depicting various human dimensions of the world have been published on the project's website (www.worldmapper.org). Since the publication of the first new world population cartogram in 2006, nearly 600 maps have been produced, going far beyond the depiction of the world's

[1] By Benjamin D. Hennig, John Pritchard, Mark Ramsden, and Danny Dorling, while all were at the Department of Geography, University of Sheffield.

population and covering topics such as education, poverty, and pollution.[2] The Worldmapper cartograms show the data for 200 territories, thus making this new view on the world to some extent an arbitrary view: territorial borders are artificial and are subject to change. Furthermore, the assignment of territories in Worldmapper is arbitrary as different opinions on the legitimacy of these territories might exist. Therefore, the world population cartogram was taken as an example to test different ways to calculate these cartograms beyond the territorial borders. [Additional information on the calculations used in and the design of existing Worldmapper cartograms is given in "Worldmapper: The World as You've Never Seen It Before," by Danny Dorling, Anna Barford, and Mark Newman, published in the September 2006 issue of *IEEE Transactions on Visualization and Computer Graphics.*]

## Data and cartogram calculation

Data used in this work were derived from the Socioeconomic Data and Applications Center (SEDAC) of Columbia University, New York. The Gridded Population of the World (GPW) database contains the distribution of the world's population on a gridded base (sedac.ciesin.columbia.edu/gpw/), including population data and estimates from 1990 to 2015. These data are available in resolutions of up to 2.5 arc minutes, leading to a population grid of 8,640 x 3,432 pixels. Data from the year 2000 has been used to make the results comparable to the original Worldmapper population cartogram.

This raster format data was imported to ArcGIS, converted to polygons, and combined with further metadata (eg, country labels) to match grid cells for further visualization tasks. The cartogram script uses a 4,096 x 2,048 pixel-sized lattice for its map results.

The cartogram itself was calculated using the Cartogram Geoprocessing tool created by Tom Gross of ESRI and available from the ESRI ArcScripts site (www.esri.com/arcscripts). It uses density-equalizing methodology developed by Mark Newman and Michael Gastner at the University of Michigan. Unlike the Worldmapper cartograms that distorts an initial projection of the boundaries of the territories, each population grid is treated as a separate part for the calculation, not taking any territorial information of borders into account. Thus each grid cell marks a border so that distinct shapes of countries are intentionally of no interest in the calculation.

Changes in the distortion of the resulting cartogram thus are only possible by adjusting the factor to smooth the original density. In addition, data from

---

[2] Editorial note: By 2011 over 1,000 maps are included on the website as every individual country is now also mapped to show its population. See www.worldmapper.org

**Figure 1:** Worldmapper population cartogram

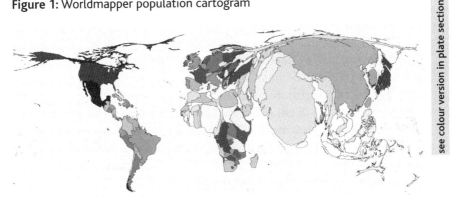

**Figure 2:** Grid-based world population cartogram (2000)

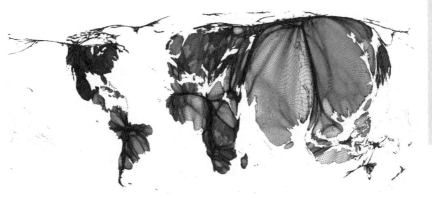

the USA has been extracted from the 2.5 arc minutes population grid and is calculated separately in the same way to produce a more detailed view of the resulting grid for that country and its interval variation.

## Results

The resulting cartograms require some final visualization steps to adapt them to appear similarly to the original Worldmapper cartograms. The polygons of the calculated world population cartogram are dissolved according to their affiliation to the Worldmapper territories and coloured according to the distinctive Worldmapper colour scheme. The gridlines in the USA cartogram are preserved to show the degree of distortion within the grid.

## A redrawn world population cartogram

Compared to its predecessor (Figure 1), the redrawn World Population Cartogram (Figure 2) shows considerable differences. For example, in

China the sparsely populated Himalayan regions can be distinguished from the densely populated eastern coastal regions. Internal variation within the United States and Mexico can also be recognized. Somewhat harder to identify, but still evident, are north-south differences in Great Britain and west–east differences in Germany. Hence, our goal to take the varying distributions of population on a subnational level and make them visible on a global view has been achieved. However, subnational variation can be difficult to analyze in more detail because the grid cells are eliminated to sustain the view on the global scale. In addition, more distinctive national shapes are far more distorted than in the original cartogram which, for some users, might appear odd when interpreting such maps.

## Down to earth: a population cartogram of the United States

To counter the loss of familiar national boundary shapes, a separate population cartogram is produced for the contiguous United States (Figure 3) and several other countries. The shape of the cartogram has more detail compared to the shape of the USA on the world population cartogram. This is because more grid cells are used in the calculation of the cartogram and no other polygons (e.g., from the European continent) influence the calculation. The different scale also allows the visualization of each grid cell so that subnational variation can be recognized.

This visualization on a different scale is an improvement that goes far beyond the current capabilities of the Worldmapper project by using gridded base data to allow a different view of population distribution not only worldwide but also within separate regions. By using cartogram techniques, a different view on the regional variations of human geography is created, which can hardly be achieved with traditional mapping techniques.

**Figure 3:** Grid-based population cartogram of the contiguous United States (2000)

see colour version in plate section

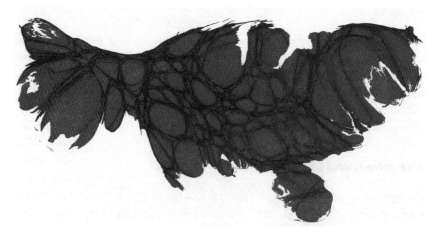

## Outlook

The most significant obstacle to the realization of gridded depiction for Worldmapper will be the vast quantity of different topics covered and the availability and reliability of data. Reliable gridded social and economic data for the whole world is rarely available and rarely of such good quality as the population data. The estimation of missing national data for some topics has already been a problem that had to be overcome to produce the existing Worldmapper cartograms. Such estimations will not meet the demands of gridded datasets, so new ways of data estimation are needed.

Current approaches to estimate data commonly use the GPW data, and these have the potential to be adapted to Worldmapper's requirements. Revised gridded cartograms offer great potential to enhance the variety of Worldmapper's visualization capabilities. A different view of the "real" location of the depicted topic can present a better understanding of human action and human patterns on the globe.

However, distortions associated with the gridded method are a disadvantage and undermine the purpose of Newman and Gastner's algorithm to preserve the familiar shapes of countries. The potential of the gridded approach and the desire to preserve the familiar shapes must therefore be carefully balanced. Nevertheless, much potential lies in adding more user interactivity and detail to Worldmapper. Grid-based cartograms have the advantage of allowing a user to zoom in to view national and regional details, within a global context.

GIS technology is a key tool to make this happen. A GIS environment not only facilitates data conversion and calculation of cartograms but also allows different geographic scales to be brought together under one map. An easy transfer to popular digital globes can thus be realized, allowing viewers to identify the regional dimension of a subject. Separate regional editions of gridded population cartograms can be generated to visualize the regional variation of population distribution.

## References

Dorling, D. (2007) 'Worldmapper: the human anatomy of a small planet', *PLoS Medicine*, vol 4, no 1, pp 13–18.

Dorling, D., Barford, A. and Newman, M. (2006) 'Worldmapper: the world as you've never seen it before', *IEEE Transactions on Visualization and Computer Graphics*, vol 12, no 5, pp 757–64, doi:10.1109/ TVCG.2006.202.

Gaffin, S.R. et al (2004) 'Downscaling and geo-spatial gridding of socio-economic projections from the IPCC Special Report on Emissions Scenarios (SRES)', *Global Environmental Change*, vol 14, no 2, pp 105–23.

Gastner, M.T. and Newman, M.E.J. (2004) 'Diffusion-based method for producing density equalizing maps', *Proc. Natl. Acad. Sci. USA*, no 101, pp 7499–504.

Hay, S.I., Graham, A. and Rogers, D.J. (2006) *Global mapping of infectious diseases: Methods, examples and emerging applications*, London: Academic Press.

Webb, R. (2006) 'Cartography: a popular perspective', *Nature*, no 439, p 800.

# 52

# If I were king[1]

*Big Issue* magazine (2008) December 1–5, p 46

If I were king for a day I'd want to be king of a country I could boast about. I'd be the Prince-Bishop of Andorra, or Albert, King of Monaco, who both head countries where a majority of the population are immigrants and to which more tourists flock per resident than anywhere else in the world. Alternatively I could be 'Henri' for a day, the Grand Duke of Luxembourg, and boast of net immigration swelling my rich country more than any other in Europe, and how I 'performed' the best of all in Europe in terms of tourist receipts (per resident).

Perhaps I should rise above mere riches? Hans (Prince of Liechtenstein to you mere mortals) can boast of how many trees are being planted per person in his little principality: more than anywhere else in Europe. But consider 'proper' countries: Harald of Norway can talk of how more hydroelectric energy is generated by each of his subjects than anywhere else in the world, and given their oil, the Norwegians also export more fuel than anywhere other than Brunei (with its Sultan) or Qatar (with its Sheikh). Norway and

---

[1] Editorial note: All the data used to make the claims in this chapter were collected by the author and are documented in www.worldmapper.org in the technical notes to the relevant map.

Sweden (monarch: King Carl) also send the most young people to university in Europe, only Finland (without a monarch) sends more.

Only three countries in Europe have female heads, Britain (Queen Elizabeth), Denmark (Queen Margrethe), and the Netherlands (Queen Beatrix). In comparison with Britain, the poorest fifth of the population are best provided for in Europe in Luxembourg (3.6 times better-off than in Britain), then Norway (2.2), then, Ireland and Denmark (1.6), Finland and Sweden (1.5), Austria, Germany and Belgium (1.4). The poor of Britain fare worse than the poor of all other Western European countries other than Malta, Greece and Portugal.

In Britain, Elizabeth is monarch of the country relying more on selling insurance and profiting from its finance industry than any other in the world. Hers is the only monarchy to have nuclear missiles. Britain has been involved in wars for the longest recently, had the highest per capita income in the world in 1900, and now has the highest United Nations calculated human poverty index of any monarchy in the rich world. If I became king of Britain, just for a day, I would ask why I had been put in this situation.

But why stop at king? In Japan Emperor Akihito presides over a country where the poorest fifth live off 1.8 times as much as they do in Britain, a country with the *lowest* worldwide teenage pregnancy rate, the *highest* secondary education enrolment rate, where people travel more by train than anywhere else. Japan is the rich country with the fewest people in prison (less than half as many as in Britain). And, of all the countries of the world, it is in Japan that people live the longest lives, followed by the monarchies of Monaco, Andorra and Sweden.

Where would you be king, just for one day?

# Bibliography

Daniel Dorling has written numerous articles and papers, many in collaboration with others, of which those in this book are just a small selection. More are available at: www.shef.ac.uk/geography/staff/dorling_danny/papers.

A complete list of all publications found be found at :http://sasi.group.shef.ac.uk/publications/CV_DannyDorling.pdf

Open Access PDF files of some earlier books can be found at www.shef.ac.uk/sasi

Danny is the sole author of the following books:

Dorling, D. (1995) *A new social atlas of Britain*
Dorling, D. (1996) *Area cartograms: Their use and creation*
Dorling, D. (2005) *Human geography of the UK*
Dorling, D. (2010) *Injustice: Why social inequality persists*
Dorling, D. (2011) *So you think you know about Britain?*

He is also co-author of many other books, including:

Dorling, D. and Fairbairn D. (1997) *Mapping ways of representing the world*.
Shaw, M., Dorling, D., Gordon, D. & Davey Smith, G. (1999) *The widening gap*.
Johnston, R., Pattie, C., Rossiter, D. and Dorling, D. (2001) *From votes to seats*.
Shaw, M., Dorling, D. and Mitchell, R. (2002) *Health, place and society*.
Dorling, D. and Thomas, B. (2004) *People and places: A census atlas of the UK*.
Thomas, B. and Dorling, D. (2007) *Identity in Britain: A cradle-to-grave atlas*.
Dorling, D., Newman, M. and Barford, A. (2008) *The real world atlas*.
Dorling, D. and Thomas, B. (2011) *Bankrupt Britain: An atlas of social change*.

# Index

The letter f represents a f figure a t a table